Sopwith Aircraft

Sopwith
Aircraft

Mick Davis

The Crowood Press

First published in 1999 by
The Crowood Press Ltd
Ramsbury, Marlborough
Wiltshire SN8 2HR

© Mick Davis 1999

British Library Cataloguing-in-Publication Data
A catalogue record for this book is available from
the British Library.

ISBN 1 86126 217 5

Typefaces used: Goudy (*text*),
Cheltenham (*headings*)

Typeset and designed by
D & N Publishing
Membury Business Park, Lambourn Woodlands
Hungerford, Berkshire.

Printed and bound by Redwood Books, Trowbridge.

Acknowledgements

I would like to express gratitude to all my friends who have shared information that has made the writing of this book possible. Photographs are credited appropriately and especial thanks must be given to Stuart Leslie, who allowed me free access to the massive photographic collection that he has built up with Jack Bruce. Finally, thanks to my wife Sue and son Chris for putting up with the lack of attention over these last months.

Contents

Glossary

AA	Anti-aircraft fire	Flt Lt	Flight Lieutenant	RAF	Royal Air Force (post-1 April 1918)
AAP	Aircraft Acceptance Park	FS	Fighting School		
AD	Aircraft Depot	FSL	Flight Sub Lieutenant	RAE	Royal Aircraft Establishment (post-1 April 1918)
AFC	Australian Flying Corps	FTS	Flying Training School		
AFC	Air Force Cross			RFC	Royal Flying Corps
AICS	Artillery and Infantry Co-operation School	HD	Home Defence	RNAS	Royal Naval Air Service
		HMS	His Majesty's Ship	RS	Reserve Squadron
AM	Air Mechanic				
AR	Admiralty Rotary	IDE	Instrument Design Establishment	SAF	School of Aerial Fighting
ARD	Aircraft Repair Depot			SAFG	School of Aerial Fighting and Gunnery
ASD	Aircraft Supply Depot	IWM	Imperial War Museum		
				SAG	School of Aerial Gunnery
BEF	British Expeditionary Force	LdeH	Legion d'Honneur	SAGF	School of Aerial Gunnery and Fighting
BR	Bentley Rotary	Lt	Lieutenant		
		2Lt	Second Lieutenant	SD	Seaplane Defence (Flt/Sqn)
CAF	Canadian Air Force			SD	Special Duties
CdeG	Croix de Guerre	MAEE	Marine Aircraft Experimental Establishment	SEAFIS	South East Area Flying Instructors' School
CFS	Central Flying School				
CO	Commanding Officer			SNDB	School of Navigation and Bomb Dropping
		MC	Military Cross		
DFC	Distinguished Flying Cross	MOS	Marine Observers' School	Sqn	Squadron
DSC	Distinguished Service Cross				
DSO	Distinguished Service Order	N	Naval (e.g. 5N Sqn)	TDS	Training Depot Station
		NEAFIS	North East Area Flying Instructor's School		
ECD	Experimental Construction Depot			TS	Training Squadron
		NTS	Night Training Squadron		
EI & ESS	East Indies and Egypt Seaplane Squadron	NWAFIS	North West Area Flying Instructor's School	USAS	United States Air Service
				USN	United States Navy
ES	Experimental Station	PC	Protective Cellulose	VC	Victoria Cross
		POW	Prisoner of War		
Flt	Flight			WEE	Wireless Experimental Establishment
Flt Comm	Flight Commander	RAF	Royal Aircraft Factory (pre-1 April 1918)		

CHAPTER ONE

Sopwith

The Man, the Company and the Legacy

Thomas Octave Murdoch Sopwith was born on 18 January 1888 and died more than 101 years later, as Sir T.O.M. Sopwith CBE. For the majority of his long life he was a major figure and prime mover in the British aviation industry and yet the registered companies that bore his name were in existence for only eight of those years. In that time, the Sopwith Aviation Company Ltd produced some of the best-known aeroplanes and seaplanes of the Great War and the name Sopwith became synonymous with fighting scouts.

T.O.M. Sopwith was also a pioneer aviator and record breaker who was a contemporary of and competitor with other early 'greats', such as Samuel F. Cody and Claude Grahame White. He made several important achievements between 1910 and 1912, before virtually giving up flying to concentrate on the manufacture of aircraft.

If a secret of successful management is the ability to attract and retain people of skill and initiative, Sopwith was a master. Under his patronage, men such as Harry Hawker, Fred Sigrist, Harry Kauper, Herbert Smith and R.J. Ashfield became famous in their own right. He had the ability to select the likes of these as his team, and team it was because the Sopwith products were almost invariably the synthesis of ideas from these men. The now famous machines that emerged, particularly during the war, were not only of sound overall concept, they also incorporated details of design that were important innovations or developments – sprung seaplane floats, the split undercarriage that gave independent suspension, adjustable tailplanes, air brakes and a gun synchronization gear are just some examples.

The young Sopwith had engineering ability and a fascination for motorcycles, speedboats, yachting, driving cars and ballooning. That he could indulge in these sports was made possible by the affluence

Thomas Octave Murdoch Sopwith dressed for flying, c.1910–11. via Bruce Robertson

of his parents, his father having also been a successful engineer. As early as 1906, at the age of 18, Sopwith had joint ownership of a balloon and moved in a circle of friends that included the Hon. C.S. Rolls.

It was his yachting that brought him into contact with the first person who was to become part of the Sopwith team. By 1909, Sopwith had joint ownership of a schooner and employed Fred Sigrist to be its engineer.

Powered flight first figured in Sopwith's life in 1910 when he decided to learn to fly aeroplanes after meeting J.B. Moisant, the first person to make a powered cross-Channel flight with a passenger. After sampling the joy of flying in an aeroplane at Brooklands, Sopwith bought a 40hp Howard Wright monoplane from its manufacturer and decided to teach himself to fly. Despite an early crash on 22 October, Sopwith persevered and began to master the skill. He then bought another machine from Howard Wright, a 60hp biplane, and took the tests for his Royal Aero Club Certificate on 21 November, receiving 'ticket' No. 31.

Sopwith's rapid development as a pilot had been remarked upon in the press and he was confident in both his own ability and that of his machine. His confidence led him to attempt to gain two prizes that were available for British pilots flying all-British machines and given the deadline of 31 December. The British Empire Michelin Cup came with £500 and went to the pilot making the longest non-stop flight in the UK. The Baron de Forest offered the much more substantial prize of £4,000 for the pilot making the longest non-stop flight between Britain and mainland Europe. Sopwith, after establishing temporary mainland records of 107¾ miles (173.37km) on 10 December and 150 miles (241.35km) on the 31st of that month, was pipped at the post for the Michelin Cup by S.F. Cody with one of 195 miles (313.76km) on that same New Year's Eve. He won the Baron de Forest prize, however, with a flight of 177 miles (284.79km) from Eastchurch to Beaumont in Belgium. That achievement led to an invitation to meet the King and Sopwith

Fred Sigrist

Frederick Sigrist was, arguably, the unsung hero of the Sopwith organization. T.O.M. Sopwith once remarked that he doubted whether Sigrist had any schooling, but that did not prevent him from being an excellent mechanic. It was in that capacity that he was first employed by Sopwith in 1909, to tend the engine of a yacht that Sopwith jointly owned with V.W. (Bill) Eyre. Sigrist was present when the flying 'bug' caught Sopwith's imagination and he was quick to adapt to tending aero engines.

Sigrist was placed in charge of the maintenance of the aeroplanes operated by the Sopwith School and was involved in the reconstruction of the Burgess Wright for instructional work. He became Works Manager of the Sopwith Aviation Company. His ideas, particularly those that simplified production, were incorporated in Sopwith designs and the line of famous rotary-engined fighting scouts can be traced back to his design that formed the subsequent basis for the 1½ Strutter.

His position in the Sopwith Company brought great financial reward and he became an original director of both the Hawker Company and (later) Hawker Siddeley.

His organizational ability was demonstrated in his work with these companies, but he continued to develop innovations. With Sidney Camm, Sigrist used his knowledge of welding to develop the Hawker method of metal airframe construction that allowed such easy assembly and replacement of components in the classic designs of the 1920s and 1930s. Sigrist's name also appeared in its own right as half of the Reid and Sigrist company that developed the first effective blind-flying system for the RAF.

Ill-health forced Sigrist to move to the Bahamas, but he worked for the British Air Commission in California during the latter half of World War II. Fred Sigrist was made an MBE for his services to aviation and died on 10 December 1956.

Frederick Sigrist in nautical attire. He was first employed by Sopwith to tend the engines of yachts but subsequently became a noted aeronautical engineer and made significant contributions to the design of Sopwith aircraft. via Bruce Robertson

dutifully flew his biplane to Windsor for the occasion. Some of the proceeds from his prize were used to buy two new aeroplanes, both monoplanes and both powered by Gnome rotary engines. They were a 70hp Bleriot and a 50hp Martin and Handasyde Type 4B. These purchases coincided with the offer of a further prize, this time by W.R. Hearst, the American newspaper giant and alleged model for Citizen Kane, for the first (obviously staged) east–west transcontinental flight across the USA. Sopwith was prepared to take up the challenge.

He took Sigrist and two other mechanics to tend to the Bleriot that he took to the USA. It was reassembled on Long Island and ready by May 1911, but crashed on its second flight. The Howard Wright biplane was sent from England and a new Bleriot from France. Sopwith made exhibition flights and participated in several aviation meetings, winning some prize money, but the transcontinental flight was not attempted. During that American visit, Sopwith had, as in his pioneering work in Britain, the enduring support and help of his sister, May. The Sopwith party returned to England in October, with the Bleriot following. It was accompanied by a new Burgess-Wright biplane that he had bought and the components of the Howard Wright that had been wrecked after engine failure forced a landing off Manhattan Beach.

Birth of the Sopwith Aviation Company

Sopwith had decided to go into the aviation business by opening his own flying school. The Sopwith School of Flying opened at Brooklands in February 1912 and offered a greater range of instructional machines than any other similar institution. The two-seater Bleriot was flown alongside the Howard Wright monoplane which had been rebuilt, the Burgess-Wright biplane that was modified for instructional work and the Martin and Handasyde monoplane. These were later joined by a Henri Farman biplane. F.P. Raynham was hired as instructor and this enabled Sopwith to pursue both his competition interests and testing work for the Coventry Ordnance Works, whose biplane he flew in part of the Military Trials at Larkhill in August. Fred Sigrist was in charge of the aeroplanes. When Raynham later left to join the firm of L.H. Flanders, his place was taken by E.W. Copland Perry – destined to become one of the first two Royal Flying Corps (RFC) fatalities of the First World War. The first pilot graduated in mid-April 1912 and, on 31 July, Major Hugh Trenchard passed his tests after undergoing a necessarily rapid course.

A first attempt at aeroplane construction had been made, and on 4 July Sopwith took to the air in the Sopwith-Wright biplane with a 70hp Gnome engine

providing the power. That machine, one name being the hybrid School Biplane, was constructed under Sigrist's supervision. It was intended for instructional work, and Sopwith soon demonstrated its ability to carry two passengers. It crashed on the 12th of that month and was rebuilt over the summer. Sopwith then tried to interest the military in the design, demonstrating it at Farnborough on 8 October, but to no avail. The Naval Wing was interested, however, and bought the machine for £900.

In 1911, two Australians had sailed for England. They were Harry Hawker and Harry Kauper, both of whom were to become part of the Sopwith organization. Hawker was a year younger than Sopwith and also had an engineering background, particularly with motor cars. He began working for Sopwith in June 1912 after being introduced by Kauper, who was already working for the firm. After taking flying lessons that summer, he gained his Royal Aero Club Certificate in September. Hawker was a natural pilot and was chosen by Sopwith to fly the Burgess-Wright in an attempt at winning the Michelin Duration prize of £500. Hawker first flew that machine on 15 October and nine days later established a new British record of 8 hours 23 minutes.

Brooklands was one of the two centres of early aviation and the number of flying schools both there and at Hendon multiplied in 1912. T.O.M. Sopwith, with the success of the hybrid School Biplane behind him, decided to abandon flying tuition and concentrate on aircraft manufacture. Premises were needed and an empty skating rink at Kingston was acquired. The Sopwith Company, as it was first known, was thus established some 7 miles from Brooklands, to where its future products could be taken for assembly and test-flying. The first designs of the new company were a three-seater biplane and a flying boat, whose original hull was replaced by one of S.E.

several that were produced were notable attempts at advancing the aircraft as a weapon. These included designs for torpedo and gun-carrying seaplanes. At a time when France was still viewed as a world leader in aircraft design, it was to Sopwith's that the Greek Navy turned for its first machines.

Sopwith was interested in further promoting his new company by successful participation in competitions and his entry was the sole starter in the 1913 Circuit of Britain that was sponsored by the Daily Mail. Despite failing to complete the course, the

the RFC. It was probably with an eye to the export potential offered by Australia that Sopwith arranged for Hawker to demonstrate the Tabloid prototype in his home country during early 1914. In Hawker's absence, a 100hp seaplane version was entered for and won the Schneider Trophy. The firm had by then been registered as a limited liability company, with the name The Sopwith Aviation Company Ltd, and had, to cope with increasing Admiralty orders, taken over further premises in Kingston, in Canbury Park Road. The company maintained its Brooklands base

The Burgess-Wright biplane that Sopwith bought in the USA was modified for school work by Fred Sigrist, being given side-by-side seating and an enclosed nacelle front. It was used by Hawker to establish a British duration record of 8hrs 23min on 24 October 1912. JMB/GSL

Saunders, construction to become the first of the Bat Boats. Both caused a sensation when they were exhibited at the 1913 Olympia Show and orders followed later.

The Naval Wing of the RFC had an agenda that was at variance with that of the Military Wing and its aircraft requirements were therefore often different. The designs of the Royal Aircraft Factory were, largely, to military requirements and so the Naval Wing turned to private enterprise for many of its machines. Sopwith began to receive orders for small batches of seaplanes to meet naval specifications and

Sopwith attempt by Hawker and Kauper was still a major achievement. The Mortimer Singer Prize, for amphibian machines, was won by the Bat Boat, and that competition, like that of the Daily Mail, reflected the jingoistic feelings of the time by the insistence that competing machines had to be of all-British manufacture.

1913 saw the first appearance of the Tabloid and that remarkable design was the forerunner of the succession of rotary-engined, single-seater machines that characterized the company's success. Examples were exported and orders for developed versions were received from both Wings of

for the testing of aeroplanes, and sheds were acquired at Woolston, on Southampton Water, for the assembly and testing of seaplanes.

The First World War

When the inevitable war came, Sopwith's was firmly established as a supplier to the RNAS, as the Naval Wing had been rechristened. The staff at Sopwith's had been expanded and Herbert Smith had been brought from the British & Colonial Aeroplane Co. to become the leading

Harry Hawker

Australian Harry George Hawker, a blacksmith's son, was born at South Brighton, Victoria, on 22 January 1889. Like Sigrist, he had little formal education but an aptitude for all things mechanical. He began work at the age of 12, being employed by a motor company. His ability with cars led to a job in Melbourne, supervising the maintenance of vehicles for one de Little at a (for the time) very attractive salary. He became acquainted with Harry Busteed, who was intent on going to England to learn how to fly. Hawker decided to join Busteed and they sailed for the mother country at the beginning of 1911. They met up with Harry Kauper on the boat, finding he had similar ambitions to Busteed.

On arrival, Busteed learned to fly at Larkhill and later became a noted figure in the Royal Naval Air Service (RNAS). Kauper landed a job with Sopwith at Brooklands, but Hawker went through a variety of jobs in the motor business, working for Commer and Mercedes before moving to Austro-Daimler and contact with aero engines. Kauper then introduced Hawker to Sopwith and he became a mechanic at the Sopwith School in July 1912. His ability was quickly appreciated, especially by Fred Sigrist.

Hawker had been saving for a return fare to Australia but used his money to pay Sopwith for flying lessons. He proved to be a natural pilot and soon gained his Royal Aero Club 'ticket'. This moved Sopwith to make him exhibition pilot for the company and Hawker went on to test-fly and demonstrate the full range of machines that

Harry Hawker, the gifted Australian engineer and airman who had a hand in most Sopwith designs and who test-flew the majority of prototypes, seen here post-war with cap in the de rigueur **reversed position.** via Bruce Robertson

were produced. He also set the records that are mentioned in the main body of the text.

With the outbreak of war and the placing of ever larger contracts for Sopwith aeroplanes, Hawker was involved in a great deal of test-flying and took the majority of the company's designs for their maiden flights. His intuitive understanding of aerodynamics also led to his being involved in design work, contributing ideas that were embodied in the famous Sopwith types. His thoughts on the layout of a single-seater 'runabout' began the evolution of the Pup. The Armistice saw a return to competition flying and Hawker's attempt at a transatlantic crossing was a brave attempt.

Hawker's work with Sopwith brought wealth as well as fame and, when the Sopwith company was placed into liquidation, it was he who took over the mortgage on the Kingston premises in preparation for the emergence of the new Sopwith company, H.G. Hawker Engineering, in 1920.

The new company may not have produced aeroplanes but that did not prevent Hawker from flying. He was in demand as a pilot and he was scheduled to fly the Nieuport Goshawk in the 1921 Aerial Derby. It was while practising for that event at Hendon that Hawker crashed to his death on 12 July 1921. It was concluded that he had passed out in the air and lost control. The nation mourned his loss and both the King and Prime Minister made eulogies. He was only 33 when he died, but his name was perpetuated in the Hawker Company.

---

draughtsman and, later, chief designer. Smith joined R.J. Ashfield in the Design Department, and with Reginald Carey as General Manager, Fred Sigrist as Works Manager, Harry Kauper as foreman of fitters and Harry Hawker as test pilot, Sopwith had a precocious, yet formidable, team and was now free to take an overall view. Most of these men, it must be remembered, were still in their mid-twenties and yet at the forefront of the industry.

The future of the company was guaranteed with the placing of large orders for Schneider and, later, Baby seaplanes. These orders were to occupy fully the existing premises, and so Robey & Co. of Lincoln was given responsibility for producing the last batch of Sopwith Gunbus pushers and became the first of many subcontractors for Sopwith designs. The real breakthrough came with the 1½ Strutter of 1915, the design that established Sopwith's as a manufacturer of rotary-engined fighting aeroplanes. The Pup, Triplane and Camel followed; each of greater engine power and improved fighting efficiency. Engine power was crucial and Sopwith had early access to what were,

arguably, the best rotary engines of the war; those designed by W.O. Bentley.

It was the Camel that introduced the classic armament of two forward-firing Vickers guns to the British air services. Interestingly, the best of the company's fighting scouts was, probably, the underrated Dolphin, which had the V8 Hispano-Suiza engine and was also the first operational British machine with a multi-gun armament. Sopwith's fortunes as a designer of fighting scouts peaked with the Snipe. By late 1917, the Sopwith organization had grown further with the acquisition of the works at Ham, but the company had been unable to supply the demand for its products and large numbers of sub-contractors were employed. A pattern had developed, from the time of the Baby, whereby Sopwith's initiated production of a type and subcontractors would then take over, leaving the parent company to develop its next machine. As a result, greater numbers of most the classic Sopwith fighters were built by manufacturers other than the parent company.

The Ministry of Munitions had concluded, in July 1917, that aircraft production

could be made more efficient if it was centralized. This led to the idea of National Aircraft Factories (NAF) where machines could be produced on a massive scale under government direction and control of raw materials and components. National Aircraft Factory No. 3 was planned for Richmond and Sopwith was asked to manage it. T.O.M. Sopwith was, however, a believer in private enterprise and recognized the potential problems of state intervention. Consequently, he declined the offer and events proved him correct. Production from those NAFs that were set up was slow and unit costs high.

The Sopwith Company played a major role in the development of shipborne naval aviation. From the early use of its seaplanes from naval vessels, developments moved on to the use of aeroplanes; at first from turret ramps and fixed platforms on warships, then from the first aircraft carriers (in the modern sense of the word). Adaptations of existing Sopwith types led to the Ships Pup, Camel and 1½ Strutter, but a development was the Cuckoo, designed as the first ship-launched torpedo-carrying aeroplane.

The need for an armoured aeroplane, for ground attack work, resulted in the Salamander, the only such British machine to achieve production status. There was a spate of designs during 1918 that included some reversions to the triplane configuration and attempted to utilize the Dragonfly radial engine, but only the Dragon was ordered in quantity and that, like the others, was a failure due to the engine's shortcomings.

Sir Thomas Sopwith CBE at the Café Royal, London, in 1970. via Bruce Robertson

The Post-War Years

The Armistice brought reductions and cancellations of orders and Sopwith's turned its attention to the potential civil market, both at home and overseas. In an attempt to tap the Australian market, a joint company was created, the Larkin-Sopwith Aeroplane Company, which was based in Melbourne. The Dove, the Gnu and others were the results, but these could

do little in the face of competition from the large stocks of cheap war-surplus machines that were available. A return to competition flying resulted in the Atlantic, Wallaby and Rainbow, but none of these achieved their intended goals.

Diversification seemed the only answer and the firm was re-registered as the Sopwith Aviation & Engineering Company Ltd, reflecting its intended production of

ABC motorcycles and car bodies. The company might have survived in this form, had it not received a massive and cruel bill for Excess Profits Duty from the Treasury. Sopwith decided that voluntary liquidation was the only answer, but first ensured that all of the company's creditors were paid in full. The works at Kingston and Ham were closed, effectively from 3 September 1920, and the overt name of Sopwith disappeared from British aviation.

Less than six weeks later, Sopwith was back in business, but his new company did not bear his name. In making a fresh start, it was considered wiser to sever links with the liquidated company and so the H.G. Hawker Engineering Company Ltd was registered on 15 November 1920. There was, however, no mistaking that it was the successor to the Sopwith Company, its first directors being Sopwith, Hawker, Sigrist, Eyre and F.I. Bennett, with its address given as Canbury Park Road, Kingston-upon-Thames.

The new company continued where Sopwith's had left off, producing cars and motorcycles, but it also began to receive government contracts to recondition aeroplanes, including Snipes, for the peacetime Royal Air Force (RAF). Hawker did not live to see the first design to bear his name, as he was killed in a flying accident on 12 July 1921. That machine was the Duiker, which did not receive any production order. Herbert Smith had been employed in Japan, where he had worked for the Mitsubishi Engineering Co and had helped to design some of that company's early aeroplanes, which incorporated several Sopwith features. Consequently Captain B. Thomson was Hawker's first designer, but the great Sidney Camm succeeded him and the company went on to become even more famous than Sopwith's as a producer of fighter aeroplanes.

T.O.M. Sopwith was made CBE and was chairman of the Hawker companies, the original name being changed, more appropriately, to the Hawker Aircraft Company in 1933. He went on to create the Hawker-Siddeley Aircraft Company, which was an amalgamation of some of the great companies in British aviation – Hawker, Armstrong Siddeley, Armstrong Whitworth and A.V. Roe. Knighted in the 1953 Coronation Honours for his services to British aviation, Sopwith was an active chairman of the Hawker-Siddeley group until his retirement in 1963. His one-hundredth birthday was reported in the press and on television, but despite the huge success of the Hawker concern, his name is still, inexorably, linked to those early machines of the Great War.

The following chapters of this book are intended to give a picture of those Sopwith aircraft and place the machines in chronological order of design. The volume of detail given to each is a reflection of importance, either in terms of numbers produced or significance of design.

CHAPTER TWO

Early Designs

Sopwith's short but prestigious association with the British flying services began in 1912, when the Admiralty purchased the hybrid School Biplane of original design. That machine had been intended to take a 50hp engine but, in the event, had a 70hp Gnome. The planform of the wings owed much to the Burgess-Wright biplane but a novel feature was the rudder, which was a balanced affair that projected equally above and below the sternpost to give a cruciform tail unit – a feature that was to re-emerge on others of the firm's early designs. The form of the engine cowling was also to be continued on several subsequent machines.

The D1

In the meantime, the Sopwith Aviation Company Ltd had been registered and the new limited liability company exhibited two machines at the February 1913 Olympia Aero Exhibition. Both were remarkable for their quality of construction and cleanliness of design. They were the Bat Boat and an 80hp three-seater biplane. The Admiralty bought the three-seater and ordered an example of the Bat Boat.

The three-seater was a clean design for its day. The slightly staggered, two-bay wings had warping for lateral control. The elegant

rigidity. The large tailplane was semicircular in plan and the rudder was lobe-shaped. The undercarriage, typically for the period, had the axle for its main wheels attached to a pair of skids, each of which had an auxiliary wheel attached to its front end. Typically, the pilot occupied the rear cockpit, while the passengers were accommodated side-by-side in the front one.

The three-seater was tested by the Naval Wing at Hendon and, modified after criticism of certain features, was delivered to Eastchurch. There it acquired the serial number 33. After 27 had been returned to Sopwith's for repair, it was

The clean lines of the first Sopwith D1 (three-seater) are shown in this photograph taken at Brooklands. The original lobe-shaped rudder is evident, as are the clear-view panels in the fuselage, the four-wheeled undercarriage unit, the lack of ailerons on the warping wings and the twin tail-skids. JMB/GSL

The offer of the biplane to the RFC Military Wing was declined, but was taken up by the Naval Wing and, with the number 27, delivered to Eastchurch by 24 November. The machine, however, was not successful, and was considered suitable only for taxiing work by May 1913, resulting in its being returned to Sopwith's for repair and reconstruction the following month.

fuselage was deceptively deep and three clear view panels were let into the aluminium covering on each side of the forward part. A fore and aft mounting carried the Gnome engine, the upper half of which was enclosed in a semicircular cowling. Such a mounting allowed the use of three crankshaft bearings, rather than two with an overhung mounting, and provided greater

reconstructed to the same layout, although it retained its 70-hp Gnome. The design was named Sopwith D1. The Naval Wing acquired a further two during September 1913, 103 and 104, and these, in company with 27 and 33, flew from Eastchurch. All were still serving at the outbreak of war and 906 joined them, as an impressed civilian three-seater. 33 went to Belgium

Specification – Sopwith D1	
Engine:	One 80hp Gnome Monosoupape
Dimensions:	Length 29ft 6in (9m); height not known; wingspan upper 40ft (12m), lower 40ft (12m); chord upper 5ft 1½in (1.56m), lower 5ft 1½ (1.56m); gap 5ft 3in (1.6m); dihedral upper 2½°, lower 2½°
Performance:	Max. speed 73.6mph (118.4km/h) Service ceiling not known Endurance 2½ hours
Armament:	None by design

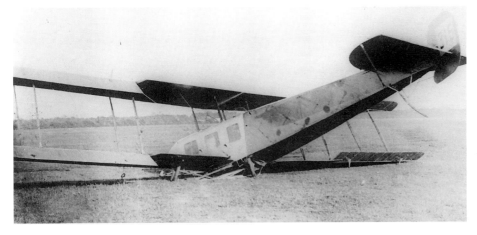

Production D1s had aileron control, an enlarged rudder and a single, taller tail-skid. 315, the subject of these photographs, went to 5 Sqn, as did most other D1s. The cause of its distress is not known. JMB/GSL

with the Eastchurch Sqn, but was damaged on 10 September 1914 and returned to England. 103 was intended to replace 33 but 3 Sqn RNAS, as the Eastchurch Sqn had been retitled, found it unsuitable. It too returned home and served at the Eastbourne and Eastchurch Flying Schools. 906 had the most war-like, if short, service history of any D1. It was with 1 Sqn RNAS in Belgium by 15 September and a week later was used by Lt C.H. Collett to bomb the German airship sheds at Düsseldorf. It was subsequently transferred to 3 Sqn RNAS during October, but was deleted that month.

The Military Wing was not, as some would believe, constrained to fly products produced by the Royal Aircraft Factory. Harry Hawker had set a new altitude record of 12,900ft (3,930m) with a passenger in a three-seater; the type was slightly faster than the B.E.2a and could carry two observers, whose downward view was enhanced by the clear-view panels in the fuselage sides. These features made the D1 appealing to the military. The design was evaluated at the end of June 1913 and nine were ordered on the basis of the subsequent report. 243 was ready by November and was delivered to Farnborough, where it was the subject of static load tests in January 1914. The remaining eight machines (246, 247, 300, 315, 319, 324, 325 and 333) were delivered to 5 Sqn at Farnborough. The unit moved to Netheravon that May, for the RFC Concentration Camp, and thence to the new aerodrome at Fort Grange, Gosport.

Military Wing D1s and, at least, the naval 27 in its rebuilt form differed from the prototype. Most significant was the introduction of aileron control, but there were also changes to the undercarriage, the style of the clear-view panels and the rudder. The latter, on these machines, resembled somewhat an exaggerated version of that on the Bleriot XI, extending both above and below the sternpost. Although known as the 'three-seater', the D1 was usually flown with just one observer, presumably in the interest of maximizing performance.

The D1 was not the success that had been hoped for and, despite their relative newness none went to France with 5 Sqn when that unit moved to Amiens on 15 August. By that date, the number in use had been reduced by the loss of 319 in a crash and of 324 and 325 in a collision. 315 had also crashed at one time. 333 was transferred to the Central Flying School (CFS) at Upavon on 6 August and was the last of the type flying with the military.

The Bat Boats

An example of Sopwith's other 1913 Olympia exhibit, the Bat Boat, was also ordered by the Admiralty, for the Naval Wing, upon the conclusion of that show. Such a flying boat had been under construction at Brooklands as early as August 1912, but it seems unlikely that the 1913 Olympia exhibit was the machine reported on in *The Aeroplane* that previous year. It was not a wholly Sopwith product, the hull having been built at Cowes by Sopwith's yachting friend, S.E. Saunders.

The Olympia machine was assembled in the former skating rink at Kingston and

The cause of 325's demise is known. It collided in mid-air near Farnborough with 324 on 12 May 1914 and its pilot, Lt C.W. Wilson, was lucky to survive. Captain E.V. Anderson and AM Carter, the occupants of 324, were killed. via K.Kelly

the triumvirate of Sopwith, Sigrist and Hawker all had a hand in its layout. The hull was, typically for Saunders, built using the Consuta double skinning of laminated planking that sandwiched a layer of fabric. After Olympia, the Bat Boat was not taken into service, but delivered to Cowes for testing. It was found to be difficult during take-off and suffered damage in bad weather.

T.O.M. Sopwith had designs on the Mortimer Singer Prize. This was for £500 and was to be awarded to the first all-British (airframe and engine) machine, of amphibian capability, that successfully achieved a series of goals including landings and take-offs at sea. The original Bat Boat was modified to meet these criteria, including replacement of the original 90hp Austro-Daimler engine with a 100hp Green. Changes were also

made to the airframe, with longer tailbooms being added to compensate for the deletion of the forward elevator, and a larger tail unit was fitted, incorporating twin rudders.

Construction of a second Bat Boat was then undertaken, in order to fulfil the Admiralty order. The first won the Mortimer Singer Prize for Sopwith. Harry Hawker completed the requisite tasks on 8 July 1913 and the awarding of the prize to Sopwith was announced four days later.

Hamble River, Luke & Co at Hamble, on the Southampton Water, had delivered the second Bat Boat to the Naval Wing at Calshot on 8 June, after receiving its components from Kingston for assembly. It never wore its given number, 38, in that form, being sunk at Brighton on 24 August. The machine was returned to Kingston for a reconstruction that involved utilization of the existing hull but modification to the tailplane layout. It was returned to Calshot in November and marked with its serial number. As 38, it moved to Grain in June 1914 and then, in the prelude to war, to Felixstowe. This was followed by a transfer to Yarmouth and then shipment to Scapa, where 38 was finally wrecked, beyond reconstruction, on 21 November. In service, 38 had acquired a triangular fin.

The original Bat Boat was bought by the Admiralty in January 1914 and delivered in its original, non-amphibian, form. It received the serial number 118 and was at

38, a Bat Boat Type 1, was delivered to the Naval Wing in the form shown in this photograph. It lacked the bow-mounted elevator of the prototype. It sank at Brighton on 24 August 1913 and was rebuilt with a revised tail unit. JMB/GSL

Specification – Sopwith Bat Boat Type 1

Engine:	90hp Austro-Daimler
Dimensions:	Length 32ft (9.75m); height 11ft 6in (3.5m); wingspan upper 41ft (12m), lower 41ft (12m); chord upper 5ft 6in (1.67m), lower 5ft 6in (1.67m); gap 5ft 6in (1.67m); dihedral upper 2°, lower 2°
Performance:	Max. speed 65mph (104km/h) Service ceiling not known Endurance not known
Armament:	None by design

Calshot by 27 February. There it was used for a variety of experiments and was a popular machine. Fitted with a headlight on its stem, 118 was flown at night in the lead-up to the Naval Review of July 1914. Fins were added ahead to the twin rudders. After the declaration of war, 118 was fitted with bomb carriers, being wrecked in a crash on 14 February 1915.

These two Bat Boats were retrospectively designated Type 1, with the appearance of a larger version in 1914. The Type 2 was of all-Sopwith manufacture, hull included. The first of these appeared in public at the Olympia Exhibition in March 1914 and maintained the quality of workmanship set by its predecessors. The wings were of increased but unequal span and their centre-section struts mounted a 200hp Canton-Unné radial engine that had a frontal radiator. An attempt to improve take-off was made by the screwing of brass plates to the hull sides, this being intended to channel air to the step in the boat's hull. Sopwith had contacts in the services and, understanding that the Navy would require wireless in future machines, had a WT set fitted. The machine was delivered to Calshot, as 127, during May but was damaged whilst undergoing acceptance tests. It was transferred to Greece, where the far-sighted Vice Admiral Mark Kerr was principal adviser to the Hellenic Navy and keen to establish an aviation section. That transfer may have been as consolation for the five pusher seaplanes intended for that country but impressed into RNAS service.

Surprisingly, given the political situation of the time, another Bat Boat Type 2 was sold to Germany. It had been tested by late May 1914 and collected, by a German pilot, in (it is believed) July. That machine was, apparently, identical to 127 and was delivered to the seaplane station at Keil. There, it was painted in German national markings and is reported to have served as a training aircraft.

One of the two Sopwiths to be intended for entry in the 1914 Circuit of Britain was a Bat Boat Type 2 that would be flown by Howard Pixton. The airframe was constructed, but the impending outbreak of war caused the challenge to be cancelled. A 225hp Sunbeam engine had been fitted, possibly to compensate for that version's greater weight which resulted, partly, from an increased span. The machine was impressed into RNAS service and numbered 879. It too went to Calshot, but was seldom serviceable. That may have been due to its engine because it was mooted that twin 100hp Monosoupape engines be fitted. The modification did not materialize and 879 was deleted in April 1915.

The HT Seaplane

The original three-seater and Bat Boat were shortly followed by a seaplane design that owed much to that of the former. The new machine was given the designation HT (Hydro-Tractor?) and had a fuselage of similar proportions to the D1. The similarity was furthered by the use of a rudder and tailplane that also resembled those of the three-seater. Dimensions are not available for these tail surfaces and it may be that they were common components, a precedent for those of the Pup and Clerget Triplane in its original form. The engine was a 100hp Anzani radial that was surrounded by an exhaust collector ring.

The wings of the HT were of greater span, however, and comprised three bays to each cellule. The upper wings were slightly longer and the overhang was strut-braced. Large aerofoil-shaped plates were fitted at the inboard end of each upper mainplane, where it joined an open centre section. Ailerons were fitted to all four of the wing panels. The main floats were widely spaced and connected, not to the fuselage but to the lower wing spars at the compression member that also supported the inboard set of interplane struts. The strains imposed on floats, particularly during take-off, were minimized by the use of an ingenious springing system that evened out stresses between the front and rear struts. The tail float was hung well below the rear fuselage, keeping the rudder clear of the water.

Three of these seaplanes were ordered by the Naval Wing and given the numbers 58–60. The first was accepted on 28 June 1913 and all were in service five weeks later. Wireless equipment was fitted to the first two, but was removed from 58 at its Calshot base to save weight during experimental work that included the fitting of bomb carriers. 59 was delivered to the new station at Cromarty, but it was wrecked on 3 September and returned to Sopwith's for reconstruction. 60 went to Yarmouth and survived only until May 1914, when it was burnt.

59 re-emerged from Kingston as a landplane, as did 58 after its reconstruction in August 1914. The wheeled undercarriage resembled that of the D1. 58 went to France, via Eastchurch, to join 3 Sqn RNAS on 27 September, but it was considered unsuited to work with the Expeditionary Force and so returned home. It was, briefly, back at Eastchurch, but moved to Yarmouth, where it was

Specification – Sopwith Bat Boat Type 2

Engine:	200hp Canton-Unné and 200hp Sunbeam
Dimensions:	Length not known; height not known; wingspan upper 55ft (16.76m), lower 45ft (13.72m); chord upper 6ft 9in (2.05m), lower 6ft 9in (2.05m); gap 7ft (2.13m); dihedral upper 2°, lower 2°
Performance:	Max. speed 70–75mph (113–121km/h) Service ceiling not known Endurance 5 hours
Armament:	None by design

wrecked on 19 November. It outlived 59, which had crashed en route for France on 7 September.

The Circuit of Britain Competition

Another that had some similarity of design, but which was built especially for competition work, followed these HT seaplanes. The Sopwith Company was still new and had not, thus far, received significant numbers of orders for its machines.

coast, with predetermined checkpoints. This had to be completed in three full days, during the last two weeks of August. The Sopwith Circuit of Britain seaplane that emerged was a four-bay biplane, with wings of equal span. Again, there were ailerons on all four mainplanes, with endplates added to the upper ones. The layout of its floats resembled that of the HT, but it had a more streamlined appearance, thanks to the use of a 100hp Green inline engine. The name SOPWITH painted, full depth, on the rear fuselage proclaimed its manufacturer.

reaching Yarmouth by mid-afternoon on the 16th. Hawker collapsed after landing, having inhaled too much of the exhaust's emissions. It was hoped that Sydney Pickles would take over, but an elevator was damaged on take-off, and the seaplane was returned to Cowes. A nine-day postponement was announced by the *Daily Mail* and this gave sufficient time for the seaplane to be repaired and for Hawker to recover. The same crew started again on the 25th, again the only entry. Beadnell, in Northumberland, had been reached by the end of the first day and Oban by the end of the

The sole starter in the 1913 Circuit of Britain was the Sopwith Seaplane seen here, marked with its entry number '1'. Hawker and Kauper made a valiant effort at completing the circuit but crashed off the Irish coast. JMB/GSL

The £5,000 offered by the *Daily Mail* to the winner of its 1913 Circuit of Britain competition for 'water-planes' was too great a prize to ignore, for reasons of prestige as well as financial ones. The use of the Bat Boat, which won the Mortimer Singer prize, was a possibility; the competition's rules specified an all-British aircraft. However, that machine had limited endurance, and the *Daily Mail* specified a 1,540-mile (2,478km) course that included the Irish

There were only four contenders prepared to stand the entrance fee of £100, but only the Sopwith entry was ready at Cowes by 16 August – the first day for the competition. Two of the other entrants could not have their machines ready and the fourth, the legendary Samuel F. Cody, was killed in an accident that Bank Holiday, 7 August.

Harry Hawker, with Harry Kauper as his passenger, was the obvious choice of pilot and he covered the first two stages,

second. After an early start on 27 August, the machine had reached Lough Shinny, just north of Dublin, where Hawker attempted to put down, in order to make adjustments to the engine. Hawker's foot slipped from the rudder bar during a banking approach and the seaplane crashed. He was unhurt but Kauper had a fracture to an arm bone. Despite the failure, the newspaper awarded Hawker £1,000. Some two-thirds of the course, 1,043 miles (1,678km), had been covered. The seaplane was salvaged and returned to Kingston for reconstruction. It re-emerged as a landplane on 4 October, but crashed soon after and, after being rebuilt once again as a seaplane, was sold to the Admiralty. It received the number 151 in the Naval Wing, after acceptance on 12 May 1914. After participation in the Naval Review at Spithead on 18 July, it was allocated to Yarmouth, but was damaged en route in a forced landing on the 30th. It was deleted on 19 August.

The Tabloid

The classic Sopwith design of 1913 was the Type St.B. The meaning of those abbreviations is still open to interpretation, but the type is well known as the Tabloid. The prime mover in its design was, undoubtedly, Harry Hawker and the reason for it was a quest for a nimble machine with a high speed. It is almost certain that Sopwith and Sigrist also had a part to play.

The components of the St.B emerged from Kingston on 27 November 1913 and were taken to Brooklands for assembly, which took place that same day, as did the first flight. Hawker was at the controls and the pace of events would suggest his faith in the machine.

It was a compact, side-by-side two seater with wing warping of its staggered mainplanes for lateral control. In tests at Farnborough, on 29 November, Hawker achieved 92mph (148km) with passenger and full fuel load. That was better than the Royal Aircraft Factory's B.S.1/S.E.2, despite the extra crew member and was achieved with only an 80hp Gnome rotary engine. Such a performance could not be ignored and it took less than three weeks for the Military Wing to order nine such machines, for use as high-speed scouts. The compactness of the design had encouraged C.G. Grey, in *The Aeroplane*, to use the description 'tabloid'. That name stuck with the type, and it became known as the Tabloid. Its manufacturer was proclaimed, as with the Circuit of Britain seaplane, by the name SOPWITH painted on the rear fuselage.

Whether for publicity purposes or in the hope of further orders, Hawker went to Australia with the St.B in January 1914 and performed in a series of flying exhibitions in front of thousands of his fellow countrymen. The rear fuselage of the aeroplane was, upon its return from that tour, stripped of its fabric and the original undercarriage was replaced by a simpler one that relied on inverted V struts to carry the axle. A cut-out had been made in the trailing edge of the centre section, presumably to improve the pilot's field of vision, and the wings rerigged to reduce the dihedral of the upper mainplanes.

While Hawker was abroad, the decision was made to enter the 1914 Schneider Cup competition, which was for seaplanes and tested the speed and seaworthiness of its entrants. The Frenchman, Maurice Prévost, who had won in 1913 at Monaco on a Deperdussin, then held the trophy, having covered the specified number of laps at an average speed of 61mph (98km/h). T.O.M. Sopwith decided to enter a floatplane version of the St.B that was to be powered by a 100hp Gnome and known as the HS. The fitting of the more powerful engine necessitated revision of the forward fuselage contours and the balanced rudder was replaced by one of half-round shape that had a triangular fin fitted in front. Wing warping was again used, rather than ailerons. Originally a single central float was envisaged, with another at each wing-tip. That undercarriage was tested but proved a failure and a more traditional pair of main floats was added. A close-mounted tail float was tried, but was replaced by one supported on longer struts. This machine was also prominently marked with the manufacturer's name and it seems likely that this was green or red, not black as may be surmised from a cursory study of photographs.

Howard Pixton was selected, in Hawker's absence, as pilot and on 20 April he won at Monaco. The Sopwith had averaged almost 87mph (140km/h) and that was with the Gnome misfiring on one

The prototype Tabloid was a very neat and compact machine, features that are evident in this rear view that was taken at Brooklands. As with the Circuit of Britain seaplane, the company name was prominently marked on the fuselage. JMB/GSL

cylinder for almost half of the twenty-eight laps. The success of the Sopwith Company was thus established internationally.

The machines on order for the Military Wing were designated SS. Again there is confusion concerning the abbreviations, one of which must have signified Scout (Sopwith Scout?) – the intended function of the type in the RFC. Unlike the St.B, the SS was a single-seater, but it did continue the use of the 80hp Gnome. Externally, there was little to differentiate the production machines from the prototype, except for the introduction of the split-axle arrangement that gave independent suspension to each wheel. This undercarriage refinement was to be a feature of subsequent Sopwith landplanes and was patented in 1916.

To the RFC the Tabloid was the Sopwith SS. The Military Wing received the first examples, in which a fin and rudder replaced the vertical tail surface of the original. The second SS was overturned on its delivery to Farnborough on 6 May 1914. The damage was not severe and it was returned to flying condition within three weeks. JMB/GSL

Plan

Front

Assembled

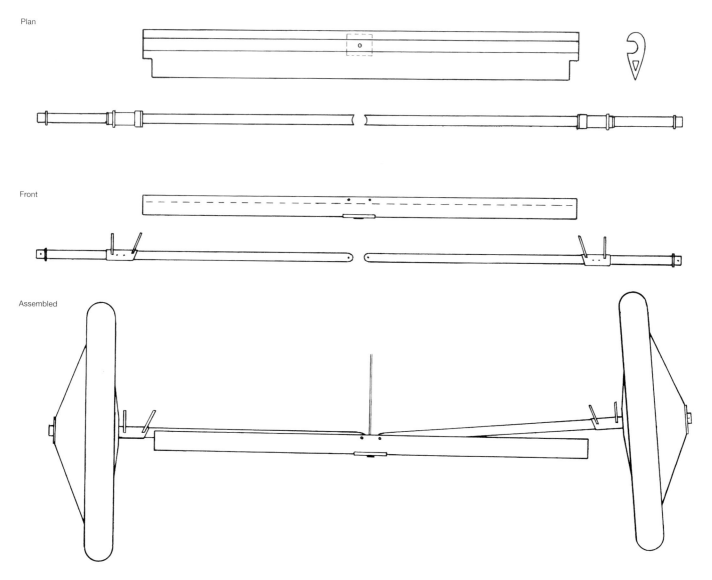

Sopwith split undercarriage.

378 was the first accepted by the Military Wing and, as was customary, was delivered to RAF Farnborough where it was load-tested to destruction. The integrity of the airframe was questioned and modifications had to be made to the interplane struts and the bracing of the fuselage box girder structure. The undercarriage was to be strengthened by an additional strut on each side. The others were then delivered from 13 May, receiving the known serial numbers 326, 381, 386, 387, 362, 392, 394 and 395. Three others were ordered, presumably for (but apparently never serving with) the CFS at Upavon, as the two known serial numbers were 611 and 654, these being in the batch reserved for that school.

The HS that won the Schneider Trophy was converted to landplane configuration but was wrecked on 27 June, in a crash that resulted from a spin. Hawker was, almost miraculously, unhurt. The machine's success at Monaco and Hawker's exhibitions on the Tabloid brought a prestigious customer for an example of the type. Louis Bleriot bought an engineless example that was delivered at the end of June. The St.B was bought by the Military Wing at the outbreak of war and numbered as 604. The military must have been unsure of how to utilize the type, as none flew to France with the original four squadrons of the Expeditionary Force. That uncertainty is further indicated by the fact that the Military Wing sold 394, 395 and 604 to the RNAS (as the Naval Wing had, by then, been unofficially but permanently renamed). In that service, the three became 167, 168 and 169 respectively, although the numbers 904 and 905 had been intended for the first two. The three were delivered to Eastchurch during the second week of September 1914.

The RNAS at Eastchurch had, at that time, another Sopwith on strength. This was 149, a twin-bay, two-seater biplane that resembled somewhat a scaled-up St.B, with aileron control. The ailerons had inverse taper. It was known as the 'Sociable', as its crew sat side-by-side, and also as the 'Churchill' because the First Sea Lord had made several flights in the machine at Hendon, where it had been delivered on 19 February.

All four of these Sopwiths went to France with the RNAS; 149, 167 and 168 on 16 September and 169 six days later. The operational use of the SS by the RNAS and RFC demonstrates the differing priorities of the two services during the early months of the war. The RFC came to

use the type as a scouting machine, but the RNAS employed it as a bomber and it was in the latter role that the type found fame.

Nos 167 and 168 went to 2 Sqn RNAS in Belgium and operated from Antwerp. Each departed on a bombing sortie on 8 October. Sqn Cdr Spenser D.A. Grey, in 167, successfully bombed Cologne railway station, after searching for his intended target of airship sheds reported at that city. Flt Lt R.G. Marix, in the other, attacked Zeppelin sheds at Düsseldorf, destroying the Z.XI. Both of these historic machines were abandoned at Antwerp in the retreat on the following day, along with 149 and, presumably, 169. All four were subsequently deleted.

The RFC did send four of its SS1s to France in mid-August, crated, with the Aircraft Park that was to supply the squadrons of the British Expeditionary Force (BEF)s. These were 362, 386, 387 and 611. The latter pair was received by 3 Sqn, but neither lasted longer than 3 September, by which date both had crashed and been struck off charge of the RFC in the field. 362 seems to have spent its time in France with the Aircraft Park, but it was assembled. It may have been cannibalized as a source of spares, as it was refurbished before being flown at St Omer in December. It crashed on 17 January 1915

and was returned to England alongside the remains of 654, which had gone to France after the original four, been issued to 5 Sqn and crashed on 2 December. There is no evidence of either being further rebuilt. 386 was, apparently, with the Aircraft Park until the beginning of December, when it was issued to 5 Sqn. Later that month, it was transferred to 4 Sqn and wrecked in January 1915, being struck off charge on the 22nd. The type's service with the RFC was brief but it is worth noting that some of these were the first Sopwith machines used to fire weaponry at enemy aeroplanes. The SS was not powerful enough to carry a machine gun, but carbines and automatic pistols were used and 2Lt N.C. Spratt of 3 Sqn is recorded as having attacked enemy machines with flechettes from 387.

The RNAS received three other machines of approximate Tabloid configuration. All retained the 80hp Gnome, but there were two distinct types. 1213 was known as the Tabloid R and was, apparently, basically an SS fitted with a racing undercarriage. By this, it is assumed that a V-strut arrangement was used. 1214 is better documented and it too had a V-strut undercarriage, whose wheels seemed disproportionally large. It and 1215 were

Specification – Sopwith SS

Engine:	One 80hp Gnome Monosoupape
Dimensions:	Length 20ft 4in (6.19m) (originally 20ft 0in (6.09m)); height 8ft 5in (2.56m); wingspan upper 25ft 6in (7.77m), lower 25ft 6in (7.77m); chord upper 5ft 1½in (1.56m), lower 5ft 1½in (1.56m); gap 4ft 6in (1.37m); dihedral upper 1°, lower 1°
Performance:	Max. speed 92mph (148km/h) Service ceiling not known Endurance 3 hours
Armament:	None by design, carbines and small bombs used operationally

Specification – Sopwith Sociable

Engine:	One 100hp Gnome Monosoupape
Dimensions:	Length 24ft 3in (7.39m); wingspan upper 36ft (10.97), lower 36ft (10.97m); height 9ft (2.74m); chord upper 5ft 1½in (1.56m), lower 5ft 1½in (1.56m); gap 4ft 6in (1.37m); dihedral upper 1°, lower 1°
Performance:	Max. speed 90mph (145km/h) Service ceiling not known Endurance 3 hours
Armament	None by design

1214 was a Tabloid type with 'racing' undercarriage. It had been constructed for the 1914 Gordon Bennett competition but was impressed into RNAS service upon the outbreak of war. It is seen at St Pol, with a Morane Type L for company. JMB/GSL

5 Wing later that month. It returned to St Pol in late June and was with 1 Sqn until at least September. By that time, 1215 had been deleted, having gone from Hendon to Chingford, but was withdrawn from use in July.

The RNAS had ordered a further twelve Tabloids and these were delivered from December 1914. They were of a revised form and designated SS3. The missing design in the sequence, the SS2, has still not been positively identified. The SS3 had the V-strut tubular undercarriage, but

differed from the SS in having a redesigned tailplane of straight leading edge, strut-connected ailerons and zero stagger. Oval-section steel tube was also used for the interplane and centre-section struts. The numbers 1201–1212 were allocated.

After testing, the first four of these were crated for HMS *Ark Royal* and service in the Dardanelles. All were aboard by the end of December, the first two having been sent to Blyth, where the ship was commissioned, and the others to Chatham, for collection en route. There was an intention to

built for the 1914 Gordon Bennett race that never took place. Wing warping was retained and a cane half-hoop was added to the underside of each lower mainplane to prevent ground damage. The engine cowling was of revised design and incorporated five cooling holes. The wing bracing utilized single flying wires, but a pair of stay cables connected the upper ends of the front interplane struts to the front engine mounting. 1215 was an almost completely different design. The mainplanes appear to have been the same as the previous machine, but the upper ones were held by a narrower centre section, of only five (not six) rib bays. This narrower centre section may have resulted from the narrow and more streamlined fuselage that was fronted by a circular engine cowling. Cooling for the Gnome was via a small frontal aperture. The tailplane was integral with the fuselage, above and below which extended the small rudder that had diminutive triangular fins placed in front.

These three machines were delivered to Hendon during October and November 1914 and comprised the Fast Flight that was formed for home defence duty. 1213 and 1214 were transferred to 1 Sqn RNAS. The latter was with that unit at St Pol by 24 April 1915 and was still on strength in June, when the squadron became 1 Wing RNAS. By that time 1214, had been fitted with a Lewis gun, mounted on the starboard fuselage side, and deflector plates on its propeller. It returned to the UK that September, joining 5 Wing at Dover. 1213 reached 1 Sqn RNAS on 6 May, but its stay was brief and it was with

1215 was the second Sopwith machine built for the 1914 Gordon Bennett competition. Its fuselage was of much greater streamlined form, with the engine enclosed in a circular cowling. Along with 1214, it served with the Fast Flight at Hendon. JMB/GSL

Tabloids ordered for the RNAS were of the SS3 type that had aileron control, zero stagger and a simple V undercarriage unit. This delightful photograph shows one of those, possibly 1202, that was sent to the Aegean. It was marked with union flags under the lower mainplanes and the picketing arrangement shown was somewhat primitive. JMB/GSL

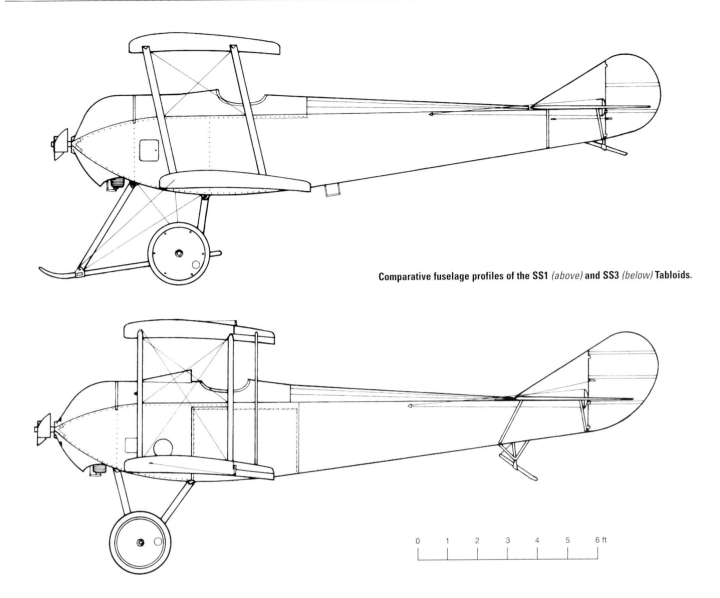

Comparative fuselage profiles of the SS1 *(above)* **and SS3** *(below)* **Tabloids.**

0   1   2   3   4   5   6 ft

use the ship's fo'c'sle to fly the aeroplanes off, but this was never put into practice. In fact, it seems that none did any flying and they were returned to the UK for deletion. 1205 and 1206 went to 1 Sqn RNAS at the beginning of January 1915, but were only in France for a month. They returned to Dover and were packed for shipment to the Aegean, where they joined 3 Sqn, later 3 Wing, RNAS for operations against the Turks. An overwing Lewis gun was fitted to each machine, but they were not popular with the pilots. As a consequence, both were returned to the UK in October and deleted. 1209 replaced them, arriving at the end of the month, but it too was found wanting and was sent home to a similar fate in December.

1209 and the final three machines of the batch had been delivered to Eastchurch for 2 Sqn RNAS, were they were used for a variety of patrol work. 1212, which, like 1211, had transferred to 4 Wing, was crashed on an anti-Zeppelin patrol on the night of 10 August, killing FSL R. Lord. 1210 lasted longest, being used by several of the development flights that operated from Eastchurch. It was finally deleted on 1 July 1916.

Yarmouth had received the remaining two machines, 1207 and 1208, on 16 March 1915. Both were not accepted immediately, but were returned to Yarmouth after repair by Sopwith's. Bomb carriers were fitted, possibly for anti-airship operations. The pair lasted for almost a year at that base, but performed no significant act of war. 1208 was deleted on 17 March 1916 and 1207 a calendar month later.

A further Tabloid type may have been intended for the RNAS. The serial number 160 was allocated for a single-seater Sopwith biplane to be powered by an 80hp Gnome. The order had been placed by July 1914 but delivery had still not been made by that December.

Despite the success achieved by Marix, the type never became popular in either service and yet it was, for its time, quite a good aeroplane. Sir Walter Raleigh, in the first volume of *The War in the Air*, suggested that the Tabloid's lack of acceptance could be attributed to its pilots, who were (by and large) not prepared, or not trained, to use it to its potential.

The Tabloid design did not, however, disappear in 1916. It would seem that a single example had been bought by Vladimir Lebedev and delivered, engineless, to Russia

(Above) The 'Sociable' or 'Churchill' was an enlarged Tabloid type and was given the number 149. It was abandoned in Belgium on 9 September 1914, during the retreat from Antwerp. JMB/GSL

The Greek naval air service ordered seaplanes from Sopwith's and one is seen here under construction. Its Monosoupape engine is already fitted. The nacelle in the foreground shows the early use of metal stampings that duplicated as brackets for longeron spacers and anchorage points for bracing wires. JMB/GSL

immediately before war broke out. In what was to become the Russian tradition, the type was copied and produced as the Lebed VII and served, in small numbers, in the Imperial Russian Air Service.

The Sopwith Pushers

Despite the performance advantages that the tractor configuration had shown over the pusher type, Sopwith's did have a flirtation with the latter. This was undoubtedly due to the fact that the pusher did offer the advantage of an unrestricted forward field of fire for any gun carried, and Sopwith's first such design was an ambitious one. The Admiralty wanted a machine that was capable of carrying a large gun (presumably a 1½lb Vickers) and, to that end, the Type S

pusher seaplane was proposed. It was allocated the service number 61 and was to be powered by twin 120hp Austro-Daimler engines. That does not necessarily imply the use of two separate engines, as it is almost certain that a double block was intended. Construction was, apparently, begun in 1913 and it is possible that this was the 80ft (24.38m) span machine that was recorded at the time. There must have been

setbacks because, even as late as August 1914, it was recorded at Woolston under allocation to Calshot. Whether it actually reached the RNAS is debatable.

A second pusher seaplane was ordered during 1913 and recorded under the contemporary generic name of Gunbus, although officially it was the SPGn (Sopwith Pusher Gun-carrier). Power came from a 200hp Salmson engine and it was, again, intended to carry a large Vickers gun. A wingspan of 80ft is also associated with this machine and it may have been a derivative of the Type S. It did go to Calshot, as No. 93, by February 1914, as it was used for tests with a Maxim machine gun. Later, a 1½lb Vickers gun was mounted and fired but, by August 1914, there were concerns about the integrity of 93's tail structure and deletion was ordered.

Nos 123 and 124 were further pusher seaplanes, both having the 100hp Anzani engine. They had also been ordered in 1913. Both were delivered to Grain in May 1914 and then transferred to Felixstowe after the declaration of war. They did some flying there and 124 was fitted with a bomb carrier, but neither was found suitable for patrol work and both returned to Grain Repair Depot, perhaps in the hope that they could be improved by reconstruction. In the event, they were deleted during February 1915, being classed as of 'poor design'.

Rear Admiral Kerr had also, during 1913, expressed interest in acquiring six armed machines for the Greek Navy that could be used for training purposes as well as patrol work. His request was passed, via the Admiralty, to Sopwith and design of another pusher seaplane, that retained use of the Anzani and four-bay, 50ft (15.24m) span wings, was undertaken. The first had been delivered during the late spring of 1914 but five were still in this country when war was declared. These were impressed, fitted with 100hp Gnomes and given the numbers 897–901. The first three were accepted at Calshot and

Specification – Sopwith SPGn, Greek Seaplane and Gunbus	
Engine:	One 100hp Anzani (SPGn & Greek Seaplane), one 150hp Sunbeam (Gunbus)
Dimensions:	Length 31ft (9.45m) (SPGn & Greek Seaplane), 32ft 6in (9.9m) (Gunbus); height 11ft 4in (3.45m) (Gunbus); wingspan upper 50ft (15.24m), lower 50ft (15.24m); chord upper 5ft 1½in (1.56m), lower 5ft 1½in (1.56m); gap 5ft 6in (1.68m); dihedral upper 3½°, lower 3½°
Performance:	Max. speed 80mph (129km/h) Service ceiling c4,000ft (1,220m) Endurance 2½ hours
Armament:	1½ Vickers gun (SPGn), one Maxim gun (Greek Seaplane & Gunbus)

The Gunbus was a very large aeroplane and the first Sopwith to be subcontracted, with most being produced by Robey & Co. of Lincoln. JMB/GSL

intended for use at Killingholme. 897 and 899 reached that station, but 898 only got as far as Yarmouth and was wrecked on 27 October. 900 and 901 were still at Kingston and were converted to landplane configuration, with strut and skid undercarriages. Both were issued to 3 Sqn RNAS in Belgium. The latter lasted less than three weeks, but 900 remained on active service until a crash on 8 November necessitated its return to England. After repair, it was on the strength of the flying school at Eastchurch until June 1915.

RNAS Seaplanes and Pushers

The Naval Wing was always keen to find ways of using aircraft as offensive weapons, and in February 1914 ordered a Special Seaplane from Sopwith's. Its purpose was to carry torpedoes and a massive machine emerged, whose span has been given as 80ft (24.38m). If so, it was the largest machine produced thus far, for the British

services. The chosen engine was the 200hp Canton-Unné cooled by lateral radiators. Wings were unstaggered and of unequal span and had four bays to each cellule, with struts supporting the overhangs. Lateral control was by comparatively small ailerons on each upper wing. Mounting the main floats under the wings created accommodation for a torpedo to be carried under the fuselage. Wingtip floats were fitted on account of the large span. The machine was delivered to Calshot on 1 July but take-off proved difficult unless the observer and a proportion of the fuel load were dispensed with. Attempts were made to rectify this problem, with modifications carried out at Woolston, but there was little improvement. 170 left Calshot for Hamble in January 1915, but was dismantled three months later.

Although total success had eluded Sopwith, in the 1913 Circuit of Britain competition Hawker's achievement had been outstanding and it was decided to enter a repeat of the event that was scheduled for August 1914. As well as a Bat Boat Type 2, a new machine, the D3, was developed for this competition. It was completed and flown at Brooklands, with a wheel and skid undercarriage. Its engine was a 100hp Gnome Monosoupape, carried on a fore-and-aft mounting and partly enclosed in a more streamlined cowling than that of the Tabloid. Each cellule of its staggered wings incorporated two bays and a triangular fin was placed ahead of the rudder.

The outbreak of war prevented that competition and the RNAS took over the proposed Sopwith entry in seaplane form. Numbered 880, it was accepted at Calshot

Specification – 1914 Circuit of Britain Seaplane	
Engine:	One 100hp Gnome Monosoupape
Dimensions:	Length not known; height not known; wingspan upper 36ft (10.97m), lower 36ft (10.97m); chord upper 5ft 1½in (1.56m), lower 5ft 1½in (1.56m); gap 5ft 7in (1.7m); dihedral upper 2°, lower 2°
Performance:	Max. speed 80mph (129km/h) Service ceiling not known Endurance 3½ hours
Armament:	None by design, light bombs carried in service

138 was the second Type 137 seaplane. It was delivered to Calshot and used for successful torpedo dropping trials. It also served at Bembridge and was not deleted until 1 January 1916. JMB/GSL

The Type 807 seaplane was known as the Folder. 919 was the first of the second batch and served at Calshot and Bembridge. JMB/GSL

with the flying school at that station until June 1915. During December 1916, long after these two machines had been withdrawn from service, the RNAS contemplated buying further examples. The serial numbers N1340–N1369 were allocated for thirty 'Daily Mail' seaplanes and a contract was drawn up, only to be cancelled.

Two large tractor seaplanes were ordered before the war and delivered to Calshot during August. These, 137 and 138, were given the designation Type 137. The first had a 120hp Austro-Daimler engine. 138 was given a 200hp Canton-Unné and had the ability to carry a torpedo, being tested with such a weapon on 25 August. 137 was re-engined to match during August 1915. Both had lengthy careers in a variety of patrol and experimental work and were finally deleted at the beginning of January 1916.

The 200hp Canton-Unné was also used in the Type C seaplane, three of which (157–159) were ordered in July 1914. These, too, were delivered to Calshot, in November, but were found wanting. 157 was tested with a torpedo, but could not take off with that load, while 158 was lost on 8 February 1915, sinking under tow after engine failure caused it to be landed in the Channel. The others did little flying and were robbed of their engines the following month, being deleted in due course.

The RNAS had appreciated the gun-carrying ability of the landplane pusher and an order was made for a further six, as the Type 806, to be numbered 801–806 and powered by Sunbeam engines. The existing 50ft (15.24m) wing configuration was again employed. The first two of these machines had the 110hp Sunbeam, but the others had the 150hp engine. All except 804 were delivered to Hendon for defence duty from October 1914. 804 was delivered to Hendon, but was transferred to the RNAS in France and issued to 1 Sqn. Its service there was brief and it returned to Hendon during August 1915. None of the others was there by that time. 801, 805 and 806 were at Chingford and the remaining two were under repair. All had been withdrawn from service by December. More, however, had been ordered on 30 June, but Sopwith's were at that time committed to mass production of the Schneider seaplane. The contract for thirty machines (3833–3862) was therefore awarded to Robey & Co. of Lincoln, which was the first of many subcontractors

and then issued to Yarmouth during that August. Bomb carriers were fitted and 880 did some operational flying. It was airborne on an anti-Zeppelin patrol on 23 January 1915 and damaged on another on 16 April. Irreparable damage was sustained on 17 May and 880 was deleted. A second such

machine had been on order for the Greek government and this, too, was impressed into RNAS service – as a landplane. Given the number 896 and fitted with a Maxim gun, that machine went to France and was based at Dunkerque until the end of 1914. It was then returned to Eastchurch and served for Sopwith designs. Production was slow and it was December before the first machine, 3835, was accepted. That aeroplane, along with 3833, 3836 and 3841, was delivered to the War Flight at Detling. It, 3833 and 3841 were wrecked in a gale on 16 February 1916, and the remaining machine was deleted some three weeks later. Eastchurch received 3849 on 13 February and others (3834, 3839–3840, 3842–3844, 3847 and 3849) over the next two months. The two-seater pusher was, by then, obsolete and all were withdrawn by that summer. 3837 was delivered, belatedly, to Hendon on 13 July, but was deleted the following month. The RNAS had no use for the balance of the order and all were delivered into storage at the White City. An attempt was made to interest the Romanian government in taking these surplus machines, but nothing came of that idea and all were scrapped.

Two developments of the 1914 Circuit of Britain machine were ordered for the RNAS and the first had the same type of engine. Four were ordered as seaplanes and designated Type 807, from the serial number of the first in the batch. The type was sometimes known as the Folder, because its mainplanes employed the Short-patented method of folding for easy shipboard stowage. Fred Sigrist later designed and patented a device whereby wings could be folded by turning a crank in the cockpit. A further eight Type 807 were ordered as 919–926. 807 and 808 were delivered to HMS *Ark Royal* at Blyth in December 1914 and taken to the Aegean, along with 922, which had been collected en route at Chatham. Their intended use was spotting for naval gunfire, but they (like the SS3s that accompanied them) were found to be of limited value and none lasted out the year.

Nos 809 and 810 were delivered to Calshot in December 1914, apparently for

Sopwith Two-Seater Scouts Flown by RNAS Squadrons and at RNAS Stations

1 Sqn RNAS Dover – 1059, 1060.
2 Sqn/2 Wing RNAS Eastchurch – 1066.
4 Sqn RNAS Dover – 1059, 1060.
Chingford – 1061, 1062, 1063, 1064, 1065, 1074.
Yarmouth (dets Bacton) – 1051, 1052, 1053, 1056, 1057, 1058.
Killingholme – 1054, 1055, 1070, 1071.
Eastchurch – 1051, 1052, 1053, 1054, 1066, 1072, 1073.
Montrose – 1067, 1068, 1069.
Dundee – 1067.
Barry – 1069.
East Fortune – 1069.

instructional purposes, and were joined by 919 and 923. The latter pair was temporarily detached to Bembridge and was augmented by 925 (ex HMS *Campania*), but all five had been deleted by September 1915. *Campania* had also taken 924 and 925 aboard and these had equally short service lives.

Nos 920 and 921 were embarked for a special operation in January 1915. They were shipped to Niororo Island, off East Africa, to provide spotting for monitors that were to shell the German warship *Königsberg*, bottled up in the Rufiji Delta. The thin tropical air made take-offs almost impossible; 922 was wrecked and 921 damaged. After languishing at Mombassa until August, 920 was transferred to the RFC Force D at Basra in Mesopotamia, where it was wrecked on New Year's Day 1917.

The Spinning Jenny

The second development of the 1914 Circuit of Britain machine was a landplane that acquired the ignominious nickname of 'Spinning Jenny'. Officially, it was the Two-Seater Scout. The inspiration for its

design was obvious from one Admiralty reference that described the twenty-four machines on order (1051–1074) as Sopwith 'Daily Mails'. That newspaper was, of course, the sponsor of the aborted competition. The Two-Seater Scout resembled, in most respects, a landplane version of the Type 807 with equal span wings, but lacked any stagger to these. A V-strut undercarriage was fitted and some had a bomb carrier slung under the fuselage behind this. These two-seaters had the 80hp Gnome and were of limited belligerent value to the RNAS. Their delivery was concurrent with that of the Type 807 and all went to home stations, initially for defence purposes, but later were relegated to training. Yarmouth, Eastchurch, Killingholme and Chingford were the main recipients, although three were detached to Montrose during the brief occupation by the RNAS of that station. The sobriquet 'Spinning Jenny' was due to the type's reputed propensity for entering that condition, but there were no recorded fatalities in the inevitable accidents that occurred. All had been withdrawn by February 1916, when the last was deleted on the 22nd.

The Type 860 Seaplane

The serial numbers 851–860 were originally allocated to Type C seaplanes, but were given to a different design that was known as the Type 860. It was a large machine, comparable with contemporary Shorts, and was powered by a 225hp Sunbeam engine. That engine had a large rectangular exhaust that could be misidentified as the radiator, which was frontally mounted. There were two configurations of wing. Some machines had equal span, three-bay cellules, while others had two-bay, unequal span wings. The overhang on the latter was strut-braced from the lower attachments of the outer interplane struts. All had close-set and sprung main floats that attached to the fuselage and wing-tip floats to counter the instability that resulted. A tail float kept the rear fuselage well clear of the water. A second order, for twelve (927–938), was placed before any from the first order had flown.

853 was delivered to Calshot on 21 December 1914 and that station initially received most others from the first batch. The type was not particularly successful and one official report concluded that there was nothing good about it. Four were

Specification – Sopwith Type 807 and Two-Seater Scout

Engine:	One 100hp Gnome Monosoupape
Dimensions:	Length not known; height not known; wingspan upper 36ft (10.97m), lower 36ft (10.97); chord upper 5ft 1½in (1.56m), lower 5ft 1½in (1.56m); gap 5ft 6in (1.68m); dihedral upper 2°, lower 2°
Performance:	Max. speed 80mph (129km/h) Service ceiling 3,000ft (915m) Endurance 3½ hours
Armament:	None by design

temporarily embarked on HMS *Engadine* and *Ben-my-Chree*, but little use was made of them. 857 and 860 were shipped to the Aegean for HMS *Ark Royal*, but received the same verdict on their usefulness as had other Sopwiths in that theatre.

Examples of the Type 860 were delivered to Dover, Dundee, Felixstowe, Killingholme and Yarmouth. 852 went to Grain, after service at Calshot and aboard the two carriers, where wings of high-lift section were fitted in October 1916, presumably in an attempt to improve the type's performance. The RNAS had, by then, realized the futility of maintaining the type in service and had cancelled a third batch (1347–1350), while later machines in the second batch were delivered directly to storage.

These were the Sopwith designs that had emerged by the end of 1914. From the foregoing, it can be concluded that none was particularly successful in service. However, the Sopwith Company had been established as a leading British manufacturer. More than 160 airframes were ordered from Sopwith's and its subcontractor, Robey. The company had achieved several 'firsts' and was well placed to handle the large contracts that were subsequently awarded. The close liaison between Sopwith and senior figures in the RNAS led to his company becoming regarded as a contractor for that service, rather than the Military Wing RFC. The machines that had been delivered may not have been outstanding, but they were of

The landplane derivative of the Type 807 was officially the Two-Seat Scout, but it was known as the 'Spinning Jenny'. This photograph shows the clean lines of the type and its lack of stagger. RNAS style cockades are marked under its mainplanes. JMB/GSL

high quality workmanship. Much use had been made of rotary engines and the most successful of the company's future products were to use that design of power plant. Lightening of structural members compensated for the limited power of rotary engines, so that spars, longerons and fuselage spacers were routed, where practical, to I-section. A practical wheeled undercarriage had been developed and much use was made of a standardized longeron clip in the assembly of

Sopwith Type 860 Seaplanes in RNAS Service
Calshot (dets Bembridge) – 851, 852, 853, 854, 855, 856, 857, 859, 931.
Dover – 859.
Dundee – 929, 930.
Felixstowe – 852, 858.
Grain – 852, 935.
Killingholme – 933.
Yarmouth – 931.
HMS *Ark Royal* – 857, 860.
HMS *Ben-my-Chree* – 852, 856, 858, 928.
HMS *Engadine* – 852, 858.

fuselage components, which facilitated mass production. The stage was set for the future development of the company.

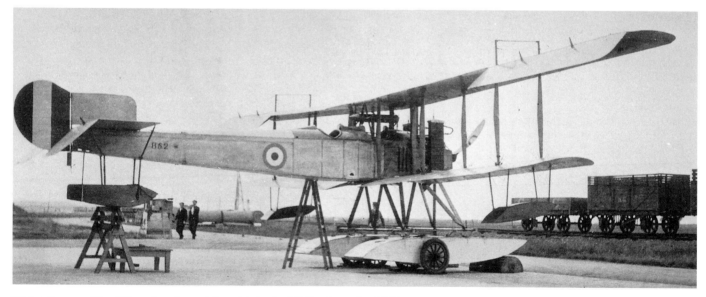

852 was the second Type 860 seaplane. It was delivered during April 1915 and served on HMS Ben-my-Chree and Engadine. It went to Grain in October 1915 and, in an attempt to improve the type's mediocre performance, was fitted with the high-lift wings shown here. It was the longest lasting of its type, not being deleted until 5 March 1917. JMB/GSL

CHAPTER THREE

Into Mass Production

The Schneider and Baby

It is surprising that the Sopwith design that lasted longest in military or naval service was a derivative of the Tabloid of 1913. That was the Baby and it was not finally withdrawn from Norwegian service until 1930. The Baby itself was a development of the Schneider, which was essentially a floatplane conversion of the Tabloid. It was also the first Sopwith design to be the subject of large-scale production.

The Schneider

It was not until the beginning of 1915 that the RNAS realized a need for a single-seat floatplane. That realization was probably the result of the Admiralty's growing preoccupation with the menace posed by the German airship. A relatively fast and armed single-seater was a possible panacea, and so machines of essentially the same configuration as the winning Schneider Cup seaplane were ordered in January of that year. That configuration included a reversion to wing warping for lateral control, even though RNAS Tabloid landplane types already in service had the more effective aileron control. The initial order was for twelve machines, numbered 1436–1447.

Construction was of typical materials for the period, although a novelty was the provision of a detachable rear fuselage, in order to facilitate stowage aboard ships. The longerons of the two fuselage portions were joined by external turnbuckles a design feature that was to re-emerge in the 2F1 Ships Camel (q.v.). Power was provided by a 100hp Gnome Monosoupape that was carried on a fore and aft mounting and enclosed on its top and sides by aluminium shields. The main floats, supported by N struts and joined by lateral ones, were widely spaced for stability, and the strut-mounted tail float carried a water rudder.

Initially, armament was envisaged as comprising light bombs that were to be

3726 was delivered to Calshot on 23 August 1915 but was wrecked the next day, in an accident that cost FSL J. MacLarty his life. It was rebuilt by Supermarine and fitted with an upward-firing Lewis, as seen here. It survived in that form until April 1917. JMB/GSL

mounted on a carrier under the fuselage, below the cockpit area. Containers for Ranken darts were a later consideration, but the type was never likely to be able to out-climb a Zeppelin and so the fitting of a Lewis gun, usually firing at an upward angle, was the logical eventual armament for anti-airship operations.

Even before the first twelve had been completed, a second order was placed for twenty-four, 1556–1579, followed in May 1915 by an order for one hundred, 3707–3806. The RNAS must have had considerable faith in the type, because another hundred, 8118–8217, were ordered that August. These were massive RNAS orders for the period, only being equalled by one for the (virtually useless) Curtiss R2.

The first production machine was delivered to Grain by late February 1915, after a brief sojourn at Calshot. It was used in experimental work at that station for more

than a year. Most initial deliveries of Schneiders were mainly to East Coast stations, notably Felixstowe, for use by seaplane carriers, although some were shipped to the Aegean for use in the Dardanelles campaign.

The Admiralty's planned use of the Schneider in the anti-airship role relied on the use of seaplane carriers, which could launch the floatplanes from prearranged positions in the North Sea, on known tracks followed by enemy airships. The carriers HMS *Vindex*, *Ben-my-Chree* and *Engadine* had been purposely converted for that role, with the provision of hangarage, but others, such as HMS *Kingfisher* and *Sir John French* were trawlers and drifters with a platform fitted aft and equipped with suitable lifting gear.

The trawlers worked in conjunction with the Yarmouth seaplane station. They would embark a Schneider, or later a Baby, when

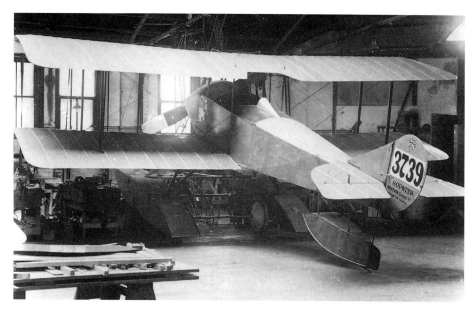

3739 is seen in the Sopwith factory before delivery. It went to Dover by road on 24 August 1915 and later served at Dunkerque. It returned to Dover, by which time it had a Lewis gun fitted, but was wrecked in an accident by Flt Lt E.J. Cooper on 24 January 1916. JMB/GSL

airships were expected and make for a station that might allow interception before the raiders could reach the coast. Seaplanes would be launched on a dusk patrol and

Changing conditions meant that pilots could be placed in the position of having to fly back to Yarmouth when return to parent vessels became impossible.

vessel was steaming into wind at 18 knots. The Schneider had a dolly fitted to its floats. Other attempts followed.

3707 had been delivered to HMS *Campania* on 11 June 1916 and in November of that year made three deck take-offs in the hands of Flt Lt R.E. Penny. The first was on the 3rd of that month and the following day he made a further two, each carrying 2¼ hours of petrol and first two and then four 16lb bombs. Penny's first such take-off was on the same day that Flt Cdr B.F. Fowler made the more widely known take-off from HMS *Vindex* in Bristol Scout C 1255. Welsh's success had been a full three months earlier.

The permanent carrier force of *Engadine*, *Vindex* and *Ben-my-Chree* was augmented with the commissioning of *Empress* and *Riviera*. There were plans, that involved Schneiders, to use these carriers to launch strikes against the bases from which Zeppelins operated, but most of these were thwarted by poor weather conditions. One that did take place was a raid mounted against Tondern, on 4 May 1916. Eleven Babies, including 8143, 8145, 8158, 8159, 8167 and 8179 participated. 8143 crashed into a destroyer on take-off, 8145 capsized, 8158 first suffered engine failure, the next two were damaged

Submarines were seen as an alternative method of transporting Schneiders to operational areas and HM E22 was fitted with a platform to test the feasibility of the idea. This print shows part of the tests, with a pair of Schneiders. Both machines have bomb carriers fitted and the rearmost has a Lewis gun mounted to fire through the propeller arc. The tests were not successful and the scheme was abandoned. JMB/GSL

then retrieved for the night. Further patrols would then be flown at dawn, in the hope of catching the enemy on the homeward journey. Sea and weather conditions in the North Sea were often unfavourable, making take-off difficult, if not impossible. Engadine attempted to launch Schneiders 1443 and 1444 on 15 May 1915 and both were wrecked, while 3711 and 3712 were lost in similar circumstances on 4 July.

The problems associated with launching seaplanes in anything other than calm conditions provoked attempts to launch machines from vessels' decks. It is often overlooked that a Schneider made one of the earliest take-offs from a moving vessel. This was achieved on 1 August 1915 by 1559, which had been delivered to HMS *Campania* at Scapa. Flt Lt W.L. Welsh made a successful take-off while the parent

on take-off. 8179 reached its target, where Flt Lt L.P. Openshaw dropped a pair of 65lb bombs, apparently without positive result.

At one stage, it was suggested that submarines could be used to transport Schneiders and Babies on such missions. The reasoning behind using such craft is not known but a possibility is that, submerged, they would have been less vulnerable in enemy waters while their charges were flying. Submarine E22 was fitted with an aft platform to test the feasibility of such operations and Schneiders were embarked. The platform was found to have a detrimental effect on underwater control of the vessel and the scheme was abandoned.

The strength of the carrier force was further enhanced in 1916, with the acquisition of HMS *Killingholme* and *Brocklesby*; a pair of converted and armed paddle steamers that could each accommodate two seaplanes. Encounters with enemy airships were few, but on 2 August 1916, *Brocklesby* sighted a Zeppelin, possibly L13, and launched Schneider 3736 and Baby 8149, flown by FSLs H.B. Smith and G.H. Bittles. Both pilots came close to making interceptions, but 3736 developed engine trouble, forcing Smith to make for Yarmouth, while Bittles could not keep up with the airship when it began to climb away.

The results of these anti-Zeppelin operations were negligible in comparison with the outlay involved and the end of 1916 saw them brought to a conclusion. Seaplanes from RNAS shore bases still flew, on occasions, against raiding airships, but the RFC had taken over responsibility for Home Defence duties. Strikes against the airship bases were then held in abeyance until that launched on Tondern by Camels from HMS *Furious* in July 1918.

The Baby

Modifications were made as production progressed and machines of the second batch of one hundred were officially given the new name of Baby and the Admiralty designation of Type 8200, the number being taken from the serial of an early representative machine. Attempts had been made to increase the strength of the main

The distinctive horseshoe-shaped engine cowling of the Baby is seen in this photograph of a machine on its beaching trolley, ready loaded with four small bombs. JMB/GSL

floats and aileron control was introduced. Later Schneiders also had an enlarged fin, with a pronounced kink in its leading edge, and also had aileron control, possibly fitted retrospectively. The first five and last thirty-one of the batch from 8118 retained the Monosoupape engine, while the others and subsequent Babies had a Clerget, initially 110hp 9Z but later of the 130hp 9B type. It was not, therefore, the change of engine type that merited the new name. The Clergets were carried on an overhung mounting

---

Specification – Sopwith Schneider and Baby

Engine:	One 100hp Gnome Monosoupape (Schneider & Baby) or 110hp Clerget 9Z (Baby) or 130hp Clerget 9B (Baby)
Weights:	Empty 1,220lb (553kg) (Schneider), 1,226lb (556kg) (110hp Baby), 1,286lb (583kg) (130hp Baby); loaded 1,700lb (771kg) (Schneider), 1,580lb (717kg) (110hp Baby), 1,715lb (778kg) (130hp Baby)
Dimensions:	Length 22ft 10in (6.96m) (Schneider & 110hp Baby), 23ft (7m) (130hp Baby); height 10ft (3.08m); wingspan upper 25ft 8in (7.82m), lower 25ft 8in (7.82m); chord upper 5ft 2in (1.57m), lower 5ft 2in (1.57m); gap 4ft 6in (1.37m); stagger 8in (20.32m); dihedral upper 2°, lower 2° on Schneider & 130hp Baby, upper 2½°, lower 2½° on 110hp Baby
Performance:	Max. speed 87mph (140km/h) (Schneider), 100mph (160km/h) (Baby) Service ceiling 7,000ft (2,130m) (Schneider), 8,000ft (2,440m) (Baby) Endurance 3 hours (Schneider), 2 hours (110hp Baby), 2¼ hours (130hp Baby)
Armament:	Schneider –1 × 65lb (29kg) bomb on under-fuselage carrier or equivalent weight of smaller bombs, grenades or darts. Lewis gun could be fitted to fire forwards from overwing position or forwards and upwards through a centre-section cut-out. Baby – 2 × 65lb bombs on under-fuselage carrier or equivalent weight of smaller bombs, grenades or darts. Lewis gun fitted to forward fuselage and synchronized to fire through propeller arc or fitted to upper centre section and fired above propeller arc. Le Prieur rockets could be fired from tubes on interplane struts.

Wing Warping

Today, aileron control is seen as the accepted method of lateral control but many early machines, including the Schneider, utilized wing warping. In the case of biplane designs, this usually involved the use of cables that ran from a chain on the control column (or wheel) to the underside of the rear spars of the upper wing at the interplane strut mountings. Rolling was induced by control movement that, via the cables, pulled the rear edge of the outside wing to increase the angle of attack and increase lift. The interplane strut transferred this movement to the lower wing. Simultaneously, the tension on the rear spar of the opposite wing was released and the angle of attack decreased to reduce lift. Biplane machines with such control can be recognized in photographs by their lack of bracing between the interplane struts.

8151 was a Baby of the first production batch and was delivered to Grain on 11 December 1915. It served with the Nore War Flight at that station and then transferred to Felixstowe, where it was fitted with the Lewis gun seen on its starboard longeron. It was wrecked on 21 May 1916. JMB/GSL

(Below) 8210 was a Baby that retained the Schneider form of engine cowling. It was delivered to the RNAS flying school at Calshot and was at Lee-on-Solent (the location for this photograph) by October 1917. JMB/GSL

and a new cowling, of horseshoe frontal shape, was fitted. The Baby had a slight increase in wing dihedral angle but, in its Monosoupape version, was virtually indistinguishable from the Schneider.

Mediterranean Operations

Early Schneiders were flight-tested from the River Thames, but that practice was soon dropped. Instead, the airframes were delivered from Kingston to Woolston, near Southampton, for erection and testing. Many were then recrated for delivery to RNAS stations.

Schneiders 1437 and 1438, the second and third production machines were delivered to the Aegean in April 1915, for use from HMS *Ark Royal* during the Dardanelles campaign. Neither lasted long, but attempts were made to equip the former with a wireless transmitting set, for use in observation duties. Others followed, *Ark Royal* receiving 1566, 1577, 1578 and 1579 and *Ben-my-Chree* bringing 1560 and 1561 when that vessel joined the Aegean force in June. The Schneiders were not as effective platforms for reconnaissance as the Shorts that were also carried, but proved more reliable. Duties included spotting for the naval bombardments that preceded the landings and, as the campaign bogged down into stalemate, observation of enemy positions. After the evacuation of Allied troops, *Ark Royal* served as a depot ship, being based at Mudros, with her Schneiders and, later, Babies flying from shore stations and on detachment to a variety of smaller vessels. Some were embarked on HMS *Peony* during 1917, when it was thought that German submarines were operating in the Aegean. That embarkation was needed because further proposed seaplane stations, to supplement that at Syra, had not been commissioned.

although he failed to hit the target. N1424 was then forced down through engine failure but Peel managed to escape the attention of enemy vessels by taxiing away.

The evacuation from Gallipoli in January 1916 led to the withdrawal of HMS *Ben-my-Chree*, which then joined the East Indies and Egypt Seaplane Squadron (EI & ESS) that was in the process of forming at Port Said. That squadron had operated French Nieuport seaplanes, but began to receive Shorts, Schneiders and, later, Babies. During May, it received a new CO,

The effect of the 90+ bombs dropped was sufficient to contain the situation and *Raven II* returned to Egypt. She was replaced by *Ben-my-Chree*, whose two Schneiders (3789 and 3790 – the latter ex *Raven II*) and Baby (8189) helped to continue the campaign.

Turkish communications in Sinai, particularly railways, were the subject of subsequent attention by the ships and seaplanes of the EI & ESS. Samson, as was typical of the man, was inclined to lead from the front and participated in several raids and spotting missions. On 27

Schneider 1438 was shipped to the Aegean for use on HMS Ark Royal and is seen here being hoisted out for a sortie in April 1915. The deep bomb carrier, as fitted to the type, is seen below the lower wing trailing edge. 1438 lasted until 29 September 1915, when it was overturned in a downwind landing that followed an engine failure. JMB/GSL

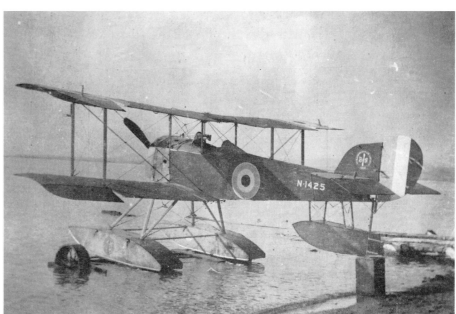

N1425 was initially delivered to Dover. It went to the Aegean for HMS Ark Royal and was later transferred to the Greek naval air service. JMB/GSL

Babies were operational in the Aegean theatre even as late as 20 January 1918, when two were involved in attacking the German cruiser *Goeben*. That vessel and its companion, the *Breslau*, had made a sortie from the Dardanelles to attack British monitors and bombard Mudros. The *Breslau* sank after striking a mine. The *Goeben* struck another and made to return to base. FSL W. Johnston (N1445) and R.W. Peel (N1424), although escorted by a Camel, were intercepted by enemy seaplanes. Johnston was shot down in flames, but Peel managed to drop his two 65lb bombs

the innovative and inspirational Commander C.R. Samson. The EI & ESS was to conduct a mobile campaign against Turkish forces in the Eastern Mediterranean and Red Sea and, living up to its name, also ventured into the Indian Ocean.

Much of its work involved spotting from British naval bombardments, with Schneiders being carried by its four ships, *Ben-my-Chree*, *Empress*, *Anne* and *Raven II*. Occasionally it conducted bombing missions. During March 1916, Arabs sympathetic to the Turkish cause were massing around the strategically important base of Aden. *Raven II*, with five operational Schneiders (3721, 3722, 3727, 3774 and 3790) and a Short, was dispatched and conducted a three-day bombing operation, beginning on the 31st.

December, for example, he flew Schneider 3770 in a bombing attack on the Chicaldare Railway Bridge, scoring a direct hit with one of his bombs.

Raven II was detailed, in March 1917, to search the Indian Ocean for the German commerce raider *Wolf*, which also embarked a seaplane. Samson's unit only embarked one Baby (N1014), along with four Short 184s – the single-seater type being less suited to observation duties. N1014 was temporarily transferred to HMAS *Brisbane*, in order to widen the search, and was fitted with twin overwing Lewis guns at that time. The quarry had, however, made for the Pacific and *Raven II*, with all her seaplanes, had returned to Port Said by June.

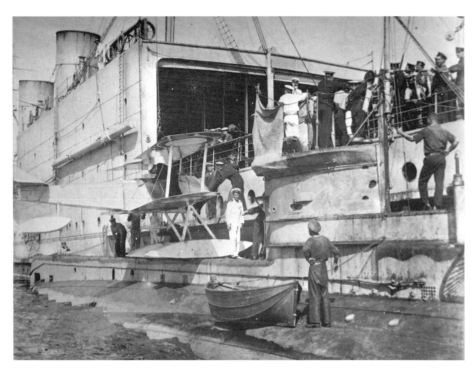

3722 was also shipped to the Aegean and served on HMS Ben-my-Chree and Raven II. It is seen here whilst serving on the former and is resting on a submarine that is moored alongside the parent vessel. 3722 was damaged at Port Said on 17 April 1916 and subsequently deleted. JMB/GSL

by Ansaldo. Those Babies produced in Italy had a fully circular cowling that housed a 110hp Le Rhone. There was also Japanese interest and 8201 was transferred to that country, as a sample, in July 1916, but, despite making a suitably good impression, no further orders were placed until, apparently, 1918. There were no replacements ordered to make good the transfer of Babies to the French and Italians, but 8201 was so covered. Its replacement, built by Blackburn's, was given the number N300. That serial was in the range reserved for experimental seaplanes and flying boats.

Sub-Contracted Production

Production by the Blackburn Aeroplane and Motor Co. has been alluded to and the reason for the transfer of production to that subcontractor requires explanation. The first order given to the Leeds-based company was dated 24 May 1916. By that time, Sopwith's Kingston factory, with its limited capacity, had been given over to the production of the first 1½ Strutters and the Pup and Triplane were in the pipeline. The first seventy machines from Blackburn's, built in three batches (N1010–N1039, N1060–N1069 and N1100–N1129), were almost indistinguishable from those of the parent company, save for the addition of the prominent logo that was applied to the fins and floats of the Leeds-built machines. They were powered by the 110hp Clerget 9Z. N300, the extra machine to replace that supplied to Japan, had a 100hp Monosoupape. Subsequent machines, from mid 1917, were fitted with the 130hp Clerget 9Bf, in an attempt to increase power for take-off. Blackburn's also introduced a new section wing, from N1031, which retained the original planform. The Blackburn factory was, of course, away from any suitable stretches of water for flight-testing and so its products were delivered, by lorry or by train, to RNAS stations for erection and testing.

That ship's subsequent operations were in the Eastern Mediterranean, against Turkish positions during the third Battle of Gaza. She was joined by *Empress* for further attacks on communications and depots, the latter having embarked Hamble Babies (N1209 and N1210) in addition to Babies (N1028, N1038, N1106 and N1139). These were some of the last operations of their type by the EI & ESS, whose ships were dispersed the following spring. Some Babies continued to operate from Port Said, but were quickly replaced by landplanes upon the formation of 269 and 270 Sqn in October 1918. A few went to Malta and were operated by 268 Sqn at Calafrana.

were joined later by four Blackburn-built specimens. These were used operationally, but further orders did not materialize from that government. 8214 and 8215 were delivered to Italy as pattern machines, to assist production of the type under licence

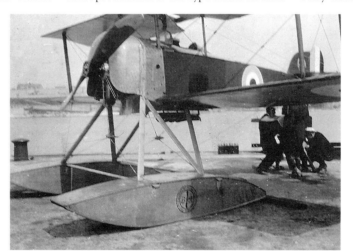

This Blackburn-built Baby was photographed at Fishguard and was, probably, N1127. That machine was the vehicle for tests of a new carrier for four 20lb bombs. Such a carrier is seen mounted close to the fuselage. N1127 had the distinction of being involved in an attack on an enemy submarine, on 22 March 1918. It was at Yarmouth by mid-June and deleted on 10 October 1918. JMB/GSL

Babies were ordered from two further subcontractors during January 1917. These were the Fairey Aviation Co. Ltd of Hayes and Hamble and George Parnall & Sons of Bristol. Fairey

Foreign Sales

There was early foreign interest in the Baby. Three machines, 8128, 8129 and 8185, were transferred to the French government from April 1916 and had received the Sopwith-built Baby 8134 by the end of May 1916 and set about a series of modifications that were designed to improve take-off performance and load-carrying ability. Increased span mainplanes, that carried larger ailerons, were first fitted, but were replaced by others that incorporated that company's Patent Camber Gear. This was a device that used the full span of all mainplane trailing edges, from the rear spars aft, as flaps that could be lowered to increase lift by turning a handle on the side of the cockpit. Those same flaps could also be applied differentially as ailerons. They were carried on wings of,

again, increased span that had distinctively rounded tips. Better adhesion of fabric to the mainplane ribs was ensured by the use of half-round wooden strips, nailed and glued, rather than stitching and tape covering. Larger and strengthened floats were fitted as a measure designed to overcome another shortcoming of the Baby, that of frequent float damage in rough seas. Parnall-built Babies were of similar design, but could be distinguished from Fairey-built examples by their retention of the Sopwith/Blackburn styles of fin and rudder. Fairey chose to modify the fin to one of a more square-cut shape and attached a

rudder of reduced area. These changes did little to improve the performance, in terms of speed and rate of climb.

The gradual modification of the airframe, combined with the adoption of the more powerful 130hp Clerget did result, however, in an increased load-carrying capacity, it being usual for these later machines to be armed with two 65-lb bombs and one (sometimes two) Lewis gun. Fairey and Parnall-built machines were generically known as Hamble Babies, as a means of differentiating them from those produced by Sopwith and Blackburn. In reality, there were in fact differences

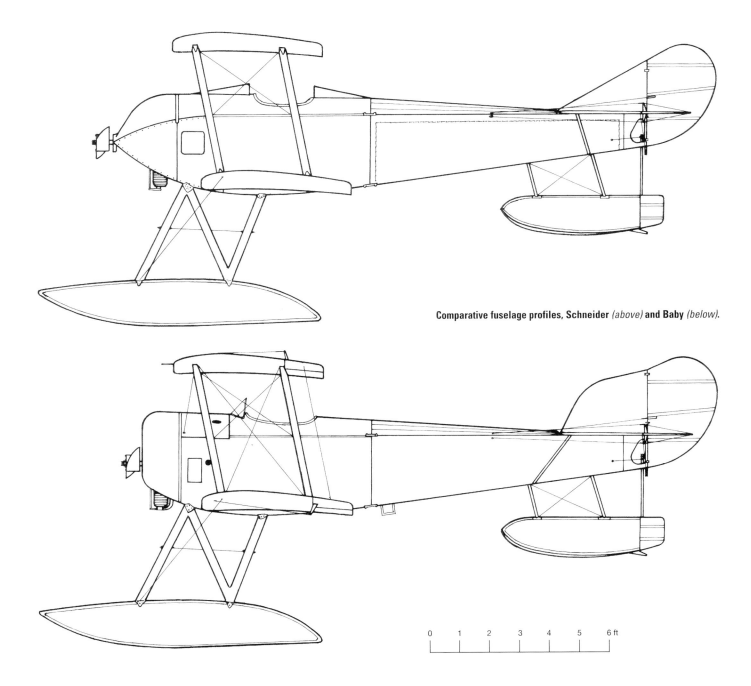

Comparative fuselage profiles, Schneider *(above)* **and Baby** *(below)*.

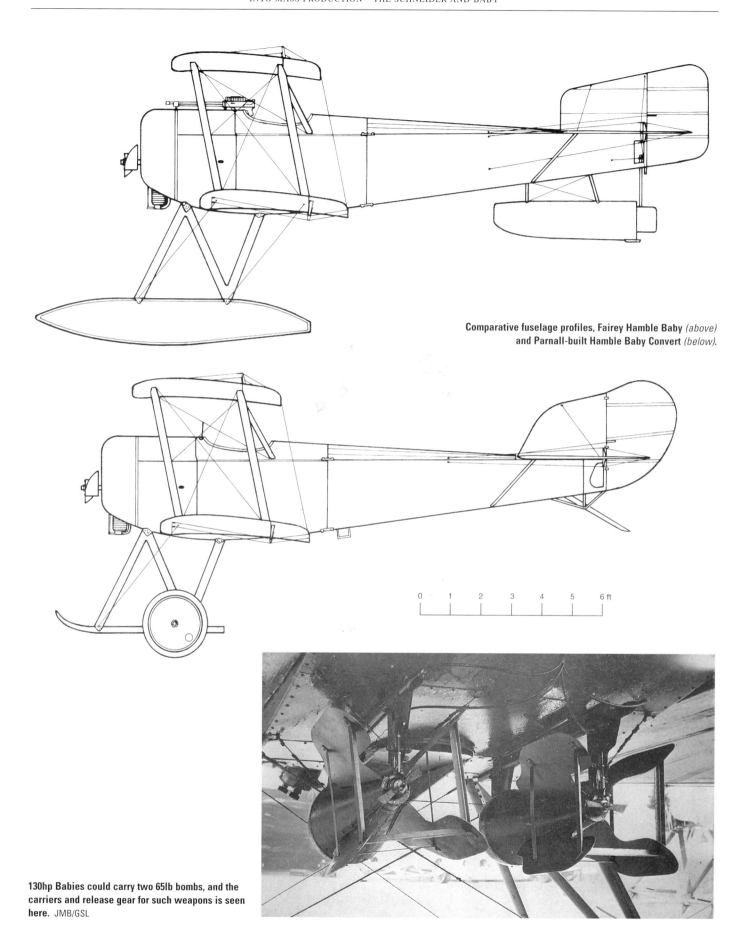

Comparative fuselage profiles, **Fairey Hamble Baby** *(above)* and **Parnall-built Hamble Baby Convert** *(below).*

0   1   2   3   4   5   6 ft

130hp Babies could carry two 65lb bombs, and the carriers and release gear for such weapons is seen here. JMB/GSL

between the Hamble Babies produced by the two firms, other than the shape of the fin and rudder, and many parts were not interchangeable.

Late War Operations

Babies were delivered to a variety of seaplane stations in the UK, usually as parts of mixed complements that included Short 184s. The bases at Dover, Grain, Yarmouth, Felixstowe, Westgate and Killingholme flew the type on anti-Zeppelin patrols after the withdrawal of the temporary seaplane carriers. Attempts were made to mount Le Prieur rockets on the interplane struts of some machines, but those weapons were not adopted. Usually, pilots relied on using the Lewis gun, Ranken darts and small bombs. The Baby's limited endurance, poor rate of climb and low service ceiling made it unsuited to that task, but there were occasions when combat could have been joined. It was probably Flt Lt G.H. Bittles who came closest to having a chance of success. On 17 June 1917, while flying from Yarmouth in N1064, he encountered the airship L42 off Lowestoft and attacked at 11,000ft

(Above) N2071 was a well photographed machine, its attraction being, perhaps, the red and white chequered cowling and white floats. It was fitted with two Lewis guns and served at Yarmouth. JMB/GSL

(Left) The Hamble Baby could be distinguished by its rounded wing-tips. One is seen here, being hoisted onto the pier at Fishguard. JMB/GSL

(Right) The Baby was seen as an anti-airship machine and Le Prieur rockets were envisaged as possible armament. The pyrotechnic effect of their firing is seen here. JMB/GSL

(3,350m) from close range. The airship did not catch fire, despite his firing a full drum of Lewis ammunition into it, and climbed away from the seaplane.

Babies from these bases also flew anti-submarine patrols and were joined by others at Dundee and Calshot. More were added as new stations opened at Seaton Carew, Hornsea Mere, Lee-on-Solent, the Cattewater, Newlyn and Fishguard. Calshot also had a training function, as did Felixstowe and Killingholme. These Babies were, by late 1917, being delivered from and underwent major repairs at the Depots sited at South Shields, Brough and Hamble.

The Baby, like other rotary-engined aircraft, was susceptible to engine choking if the mixture settings were not adjusted at the appropriate time on take-off or after applying full throttle. Several were lost after this cause of engine failure, an example being N1063 from Dundee. The type was by no means aerobatic, but the seaplane station at Dundee was just downstream of the Tay Bridge which, like similar structures elsewhere, exercised a fascination for pilots. During August 1918, Lt V.D. Grant (who claimed to have already rolled a Baby) received his station commander's permission to attempt to fly between the spans of that bridge. He accomplished that feat successfully but, after a low flypast of the slipways at Dundee, opened up his engine too far. It choked and N1063 ended wrecked on the shingle downstream. Grant managed to walk away from the crash.

By late 1917, there were more Babies, of both types, on order than the RNAS anticipated it could use. As a consequence, the Parnall firm was instructed to deliver its second batch of seventy-five machines (N1986–N2059) as landplane conversions, that type becoming known as the Hamble Baby Convert. It was not a pretty conversion. The undercarriage struts of the floatplane were retained, but connected to a pair of short skids, onto which was mounted the axle for a pair of wheels. A skid supported the tail. On some machines, at least, a headrest was fitted and provision was made for carrying a Lewis gun that was synchronized to fire through the propeller arc.

The first six of these Converts were shipped to Otranto in December 1917, for use by 6 Wing RNAS, but three were lost when their transport was torpedoed. The survivors served on after the formation of the RAF, being on the strength of 225 Sqn during April 1918. They were not the only

Babies to operate in Italy. Baby and Hamble Baby floatplanes of 441 Flt, 263 Sqn flew from St Maria di Leuca. The next four and N2007–N2009 were delivered to Yarmouth, after a period in storage at Killingholme, and lasted until the summer of 1918, latterly on the charge of 490 Flt. N1996–N2003 were delivered to Cranwell for training purposes, most surviving long enough to be on 201 TDS, after the formation of that unit on 1 April.

There was no further use for the remainder of the Hamble Baby Converts and all were delivered to store at Killingholme. Their fate after the formation of the RAF is unknown, but it may be that some were transferred abroad. It is known that Norway bought ten Babies, but known photographs show these to have been of the original type, as built by Sopwith and Blackburn. Japan is reported to have acquired twenty Babies in 1918 and these might have been Converts. The fate of the vast majority of Babies is quite well documented and the only other possible source of the reported Japanese Babies could be these stored Parnall machines.

The RNAS Dover-Dunkerque Command sought to protect its Short 184s from attack by enemy seaplanes and to that end created the Seaplane Defence Flt at Dunkerque in June 1917. Its initial equipment was Babies, but these proved unsuitable and were supplemented and then replaced by Pups which flew from the nearby St Pol aerodrome. Babies still flew from Dunkerque, however. N1106, N1121, N1430 and N1431 joined the initial French deliveries from August, and were flown operationally.

Babies continued to serve in the Aegean with 62 Wing, which used *Ark Royal* as its HQ, after that unit was formed by the RAF from 2 Wing RNAS. N1425 was transferred to the Royal Hellenic Naval Air Service and that force also received 20 Hamble Babies. Those were of both Fairey and Parnall manufacture and most had seen previous service with RNAS units in the UK. Although prepared for shipment during May and June 1918, it was the beginning of September before they were dispatched.

The type also served on the other side of the Atlantic. The Royal Canadian Naval Air Service (RCNAS) planned to create an anti-submarine force to protect shipping on its eastern seaboard. It received four Schneiders (3707, 3708, 3765 and 3806) and five Babies (8124, 8125, 8197, 8204 and 8209).

Most of these had seen previous service with RNAS units and were reconditioned by Blackburn's before dispatch in the spring of 1917. The RCNAS had little use for them, presumably due to its decision to adopt Curtiss flying boats as the mainstay of its proposed anti-submarine force. At least two of its Schneiders (3709 and 3765) and one Baby (8209) had been transferred to the US Navy by 1918. Further south, the Chilean government received three Babies (N1068, N2103 and N2104), probably as part of the exchange that included Bristol monoplanes. These Babies, too, had seen previous service, but were packed during May 1918 and shipped some two months later. The last survivor of these was still flying in 1921.

Floatplane operations from the UK were often conducted from sites of primitive conditions, several seaplane stations being very temporary in nature. The operation of Baby seaplanes in the anti-submarine role was typified by the experience of the base at Seaton Carew, originally known as Tees. The site had opened in September 1917 and was intended as an interim base until a permanent station could be opened on Holy Island. Consequently, only Bessoneau hangars were erected and the ground crew of its War flight were accommodated under canvas. The inhospitable conditions in winter on the north-east coast and the deprivation suffered led to the need to billet the ratings on the local population. With the abandonment of plans for Holy Island and the arrival of spring, a permanent seaplane shed was erected. The War Flight was amalgamated into 252 Sqn, when that unit formed on 25 May 1918, becoming 451 and 452 Flts under a new numbering system that allotted 450–469 Flts to units operating Babies. Only the first six flights of this block were taken up, the Baby being, by that time, regarded as virtually obsolete and inferior to both landplanes and the two-seater Short 184 in terms of endurance and bomb-carrying capacity. The other remaining Baby flights were at Dundee, Hornsea Mere and Yarmouth. Further Babies were still used, in increasingly smaller numbers, at Fishguard, Calshot, Westgate and Felixstowe.

The two Seaton Carew flights continued to operate Babies for a further five months and performed some useful work. Although no submarines were sunk, attacks were made on eleven. FSL E.F. Waring, in N2101, made an early one of these on 25 March 1918. That pilot sighted a submarine 15 miles (24km) east of Hartlepool and dropped the seaplane's 65lb bomb, which fell astern of its target. Further attacks were made in the following months by Lt E.J. Addis, Lt L.C.F. Clutterbuck, Lt R.R. Richardson and Lt G.F. Taylor. Only one was classified as having, perhaps, caused slight damage, that being on 31 May when Clutterbuck dropped his bomb from N2111 an estimated 6yd (5.5m) on the starboard bow of a U-boat that was sighted 12 miles (19km) off Whitby.

Transfer of 451 and 452 Flts to 246 Sqn control took place when that unit formed as part of the 68th Wing on 15 August. It would seem that the squadron was short of aircrew as some of the pilots also flew land-planes from the nearby Seaton Carew aerodrome, Richardson being recorded as making at least two attacks on U-boats in Kangaroo B9975.

Pilots who were posted to seaplane stations had long spells at those bases. The experience of FSL G.F. Hyams exemplifies this. After preliminary training and a 'boat' course at Killingholme, he was posted to the War Flt at Hornsea Mere, which provided a sheltered stretch of fresh water for floatplane operations. His initial flights there were on FBA 9616, which he had brought from Killingholme, but on 1 October 1917 he had his first flight on a 110hp Baby N1411, making a 1-hour search for a wrecked airship. Almost all of his subsequent flights until July 1918 were in Babies, of either Sopwith

N2099 was delivered to Killingholme and marked with the distinctively large serial presentation adopted by that station. It subsequently went to Seaton Carew. JMB/GSL

or Hamble varieties. His logbook reveals that most were patrols of a fairly standardized pattern that must have involved a degree of monotony. On 26 March 1918, however, he sighted and bombed a submarine 10 miles (16km) north-east of Scarborough. On other occasions, he was called out on 'Special Patrols', when submarines had been reported. Hyams was Mentioned in Dispatches for his perseverance in

drawing aid to the crew of an H12, which he had observed to crash on 19 July.

The Baby was withdrawn from 246 Sqn during October, 451 Flt disbanding on 10 October and 452 Flt on the last day of that month. The unit's remaining Babies were returned to the Depot at South Shields. The other numbered Baby flights were disbanded at about the same time, 450 Flt at Dundee and 454 Flt at Yarmouth on 30 September, and 455 Flt at Yarmouth on the same day as 452 Flt and 453 Flt at Hornsea Mere on 30 November. The type had not been numerous during 1918. From 1 May until the signing of the Armistice the average number in service at home was forty-six, of which an average of nineteen were serviceable on any one day. This serviceability rate of 41% may seem low, but it was greater than that of either the Short 184 or the 'Large America' flying boats. Patrols by the Baby averaged 1 hour 49 minutes and were less susceptible to curtailment by either the weather or engine trouble than those of the other types.

Post-War Use

The Norwegian government, as noted above, bought ten Babies in 1917. As a neutral country, with thousands of miles of fjord coastline to patrol and few bases to operate from, the easily launched Baby was an obvious choice. The first machines

The Chilean government acquired three Babies, which were delivered in July 1918. N2103 was one and was photographed at Talcahuano. via D. Brown

landplane configuration. The undercarriages of these were a lot more refined than those of the Hamble Baby Convert. The Norwegian government lent a Baby to their intrepid polar explorer, Roald Admunsen, for his 1921 expedition, and it was another nine years before the last was withdrawn, almost certainly the last Sopwith type in service.

Today, the FAA museum at Yeovilton is graced by the presence of a Baby replica that contains some original parts. Marked as a Blackburn-built machine, N2078, carrying the name *The Jabberwock*, it represents a machine flown from Hornsea Mere by 453 Flt. Its small size is immediately apparent and allows latter-day enthusiasts to wonder at the undoubted bravery of pilots who flew the type from and over inhospitable stretches of water.

were delivered and in use by the end of that year and it seems probable that N2125–N2130, which were taken from storage at Brough and delivered to a foreign government, made up the balance.

In Norwegian service the Babies' duties included patrolling for alien vessels and loose mines. The machines lasted well, this being the result of a rebuilding programme that also saw some converted to

---

Representative Schneiders and Babies with Ships, RNAS Stations and RAF Units

RNAS Bembridge: 3780, 3781, 3785, N1198, N1202, N1333.

RNAS Calshot: N1017, N1436, N1437, N1960, N1961, N1965, N1969, N1970, N1971, N1972, N1973, N1974, N1975.

RNAS Cattewater: N1023, N1191, N1206, N1207, N1208, N1330, N1414, N1433, N1456, N1963.

RNAS Dover: 8145, 8171, 8195, N1069, N1194, N1410, N1425.

RNAS Dundee: N1063, N1067, N1197, N1219, N1432, N1438, N1439, N1440, N1441.

RNAS Felixstowe: 3711, 3712, 3746, 3747, 3748, 3794, 8137, 8165, 8166, 8198, 8199, N1118, N1190.

RNAS Fishguard: N1033, N1127, N1199, N1205, N1433, N1457.

RNAS Grain: 3753, 8118, 8119, 8123, 8151, 8168.

RNAS Hornsea Mere: N1204, N1448, N1449, N1469, N1471, N2079, N2087, N2088, N2089, N2096, N2097.

RNAS Houton Bay: N1978.

RNAS Killingholme*: 3800, 3801, 8130, 8141, 8147, 8148, 8154, 8155, 8161, 8162, 8206, 8207, N1037, N1068, N2102.

RNAS Lee-on-Solent: N1211, N1331, N1332, N1458, N1463, N1960, N1961, N1969, N1971, N1972.

RNAS Newlyn: N1023, N1062, N1191, N1205, N1420.

RNAS Otranto: N1030, N1442, N1443, N1981, N1982, N1983, N1989, N1990, N1991, N2080, N2081, N2090, N2091, N2093.

RNAS Scapa: 3707, 3806, N1964, N1965, N1978.

RNAS Tees (Seaton Carew): N2063, N2064, N2067,

N2098, N2099, N2100, N2101, N2106, N2107, N2108, N2109, N2110.

RNAS Tresco: N1191.

RNAS Westgate: 3756, 3757, 3758, 3766, 8119, 8146, N1065, N1203, N1025, N1212, N1450.

RNAS Windermere: 3781.

RNAS Yarmouth**: 3715, 3716, 3744, 8122, N1061, N1206, N1207, N1208, N1977, N2068, N2069, N2070, N2071, N2116.

EI & ESS – Port Said (HMS *Raven II*, *Empress*, *Anne*, *Ben-my-Chree*): 3774, N1014, N1060, N1209, N1210, N2072, N2073.

2 Wing RNAS – Mudros/Syros/Thasos/Talikna/HMS *Ark Royal*: 3772, N2074, N2075, N2076, N2077, N2082, N2083, N2086.

Seaplane Defence Sqn & RNAS Station – Dunkerque: 8126, 8171, N1011, N1015, N1017, N1019, N1024, N1031, N1069.

212 Sqn 490 Flt – Burgh Castle/Yarmouth: N1992, N1993, N1994, N1995, N2007, N2008, N2009.

219 Sqn – Westgate: N1962.

225 Sqn – Andrano: N1989, N1990, N1991.

229 Sqn 454/455 Flts – Yarmouth: N2114, N2115, N2116.

246 Sqn 451/452 Flts – Seaton Carew: N1447, N2063, N2064, N2067, N2107, N2108, N2109.

248 Sqn 453 Flt – Hornsea Mere: N2087, N2088, N2089, N2094, N2095, N2097, N2099, N2112, N2113.

249 Sqn 450 Flt – Dundee: N1438, N1439, N1440, N1441.

252 Sqn 451/452 Flts – Seaton Carew: N1447, N2063, N2064, N2067, N2101, N2107, N2108, N2109, N2111.

263 Sqn – Otranto/Santa Maria di Leuca: N1336, N2090, N2091, N2092, N2093.

268 Sqn – Calafrana: N2132, N2133, N2134.

269 Sqn – Port Said: N2073, N2132, N2133.

270 Sqn – Alexandria: N2131.

271 Sqn – Otranto: N1981.

201 TDS/57 TDS – Cranwell: N1996, N1997, N1998, N1999, N2000, N2101, N2102, N2103.

HMS *Campania*: 3709, 3796, 3797, 3798, 3806, 8124, 8125, 8183, 8184, 8190, 8191, 8192, N1026, N1027, N1416.

HMS *Engadine*: 3711, 3712, 3714, 8142, 8162, 8175, 8176, 8177, 8178, 8181, 8182, N1021, N1022, N1100.

HMS *Manxman*: N1020, N1021, N1022, N1967, N1968, N2119, N2120, N2122.

HMS *Pegasus*: N1415, N1416.

HMS *Riviera*: 8138, 8145, 8179, N1031, N1124, N1414, N1982, N1983, N2124.

HMS *Vindex*: 3750, 3755, 8145, 8152, 8153, 8157, 8158, 8159, 8167, 8171, 8179, 8181.

HMS *Nairana*: N1440, N1441.

* Machines from Killingholme were embarked for operations on HMS *Killingholme* and *Princess Margaret*

** Machines from Yarmouth were embarked for operations on HMS *Brocklesby*, *Canatrice*, *Christopher*, *Dryad*, *Halcyon*, *Jerico* and *Kingfisher*.

CHAPTER FOUR

The 1½ Strutter

The First True Fighter

Affectionately known as the 1½ Strutter, the Sopwith LCT was a remarkably clean aeroplane for its time and it introduced design features that would be carried on with the Pup, Triplane and Camel. Although not positively resolved, the initial letters LCT are generally accepted to have represented Land Clerget Tractor. The tractor configuration was not something new to Sopwith designs, but hitherto the majority of its machines had been seaplanes and the use of the 110hp Clerget 9Z introduced a more powerful rotary engine than had previously been used.

Inception

The origins of the LCT lay in a private company design that was known as the Sigrist Bus, or Sigrist's bus. Apocryphal as it may seem, Fred Sigrist had, in late 1914, chalked out the design of a new machine on the workshop floor at Kingston and work on its production proceeded as and when time allowed. What emerged, when completed, was quite a remarkable machine. It was a compact, two-seat, single-bay biplane with uneven span wings. There was no centre section as such, only a central box rib that was carried above the fuselage on inverted-V struts. The upper mainplanes were attached to the fuselage at the base of these V struts, each by a pair of fairly long bracing struts. This gave a frontal W shape to the central strutting arrangement, of one long and one half strut to each mainplane spar. The engine was an 80hp Gnome. The undercarriage featured a central skid. The machine was completed by December 1914 and was used by Harry

Hawker on 6 June 1915 to establish a new British altitude record of 18,393ft (5,606m). That record-breaking flight was made from Hendon and the altitude reached was the corrected figure from a barograph reading of more than 6,000m. Contemporary reports suggest that the machine had a maximum speed of about 90mph (145km/h).

On 12 December 1915, almost exactly a year after the Sigrist Bus had first appeared, a new machine was passed by Sopwith's Experimental Department. This was the LCT. It was completed four days later and its wing layout owed much to the previous

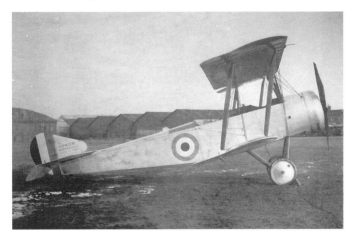

The 1½ Strutter was a radical design for its day and the lack of drag-inducing encumbrances is evident in this view of the prototype, which became 3686 in RNAS service. At the time that the photograph was taken, the machine had a fixed tailplane and was completely unarmed. JMB/GSL

design. There were differences, however. Although the central box rib was retained as a centre section, as was the characteristic W-strut arrangement, the mainplanes were of equal span. There was a lower centre section, whose spars passed through the lower fuselage. The engine was a 110hp Clerget, carried on an overhung mounting. The extra power was necessary to accommodate

anticipated war loads, although at this juncture the machine was unarmed. That engine was neatly enclosed in a fully circular cowling, adding to the cleanliness of the design. The LCT introduced what was to become the standard Sopwith method of mounting rotary engines. It had a circular front mounting plate, with a lower V-shaped exhaust channel, and a rear one of steel channelling that was carried between a pair of diagonal struts in the first bay of the fuselage. The cowling was faired into the slab sides of the fuselage with curved formers, which supported longitudinal stringers. The first bay of the fuselage was panelled with aluminium, the sides having perforations for the carburettor intakes. The rounded fuselage top was ply-covered to a point behind the observer's cockpit. That cockpit was placed behind the wing trailing edge, probably with consideration to the use of a defensive gun that could fire through 360 degrees. Its placing set it apart from the pilot's, which was under the upper wing, and the fuel tank separated the two. The sensible arrangement of having the observer to the rear was in marked contrast to that of the B.E. series that was, and would continue to be, in quantity production for both British air services.

There were other innovations. The clean lines of the airframe were anticipated as producing a high landing speed and long landing run. Air brakes were consequently fitted, being let into the trailing edge of the lower centre section. An adjustable tailplane, of Sopwith patent, was fitted, presumably to allow compensation for trim changes resulting from disposal of war-load and what, for the time, was a large fuel load (40 gallons/182 litres).

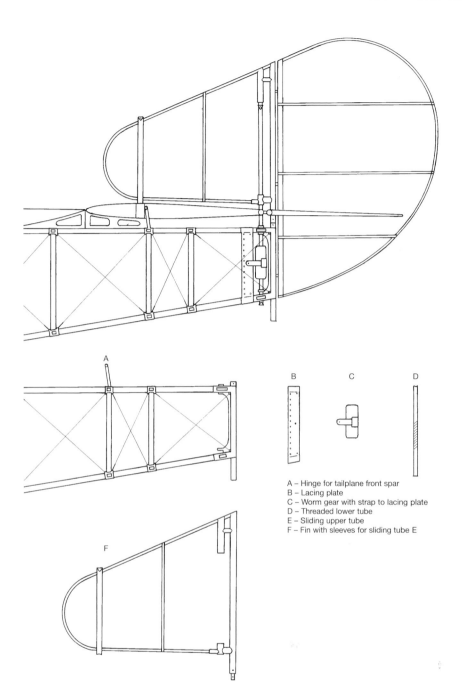

A – Hinge for tailplane front spar
B – Lacing plate
C – Worm gear with strap to lacing plate
D – Threaded lower tube
E – Sliding upper tube
F – Fin with sleeves for sliding tube E

The adjustable tailplane mechanism was patented in the names of T.O.M. Sopwith and the Sopwith Aviation Company Ltd. The front spar of the tailplane was hinged to the upper fuselage. The rear spar was attached to a vertical tube that led into sleeves, one at the bottom of the fuselage and another that was an integral part of the fin structure, allowing vertical movement in either direction. The rear tailplane bracing wires were attached to this tube, which was threaded in the part that passed through the fuselage. A bottle-shaped worm gear was attached to the sternpost inside the rear fuselage and the threaded part of the tube passed through this. The worm gear was actuated by cords, connected to a handwheel on the starboard side of the cockpit. Turning the handwheel actuated the worm gear, causing the vertical tube to move upwards or downwards, depending on the direction of rotation. As the tube moved upwards, the angle of tailplane incidence was decreased from its neutral setting of 2 degrees positive and vice-versa. The fact that the bracing wires were attached to the tube meant that the integrity of the bracing was maintained, regardless of the angle of incidence.

The cleanliness of design resulted in a high landing speed and air brakes were added to improve the landing run. They are shown here in the fully extended position. Pilots did not like them, as their use produced much airframe vibration. Also evident in this view is the centre-section strut arrangement that gave the machine its nickname. JMB/GSL

This prototype LCT, as yet unarmed, was sent for evaluation to the CFS at Upavon. Its testing took place on 24 January 1916 and the ensuing report was generally favourable. It had carried a Lewis gun but no mounting during its tests and was reported to have a ground-level speed of 105mph (169km/h). The handling qualities were considered good, but criticism was made of the wing bracing and the vibrations created when using the airbrakes.

The RNAS immediately ordered the LCT and contracts for 156 were in place with the parent company by April. That total included a small batch of six, 9892–9897, which was an unusually small contract, the purpose of which has yet to be explained. The RFC was also impressed with the CFS report and wanted the type. Sopwith's, however, was regarded as a naval contractor and so the Lincoln-based firm of Ruston Proctor and Co. was given an initial contract for fifty machines (7762–7811) during March 1916. Ruston's had experience of aeroplane manufacture, having built the B.E.2c under subcontract.

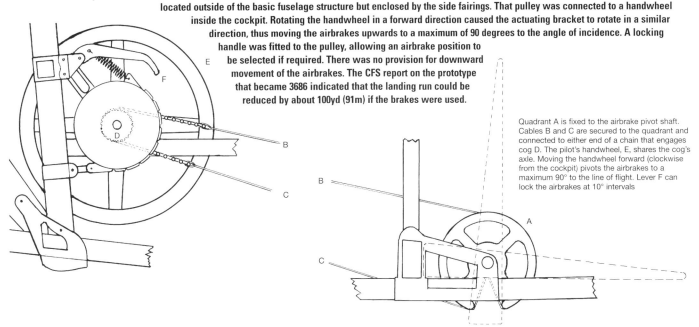

The airbrakes extended from the rear spar to the trailing edges of the lower centre section and were connected by a tube, at approximately one-sixth chord, that passed through the fuselage on bearings. A circular bracket was fixed to the connecting tube and partly projected below the port underside of the fuselage. A pair of cables was attached to this bracket and connected to either end of a chain that passed around a pulley, located outside of the basic fuselage structure but enclosed by the side fairings. That pulley was connected to a handwheel inside the cockpit. Rotating the handwheel in a forward direction caused the actuating bracket to rotate in a similar direction, thus moving the airbrakes upwards to a maximum of 90 degrees to the angle of incidence. A locking handle was fitted to the pulley, allowing an airbrake position to be selected if required. There was no provision for downward movement of the airbrakes. The CFS report on the prototype that became 3686 indicated that the landing run could be reduced by about 100yd (91m) if the brakes were used.

Quadrant A is fixed to the airbrake pivot shaft. Cables B and C are secured to the quadrant and connected to either end of a chain that engages cog D. The pilot's handwheel, E, shares the cog's axle. Moving the handwheel forward (clockwise from the cockpit) pivots the airbrakes to a maximum 90° to the line of flight. Lever F can lock the airbrakes at 10° intervals

A1031 was Fairey-built and served at Gosport, the locale of this mishap. The photograph gives a good view of the adjustable tailplane mechanism. JMB/GSL

Into Service

Production LCTs for the RNAS were delivered from February 1916. Initial deliveries had no provision for armament to be fired by the pilot, but relied instead on the observer's use of a Lewis gun on a rotating mount. Some had a pillar mounting for the Lewis, but the French Etévé gun ring was more common. Movement during use of the gun by the observer was catered for by the use of an especially designed seat. This was on an eccentric mounting and was free to rotate when relieved of the observer's weight, but locked in position when used.

Later RNAS Service

5 Wing RNAS, based at Coudekerque, was the first RNAS unit to receive the type in quantity. It received most of the early deliveries from the first Sopwith-built batch, 9376–9425. In RNAS parlance they were of the Type 9400S, the designation being taken from the serial number of a typical early machine and the suffix indicating short-range fighter. The second batch, 9651–9750, comprised Types 9400S, 9400L and 9700. The 9400L was, of course, a long-range, two-seat fighter and had extra tankage in the form of a gravity tank, located under the turtle decking between the cockpits.

The 9700 was a single-seat bomber and was not just a 9400 with the observer's cockpit faired over. It had a completely revised fuselage structure, with the under-fuselage spacers deleted from the bays aft of the cockpit and transferred to auxiliary longerons at approximately mid-fuselage depth. This created a bomb bay. A new fuel tank was fitted. The bomb bay was fitted with doors that were held in the closed position by elastic cords. These cords allowed the doors to open under the weight of released bombs and close afterwards. Metal inspection panels were let into the fuselage sides, to allow

Early 1½ Strutters went to 5 Wing RNAS, which operated both Type 9400 two-seaters and Type 9700 single-seat bombers. Both types are shown here and the Type 9700s have over-wing Lewis guns rather than fixed Vickers. JMB/GSL

access to stowed bombs. Mainplane bracing was revised, with the flying wires converging towards the fuselage, rather than being parallel as on the Type 9400.

5 Wing RNAS had moved to France during March 1916, to provide a bombing force that would be capable of attacking German-occupied ports on the Belgian coast. It flew an assortment of types that included Caudron G.IVs and Breguets de Chasse. By the end of April it had received three of the new Sopwiths, 9376,

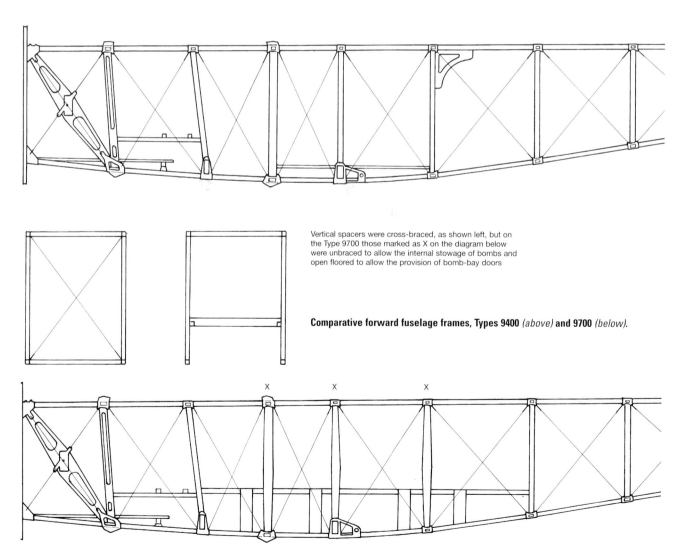

Vertical spacers were cross-braced, as shown left, but on the Type 9700 those marked as X on the diagram below were unbraced to allow the internal stowage of bombs and open floored to allow the provision of bomb-bay doors

Comparative forward fuselage frames, Types 9400 (above) and 9700 (below).

9378 and 9383, and these were allotted to 5 Flt of its A Sqn. Further Sopwiths were received, but by September it only had ten. Six of these (9379, 9405, 9663, 9896, N5080 and N5084) were with 5 Flt. The others (9383, 9415, 9423 and 9658) were with 8 Flt of B Sqn. The remainder of the Wing still flew its, by then outdated, French machines.

The aerodynamic cleanliness of the design and the potential difficulties facing pilots in adjusting to the higher landing speed of the type may have been the reasons for the ordering of 9891. This was known as the Sopwith School Tractor Biplane and was, essentially, the prototype of a proposed trainer version, powered by an 80hp Gnome engine. 9891 was delivered to Detling, for 3 Wing RNAS, on 18 May 1916 and subsequently served with that unit at Manston. It survived until that October, but no further orders were placed. Perhaps the anticipated problems never materialized.

Further orders for the type had been placed. The parent company produced a further one hundred, but had an order for another thirty-three (including eight for the Aviation Militaire Belge) cancelled. The Westland Aircraft Works of Yeovil produced seventy-five and Mann, Egerton and Co. Ltd of Norwich the same amount. Oakley & Co. of Ilford received an order for twenty-five, but this was changed to one of a similar number of Triplanes. Contracts for all of these had been agreed by November 1916 and no more were ordered for the RNAS.

The inability of 5 Wing to completely re-equip with the Sopwith LCT was the result of two factors. The main one was the need of the RFC with the BEF to have effective fighting machines to operate in the Somme offensive. That need had been realized during the early spring. RFC units in the UK had too few up-to-date machines that could be used operationally and so the RNAS, not for the last time, was asked to help. The result, ratified by 15 May, was an agreement to transfer forty of its LCTs, at a rate that equalled one-third of deliveries. Eventually, however, the agreed total was almost doubled.

The second factor was the formation of 3 Wing at Detling and Manston. This new unit (the original 3 Wing had disbanded in the Aegean area) was scheduled to move to north-eastern France in order to conduct a bombing campaign against industrial targets in Southern Germany. It was

intended to build the Wing up to a strength of one hundred aeroplanes, most of which would be Sopwiths. LCTs from the first Sopwith-built batch were also delivered to 3 Wing. However, RNAS policy, of attempting to equip two Wings simultaneously, meant that neither could be provided fully with the necessary machines, and 3 Wing suffered equally from the deficit created by assisting the RFC. By mid-September 1916, sixty-two LCTs had been diverted to the military.

LCTs in RFC Service

The diversion of LCTs to the RFC was the result of an agreement reached early in 1916 and deliveries to the military began

became the 1½ Strutter. The need of the RFC in France for up-to-date machines was so great that 70 Sqn's move to the continent differed from that of other squadrons, which had been dispatched as entire units. As flights of 70 Sqn were equipped and mobilized, they were sent to their designated base at Fienvillers. Machines from the initial transfer were used by A Flt and their significance lay in the fact that they were provided with forward-firing Vickers guns, the muzzle casings of which were faired into the fuselage contours. The synchronization gear for the pilot's gun was of the Vickers-Challenger type and prone to breakage. At first, there was no standardized mounting for the observer's Lewis gun. Some machines had the Strange mounting, a cranked pillar,

A981 served with C Flt of 70 Sqn as 'C5', with its fin over-painted in blue as a flight marking. It was lost in action near Menin on 3 June 1917 and its Canadian pilot, Lt A.S. Bourinot, is seen here with his captors. The Canadian observer, Cpl A. Giles was less fortunate, being killed when he fell from the machine during combat with, probably, Jasta 8. via CCI

during April, when 9381, 9386, 9387, 9389 and 9391–9393 were delivered to Farnborough and renumbered 7942, 5719–5721 and 7998–8000. It should be noted that these, and subsequent transfers, were of the Type 9400S, the RNAS retaining the 9400L and 9700 machines. These transfers, that represented a major loss to RNAS strength, were used to create 70 Sqn at Farnborough. The official RFC name for the new machine was the Sopwith Two-Seater, but to its aircrews it

and others the Etévé type. Such was the haste to dispatch the machines to France that when A Flt flew to war on 24 May 1916, observers carried Lewis guns, still in greased wrappings, on their laps. Once established on a war footing, those Sopwiths were the first fully armed two-seat tractor aeroplanes in RFC service and the only examples of their type available when the Somme offensive opened on 1 July.

The initial equipment of B Flt of 70 Sqn consisted of A380–A385, and this flight flew to join the war on 3 July, with C Flt following on 1 August, its machines being fitted with a new type of mounting for the observer's gun, one which would become the standard such fitment on armed two-seaters. This was the Scarff mounting, a rotating ring that carried an elevating arm. The arm elevated through a pair of toothed guides and was counterbalanced by elastic cords. A single movement could easily lock both ring and bracket. It had been designed by Warrant Officer F.W. Scarff RNAS, who also had a hand in the design of the improved synchronization gear fitted to C Flt's machines. They were fitted with the Scarff-Dibovsky gear, another mechanical system. The major shortcoming of this and all mechanical gun-timing gears was the inertia imposed on the moving parts. In the fraction of a second that it took those parts to begin moving, the propeller blades would already have moved and there was the chance of bullets penetrating them. Over-compensation for that inertia resulted in the gun having a lower rate of fire. This was certainly the case with another mechanical gear, the Ross type that had been devised by Sgt Ross in France and was fitted to some machines of 45 and 70 Sqns.

The mounting of the Vickers gun brought its breechblock uncomfortably close to the pilot's face and the consequences of this in the event of a crash were all too apparent. Sopwith's solution was a patented padded windscreen that attached to the gun. However, many pilots chose to dispense with the screen in operation service, as it impaired the field of vision.

Ruston Proctor began to deliver the first of its 1½ Strutters during June and July, by which time others were on order for the RFC. The Fairey Aviation Co. of Haynes was contracted to deliver one hundred (A954–A1053) and Vickers Ltd of Crayford a similar number (A1054–A1153). Hooper & Co. of Chelsea received an initial order for fifty, to be numbered A1511–A1560 and, later, the co-located Wells Aviation Co. Ltd received one for one hundred (A5238–A5337). Subsequently, further contracts were placed with Vickers (A8744–A8793) and Ruston

Proctor (A2381–A2430, A8141–A8340 and B2551–B2600).

70 Sqn was regarded as a fighter-reconnaissance and escort unit, the long endurance of its machines making deep penetration of enemy airspace possible. Unfortunately, that often put the aircrews in exposed situations and resulted in a considerable number of casualties. The first of these occurred on 8 July, when A384 was brought down by anti-aircraft, with Captain D.M.V. Veitch killed and Lt J.L. Whitty fatally wounded as a POW. On that same day, 5719 was damaged and its observer fatally wounded. Casualties continued to be incurred, but the aircrews of

At one time, it was thought that the American Smith Static radial engine could be used on the 1½ Strutter and was tested in 9712 but was found unsatisfactory. JMB/GSL

70 Sqn were also learning to use their machines in a more offensive capacity. On 28 August the unit claimed its first combat successes, a pair of Albatros D IIs sent down out of control during an Offensive Patrol near Bapaume. The crews involved were Capt H.A. Salmond and Lt D.A. Stewart in A888 and Lt A.W. Keen and Capt F.G. Glenday in A2432.

The air war over the Somme became more heated with the opening of a further offensive on 15 September, and that day saw a dramatic increase in the number of casualties suffered by 70 Sqn. Two machines were lost, with three crew members killed and another made POW, while a further two observers, including Glenday, were killed, although their pilots survived forced landings. These losses were the result of encounters with the latest generation of

German fighting scouts and Hptm Oswald Boelcke brought down two of the four. Boelcke had recently brought the newly formed *Jasta* 2 to operational status and that unit was to have a major impact on allied casualties. On the credit side, Lt A.M. Vaucour MC added to his existing two 'victories', when he and his observer, Lt A.J. Bott, in their usual machine A892 destroyed a Fokker E Type. A further three machines were lost by 70 Sqn over enemy territory during the rest of September and a further five during October, including two on the last day of that month.

A second RFC squadron was in the process of working up during the early autumn of 1916. This was 45 Sqn at Sedgeford, which began to receive Ruston Proctor machines direct from Lincoln. The unit joined 70 Sqn at Fienvillers on 15 October, and its 1½ Strutters, like most of 70 Sqn's, were fitted with the Etévé mounting for the Lewis gun, the RNAS then having priority over deliveries of the superior Scarff mounting.

A bloody introduction to war flying awaited 45 Sqn. 7782 was damaged in combat five days after arriving in France and then, on the 22nd, 7777, 7786 and A1061 were lost with all six crew killed and A1066 was damaged in combat with five enemy machines. Fortunately, the pace of the fighting slowed as winter approached and there were no further combat casualties that year for 45 Sqn and only one for 70 Sqn.

The RFC units supporting the Somme offensives were reinforced on 26 October by a detached squadron of the RNAS, that initially included a flight of Type 9400s from 5 Wing. The other flights were of Nieuports and Pups. That squadron became 8N Sqn, but even at that early juncture, the two-seaters that formed B Flt were found inadequate for the task of air fighting and were soon relinquished in favour of its single-seat stablemate. The 1½ Strutters that are known to have been flown by Naval Eight included 9896, N5080, N5084, N5090, N5096 and N5102 – all Type 9400S.

The original 110hp Clerget 9Z provided only just enough power and attempts were made to fit more powerful engines. The ten-cylinder Smith Static, a radial engine of American design, which promised to deliver 150hp, was tested in 9712 but was not considered suitable. The availability of the 130hp Clerget 9B led to the adoption of that engine. The RNAS was fitting that power plant to its Sopwiths during late 1916, but it was in short supply and most RFC machines in operational service had to continue with the lower-rated unit. As limited supplies became available to the military, it was decided that, to simplify supply and maintenance, machines so fitted would be issued to 70 Sqn only.

Other than the engine change, very few modifications were made to the type once it was in service. The only one of any great significance was the introduction of longer ailerons, from late 1916, in an attempt to improve the type's lateral response. Longitudinal response was also regarded as poor and attempts were made to use a smaller tailplane, but that modification was never introduced on service machines.

The bombing campaign of 5 Wing RNAS continued throughout 1916. However, on the last day of that year 5 Wing RNAS formed the basis of two new numbered squadrons, 4N and 5N Sqns. The 1½ Strutter formed part of their initial equipment, and 5N Sqn was to continue bombing the German-occupied Belgian ports, usually in the form of high-altitude attacks. Its Sopwiths were mainly of Type 9400S and were used for photography and escort work. The other squadron, 4N, was intended for fighting and its Type 9400S machines were seen as interim equipment until Sopwith Pup replacements could be delivered. A further naval squadron to fly the type was 2N. It had reformed from elements of 1 Wing at St Pol on 5 November 1916 and had similar duties to 5N Sqn. It,

Specification – Sopwith 1½ Strutter	
Engine:	One 110hp Clerget 9Z or one 130hp Clerget 9B or one 110hp Le Rhone 9J (some French a/c)
Weights:	Empty 1,259lb (571kg) (Type 9400), 1,354lb (614kg) (Type 9700); loaded 2,149lb (975kg) (Type 9400), 2,362lb (1,071kg) (Type 9700)
Dimensions:	Length 25ft 3¼in (7.72m) (British-built a/c), 25ft 3in (7.69m) (French-built a/c); height 10ft 3in (3.12m); wingspan upper 33ft 6in (10.21m), lower 33ft 6in (10.21m); chord upper 5ft 6in (1.68m), lower 5ft 6in (1.68m); gap 5ft 4¾in (19.74m); stagger 2ft (0.6m); dihedral upper 2½°, lower 2½°
Performance:	Max. speed 96mph (154km/h) (Type 9400), 94mph (151km/h) (Type 9700)
	Service ceiling 8,000ft (2,440m) (Type 9700), 14,500ft (4,420m) (110hp Type 9400), 15,500ft (4,725m) (130hp Clerget Type 9400)
	Endurance 2¼ hours (Type 9700), 3¾ hours (130hp Type 9400), 4 hours (110hp Type 9400)
Armament:	One fixed Vickers + observer's Lewis on two-seater. 300lb (136kg) bomb load (Type 9700)

Engine Cowling Security

The overhung engine mounting offered very little support for the engine cowling and that component was in danger of detaching under vibration, with potentially catastrophic results. A simple Sopwith solution was patented (Patent 127847). The cowling ring that attached to the fuselage longerons was made of V section. The engine cowling had a V-shaped channel around its rear end, that engaged the cowling ring. A cable was then fitted into the recess and tensioned by use of a turnbuckle. This innovation was continued on the Pup, Triplane and Camel, but it was found that engine vibration could loosen the turnbuckle and so retaining clips had to be strapped across, to secure the cowling to the fuselage.

too, operated the Types 9400S. These units continued to fly the 1½ Strutter into 1917, 4N Sqn receiving Pups during March and the others DH4s from the following month. The Seaplane Defence Sqn and 9N Sqn were issued with a small number each, until re-equipment with single-seaters was completed.

Most of the initial Types 9400L and 9700 were delivered to 3 Wing RNAS. After the delay caused by the transfer of machines to the RFC, the Wing was mobilized at Manston and, although still under intended strength, had moved to its operational base at Luxeuil in north-east France on 16 October 1916. The mobilization of 3 Wing was another expression of the Admiralty's desire to take the war to the enemy and was intended to conduct a bombing campaign against industrial targets in south-west Germany. It was to work in conjunction with French units that were conducting similar operations. An advanced base was set up at Ochey.

3 Wing had a mixed complement of aeroplanes that included Short bombers and Breguets de Chasse. Under the command of Wing Cdr W.L. Elder, it conducted operations through to the late spring of 1917. It was a bold concept for its time but it has to be said that its results, like those of most bombing campaigns, caused less damage than was claimed.

The first major raid took place on 12 October 1916, when a mixed force of Sopwiths and Breguets attacked the Mauser factory at Oberndorf, in conjunction with

sixteen French bombers. Enemy fighters brought down 9660 and two Breguets were also lost – an early indication of the risks involved in conducting daylight bombing missions. Hagendingen, Volklingen St Ingbert and Dillingen were subsequent targets of raids aimed at disrupting steel production. Some 3 Wing pilots claimed successes against enemy scouts. FSL R. Collishaw made his first two of many 'victories' on 25 October, and Flt Lt C. Draper claimed four during November.

The last strategic raid by 3 Wing took place on 26 March, but on 14 April it was called on to made a retaliatory raid against Freiburg, as a reprisal for Allied civilian losses. It was an unfortunate decision, with the Wing losing three machines (9667, N5117 and N5171), one to AA and the others to Albatros scouts of *Jasta 35*. Although 3 Wing had a nominal existence until June, it was run down from April, both in men and machines. Pilots were in demand to man the squadrons that the RNAS had promised as help to the RFC for the Battle of Arras and many of the personnel of 10N Sqn were ex-3 Wing, as were a number of personnel in 3N Sqn. The 1½ Strutter had, by then, little application on the Western Front and many of 3 Wing's machines, mainly of Type 9700, were transferred to the French, with a few diverted to 2 Wing in the Aegean. French units that operated alongside 3 Wing had previously been loaned Sopwiths and one of these may have made what was an early, if not the earliest, shuttle bombing raid. This took place on 17 November 1916 and was made by a single-seat bomber that was probably a Type 9700 – the date seems too early for it to have been a SOP 1B1 of French manufacture. Capt L. de Beauchamp made an 8-hour flight from Luxeuil, bombing Munich and continuing his flight to land in Italy.

The RFC training organization responded to the need for pilots who were familiar with the 1½ Strutter by the re-equipment of 28 RS at Castle Bromwich. That unit had been dedicated to training R.E.7 pilots, but the withdrawal of the type allowed conversion to the Sopwith. Its establishment was set at nine Avros, three Bristol Scouts and nine 1½ Strutters, while 34 RS at Ternhill was similarly equipped. The first Sopwiths to reach 28 RS were from the first Vickers-built batch, with A1057–A1060 being early deliveries. Others were delivered to the CFS at Upavon. The output from these three training units was considered sufficient to maintain three operational squadrons with the BEF.

RNAS pilots under training had little opportunity to handle the type. A few were issued to the main training base at Cranwell and the Gunnery School Flights at Eastchurch and stations such as Dover and Redcar had the odd example. However, for most pilots destined to fly the type operationally, first contact was usually at the squadrons or wings to which they were posted.

Later RFC Operations

The third and last 1½ Strutter squadron for the RFC with the BEF, 43 Sqn, had left Northolt for France on 17 January 1917. It set up base at Treizennes, later moving to Lozinghem. The unit was fortunate to have joined the war during the relatively quiet winter period, but did not escape the inevitable losses. Lt H.D. Addis and AM1 F. Foott were killed in the crash of A2392 on 24 January, presumably on a delivery flight from Lincoln. First combat casualties were on 10 February, when three of 43 Sqn's machines were badly damaged, two by enemy scouts and the other by AA, with four crew members wounded, one fatally. Air action again intensified during

March, as the German ground forces prepared for withdrawal to the Hindenburg Line, with 43 Sqn suffering its first combat losses on the 5th, losing A1108 and A1109 with both crews being killed. That same day also saw the squadron's first combat victory, when 2Lt C.P. Thornton and Sgt R. Dunn sent an enemy two-seater down out of control.

Combat victories for 1½ Strutter crews were few, due largely to the fact that the type had quickly become outdated. There were, however, exceptions and the leading combat exponent of the type was Lt, later Capt G.H. Cock MC of 45 Sqn who, with the undoubted assistance of a variety of observers, was credited with no fewer than thirteen enemy brought down. All were scouts, five of these being classed as destroyed.

No.70 Sqn had a quiet start to 1917, but suffered heavily on 24 March, when it lost two machines (A957 and A1907) and had a further three (A956, A1925 and A2983) damaged in combat when twelve enemy scouts intercepted a reconnaissance patrol. The following day was even worse, when five machines (7763, A884, A954, A958 and A2986) and their crews were lost, with all men killed or fatally wounded.

April 1917, Bloody April, was not so bloody for the 1½ Strutter squadrons as it was for many other units. Only eleven of the type were lost to enemy action, mainly on distant reconnaissance patrols. 45 Sqn lost three machines on 6 April with all crew members killed, but the remainder of casualties on the type were spread throughout the month, and 70 Sqn, recovered from its March losses, only had one operational loss that month.

Outdated as the 1½ Strutter had become, the temporary supply of some Nieuport 12 and 20 machines to 45 Sqn reduced the

Sopwith 1½ Strutters Loaned or Transferred to the French Authorities (*Type 9700)
9413, 9651*, 9655*, 9657*, 9661*, 9664*, 9666*, 9669*, 9673*, 9706*, 9714*, 9720*, 9729*, 9736*, 9738*, 9742*, 9745*, 9895, N5088*, N5091*, N5092*, N5094*, N5095*, N5097*, N5098*, N5100*, N5101*, N5103*, N5104*, N5113*, N5115*, N5116*, N5118*, N5122*, N5123*, N5125*, N5126*, N5127*, N5128*, N5129*, N5130*, N5132*, N5133*, N5134*, N5135*, N5136*, N5137*, N5138*, N5139*, N5140*, N5141*, N5142*, N5143*, N5144*, N5145*, N5146*, N5147*, N5148*, N5149*, N5157*, N5158*, N5160*, N5502*, N5507*, N5511*, N5514*, N5522, N5523*

Vickers-built A1081 served with 43TS at Ternhill and carried distinctive markings. No complete record survives of the markings used by training units at home, but this one can also be seen on a Camel illustrated in Chapter 7. JMB/GSL

effectiveness of that squadron further. The French machines were issued because a hiatus had developed in the delivery of replacement Sopwiths, due to industrial action at home.

The daily routine continued for the three RFC squadrons during May, one of escort work, photography missions and reconnaissance, interspersed with offensive patrols. Occasional combat success was achieved, mainly by 45 Sqn, with 2Lt JD Belgrave of that unit adding another four 'victories' to his existing two and other pilots, such as Lts J.C.B. Firth and O.L. McMaking learning their trade. However, if enemy opposition was encountered, the 1½ Strutter was not capable of holding its own in combat gyrations and its crews had to adopt defensive tactics. The pilots of 70 Sqn found that the greatest chance of escape from attack by enemy formations was to circle in line astern formation, in order to allow gunners the chance to cover each other's machines. That defensive circle could then edge towards the lines and safety.

Unfortunately, 5 June was a bad day for 45 Sqn; its 9am offensive patrol met determined enemy opposition and three Sopwiths were shot down and another two damaged. However, that day also saw the first combat successes of two of its most distinguished pilots, when 2Lt M.B. Frew, with 2Lt M.J. Dalton as observer, sent an Albatros scout down out of control for his first 'victory'. Frew was to become the 'star turn' of 45 Sqn, eventually being credited with twenty-three combat successes, five of them on 1½ Strutters. 2Lt Norman MacMillan sent another Albatros down in a similar manner.

MacMillan later wrote the classic aviation book *Into the Blue*, which gives an insight into life on 45 Sqn. The 1½ Strutter is quite well covered in classic literature. Harold Balfour, later Lord Balfour of Inchrye, who, as Capt H.H. Balfour MC, flew and fought with 43 Sqn, painted a good picture of his former unit in *An Airman Marches*. That book includes reference to the CO, Maj W. Sholto Douglas, looping a 1½ Strutter twelve times in succession, in order to demonstrate its structural integrity to dubious new pilots. Sholto Douglas (later Lord Douglas of Kirtleside) himself left us *Years of Combat*. 70 Sqn was also chronicled, at least for its early operational period, by 'Contact' in *An Airman's Outing With the RFC, June – December 1916*. 'Contact' was A.J. Bott who, as an observer, was awarded the MC for his courageous action in fighting

a fire in A890 on 24 August 1916, undoubtedly saving the machine and his pilot 2Lt A.M. Vaucour. All four of these authors wrote about the type's inferiority of manoeuvre compared to contemporary German fighting scouts, but they did not condemn it out of hand. In order to further the record, mention should also be made of the Belgian, Willy Coppens, whose *Days on the Wing* included reference to those machines supplied to the Aviation Militaire Belge (AMB). Coppens illustrated the difficulty of landing the type onto small aerodromes, noting that it was due to the cleanliness of the design, but not making mention of the airbrakes.

The Battle of Messines opened on 7 June and 43 Sqn was given the unenviable duty of ground-attack work, losing A8221 that day and having A8248 badly damaged in the process. That battle was a prelude to the Third Battle of Ypres and for the remainder of June the 1½ Strutter squadrons were engaged on many photographic and reconnaissance missions. The Camel was beginning to be delivered to the RFC and 70 Sqn was scheduled to be the first to equip with the new type. Its first machine, N6332, had been delivered on 13 June and B3755 was on charge by the end of that month. Others followed during the first few weeks of July, but the unit was not withdrawn from duty to re-equip, and operated its 1½ Strutters in decreasing numbers until the full complement of Camels had been received. Just as this was about to be realized, two of the two-seaters were lost to enemy action with one crew being killed and the other made POW. This loss of A8335 and A8786 represented 70 Sqn's last casualties on the type.

Nos 43 and 45 Sqns were also scheduled to re-equip with the new single-seater. That process was delayed by the diversion of some of the early Camels to Home Defence work and it was 25 July before 45 Sqn received its first and 3 September before 43 Sqn did. The latter had a return to ground-attack work on 15 August and lost two machines, A1079 and A8294, to ground fire. Both crews were killed and crew members of a further three machines were wounded. As with 70 Sqn, 43 and 45 continued to operate the two-seaters until full complements of Camels had been received. By the end of September the venerable Sopwith 1½ had gone from the RFC on the Western Front. The type had performed useful, though seldom spectacular, work, but at the cost of 146 of its aircrew killed and many others made POW or wounded in action.

Mediterranean Operations

The 1½ Strutter had been shipped in considerable quantities to the Aegean during the spring of 1917, for use by 2 Wing RNAS. Both Types 9400 and 9700 were supplied. In that formation, it at first supplemented and then superseded both the aging Nieuport 10/12 and Farmans that had been bought from France, and the Bristol Scouts and B.E.2cs that had earlier been shipped from Britain. 2 Wing was subdivided into lettered squadrons that operated, mainly, from various island bases and each had its specific function, with A and D Sqns operating over Southern Bulgaria from Thasos and Stavros, while C Sqn was based on Imbros and was charged with reconnaissance and bombing duties in the Dardanelles area. Similar operations were performed by B Sqn over Southwest Turkey from its base of Thermi on Mitylene, while E and F Sqns were mobile fighting and bombing units, respectively, and were formed to counter German bombing in Macedonia. Initially, they were detached to the Greek mainland. All six squadrons had 1½ Strutters issued to them. Enemy communications and crops were major targets for the Type 9700s and the 9400s supplied an escort. Anti-submarine patrols and general reconnaissance work were other duties, as well as defensive fighting. The 1½ Strutter lingered on in this 'forgotten' theatre of operations. Some were still in service at the time of the RAF's formation, serving with 222 Sqn, and N5248 and N5249 were still surviving in January 1919. The Greek government received at least ten of the type from 2 Wing during 1918 and used them as training machines. In the same region, Romania was an ally and was provided with 1½ Strutters from RFC orders. The first machine for that country was the Ruston Proctor-built A8194, which was delivered in Romanian marking to Martlesham Heath for test in June 1917, fitted with a 110hp Le Rhone engine.

Further west, the RNAS operated 6 Wing from southern Italy against Austro-Hungarian forces across the Adriatic. Aerodromes were set up at Taranto and Otranto and 1½ Strutters were part of the Wing's initial equipment. A major duty was the patrolling of the Straits of Otranto to prevent the passage of enemy submarines. Although the first D.H.4 replacements were delivered during 1918, it was in insufficient numbers and the Sopwiths survived to serve with 224–227 Sqns of the RAF.

2 Wing operated the type in the Aegean, principally with F Sqn. Seven of that unit's machines are in this line-up. All are Type 9700 bombers, with N5119 nearest. JMB/GSL

Sopwith 1½ Strutters Transferred to the Greek Government
N5083, N5159, N5176, N5205, N5213, N5506, N5515, N5516, N5527, N5529.

The Sopwith Bomber

The single seat version of the 1½ Strutter was known, officially, to the RFC as the Sopwith Bomber and the type was ordered from Morgan & Co. of Leighton Buzzard and from Hooper & Co., with contracts issued for 300 machines (A5950–A6149 and A6901–A7000). Once produced, the RFC had no front-line use for these machines. The superior D.H.4 was in service as a day bomber and so many were placed into storage. It would seem that the Morgan contract might have been curtailed. It was intended to offer a substantial quantity of those stored for transfer to the Imperial Russian government. During early 1917, the Imperial Russian Air Service had received two Mann, Egerton & Co.-built machines, N5219 and N5244, which were of Types 9700 and 9400S respectively. These may have been sample machines; certainly the latter was photographed without camouflage. The Russians eventually received at least another 214 1½ Strutters from British stocks and others from France. Some Russian machines were fitted with 110hp Le Rhone engines, presumably making use of whatever power plants were available.

Some of the surplus Sopwith Bombers were issued to RFC squadrons that were in the process of 'working up' for operational service. At Lilbourne, for example, 84 Sqn used A6915, A6943 and A6945. Others were taken on charge by Training Squadrons, 36 TS at Montrose being typical in operating A6046 and A6984 alongside its Pups and Avros until issued with Camel replacements. Some training 1½ Strutters were converted to full dual control. The rear

Sopwith 1½ Strutters Transferred to Imperial Russian Authorities (*Type 9700)
A968–A969, A1081–A1126, A1131, A1135–A1136, A1147, A1511, A1516–A1560, A2421–A2423, A2425, A2427–A2430, A5246–A5251, A5256, A5973–A5976*, A6011*, A6015*, A6017*, A6924–A6926*, A6929–A6942*, A6949–A6951*, A6953–A6955*, A6957–A6958*, A6960*, A6973–A6978*, A8141, A8143–A8145, A8154–A8155, A8157–A8161, A8175–A8181, A8185–A8192, A8264–A8266, A8309–A8313, A8316, A8318– A8324, A8327–A8331, A8344–A8346, A8348– A8349, A8351–A8357, A8388, A8772–A8776.

cockpit shape was modified and duplicate instrumentation provided. Even so, there were still numbers of the type left in storage and at least fifty-three of these were transferred to the RNAS, in a reversal of previous situations, for conversion to Ships Strutter configuration.

Anti-Submarine Operations

The introduction of unrestricted U-boat attacks had led to a sharp rise in merchant losses and the South West Approaches, being the focal point for shipping arriving from the Americas, became one of the most dangerous areas. The RNAS already had airship and seaplane stations in the area, but operations of those types of aircraft were often restricted by weather

Hooper & Co. built Sopwith Bombers for the RFC and A6936 is shown in their Chelsea works. The flying wires of the single-seat 1½ Strutter were not parallel, unlike those in the Type 9400 and remained so even if a machine was converted to two-seat configuration. JMB/GSL

conditions. The simple solution was to establish three flights of 1½ Strutters during April 1917, one each at the existing airship stations of Mullion and Pembroke and the third at Prawle Point. Both Types 9400 and 9700 were issued, drawn from stocks of the types that were, by then, surplus to operational requirements. Both types were used as bombers, but success was restricted to keeping U-boats submerged and thus less dangerous. The *Official History* states that these flights were withdrawn during August of that year, in order to release pilots and make up the shortfall in the squadrons operating in France. The machines, however, remained at their stations throughout that year and it seems unlikely that they would have just stood there; return to a depot or transfer to a training station would have been more probable.

There were major internal differences between the Types 9400 and 9700. This photograph, taken in the Westland works at Yeovil, shows the revised fuselage structure of the bomber. JMB/GSL

Home Defence

The 1½ Strutter was one of those types that was hastily impressed into the Home Defence role, following the start of the German daylight bombing campaign against England in the summer of 1917. The first recipient was 37 Sqn, which initially operated examples in all three of its dispersed flights, where they served alongside its existing B.E. variants and R.E.7s. This must have created servicing problems, as, by June, its Sopwith two-seaters were concentrated in C Flight at Rochford. The Squadron's acquaintance with the type was brief, as it reverted to B.E. types upon a reorganization during July. 44 Sqn was scheduled to reform by that time and that unit is often quoted as having operated the 1½ Strutter. No serial numbers have come to light and it is known that Camels were available at Hainault Farm from the date of its reformation, so perhaps the larger Sopwith had been intended, rather than actual, equipment.

The main Home Defence user of the type was 78 Sqn which began to receive the type during August, with at least one of its machines having served in 37 Sqn. Its re-equipment was complete by the time the unit's flights were concentrated on Sutton's Farm during September. It was 78 Sqn and one of its flight commanders in particular that created the single-seat night-fighter conversion that became irreverently known as the 'Comic'. The Flt Cdr was Capt F.W. Honnett and his ideas were tried on B762, a reconstructed two-seater from the Southern Aircraft Repair Depot at Farnborough. The cockpit location of the two-seater and single-seat bomber was all but useless from a fighter pilot's viewpoint and so the pilot's position was moved aft to a point behind the wing trailing edge and the fuel tank was moved forward. Fittings for the single Vickers gun were then out of the pilot's reach and so that weapon was discarded and a new armament of twin Lewis guns was mounted on a tubular

The internal bomb bay of the Type 9700 necessitated a revision of the fuel tank arrangement and the twin filler ports, for main and gravity tanks can be seen here. Also visible are the padded windscreen that attached to the Vickers gun and the inspection panels for the bomb bay. JMB/GSL

bracket ahead of the new cockpit and fired above the upper wing. B762 was tested at Martlesham Heath and the conversion was declared structurally sound. At least a further eleven machines of 78 Sqn were similarly modified, although some did, but probably only initially, retain the Vickers armament in its original location. Increasing stocks of the Camel, which had proved to be suitable as a night-fighter, allowed for the re-equipment of 78 Sqn and the last of its 1½ Strutters had been withdrawn by February 1918.

Foreign Service

The French authorities were much impressed by the Sopwith 1½ Strutter and six were built by the parent company especially for the Aviation Militaire Française. French stocks of the type were increased after acquisition of the ex-3 Wing machines, and agreement was reached for production in that country. It is often forgotten that almost four times as many of the type were manufactured in France as in its country of origin, with some 4,500 airframes being produced by almost a dozen manufacturers, including Amiot, Bessoneau, Darracq, Hanriot, Loire et Olivier and REP, all well-known names. The French produced the 1½ Strutter in three versions, with the designations SOP

1A2 (two-seater artillery and reconnaissance), SOP 1B2 (two-seater short-range bomber) and SOP 1B1 (single-seat bomber – equivalent to the Type 9700). Initially, the two-seaters were fitted with an Etévé gun mounting for the observer and no Vickers guns were fitted. Later machines had provision for fitting Vickers

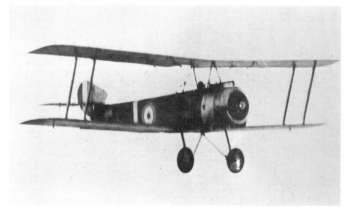

A rare in-flight view of a Type 9700. The machine belonged to 2 Wing RNAS. JMB/GSL

guns, but they were not always carried. Just as in the British air services, the French changed to the Scarff ring, which was produced in France under the designation TO3 and TO4.

Unfortunately, French production did not begin until the type was well outclassed by enemy fighting scouts, but it was not halted. As machines came forward,

they were used to re-equip escadrilles that were operating obsolete Caudrons, Voisins and Farmans. Escadrilles F29 and F123 were possibly the first to receive the new type, in December 1916, probably receiving ex-RNAS machines. It was March 1917 before another unit, VB111, re-equipped with them and further units followed. Other units formed with the type and at least seventy-five escadrilles were issued with Sopwiths. Others served with training establishments, and it was not until August 1918 that the last escadrilles had given up the type, almost a full year after the RFC and RNAS. These were Escadrilles SOP 141, 251 and 281, all of which re-equipped with Breguet 14s. What is even more surprising than the belated use of the type is the fact that photographs show operational SOP 1B1s that were totally unarmed.

By the time of the RAF's formation, on 1 April 1918, very few 1½ Strutters remained with units at home. Pups had replaced them in scout Training Squadrons, and Service Squadrons in the process of 'working up' were issued with more up-to-date types. Most had been dismantled, their 130-hp Clerget engines being needed for Camels and, such was the rapidity of the type's disappearance, when plans were made to produce a shipborne conversion some machines had to be acquired from French production. Some of the last in use as landplanes in the UK were with the Transport Flight that was attached to 491 Flt of 233 Sqn at Dover. The unit, as its title suggests, ferried personnel across the Channel and was still operating 1½ Strutters during late 1918.

America's entry into the war, bringing vast quantities of men and matériel, hastened its conclusion. However, the US Air Service (USAS) was short of combat aeroplanes and had to rely on British and French production. The French sold 514 Sopwiths to the US government and many were issued to the vast American training centres at Tours and Issoudun. The USAS was keen to field as many combat units as possible and the 88th, 90th and 99th Aero Sqns were equipped with SOP 1A2s, flying these operationally until replacement Salmson 2A2s were procured. Some of the USAS Sopwiths were taken to the USA in

The RFC had no operational use for its Sopwith Bombers and most were transferred to training units. A6034, like several others, ended up in the Middle East, where a training organization had grown up along the Suez Canal. JMB/GSL

More 1½ Strutters were built in France than in England and an early and uncamouflaged French machine is shown here with a Nieuport and a Farman for company. Like the first British machines, early French ones had the Etévé mounting for the observer's Lewis gun. JMB/GSL

the post-war period and several were transferred to the US Navy, for use as shipborne aeroplanes.

Belgium also received numbers of the 1½ Strutter. It will be recalled that Sopwith's had been intended to produce eight machines for the AMB, but that contract was cancelled. What the Belgian authorities did receive, instead, were eight Type 9400s from Mann, Egerton & Co., N5235–N5252. These became S1–S8, respectively, in Belgian service. At least a further nineteen British-made 1½ Strutters, including A8166, were transferred to that country, but others were also delivered from French production. They served with the 2ème, 3ème, 4ème and 6ème Escadrilles and were in service until 1921.

The air service of the Netherlands, the Luchtvaart Afdeling (LVA), acquired at least five 1½ Strutters, purchased after internment that followed their forced landings by crews avoiding enemy-held territory. Two of these machines, No.9396 and 9420, were from 5 Wing RNAS and were flown by the LVA as LA33 and LA38 respectively. 9376 of 5N Sqn was interned on 22 April 1917 to become LA42 and N5154 of 2N Sqn followed on 12 May, becoming LA34. The last known interned Dutch 1½ Strutter was a French SOP 1B1, of Escadrille SOP 111, that was acquired on 7 July to become LA45. There may have been a further example, however. An unknown Sopwith was force-landed and burnt by its crew on 19 January 1918. That

crew was Capt Biheller and Lt Brans, from 42 TS Wye and it has been suggested that a subsequent court-martial found Biheller to have been a German spy.

After the Bolshevik Revolution, the new regime in Russia inherited machines from the IRAS and used these in the interventionist wars that followed. Others fell into White Russian hands. Ski undercarriages were fitted to some of these machines, for operations in the extreme winter conditions of the continental interior. Some 1½ Strutters helped form the equipment of the air services of the newly emerged Baltic States. Three are known to have flown in Latvia, A5254, A6987 and F7590. All three had been Ships Strutters and were,

Later French machines were camouflaged and were fitted with the TO3 or TO4 gun mounting that was derived from the Scarff ring. JMB/GSL

The Japanese government bought several British types post-war, including examples of the 1½ Strutter. One is seen here in full Japanese markings and fitted with a gun ring for the observer. JMB/GSL

presumably, delivered at some time in 1919. In Latvian service they were numbered 13, 2 and 14, respectively, and 13 is known to have had a Siemens Halske radial engine fitted at some point in its career. Neighbouring Estonia and Lithuania also operated the type. Among those flown in the latter was A1527, a Hooper-built machine that had been captured from Bolshevik forces.

The other country to use the 1½ Strutter in quantity was Japan. Post-war, that country received at least fifteen from British stocks and it seems likely that others were purchased from France.

Post-War

Some 1½ Strutters acquired civilian identities in the post-war period. Several French machines appeared on that country's civil register, some of them having enclosed cabins and being capable of carrying two passengers. There was also civilian use in the USA, but the type (as with other Sopwiths) found little favour in its home country. Only G-EAVB, ex N5504, was registered and that machine flew as a three-seater.

It is still possible today to appreciate the clean lines and attractive design of the 1½ Strutter. The RAF Museum exhibits a superb replica, marked as a machine of 45 Sqn and two genuine machines survive across the Channel. The Royal Army Museum in Brussels holds and displays S85 while, at Le Bourget, the Air and Space Museum has Sopwith 1A2 1263.

Representative 1½ Strutters with RNAS Units

1 Wing – St Pol/Petite Synthe: 9376, 9378, 9417, 9419, 9422, 9423, 9425, 9658.

2 Wing – A Sqn Thasos; B Sqn Thermi; C Sqn Imbros; D Sqn Stavros; E Sqn Hadzi Junas; F Sqn Amberkoj/Stavros/Marian; G Flt Imbros/ Mudros: 9718, 9727, 9748, 9750, N5083, N5086, N5087, N5099, N5108, N5110, N5112, N5119, N5159, N5161.

3 Wing – Detling, Manston, Luxueil, Ochey: 9400, 9401, 9407, 9408, 9410, 9413, 9414, 9651, 9652, 9654, 9655, 9657, 9661.

4 Wing – Petite Synthe: 9376.

5 Wing – A Sqn 5 Flt and B Sqn 8 Flt Coudekerque: 9376, 9378, 9379, 9382, 9383, 9384, 9385, 9388, 9394, 9395, 9396, 9397.

6 Wing – Otranto: N5212, N5229, N5231, N5232, N5233, N5243, N5640, N5641, N5642.

2N Sqn – St Pol: 9378, 9417, 9425, 9722, 9744, 9897, N5080, N5081, N5082, N5150, N5154, N5172, N5503, N5518, N5524.

3N Sqn – St Pol: 9897, N5080, N5105.

4N Sqn – Coudekerque: N5082, N5093, N5096, N5102, N5222.

5N Sqn – Coudekerque, Petite Synthe: 9376, 9379, 9382, 9383, 9385, 9394, 9395, 9423, 9672, 9896, N5081, N5114, N5150.

7 Sqn – Coudekerque: N5504, N5505, N5509, N5519, N5520, N5528.

8N Sqn (formerly Detached Sqn) – B Flt only at Vert Galand: 9896, N5080, N5084, N5090, N5096, N5102.

9N Sqn – St Pol: 9897, N5105.

Seaplane Defence Squadron – St Pol: 9744, N5150.

War Flt – Eastchurch: 9400, 9700.

Central Training Establishment – Cranwell: 9399, 9741, 9893, 9894, N5164, N5165, N5166, N5167, N5230, N5605, N5606.

Aeroplane School – East Fortune: 9423, 9744, 9894,

N5215, N5230, N5617, N5636, N5643, N5646, N5647.

Finishing School – Dover: 9414, 9670, 9744, N5153, N5162, N5208, N5503, N5508, N5518, N5525.

War School/War Flt – Manston: 9422, 9724, N5089, N5109, N5153, N5162, N5170, N5208, N5503, N5524, N5525, N5528.

Gunnery School Flights – Eastchurch: 9422, N5234, N5607, N5608, N5612, N5613, N5617.

Anti-Submarine Flight – Mullion: N5601, N5602, N5603, N5607, N5608, N5617, N5624.

Anti-Submarine Flight – Prawle Point: N5603, N5604, N5619, N5623, N5624.

Anti-Submarine Flight – Pembroke: N5213, N5214, N5215, N5234.

RNAS Station – Yarmouth: N5622, N5633, N5634, N5635.

RNAS Station – Dover: N5508.

Representative 1½ Strutters with RFC/RAF Units

37 Sqn – C Flt Rochford: A8233, A8249, A8250, A8251, A8271, A8274, A8275, A8305.

43 Sqn – Northolt/St Omer/Treizennes/Lozinghem: 7804, A961, A973, A978, A993, A1073, A1098, A2406, A8221, A8248.

45 Sqn – Sedgeford/St Omer/Fienvillers (det Boisdinghem)/Ste Marie Cappel: 7806, A963, A1080, A1093, A8291. A8293.

46 Sqn – Droglandt (1 machine only): A882.52 Sqn – Hounslow (1 machine only): 7942.

54 Sqn – Castle Bromwich: 7736, A1068.

70 Sqn – Farnborough/Fienvillers/Vert Galand/Fienvillers/Boisdinghem: A957, A981, A1002, A1012, A1028, A8335, A8786.

71 Sqn – Castle Bromwich: A1091, A8262.

78 Sqn – Suttons Farm: A1040, A1050, A1051, A6907, A8275, A8277, A8278, B715, B762, B812, B2565, B5238, B5259.

80 Sqn – Montrose:

81 Sqn – Scampton:

84 Sqn – Beaulieu, Lilbourne: A6915, A6943, A6945.

143 Sqn – Throwley (possibly 1 machine only): A8233.

222 Sqn – Mudros: B2582.

225 Sqn – Otranto: N5232.

233 Sqn Transport Flt – Dover: 9378, 9414, 9670, N5082, N5090.

Central Flying School, B Sqn – Upavon: 7811, A378, A1085, A1089, A1090, A1104, A1109, A1114, A6105.

1 TS – Beaulieu:

6 TS – Catterick, Montrose: A5950, A6046, A6901, A6946.

10 TS – Gosport:

11 RS – Rochford:

18 TS – Montrose: A6030.

28 RS/TS – Castle Bromwich: 7801, 7805, A1056, A1057, A1058, A1059, A1060, A1113, A8243.

30 (Australian) TS – Ternhill: 7781, A1114, A6903, A6945.

31 TS – Wyton: A2855.

34 RS/TS – Ternhill: 7807, 7942.

36 TS – Montrose: A6046, A6984.

40 TS – Croydon: A2394.

43 RS/TS – Ternhill: A2403, A5964.

45 TS – South Carlton: A891.

54 TS – Castle Bromwich: A8203, A8204, B2591.

58 TS – Suez:

60 TS – Scampton:

62 TS – Dover: A5953, A5955.

67 TS – Shawbury: A2387, A5966, A8243.

198 NTS – Rochford: A8250, B2587.

6 TS AFC – Minchinhampton: A5293.

202 TDS – Cranwell: N5632.

204 TDS – Eastchurch: A5261, N5220, N5234.

207 TDS – Chingford: N5172.

208 TDS – East Fortune: N5612.

1 (Observers) SAG – Hythe: A8231.

3 (Aux) SAG – New Romney: A1014.

School of Special Flying – Gosport: B8912.

Armament Experimental Station – Orfordness: 7942, A1067, A8255, B2574.

Aeroplane Experimental Station – Martlesham Heath: B744, B862.

Wireless Experimental Station – Biggin Hill: A2409.

Fleet School of Aerial Gunnery & Fighting – Leuchars Junction: 9741, B2597.

Marine Observers School – Leysdown: 9408, N5153, N5530.

The Pup

Success with a Single-Seat Scout

Of all British World War I aeroplanes, the one that was remembered by ex-pilots with the most affection was the Sopwith Pup. Its docility, combined with superb manoeuvrability, made it an instant favourite. The Pup lacked the latent viciousness of its successor, the Camel, and the control heaviness of its progenitor, the 1½ Strutter. It was a pilot's aeroplane.

Development

Just as the 1½ Strutter had been developed from a private Sopwith creation, so too was the Pup. Harry Hawker was well recorded as having chalked out the design of a 'runabout' on the workshop floor at Kingston and the resultant machine was known as the SLTBP. Again, there is no known record to clarify these abbreviations; Sopwith Light Tractor Biplane may be a suitable interpretation.

The SLTBP had been flown by November 1915, with Hawker giving a demonstration of its aerobatic abilities on the 14th of that month. The machine was a neat single-bay biplane, with lateral control induced by wing warping. The planform of its wings and tailplane resembled those of the later Pup, but the centre-section struts were vertical to the upper fuselage longerons. The narrow centre section was of fuselage width. The SLTBP displayed typical Sopwith features, with a split axle and characteristic vertical tail surfaces. The combined fuel and oil tank was carried behind the engine front mounting plate, hung from the upper longerons, and the engine backplate was carried on diagonal struts. The engine itself was a 50hp Gnome and this bestowed a speed of 84.6mph (136.1km/h). That engine was carried in a horseshoe-shaped cowling. Stalling speed was, apparently, only 22mph (35km/h). Although the SLTBP was designed as a 'one-off' for Hawker, drawings were later

prepared and a general arrangement set were in existence by December 1915. It would appear at least five further machines of that or similar type were built. One of these was in Australia, by a former Sopwith employee, one Basil Watson. Watson's machine differed slightly from the original in having a fully circular engine cowling and aluminium side panels that extended as far aft on the fuselage as the rear line of the cockpit. Its propeller was, apparently, of local manufacture. It also carried fuselage cockades and rudder stripes. For Watson to have built such a machine in the Antipodes would have required his being in possession of factory drawings. That SLTBP was flying by November 1916 and crashed, killing its maker, on 28 March 1917.

What were also likely to have been SLTBPs were the four Sopwith machines, known as Sparrows, that were allotted, but probably never carried, the serial numbers A8970-A8973. These were described as having warping wings and provision for 50hp Gnome engines. They must have been built privately by Sopwith's but the RNAS and RFC did not want them. It is a matter of speculation as to whether they were actually acquired, although a Sparrow was fitted with a 35hp ABC Gnat engine, for use as a radio-controlled pilotless aeroplane. That machine was photographed in full factory finish. It may have been one of the four, or another built especially for that purpose.

At least one and possibly two of the type came onto the civil register after the war,

Specification – Sopwith Sparrow	
Engine:	One 50hp Gnome or one 35hp ABC Gnat
Dimensions:	Length 19ft (5.79m); wingspan upper 26ft 9½in (8.17m), lower 26ft 9½in (8.17m)
Armament:	None

The Pup was derived from the SLTBP which is shown here. The machine had a narrower centre section with vertical struts and a 50hp Gnome, but the major airframe features were carried on in the Pup. JMB/GSL

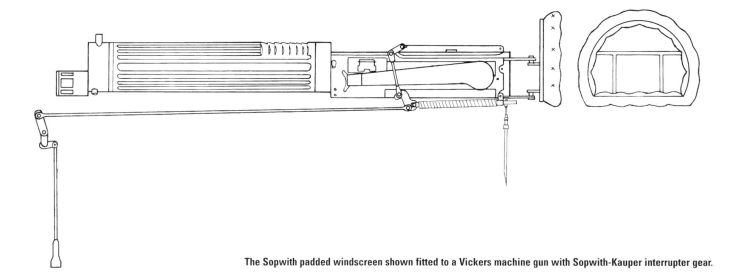

The Sopwith padded windscreen shown fitted to a Vickers machine gun with Sopwith-Kauper interrupter gear.

although neither carried any registration letters. Photographs show a machine, or machines, fitted with a full cowling. One is fairly well recorded and first appeared at Northolt in a colour scheme that suggests use as an instructor's 'personal' aeroplane. The other shows a two-seat conversion, which had long-span ailerons on its lower wings.

Construction of the first Sopwith Pup followed shortly after that of the original SLTBP. The design influence of Hawker's 'runabout' was obvious. The Pup tailplane and mainplanes, although differing structurally, retained the planform set by its predecessor, with raked back tips. A wider centre section was fitted, necessitating the use of splayed struts. Ailerons were carried on all four wings.

The Pup fuselage was somewhat deeper, but retained the fuel/oil tank position. The engine was enclosed in a circular cowling. Armament was a single Vickers gun, mounted centrally on the decking ahead of the cockpit and fitted with the Sopwith patented padded windscreen. An 80hp Le Rhone 9C engine gave the extra power needed to compensate for the military load.

That prototype was completed by 9 February and tested by the CFS at Upavon during late March. Sopwith's was, however, still regarded as a naval contractor and the RNAS was quick to order the machine and two further examples. The three became 3691 and 9496–9497. Sopwith's also received an order for a further three pre-production machines, which became 9898–9900. These may have been intended for the French government; certainly they were recorded as such on 1 September.

All three, however, saw out their service lives with the RNAS.

9496 was accepted into service on 10 July 1916 and was sent to France. After a brief spell with 1 Wing RNAS at St Pol, it was transferred to 3 Wing RNAS at Luxeuil. That transfer was via Villacoublay and may have given French authorities the opportunity to examine the type. At Luxeuil, 9496 carried the name '*The Pup*' in white letters, painted on the fuselage below the cockpit. It is tempting to speculate that this early use of the name may have been the origin of the appellation that came to be applied generically to the type. Service lore has it that the type was regarded as a pup of the 1½ Strutter, and 3 Wing was certainly operating that

machine. To the RNAS, the Pup was the Sopwith Type 9901 (or 9901a, if fitted for shipboard operations), the designation being taken from a serial number of an early machine, just as the Types 9400 and 9700 were from early 1½ Strutters. The RFC preferred the name Sopwith Scout and its hierarchy frowned on the use of frivolous names. Service units were notified that the type was to be known as the Sopwith Scout and not Pup, but the name had achieved almost universal acceptance and could not be suppressed. Pup was the first animal name to be associated with the Sopwith 'zoo', although its use was at the inspiration of service pilots and not, as subsequently, from the Sopwith factory.

3691 was the Pup prototype and it had a long and eventful career, serving operationally in France from 1 June 1916 until 10 February 1917. Withdrawn to England, it flew on anti-Gotha patrols from Dover. It went to the USA for exhibition and was scheduled for preservation post-war. JMB/GSL

Early Service

9497 was not delivered until October, from when it spent a long and useful service life at Grain, being a vehicle for many of the experiments in the development of shipboard aeroplanes that are detailed in a later chapter. The other three pre-production Pups built by Sopwith's were delivered in November and December and all saw active service, notably with 3N Sqn. Although intended to be powered by the 80hp Clerget 7Z, it is unlikely that such engines were fitted. 9899 and 9900 survived until written off as time-expired in October 1917, but 9898 later joined 9497 at Grain.

The RFC was impressed with the CFS report and also ordered the type. Sopwith's was committed to naval production and so the Standard Motor Co. of Coventry was given the first RFC contract for the type on 22 May. This was a month before the first RNAS contract was given to Wm Beardmore and was probably the result of Trenchard being impressed with the CFS report. The RFC contract covered the serial numbers A626–A675, Beardmore's from the RNAS 9901–9949. Most of those RNAS machines were built to that service's specification for an anti-airship machine and, as such, had an upward-firing Lewis gun in place of the Vickers, although the fittings to accept the belt-fed machine gun were retained. The Type 9901 Ships Pups are detailed in Chapter 8.

Further Pups were ordered from the parent company. Twenty, to be numbered N5180–N5199, were ordered in July 1916 and deliveries began just one month later. Most of this batch were delivered for service in France. Initial deliveries were to 1 Wing RNAS, but the naval service was soon to create numbered squadrons and it was with these that the Pup was truly blooded in action.

As the battles on the Somme dragged on into October 1916, the RFC was hard pressed. The newly formed German *Jagdstaffeln* had made their presence felt, as rising combat losses showed. The RNAS was asked to help and agreed to create a mixed squadron that would be detached for service on the Somme. Flights were drawn from 1, 4 and 5 Wings, equipped with Pups, Nieuports and 1½ Strutters respectively. The new squadron was with the RFC at Vert Galand by 26 October and was soon titled 8N Sqn. Interestingly, another 8N Sqn was concurrently serving in East Africa. Combat

The RNAS achieved major success with the Pup, 3N Sqn being its most successful unit. N6183 was a machine of that unit and achieved four combat 'victories' in the hands of FSL J.A. Gen. JMB/GSL

experience soon proved the Pup to be the most superior of the three types operated and the other two were soon replaced with the Sopwith Scout. Under the command of Flt Cdr (later Sqn Cdr) G.R. Bromet DSO, 8N Sqn quickly established a reputation as a fighting unit. Its pilots included several who later became leading fighter pilots: Flt Comm B.L. Huskinson, FSLs R.A. Little, D.M.B. Galbraith, C. Draper and R.R. Soar. It was 8N Sqn that, apparently, began the

common RNAS practice of decorating machines with names painted in large letters on the fuselage.

8N Sqn remained on the Somme until 3 February 1917, when its place in 22 Wing RFC was taken by 3N Sqn. The unit had achieved many combat victories, with the loss of three Pup pilots killed and another two made POW. In the meantime, Standard-built Pups had begun to come forward for the RFC. The first of

Specification – Sopwith Pup	
Engine	One 80hp Le Rhone 9C with alternatives being the 80hp Gnome, 80hp Clerget and 100hp Monosoupape
Weights:	Empty 787lb (357kg) (Le Rhone), 850lb (386kg) (Clerget), 856lb (388kg) (Monosoupape); loaded 1,225lb (556kg) (Le Rhone), 1,290lb (585kg) (Clerget), 1,297lb (588kg) (Monosoupape)
Dimensions:	Length 19ft 3¾in (5.87m); height 8ft 10½in (2.71m); wingspan upper 26ft 6in (8.07m), lower 26ft 6in (8.07m); chord upper 5ft 1½in (1.56m), lower 5ft 1½in (1.56m); stagger 1ft 6in (45.72cm); gap 4ft 5in (1.35m); dihedral upper 3°, lower 3°
Performance:	Max. speed 104mph (167km/h) (Le Rhone), 104mph (167km/h) (Monosoupape) Service ceiling 20,000ft (6,100m) (Le Rhone), 21,000ft (6,400m) (Monosoupape) Endurance 3 hours (Le Rhone), 2 hours (Clerget), 1¾ hours (Monosoupape)
Armament:	One Vickers gun synchronized to fire through propeller arc, sometimes supplemented by an overwing Lewis

these, A626, had been delivered to the CFS by 12 October 1916. It underwent official tests on the 21st, returning performance figures that were slightly inferior to those of 3691 that had been tested earlier. A626 was in France by 4 November and went, temporarily, to 70 Sqn, which was then equipped with 1½ Strutters. before moving to 8N Sqn in late December. Because 8N Sqn was operating under RFC control, it could draw on military stocks to replace losses, but A626 did not last long,

being lost on 4 January 1917, with its pilot, Flt Lt J.C. Croft, being made POW. The plane itself was hardly damaged and, restored to flying condition, it presented the Germans with the opportunity to make a detailed evaluation of the latest British fighting scout. Another Pup had been lost by 8N Sqn on 4 January, when Flt Lt A.S. Todd was shot down and killed by Ltn M. Fr v Richthofen of *Jasta 2*. Von Richthofen was a rising star of the German Air Service and his appraisal of the

type, from his combat encounter with Todd, was complimentary with regard to the Pup's handling and manoeuvrability. The Pup could hold its own in the gyrations of combat with the latest German types and von Richthofen concluded that it was only because Todd was outnumbered that he was brought down.

54 Sqn had arrived in France with its Pups on Christmas Eve 1916, being based at Bertangles from Boxing Day and moving to Chipilly on 11 January 1917. Slow delivery of Standard-built machines meant that it was to be another two months before that service had a second Pup squadron.

Whitehead Aircraft Ltd, of Richmond, had received a contract for one hundred Pups (A6150–A6249) in September 1916 and the first of these was delivered some four months later. Initial deliveries had the adjustable tailplane, but that was dispensed with by the time production had reached A6228. This created problems of spare parts, particularly when units in the field were forced to make repairs. The fixed tailplane variant had a revised fuselage structure and new fin. The integral fittings on the tailplane meant that this component was also not interchangeable. It took some time for this to be realized by the services.

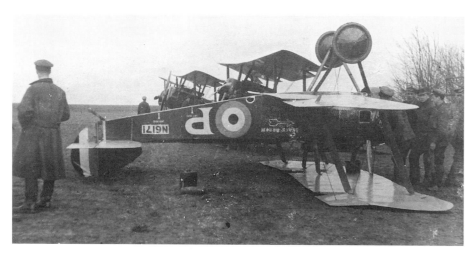

N6171 was another 3N Sqn machine and was the usual mount of FSL E. Pierce. After its operational life, it was used as a trainer at Cranwell. JMB/GSL

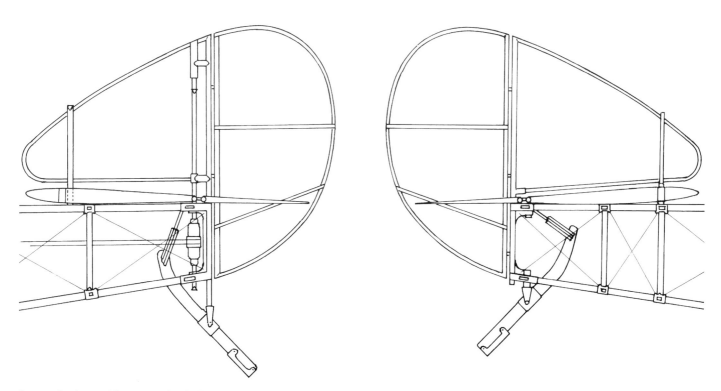

Pup rear fuselage and fin constructional differences – adjustable tailplane version *(left)* **and fixed tailplane** *(right).*

1917

The second RFC Pup squadron was in the process of formation by February 1917, with 66 Sqn at Filton beginning to receive its operation machines at the beginning of that month. Its initial complement included A7313 and A7315, which were delivered on the 24th. These were from a second batch of fifty built by Standard. 66 Sqn joined the BEF at St Omer on 3 March and was installed at its first operational base, Vert Galand, fifteen days later.

With the Pup already in large-scale production, further orders were placed, to a total of 250 airframes. B1701–B1850 were ordered from Standard and B2151–B2250 from Whitehead. These were placed to maintain the operational squadrons in France, although some did find their way to training units.

3N Sqn had been on the Somme Front since 1 February, to replace Naval Eight when that unit was withdrawn to re-equip with the later Triplane. 3N Sqn had taken over its predecessor's base, but had to vacate Vert Galand to make room for 66 Sqn. The naval unit transferred base to Bertangles and then to Marieux, where it remained until June. During that spell with the RFC, the unit was engaged in much heavier fighting than Naval Eight had known and achieved a significant number of combat successes. There were also the inevitable losses, although these were low compared to those suffered by other squadrons. Indeed, that could be said for all operational Pup squadrons. Naval Three must have had a skilled sign-writer among its ranks, because many of the unit's Pups were marked with individual names, tastefully painted in a neat shadow effect.

The early spring of 1917 was a time of build-up for the spring offensive that was planned for April and all three Pup squadrons with the RFC were heavily involved in combat. As German ground forces withdrew to the Hindenburg Line, the RFC maintained a steady programme of reconnaissance that needed protection from the growing number of *Jagdstaffeln*. From late March, the Pup units were involved in an escalating air war that was to test the British air services to the limit during the month that became known as 'Bloody April'.

There were several pilots in 3N Sqn who had been transferred from 3 Wing after the reduction in the establishment of that unit. These included Flt Lt L.S.

Breadner and FSLs J.J. Malone and R. Collishaw, all of whom were to achieve considerable combat success, with Malone becoming the unit's leading scorer during its early months with the RFC. Its other noted Pup exponents included FSL J.S.T. Fall, who became the squadron's most successful pilot on the type.

Plans designed to ensure a supply of trained RFC pilots for Pups had been in hand by 23 December 1916. On that date, the intended establishment of 43 RS at Ternhill was set at six Avros plus six Bristol Scouts plus six Pups. When pusher-type scouts were withdrawn in May 1916, Reserve (later Training) Squadrons that had operated D.H.2s and/or F.E.8s were re-equipped with Pups as part of their new equipment. These included 6 RS at Catterick, 40 RS at Portmeadow and 45 RS at South Carlton, with 63 RS receiving Pups after it had formed at Ternhill. The training procedure at that time saw successful pupil pilots moving from Elementary RS to Higher RS. At the latter, prospective Pup pilots received training on Avros, which had similar (although more sedate) flying characteristics, before graduating to the front-line type.

The first combat losses by 3N Sqn were suffered on 4 March, when two pilots were killed and another was fatally wounded. A fourth Pup was damaged in combat but its pilot, FSL H.F. Beamish was unhurt. Beamish had achieved an early, shared 'victory' with the squadron, that of a Roland D.II driven down on 16 February with the assistance of FSL J.A. Glen who had been flying 9898. This was one of the pre-production Pups, and it became a favourite mount of FSL J.J. Malone, who achieved four successes whilst flying it. These included a triple 'victory' on 17 March, a two-seater sent down out of control and two Albatros D IIs destroyed. Malone continued to score at a rapid rate, achieving a total of ten successes by 24 April. He had been made a DSO and was regarded as a rising 'star', but was killed in combat six days later. The losses of 3N Sqn had been light during 'Bloody April' in comparison with most other British units. Malone was one of only two fatalities, although one pilot was made POW and other Pups were brought down with their pilots uninjured. On the credit side, the squadron was recorded to have brought down (either destroyed or out of control) no fewer than forty-two enemy machines, several of these being shared 'victories'.

An action by the Canadian FSL J.S.T. Fall on the 11th typified the aggressive character of that pilot and merited mention in the *Official History*. Fall was one of an escort for B.E. machines of 4 Sqn that were detailed to bomb Cambrai. The attacking force was met by a formation of Halberstadt and Albatros scouts and an intensive fight ensued. Fall sent one Albatros D II down completely out of control and then destroyed another from a range so close that the head of the enemy pilot filled the ring in the Pup's Aldis sight. He was, by then, detached from the remainder of his colleagues and made for home at low level, being fired on by ground troops. A Halberstadt scout attacked him and Fall engaged this, finally sending it down to crash after his fire had struck the enemy pilot in the back. In his report, Fall noted that 'My machine was badly shot about'. The machine in question was A6158; another Pup issued to the RNAS from RFC stocks. It was so badly damaged that it was returned to 2 AD at Candas, but was back with 3N Sqn by early May and lost on the 14th of that month, when FSL W.R. Walker was shot down to become a POW. Fall's outstanding performance resulted in his being awarded a DSC.

During March, 4N Sqn had re-equipped with Pups and operated the type for three months until the first Camels arrived. This squadron was not attached to the RFC, but operated over the Channel coast from its permanent base at Bray Dunes. It suffered only one fatality, when Flt Lt C.J. Moir was shot down near Zeebrugge on 10 May. The squadron was credited with several successes, four of its leading pilots being Flt Lts A.J. Chadwick and A.M. Shook and FSLs A.J. Enstone and L.F.W. Smith. Among the latter's combat successes were two enemy kite balloons. Between them, these four pilots were to account for twenty-one 'victories' whilst flying Pups.

The RNAS also operated a systematic training scheme to supply its squadrons. From its Preliminary Training Schools, such as Redcar and Chingford, trainee pilots were posted to Cranwell for advanced training and selected there for aptitude as scout pilots. After graduation, many destined for France were posted to Dover for advanced training on types that included the Pup. From April 1917, 12N Sqn served in France as a 'finishing school' for scout pilots, continuing in this role until disbanded upon the formation of the RAF. Many of its early machines were Pups.

4N Sqn flew its Pups on operations over the Channel. Like those of other naval units, its pilots marked their machine with large names. 'Bobs' was N6200 and was used by Flt Lt A.M. Shook to achieve four combat 'victories'. It later served with the War Flight at Manston. JMB/GSL

From February and March 1917, 9 and 11N Sqns, respectively, also flew the type as part of mixed equipment that also included Triplanes and, in the case of 11N, some early Camels. Like 4N Sqn, 11N flew patrols over the Channel coast and it had

some combat successes. These included a first 'victory' for FSL A.R. Brown, later to achieve (probably unwarranted) fame. On 17 July he sent an Albatros D III down out of control while flying N6174. That incarnation of the squadron was short-lived, however, as it was disbanded, along with 6N Sqn, during August as part of an attempt to bring other RNAS units up to establishment. From 15 June 9N Sqn replaced 3N with the RFC, but Camels soon replaced its Pups and Triplanes.

The first combat victory of 54 Sqn occurred on 25 January, when Capt A. Lees destroyed an Albatros scout and captured an enemy two-seater. He was flying A635, one of the original Pups issued to the unit. The squadron suffered losses, however; 15 February was a bad day, with two of the unit's initial Pups shot down (A645 and A654 with their pilots killed) and a third, A647, severely damaged. It continued to maintain a steady rate of 'victories', but on 5 April was given a much more dangerous task. German observation balloons could have been a hindrance to the Allied advance scheduled for 8 April and an all-out attack on these dangerous targets was

The Standard Motor Co. was the main supplier of Pups to the RFC and this crowded scene was taken in its Coventry factory in 1917. B6104 and B6107 are visible among the mass of airframes in various stages of completion. JMB/GSL

ordered. Four pilots of 54 Sqn were successful in destroying the balloon allotted to the unit. A further ten enemy machines were credited to the unit during April.

The victory tally of 66 Sqn had opened on 8 April, when Capt G.W. Roberts, Lt C.C. Montgomery and 2Lt A.J. Lucas each sent a Halberstadt D II down out of control. The unit only claimed a further five 'victories' during that month of heavy fighting, for the loss of one pilot – 2Lt R.S. Capon, who was made POW in A6175 on the 26th. Capon was not the first squadron casualty, however. On 27 March, Lt S. Stretton had been killed in an accident whilst flying A6163.

A third RFC squadron had received the Pup during April 1917. This was 46 Sqn, which re-equipped from the Nieuport 12/20 two-seat general-purpose machine to become a scout unit. The four Pup units then with the RFC continued their routine of patrol and escort work over the Somme area and, despite losses, continued to achieve combat success against an increasingly well equipped enemy air service.

Dunkerque and Walmer. The former, as already related, flew Babies, but soon switched to Pups, which then operated from St Pol. That at Walmer flew Pups and Bristol Scouts, but both units were charged with the aerial protection of shipping in the Channel, as well as the protection of Short 184s. This was in response to seaplane-launched torpedo attacks, that had begun on vessels moored in the Downs. It was to Walmer that Flt Lt R.A. Little was posted after his successful combat tour with 8N Sqn and a memorial to that Australian pilot was erected there after his death in France.

Further Pups had been ordered from the parent company: a batch of fifty (N6160–N6209), followed by one of seventy (N6460–N6529), although only thirty of the latter were completed. The majority of these were issued to maintain the RNAS units in France. Beardmore's received a further order for Type 9901a Pups; thirty machines numbered N6430–N6459. Most of these were for shipboard use, but N6435–N6442 were fitted with Vickers gun armament and issued to the Defence Flights at St Pol and Walmer.

The trailing edge of the centre section was cut away behind the rear spar, forward of which was a semicircular cut-out for access to the cockpit. The pilot's head must have projected through this cut-out to give an excellent view forwards and upwards. The Bee, at some point, was re-engined with an ABC Gnat, as fitted to the Sparrow, and it may have been that it too was used for radio-control experiments.

The Pup squadrons serving with the RFC saw further combat during May and June. 3N Sqn had emerged well from 'Bloody April', having achieved victory over forty-two enemy machines, for the loss of one pilot killed and another made POW. The RNAS unit was much more

Whitehead Aircraft of Richmond was another major RFC supplier, many of its Pups having the 100hp Gnome Monosoupape engine, as shown in this factory shot. via K Kelly

The RNAS used some of its Pups operationally from home bases. War Flights, for Home Defence, were formed at Manston and Dover, with mixed equipment that included the Sopwith type. The stations at Eastchurch and Grain also operated the Pup and could field machines for Home Defence duty. During May and June 1917 respectively, Defence Flights were established at

1917 also saw the flight of a new Sopwith design that employed some Pup components. This was the Bee, a diminutive biplane that was built as another 'runabout' for Harry Hawker. Its 16ft 3in wingspan was 2ft greater than its length and power came from a 50hp Gnome that was enclosed in a circular cowling. It had wing warping rather than aileron control.

Exploits on Pups

The following descriptions are taken directly from RFC Communiqués (known to all as 'Comic Cuts') and illustrate aspects of aerial combat by Pup pilots during 1917. The action by Pritt emulated that of 2 June which had brought the award of a Victoria Cross to Capt W.A. Bishop of 60 Sqn.

April 27 – Flight Sub-Lt J.J. Malone, 3 Squadron RNAS, attacked a hostile machine over Cambrai. Three other HA joined in the engagement which took place at a height of 7,000ft. Flight Sub-Lt Malone followed one machine down to 3,000ft, firing at it, and was in turn followed by the three HA. Eventually the first machine was destroyed. When at a height of 1,000ft Flight Sub-Lt Malone turned west, but finding it impossible to evade the attacking HA, he pretended to land. As soon as his wheels touched the ground he saw that the HA were also about to land and once more put on his engine and flew off and though he was pursued by the three HA they were unable to overtake him and were driven off east by heavy fire from our trenches.

May 24 – Lt O.M. Sutton, 54 Squadron, engaged a German single-seater which flew straight at him, and it was only by a quick turn that Lt Sutton avoided crashing into the HA. As it was, his right-hand top plane hit the HA which broke to pieces in the air and fell. Although his top plane was badly broken, he succeeded in landing safely.

15 August – Lt W.A. Pritt (66 Sqn) flew to Marcke aerodrome in the dark and dropped one 20lb bomb from 100ft right in the middle of a group of machines on the aerodrome. He dropped a second which fell in a road, and a third which just missed the machines, then dropped a fourth on Herelbout siding which was full of troops. Just as he was doing this he saw an Albatros scout getting off the aerodrome so attacked it and saw it crash on the houses north-east of the aerodrome. On turning round he saw another machine getting off the aerodrome. This he also attacked and it made a half turn, side-slipped, then crashed on the aerodrome. He then silenced a machine gun that was firing at him and returned home.

(Above) The Sopwith Bee was built as a 'runabout' for Harry Hawker and employed some Pup components. Its diminutive size is evident in this photograph. JMB/GSL

46 Sqn was the third RFC Pup squadron in France. A6157 of that unit had additional cockades on its centre section and wheel discs. It was delivered to 46 Sqn on 5 June 1917 and was lost two days later, with Lt A.P. Mitchell being made a POW. via GSL

successful than its RFC counterparts in terms of combat 'victories' and had achieved these with similar minimal losses. May, however, would see those losses increase. Pilots such as Breadner, Fall and Armstrong were able to add, at a slower rate, to their existing tallies and others, such as FSL L.H. Rochford, began to score, but the nature of the air war was changing. British patrols, at flight strength, were encountering more and more opposition in the form of large numbers of enemy aeroplanes, either at *Jagdstaffel* strength or groups of these formations. Before being returned to the RNAS at Furnes on 15 June, 3N Squadron lost four pilots, who were made POW, and a further two were wounded, one fatally. Within weeks of retiring to Furnes, the squadron was re-equipped with Camels.

In 66 Sqn, Capt J.O. Andrews DSO MC* emerged as a leading exponent of the Pup in combat. He had previous experience from fighting on D.H.2s with 24 Sqn and consolidated his reputation with a successful run of five 'victories', before being posted home in mid-July. Other pilots, such as Lt T.C. Luke, were similarly successful, but the increasing strength of enemy opposition was being felt in 66 Sqn's sector too. A good account of life on this unit can be found in the book *Sopwith Scout 7309* by P.G. Taylor, who flew and fought on Pups with 66 Sqn.

46 Sqn had received its full establishment of Pups by mid-May, but it was slow to achieve a combat victory. The squadron had its first Pup casualty on 23 May, when A665 was lost, with 2Lt J.P. Stephen killed. Further pilots were wounded that month, but it was not until 2 June that the unit had its first combat successes. On that date, Lt C.A. Brewster-Joske and 2Lt F. Barrager both sent Albatros D IIIs down out of control. Brewster-Joske had a further two 'victories' that month and was the squadron's most successful pilot of the period. His usual Pup was B1709. The

activities of 46 Sqn, too, were chronicled by one of its pilots: A.S.G. Lee provided details of the squadron's work and characters in his masterly books *No Parachute* and *Open Cockpit*.

54 Sqn had a similar story to tell. Several of its pilots flew successful combats, notably Capts W.V. Strugnell MC* and O. Stewart MC and Lt O.M. Sutton. Oliver Stewart, whose usual Pup was A6156, was one of the RFC's most gifted pilots and he too had his memoirs published, *Words and Music of a Mechanical Man*. The squadron was moved north to the naval aerodrome at Bray Dunes for the Flanders campaign scheduled for July, and fought over the Channel coast area for the remainder of its time using Pups.

Seven Pups were dispatched to the Aegean theatre, for use by 2 Wing RNAS, later 62 Wing RAF. Of these four were built by Beardmore (9941, 9942, N6432 and N6433) and three by Sopwith's (N6463, N6470 and N6471). Some of the Beardmore machines retained the Lewis gun armament that characterized Ships Pups. The seven served with C, F and G Sqns of 2 Wing, being used for escort work and interceptions. None is known to have had any combat success.

Home Defence

The type had an early introduction to Home Defence duties. The initial daylight Gotha raid of 25 May 1917 had seen Pups airborne in attempted interceptions from Manston, Dover, Grain and Walmer. The closest to achieving any success was the prototype 3691, flown from Dover by FSL R.F.S. Leslie from Dover. Leslie fired about 150 rounds into a Gotha, which was seen to lose height and emit smoke, although it is unlikely that this was a successful combat. However, further Pups from 4N and 9N Sqns intercepted the raiding force near the Belgian coast. One Gotha was shot down 15 miles off Westende, probably the victim of 4N Sqn pilots, FSL E.W. Busby (N5196), FSL L.F.W. Smith (N6168), FSL A.J. Chadwick (N6176) and FSL G.M.T. Rouse (N6198).

Leslie's mount of 25 May, 3691, had a long and auspicious career. After delivery to the RNAS, it was sent, via Chingford and Grain, to Dunkerque. There it was taken on the strength of 5 Wing RNAS at Coudekerque, serving with flights of A Sqn. On 10 July 1916 it transferred to 1

Wing at Furnes and St Pol, being used by FSL S.J. Goble to send an LVG down out of control on 24 September. It then joined 8N Sqn (Naval Eight) on 16 November and was used by that unit's pilots to achieve a further combat victory. When Naval Eight returned north to re-equip with Triplanes 3691 was transferred to 3N Sqn, which replaced 8N on detachment with the RFC. After its spell at Dover, it went to the USA for exhibition and was presumably returned as, in September 1918, it was to be delivered to the Agricultural Hall at Islington and scheduled for preservation. Unfortunately, like other machines so scheduled, 3691 was scrapped.

Attempts were made to augment the single Vickers gun with an overwing Lewis. B2162 of 66 Sqn was flown operationally with that extra armament and on 30 September 1917 Lt W.A. Pritt MC achieved a victory with his 'top gun'. via K Kelly

That initial raid prompted the RFC to take measures to bolster its Home Defence force which consisted of obsolete B.E. types. Selected Higher Training Squadrons were ordered to make machines available. In order that these could be brought into the area of operations, 40 TS was moved from Portmeadow to Croydon and 63 TS from Ternhill to Joyce Green. Pups from these two units flew a number of unsuccessful patrols during the daylight raids of that summer.

Pups were added to the front-line Home Defence force. Initially, the expediency adopted was to equip B Flts of 37 Sqn and 50 Sqns based at Stowe Maries and Throwley respectively. As more machines became available, new Home Defence squadrons were created and subsumed the existing flights. These were 61 Sqn, which reformed at Rochford on 24 July, and 112 Sqn, which formed at Throwley the

following day. The first Pups operated by these HD units were standard 80hp Le Rhone versions, but later that summer the 100hp Gnome Monosoupape powered Pup became the standard variant for that duty. The adoption of that engine gave the Pup an improved rate of climb, important to its new role of interceptor. A Mono Pup could reach 15,000ft (4,572m) in approximately three-quarters of the time that it took a Le Rhone-powered one. Capt R.M. Charley, of the Experimental station at Orfordness, reported that the variant was 'almost as good as a Camel'. The drawback was a reduction in endurance to just over half that of the original. A new form of engine cowling was adopted, one of horse-shoe shape, with strengthening ribs and frontal cooling slots. There were attempts to increase the type's fire power, by adding an overwing Lewis gun, but these were not regarded as being successful and most were soon discarded. It may have been that the standard centre section, unlike that of the Beardmore-built Type 9901 and if left unmodified, was not of sufficient structural strength to withstand the added weight and accompanying vibration. In addition, there was no provision for changing ammunition drums and the extra weight of the Lewis would have had a detrimental effect on performance.

Pups flew against the remainder of the daylight raids and one was lost to enemy action. This was A6230 of 63 TS. Its pilot, 2Lt W.G. Salmon, was killed on 7 July in unknown combat circumstances. Another 63 TS pilot, who flew Home Defence

Pup Engines

Much of the Pup's tractability was due to the use of the 80hp Le Rhone engine. That engine was a product of the Société des Moteurs Gnôme & Rhône of Paris. It was a nine-cylinder rotary that was easily recognized by its induction pipes that led from the front of the crankcase. A single push-rod for each cylinder operated both inlet and exhaust valves. Its selection was undoubtedly due to its lightness; it only weighed 199lb (90kg). It was manufactured under licence in the UK and cost a mere £620.

The 100hp Monosoupape, from the same manufacturer, took its name from the single external (exhaust) valve in each cylinder head that was operated by a prominent frontal push-rod. The engine's greater power came at the expense of weight, as it was 61lb (28kg) heavier than the Le Rhone and less economical on fuel. The extra power did not improve the Pup's top speed, but greatly improved its rate of climb. Few Mono Pups were delivered to the BEF, but the variant was standardized for those Home Defence squadrons that operated the type.

Pups were issued to the VI Brigade in 1917 in an attempt to update the force of B.E. and F.E. variants that were unsuitable for countering aeroplane raids. Most had the 100hp Monosoupape engine. Here one of 61 Sqn's machines is seen after a landing accident. JMB/GSL

these combat-experienced units managed to achieve contact with the enemy, and 66 Sqn was returned to its base at Estrée Blanche after less than three weeks. The pilots of 46 Sqn were more fortunate, with their posting to England continuing until the end of August. In that time, the unit's rapid formation take-off impressed resident pilots.

It was an RNAS Pup that achieved the type's sole successes in the Home Defence role. Flt Lt H.S. Kerby was flying N6440 from Walmer against the raid of 12 August and used his Pup's height advantage to make a diving attack on Gotha G IV 656/16. The enemy machine went straight down into the sea and, despite Kerby's efforts to attract the attention of shipping, the crew was drowned. Kerby was awarded a DSC. Kerby and N6440 were again in action ten days later, when he and Flt Cdr G.E. Hervey, from Dover in Pup N6191, shared in the destruction of another Gotha.

The German tactical switch to night bombing resulted in the withdrawal of Pups from the RFC squadrons based in southern England. Whereas the Camel was found to be suitable as a night fighter, the Pup's low wing loading made it unsuitable for operations from the small aerodromes of VI Brigade (which had evolved from the Home Defence Group). Pilots found it difficult to make positive night landings and so 61 and 112 Sqns were given temporary, unnecessary, day duties until they could be re-equipped. When that happened, their Pups were transferred

sorties, was Capt J.T.B. McCudden MC. His usual Pup, A7311, was armed with an over-wing Lewis and had a home-made sighting arrangement. The Pup's ability to reach high altitude before attacking is suggested by the fact that McCudden had this machine's under-surfaces doped light blue. He was posted to France and briefly joined 66 Sqn, with which unit he achieved a single 'victory' while flying B1756 – an Albatros D V sent out of control on 26 July. He was then transferred to 56 Sqn and went on to achieve great fame as an S.E.5a pilot.

The shortage of efficient machines in the Home Defence Group and the public outrage generated by the raids led to the temporary withdrawal from 10 July of 46 Sqn from France to Sutton's Farm, while 66 Sqn had already been detached to Calais, in the hope that its Pups would be able to intercept returning Gothas. Neither of

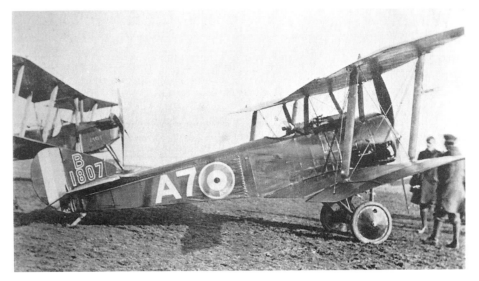

When the Southern HD squadrons received Camels, some Pups were transferred to 36 Sqn in the north-east. B1807 was one such machine and, like other HD Pups, was for day use only – hence the lack of navigation lights and brackets for Holt flares. JMB/GSL

(Above) **Pups were issued to squadrons working up in the UK for operational service. One such unit was 96 Sqn at North Shotwick and C231 was one of its Monosoupape-engined machines.** JMB/GSL

81 Sqn spent a long working-up period at Scampton and flew a variety of types that included Pups. B6124, named 'Mummy', was on the squadron's strength during 1917. JMB/GSL

to other units. Some were passed to 36 Sqn in the north-east, while others were taken on charge by the three Night Training Squadrons (188, 189 and 198 NTS) that were allocated, one each, to the three Southern Home Defence Wings. At these NTS, the Pups served as useful intermediate trainers, linking preliminary training on Avros and final training on Camels.

By the autumn of 1917, when the Camel was being introduced in ever increasing numbers, the Pup still had one advantage over its successor – its ability to hold its own at altitude. The standard F1 Camel's manoeuvrability decreased significantly over 15,000ft (4,570m), but the Pup could hold its own at that and greater heights. The only drawbacks were its low

power and single gun armament. Attempts were made to counteract both.

The 110hp Le Rhone 9J was seen as a possible alternative engine for the Pup and installations were made to test its compatibility with the airframe. This revived an idea from July 1916, when the RNAS serial N503 was allotted for a Pup with just such an engine but that proposal, as well as work on the machine, had been abandoned. An improved performance was bestowed by the Le Rhone and the rate of climb, in particular, was increased. The disadvantage was that the greater weight of the more powerful engine made landing more difficult, as the machine had to be flown in, rather than being allowed to settle in a neat three-point landing. In addition, and just as with the

100hp Monosoupape Pup, the larger and thirstier engine would have reduced endurance. Once the decision had been made to re-equip the existing RFC Pup squadrons with Camels, further work on the Le Rhone Pup was shelved.

The Pup was operated successfully by 66 Sqn throughout that autumn, until its Camels began arriving on 14 October. On the 12th, the squadron suffered its last casualties on the Pup; three were lost and two damaged in combat, with one pilot killed, one wounded and another two made POW. The unit had, however, some outstanding fighter pilots in its ranks and they too made attempts to augment the Vickers with overwing Lewis guns. It is not known whether the centre sections of the

Pups so modified were strengthened, but two-gun Pups were flown operationally by the squadron. On 30 September Lt W.A. Pritt MC was credited with sending an Albatros D V down out of control with fire from his 'top gun' on B2162.

Final Operations

On 30 August, 46 Sqn returned to France after its sojourn on Home Defence duty, initially to Ste Marie Cappel but moving to its permanent base of Filescamp Farm on 7 September. By then, the Pup was becoming outclassed, as witnessed by an action on 3 September when three of the unit's machines were lost with their pilots made POW and a further machine damaged and its pilot wounded. The squadron had to soldier on with the type for a further two months, suffering losses but also still achieving victories. Camel replacements began to arrive in November, but even as the Battle of Cambrai opened, mixed equipment was being operated and its remaining Pups were involved in the ground-attack work that characterized the battle. A6188 and B2186 were damaged on bombing raids on the 20th and two days later 46 Sqn had its final Pup loss, when Lt T.L. Atkinson was made POW after being brought down while engaged on a similar mission.

The last RFC squadron to fly the Pup operationally in France was 54 Sqn. Its Camels began to arrive during December, almost a month after it had suffered its final Pup casualty, that of B1757 lost on 9 November with 2Lt A Thompson made POW. The squadron had flown the type operationally for longer than any other squadron and had achieved some fifty-five 'victories', a rate of approximately one per week, the last being achieved on 4

Prior to operational service, pilots were posted to one of the Fighting Schools for instruction in combat techniques. Most of these had some Pups and this one from 2 FS at Marske met a nasty end. JMB/GSL

Most training unit Pups were delivered unarmed and C266 of 157 Sqn was no exception. It was embellished with further cockades on the wheel covers and had a fire extinguisher fitted aft of the cockpit. JMB/GSL

November – 2Lts S.J. Schooley and H.H. Maddocks in destroying an Albatros D.V.

A few Pups continued to serve in France until the late spring of 1918. The Scout School at 2AD Candas had at least seven (A6165, A6173, B1724, B1827, B1832, B7309 and B7324) and the Special Duty Flight, attached to 101 Sqn at Clairmarais South, had B2188 for use in its intelligence work.

The withdrawal of the Pup from first line operations in France did not mean the end of the type's production. The massive expansion that had taken place in the training programme created the niche for an intermediate trainer and the type's docile handling characteristics made it an ideal choice, onto which the trainees graduated from the ubiquitous Avro 504J/K and from which they moved to front-line

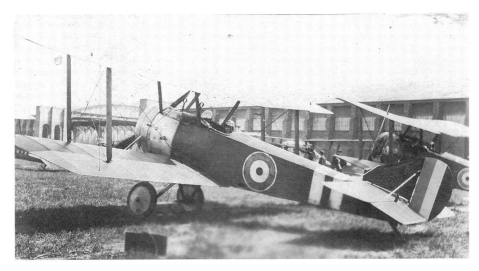

B7513 served with 4 TDS at Hooton Park. Although intended as a Dolphin training unit, 4 TDS operated a large number of Pups. B7513 has brackets on the forward fuselage that seem too large for an Aldis sight and may have housed a camera gun. JMB/GSL

(Below) The fitting of a camera gun to a Pup is well illustrated in this shot of B7525, which served at Scampton with 60 TS in 1917. JMB/GSL

types. Large numbers continued to be delivered; B5901–B6150 and C201–C400 from Standard, C3707–C3776 from Sopwith's, B7481–B7580, C1441–C1550 and D4011–D4210 from Whitehead. Some were delivered as spares, but a vast stock of airframes was available to the Training Brigade.

Accordingly, most late-production Pups were delivered directly to training units. All of the Training Squadrons and, later, Training Depot Stations that were designated as providers of Camel and Dolphin pilots had Pups on strength. A typical example was 4 TDS at Hooton Park, which was intended to have Dolphins and Avros. In the period April to June 1918 it operated at least twenty Pups (for example C222, C225, C402, C404). Similarly, 32 TDS at Montrose, when formed on 15 July 1918, received Pups from each of the Training Squadrons that disbanded to create it (for example B2207, B7573 and D4032 from 6 TS).

Training unit Pups, particularly the 'personal' aeroplanes of senior instructors, were often marked in distinctive colour schemes. These tended to utilize existing dope stocks and so usually comprised the national colours plus black. A wide variety of striped and chequerboard schemes are evident from the study of photographs, although sepia-tinged prints from orthochrome film do little justice to the colourful original machines. A typical example of such markings appeared on C417 of 3 Fighting School at Sedgeford in late 1918. This Pup had an overall finish of blue and white checks and was known, irreverently, as the 'Flying Lavatory'.

Scout squadrons working up prior to mobilization were also issued with Pups. This applied to those scheduled to receive the S.E.5a, as well as those destined to fly Camels and other Sopwith types.

The popularity of the type and its simple structure meant that reconstructions were made from crashed machines. At least twenty-nine were created in this way, most at the instigation of the Repair Sections of various Training Wings.

At least one Pup was converted to 'penguin' configuration. This was at Catterick and the machine in question, serial number unknown, had the area of its mainplanes reduced to approximately three-quarters of the original. For some unknown reason, it also had horn-balanced ailerons. The resultant wing-loading figure would have prevented the machine becoming airborne and so it must have been used as a taxiing trainer.

The last home-based Pups in front-line service were those of 36 Sqn. In the autumn of 1918, each of that unit's three flights, at Hylton, Ashington and Seaton Carew, had an establishment of four Bristol F2Bs and four Pups. Although the unit was scheduled to receive the Avro 504K (NF), that never materialized and the Pups were certainly in use until at least January 1919, Lt H. Croudace being killed on the 13th of that month in an accident with B1763.

On 31 October 1918, the RAF still had 877 Pups on charge. No fewer that forty-eight had been struck off that month, while 376 were in storage or at Aircraft Acceptance Parks and a further 361 were with training units. Others were in Egypt and the Mediterranean and one was in Italy. Only thirty-four remained with VI Brigade and thirteen with the Grand Fleet. The

Pups were favourite mounts of training unit instructors and senior officers, and many were finished in outlandish colour schemes. C417 was with 3 Fighting School at Sedgeford and had an overall scheme of white and blue checks. via author

(Below) Another gaudy Pup was C305 of 189 NTS at Sutton's Farm, the unit's nocturnal activities being reflected in the starred fuselage. JMB/GSL

Representative Pups with RFC/RAF Units

28 Sqn – Yatesbury: A7334, A7345, B803, B1753, B2196.

36 Sqn – Hylton/Ashington/Seaton Carew: B1763, B1805, B1807, B5905, C303, C306.

37 Sqn B Flt – Stowe Maries: A651, A653, A6228, A6246, A6248, B735, B1723, B1764, B1765, B1771, B2194, B5907.

46 Sqn – Boisdinghem/La Gorgue/Bruay/Suttons Farm/Ste Marie Cappel/Filescamp Farm: A673, A677, A6157, A6188, A7321, A7330, A7335, A7348, B1709, B1716, B1719, B1777, B1802, B1810, B1828, B1837, B1842, B1843, B2180, B2186, B2191.

54 Sqn – Castle Bromwich/St Omer/Bertangles/Chipilly/Flez/Bray Dunes/Leffrinckhoucke/Teteghem/Bruay: A633, A635, A640, A645, A646, A649, A668, A673, A6156, A6168, A6192, A6211, A6238, A7306, A7330, A7344, B1730, B1776, B1795, B1799.

50 Sqn B Flt – Throwley: A638, A6153, B1711, B1769.

61 Sqn – Rochford: A653, A6243, A6245, A6246, A6248, A6249, B735, B1723, B1764, B1765, B1771, B1774, B1806, B1809.

64 Sqn – Sedgeford: B1778, B1786, B1787, B1788, B1789.

65 Sqn – Wye: B2165, B2199.

66 Sqn – Filton/St Omer/Vert Galand/Liettres/Calais/Estrée Blanche: A635, A663, A665, A670, A6151, A6152, A6159, A6183, A6190, A6201, A7301, A7302, A7309, A7323, A7340, B1703, B1745, B1746, B1826, B1835, B2168, B2182, B2185, B2221.

73 Sqn – Lilbourne: A6222, A7317, A7343, B1705, B5932, B5957, B5965, B7504, B6040.

74 Sqn – London Colney: A6232, A6235, B1737, B2163.

76 Sqn – Catterick: B1807.

79 Sqn – Beaulieu: B6016, B6143.

81 Sqn – Scampton: B1840, B6124, B6126, B7502, B7504, C257.

84 Sqn – Lilbourne: A7326, A7343, B1705, B2201.

85 Sqn – Hounslow: B735.

87 Sqn – Hounslow: B2250, B5251.

88 Sqn – Harling Road: B5955.

89 Sqn – Harling Road: B5287, B5306, B5925, B5952, B5955, B6008.

90 Sqn – Shotwick: A6203, C230, C231, C276, C279, C1522.

91 Sqn – Chattis Hill: B2217, B5265, B5360, C267, C269.

92 Sqn – Chattis Hill: B5269, B5270.

93 Sqn – Chattis Hill: B5297, C266.

94 Sqn – Harling Road: A6236, A7318, B2165, B2198, B5289.

95 Sqn – Shotwick: A6203, B1813, B5331, B6164, B7513, C231, C275, C278.

96 Sqn – Shotwick: A6203, C279, C331, D4154, D4013.

112 Sqn – Throwley: A638, A6153, B1711, B1763, B1769, B1772, B1773, B1803, B1806, B1810, B2158, B2194, B2195.

143 Sqn – Detling: A6245, B1724, B4125.

157 Sqn – Upper Heyford: B5297, C266.

SD Flt – Clairmarais South: B2188.

1 TS – Beaulieu: B7517.

3 TS – Shoreham: B2152, B5336.

6 TS – Catterick/Montrose: B5260, B1751, B2207, B2242, B5329, B6077, B7345, B7485, B7486, B7491, B7528, B7592.

8 TS – Netheravon: D4191.

10 TS – Ternhill/Shawbury/Lilbourne/Gosport: A6230, B804, B1849, B5390, B6038, C218.

11 TS – Scampton: B1743.

17 TS – Yatesbury: A7317.

18 TS – Montrose: B5260, B5329, B5349, B5350, B5379, B6077, B6081, B7345, B7489, B7491, B7575, C287, C4295, D4024.

21 TS – Ismailia: C1547.

22 TS – Aboukir: B6053, C478, C480, C1493, D4114.

23 TS – Aboukir: D4107, D4117.

25 TS – Thetford: C299.

28 TS – Castle Bromwich: B5943, B5952, B5957, B7533.

30 (Australian) TS – Ternhill: A6249, B6089, B6090, B6091, B7529.

32 (Australian) TS – Yatesbury: B6105.

34 TS – Ternhill: A651, B5283.

36 TS – Montrose: B2207, B5278, B5351, B7459, B7489, B7495, B7496, B7529, C285, C288, D4035.

39 TS – South Carlton: B6127.

40 TS – Portmeadow/Croydon: A650, A6187, A6228, A7318, A7319, A7341, A7349, B1738, B5252, B5314, B5370, B6094.

42 TS – Wye: A7311, B5288, D4079.

43 TS – Ternhill: A651, A655, A656, B6040, B7510, B7517.

45 TS – South Carlton: B1734, B5359, D4126.

46 TS – Catterick: A6206, B6127.

48 TS – Waddington: B1736.

54 TS – Castle Bromwich: B2245, B2246, C215.

55 TS – Yatesbury: A6193.

55 TS – Lilbourne: B5990, B7518.

56 TS – London Colney: A6185, B1739, B2152, B2154, B2214, B2233, B2234, B5259, B5281, B5284, B9931.

58 TS – Suez: B2233, B6111.

60 TS – Scampton: B2166, B5345, B7525.

61 TS – South Carlton: B1706, B7505.

62 TS – Dover: B1714, B1740, B6067.

62 TS – Hounslow: C209, D4175.

63 TS – Joyce Green: A662, A6221, A6223, A6230, A6234, A6235, A7301, A7311, B9440.

65 TS – Sedgeford: B5312, C3502.

67 TS – Shawbury/Shotwick: B1844, B5339, B5399, B6092, B6141, B6145, C216, C218, C219, D4014.

70 TS – Beaulieu: B5310, B5901, B6015, B6074, C294, D4076, D4077.

73 TS – Turnhouse: B2247.

188 NTS – Throwley: B2209.

189 NTS – Sutton's Farm: B5907, C303, C305, C306, C308, C309, C312.

195 TS – El Rimal: B6048.

198 NTS – Rochford: A6247, B849, B1803, B1807, B2216, B5903, B5907, C303, C306, C309.

5 TS AFC – Minchinhampton: D4152, D4170.

6 TS AFC – Minchinhampton: B1764, B6089, B7506.

8 TS AFC – Leighterton: D4191.

2 TDS – Gullane: B5349, B5350, B7496, D4027, D4031.

3 TDS – Lopcombe Corner: B5253, B5254, B5967, B5995.

4 TDS – Hooton Park: B6035, B6036, B6039, B6150, C227, C230, C270, C275, C402, C404, D4011, D4012, D4139, D4158.

7 TDS – Feltwell: B6026, C9990, C9991.

11 TDS – Boscombe Down: B5327.

19 TDS – El Rimal: B4032, B6047, B6054, B8064, C247, C249, C348, C473.

26 TDS – Edzell: B7575.

32 TDS – Montrose: B2203, B2207, B7573, B7575, C235, C285, C288, D4027, D4028, D4032, D4074.

34 TDS – Scampton: B2227, D4127, D4128, D4129.

38 TDS – Tadcaster:

42 TDS – Hounslow:

43 TDS – Chattis Hill: B5314.

44 TDS – Bicester/Portmeadow: B6128.

46 TDS – South Carlton: C258.

47 TDS – Doncaster: C420.

49 TDS – Catterick: B4128.

201/56 TDS – Cranwell: B2173, B2203, B6061, B6063, C201, C202, C205, C238, C241, C261, C326, C406, C423, C424.

204 TDS – Eastchurch: N6169, N6458.

205 TDS – Vendôme: C307, C310, C313, C316, C319, C322, C325.

206 TDS – Eastbourne: B6100, C229, C314.

207/54 TDS – Chingford/Fairlop: B6086, B6097, C350, C367, C368, C369, C370, C1555.

208 TDS – Leuchars: D4034.

CFS – Upavon: A658, A659, A666, A6150, A7317, A7343, B2169, B2171, B2237, B2238, B4116, B5936, B5998, C374.

1 SSF – Gosport: B2192.

SEAFIS – Shoreham: B5390, C1510, D4192, N6199.

NEAFIS – Redcar: B6049.

Pool of Pilots – Manston/Joyce Green: B5992, C240, C244, C247, C250, C256, C271, C277.

Scout School 2 ASD – Candas: A6165, A6173, A7309, A7324, B1724, B1827, B1832.

1 SAF – Ayr:

1 FS – Turnberry: C289.

2 FS – Marske: B6008, C271, C414.

3 FS – Bircham Newton/Sedgeford: C417.

4 SAFG – Freiston: N6160.

SAF/5FS – Heliopolis: B6042, B6043, B6044, B6045, B6046, C247, C249, C250, D4114, D4123, D4124.

Fleet SAGF – East Fortune/Leuchars: C238, C283.

1(Obs) SAG – Hythe: B1815.

1 SNBD – Stonehenge: C284.

AICS – Worthy Down: C431.

MOS – Leysdown: C269.

Medical Flt – Hendon: B6074.

Experimental Station – Orfordness: B1717, B1755, C9924.

type was withdrawn during 1919, although a few examples, such as B7565, remained with experimental units. That Pup was still at Farnborough as late as July 1923, almost certainly the last in RAF service.

Those in Egypt and the Mediterranean Area were, by that time, training machines. Most were on the strength of 5 Fighting School at Heliopolis, which is known to have operated B6043, B6044, B6046 and D4123. Others (such as B6047, B6054, C247 and C249) served with 19 TDS and its precursor, 195 TS, at El Rimal.

The RAF may have had no further use for the type, but its availability from large stocks and its relative simplicity made it an ideal acquisition for emergent air services. Fifty of the type were bought for the Japanese air services and a further twelve were part of an Imperial Gift to the Australian government. The Royal Hellenic Naval Air Service had received four Pups (N6432, N6433, N6470 and N6471) from 2 Wing RNAS/62 Wing RAF and continued to operate these in the post-war period. Belgium received six and these were, apparently, built especially by Sopwith's and the identities SB1–SB4 were associated with four of these. A single example was in Dutch service, this having been N6164 of 9N Sqn which was taken on charge after being force-landed in that neutral country on 1 March 1917. It had been intended to

What must have been the most bizarre Pup colour scheme is seen on this anonymous machine which had the smaller radius to the cowling lip that characterized later Standard-built machines. via K. Molson

send N6204 to Russia, but there was (presumably) a change of heart after the Revolution and the machine was delivered to storage on 3 December 1917.

It is possible, today, to appreciate the classic lines of the Pup. Although the Shuttleworth Collection's 'N5180' is a conversion from a Sopwith Dove, it conveys the feeling of the original and to see it in flight is a treat for all enthusiasts. The RAF Museum at Hendon displays a static example alongside other classics of the era and another is available to public view at the Museum of Army Flying, Middle Wallop.

A Pup which served with the Australian Training Wing in the UK. The Kookaburra marking was repeated on the port side of the fuselage. via CCI

Representative Pups with RNAS Units	
1 Wing – B/C Sqn St Pol: 3691, 9496, N5180, N5181, N5182, N5183,N5184, N5185, N5186, N5187, N5188. 2 Wing – Imbros/Mudros/Stavros/Hadzi Junas: 9941, 9942, N6432, N6433, N6463, N6470, N6471. 3 Wing – Luxeuil: 9496, 9906. 5 Wing – Coudekerque: 3691. 3 Sqn – St Pol/Vert Galand/Bertangles/Marieux/Furnes: A6158, A6160, N6197, N6202, N6207, N6208, N6209, N6460, N6461. 4 Sqn – Coudekerque/Bray Dunes: 9899, N6185, N6187, N6188, N6190, N6192, N6196, N6198, N6200, N6462, N6475, N6476. 8 Sqn – Vert Galand/Furnes: A626, N5181, N5182, N5183, N5184, N5185, N5186, N5187, N5189, N5190, N5191, N5192. 9 Sqn – St Pol/Furnes/Flez: N6163, N6177, N6178, N6184, N6188, N6189, N6191, N6193, N6195, N6196, N6199, N6201. 11 Sqn – Dunkerque/Hondschoote: B1816, B1817, B1818, N6178, N6180, N6183, N6188, N6190, N6192, N6196, N6199. 12 Sqn – St Pol/Petite Synthe: B1816, B1817, B1818, N5189, N5196, N6167, N6180, N6196, N6202, N6468, N6476.	Seaplane Defence Flt – St Pol: 9916, B1819, B1820, B1821, N6179, N6203, N6435, N6436, N6437, N6459, N6477, N6478. Defence Flt – Walmer: 9900, 9915, 9947, B1822, N5182, N6205, N6438, N6439, N6440, N6441, N6442. War School – Manston: B2213, B5959, B5960, B5992, B5993, B5994, B6001, C229, C244, C247, C250, C271, N6195, N6475. War Flt – Dover: 9915, 9916, N5182, N5197, N6171, N6177, N6189, N6191, N6192, N6197, N6198, N6199, N6200, N6201. War Flt – Grain: 9912, 9940. War Flt – Yarmouth: 9904, 9905. Central Training Establishment – Cranwell: 9902, 9903, 9908, 9909, B6021, B6022, B6023, B6024, N6160, N6168, N6196. Flying School – Chingford: B6085, B6086, B6087, B6088, B6097, B6098. Flying School – Eastbourne: B1821, B6099, B6100. Flying School – East Fortune: B1822, C283, C284, C286, C289, C292, N6478. Flying School – Vendome: B1818, B1820, C307, C310, C313, C316, C319, C322, C325. Preliminary Flying School – Redcar: 9930, B6049, B6050, B6051, B6052.

Triplanes 1916–1917

The triplane configuration was not new in 1916. It had been tried before, but never in an armed single-seater machine designed for air fighting. The Sopwith design appeared on 28 May 1916 and obviously owed much to that of the Pup. The triplane layout was an audacious break from tradition, but the subsequent success of the type had its legacy in the proliferation of triplane designs by the Central Powers. Even the French tried, unsuccessfully, to adapt the successful Nieuport Scout to that configuration.

Construction

Although the Triplane is often regarded as embodying many Pup components, the fuselages of the two types were not identical, having different dispositions of vertical spacers. That of the Triplane was also marginally shorter and shallower, but some 3in (7.6cm) wider. The basic box girder structure was similar, however, with the typical Sopwith bracket being used to secure spacers to the longerons and simultaneously provide anchorages for bracing cables. An adjustable tailplane was added, being identical to that of the Pup, as were the fin and rudder. In the forward fuselage, the alignment of the diagonal strut, that supported the rear engine mounting, was reversed. The centre-section struts ran from the lower fuselage longerons, being lightened planks within the fuselage but of airfoil shape where exposed between the middle and upper wings. The undercarriage embodied the typical Sopwith split axles.

The wings were of identical span to the Pup's, but were of much narrower, 3ft 3in (99cm), chord. Wing spars were centred 15in (38cm) apart and each mainplane had wooden four compression struts. The tubular strut mountings served as a fifth, to give an extremely strong structure. Ailerons were carried on all mainplanes and served to make the machine very agile in the rolling plane. The wings were set at 2½ degrees dihedral, with 2 degrees of incidence.

The Sopwith-patented padded windscreen was not popular in service – it restricted the pilot's view and many chose to replace it with more practical designs. That shown here was typical and necessitated the addition of padding to the rear of the Vickers gun. The sighting arrangement, shown here, could then comprise a rear bead sight and an open, rectangular forward one. Compression struts, between the centre-section struts and the rear Vickers mounting were a frequent modification. The photograph clearly shows the fuel pump and the disposition of the cockpit instrumentation. JMB/GSL

Interplane bracing was minimal, with a doubled flying wire and single landing wire supporting each set of three wings. Drag and anti-drag wires ran from mid-point on the centre wing to the upper longerons at the engine backplate and to a point just aft of the cockpit. Another set of these wires braced each lower wing to the lower longeron at equivalent points. Centre-section bracing comprised a wire from the upper wing to the cowling ring.

As on the Pup, an internally divided fuel and oil tank was hung on the upper longerons, immediately behind the front engine plate. The magazine for the single, centrally mounted Vickers gun was behind this, on the starboard. The Vickers was, as also on the Pup, still-belt fed and a drum for used belts was mounted on the reverse port side of the instrument board, with a winding handle projecting through to enable slack to be taken up. Spent cartridges were ejected through the cockpit floor, via a chute from the underside of the Vickers. The Vickers was fitted with the Sopwith patented padded windscreen.

The cockpit was simply furnished with a wicker seat, secured to the interplane struts, and a minimal array of instruments that comprised an ASI, altimeter, compass, tachometer and watch. The handwheel, for adjusting tailplane incidence, was fitted on the starboard side. The control column and rudder bar resembled those of the Pup.

At 1,561lb (708kg), fully loaded, the Triplane was some 236lb (107kg) heavier than the Pup and so a more powerful engine was called for. The simple expediency was to use a 110hp Clerget 9Z, which was then being used to power the 1½ Strutters being built at Kingston.

Flight Testing

The first prototype made its maiden flight on 30 May and was, very shortly thereafter, tested for the RNAS by Flt Lt L.H. Hardstaff. It exceeded all expectations. The triplane layout gave a phenomenal rate of climb and its speed was quoted as 120mph (193km/h) at 10,000ft (3,050m).

It was delivered to the RNAS at Chingford on 16 June, with the serial number N500. A second prototype was ordered as N504. That second machine, again with a 110hp Clerget, was reportedly first flown on 26 August, but that date may be incorrect as a Triplane was recorded at Brooklands on 2 July. N500 had gone to France ten days earlier, still in its original uncamouflaged finish.

Machine-Gun Timing Gear

The realization that accurate firing of machine guns in aerial combat was best achieved by aligning weapons with the line of flight led to the need for ensuring that rounds did not strike the propeller. That could be achieved by mounting a light machine gun, such as the Lewis, on the top centre section of the wings, thus clearing the propeller arcs. A heavier and belt-fed weapon, such as the Vickers, had to be mounted on the fuselage and necessitated a mechanism that prevented firing during the split second that a propeller blade passes the muzzle. A variety of such devices were used by the air services of the warring nations, some mechanical and some hydraulic.

The Sopwith-Kauper gear was used in conjunction with Vickers guns in most Clerget-engined Sopwith machines, including the Triplane, having been devised by Harry Kauper and patented in his and the company's name. It was an interrupter gear that cut off the pilot's firing at the passage of a propeller blade.

Triggers for Vickers guns were carried in the triangular handhold at the top of the control column on Sopwith designs. Bowden cables led from each trigger, down through the hollow control column and via the fuselage side fairings to each gun. Activation of the trigger caused the inner cable to fire the weapon. The Sopwith-Kauper gear was designed to override that action at the appropriate times.

The Bowden cable did not lead directly to the gun firing mechanism, but to a spring and thence, via cranks, to the weapon's trigger. Activating the cable pushed the compressed spring against the cranks and fired the gun. A mechanical device linked to the engine interrupted this.

A pair of cams was added to the rear of the crankshaft, set at 180° to each other. The propeller blades were aligned with these cams. The rear engine casing was drilled to accept bell-shaped housings that enclosed tappets. The passage of a cam forced the tappets upward and activated push rods. These rods temporarily disengaged the firing mechanism. That firing resumed when the cams passed and the springs returned to their compressed state.

The problem with such mechanical gears was the inertia of the moving parts, which resulted in a time lag and reduced the rate of fire. Later machines, such as the Le Rhone Camel, used the Constantinesco hydraulic gear, where crankshaft cams operated pistons in a similar manner to a car's braking system.

N500, the prototype Clerget Triplane, is seen here at Brooklands in its original factory finish of clear-doped natural fabric, with aluminium cowling and forward fuselage panels. At the time that this photograph was made, it was still unarmed. N500 went to France in June 1916, still in this finish, but fitted with a Vickers gun. It was subsequently camouflaged. JMB/GSL

The second prototype spent time with the Design Flight at Eastchurch, where it was subjected to tests, and then returned to Sopwith's on 9 September for the substitution of a 130hp Clerget 9B. In that more powerful form, it returned to Eastchurch for further trials and was then dispatched to the RNAS in France on 15 November. There, it joined N500, which had returned during late September, on the strength of A Sqn, which soon became the reformed 1N Sqn. Dallas achieved a further success on N500 on 29 September, driving down an enemy scout. By that time the first prototype had been camouflaged and bore the nickname 'Brown Bread'.

The RNAS recognized the value of the type and placed orders soon after the prototypes had flown. N5350–N5389 (40) were ordered from Clayton & Shuttleworth of Lincoln on 23 July and the parent company received an order for seventy-five (N5420–N5494) on 1 September. The 130hp Clerget 9B had been adopted

Triplanes were produced concurrently with Pups at Kingston. Taken during the royal visit to the Sopwith factory, this photograph illustrates well the internal structure of the Triplane, including the close spacing of the mainplane spars and location of the split oil/petrol tank. JMB/GSL

It is part of RNAS lore that N500 was in action on the day of its arrival in France. It went there for trials with A Sqn of 1 Wing at Dunkerque. It was certainly in action on 1 July, when FSL R.S. Dallas had an inconclusive engagement with two enemy machines, although RNAS reports credited him with one of the two-seaters being sent down out of control. Damaged by flak on the 28th, N500 was returned to Sopwith's for the fitting of new wings.

as the standard power plant. Sopwith-built machines began leaving the production lines during November, but it was a month later that the first Clayton & Shuttleworth machine flew and a further two months before deliveries to the RNAS began. The second Sopwith production machine had been delivered to Lincoln, presumably to serve as a pattern aircraft. Many of the first twenty Sopwith-built Triplanes were delivered to 1N Sqn, the first and last RNAS squadron to operate the type. A third contractor was Oakley & Co. Ltd of Ilford. Although having no experience of building aeroplanes, the firm's woodworking experience was considered sufficient to bring them an order for twenty-five Sopwith Type 9700 bombers, to be numbered N5910–N5934. That contract was amended to one of the same number of Triplanes and was accepted in December 1916.

N5350, the first Triplane built by Clayton & Shuttleworth, was delivered on 2 December 1916 and is seen here in flying attitude on a trestle. A Rotherham, wind-driven fuel pump was mounted as standard on the starboard centre-section strut. Like those Triplanes produced by the parent company, those built at Lincoln also had the Sopwith padded windscreen fitted. After being tested at Eastchurch, N5350 went to 10N Sqn and was ditched in the Channel on 23 April 1917 by FSL R.F. Collins. It was salvaged, but not (apparently) rebuilt. JMB/GSL

The Clerget 9Z, 9B and 9Bf Engines

The firm of Clerget Blin et Cie, of Lavallois (Seine), was one of the foremost in the early development of the rotary engine. The British firm of Gwynnes Ltd of Hammersmith initially had sole manufacturing rights for their products in the British Empire. Clerget engines developed through the seven-cylinder 80hp Type 7Z and the nine-cylinder 110hp Type 9Z to the 130hp Type 9B, which powered most Triplanes and Camels. That last engine was improved to produce the Type 9Bf, which had a nominal output of 140hp.

The 9Z was a very robust engine that utilized cast-iron cylinders. Like all nine-cylinder rotaries, it had a 1-3-5-7-9-2-4-6-8 firing order. It had a very heavy-duty crankshaft and was less prone to crash damage than other rotaries. It was also designed with maintenance in mind and the front of the crankcase was easily removed in situ, allowing a skilled mechanic to strip, examine and replace the internal components in less than half an hour. The design of its timing gear was such that tappet wear was minimal. Its greatest failing was a tendency for cylinders to become distorted due to differential cooling of the front and rear faces.

The Clerget 9B was of identical bore and stroke to the 9Z, but had a higher compression ratio and was less thirsty than its predecessor. It suffered from the same cooling problems and aluminium pistons were introduced on Gwynnes-built units at the suggestion of W.O. Bentley. Concurrently, the stroke was increased by 12mm and this produced the Type 9Bf, sometimes known as the Long Stroke Clerget. The engine was even more fuel-efficient than the smaller ones and was, in reality, very little different from the BR1. However at £907-10s it was more expensive.

In all, 3,650 of these engines were manufactured in Britain, 1,750 by Gwynnes and the rest by Ruston Proctor, and a further 2,045 were delivered to the British air services by French contractors.

During January 1917 a further twenty Triplanes were ordered for the RNAS from Sopwith's, bringing the total ordered for that service to 168. The extra six were N533–N538, machines with twin Vickers armament delivered by Clayton & Shuttleworth to an order dated 2 September 1916. These have been suggested as being related to the RFC order that was supposed to have been subsequently transferred to the RNAS, but the date of allocation is much too early. Deliveries of the six did not begin until July 1917, following directly on from Clayton & Shuttleworth's first batch. It seems that, in light of the Camel's development, the decision to double the armament was retrospective. The total of 168 does not include those Triplanes

Specification – Sopwith Triplane (Clerget)	
Engine:	One 110hp Clerget 9Z or one 130hp Clerget 9B
Weights:	Empty 993lb (450kg) (110hp Clerget), 1,103lb (500kg) (130hp Clerget); loaded 1,415lb (642kg) (110hp Clerget), 1,543lb (700kg) (130hp Clerget)
Dimensions:	Length 18ft 10in (5.51m); height 10ft 6in (3.2m) (110hp Clerget), 9ft 9in (2.9m) (130hp Clerget); wingspan upper 26ft 6in (8.08m), middle 26ft 6in (8.08m), lower 26ft 6in (8.08m); chord upper 3ft 3in (0.99m), middle 3ft 3in (0.99m), lower 3ft 3in (0.99m); gap middle to upper 3ft (0.91m), lower to middle 3ft (0.91m); stagger middle to upper 1ft 6in (45cm), lower to middle 1ft 6in (45cm); dihedral upper 2½°, middle 2½°, lower 2½°
Performance:	Max. speed 112mph (180km/h) (110hp Clerget), 116mph (187km/h) (130hp Clerget) Service ceiling 20,500ft (6,250m) (110hp Clerget), 22,000ft (6,700m) (130hp Clerget) Endurance 2½ hours (110hp Clerget), 2 hours (130hp Clerget)
Armament:	One fixed Vickers (two on some machines) synchronized to fire through propeller arc

Close examination of this frontal aspect of a Clerget Triplane illustrates many minor details. These include the split undercarriage, the cooling and exhaust slots in the cowling and the ejection chute for spent cartridge cases that projected below the fuselage. The plate on the front of the engine cowling was a reminder that the gun timing gear had to be reset after engine changes. JMB/GSL

inherited from the French government. A further ten Triplanes, N5550–N5559 were ordered from Sopwith's, but the contract was cancelled before any was built.

Sopwith did, however, build a further ten machines but it is unlikely that they were N5550–N5559. These further ten were for the French government and (most) had the 130hp Clerget. It is not known when they were ordered, but deliveries began in November 1916. The machines were numbered F1–F10 and were delivered to Dunkerque for an (as yet) unidentified naval Escadrille de Chasse. The Triplanes were given French national markings at the factory and, interestingly, had their fuselage lifting points marked 'Lift Here' and not 'Lever Ici'. At least a further seven Triplanes served with that French unit, these being transferred RNAS machines that were renumbered in the 'F' series. One, or possibly more, of these French-operated triplanes was fitted with a 110hp Le Rhone engine. F17 was wrecked in an accident with a D.H.4. Some, upon withdrawal from French service, were returned to the RNAS. Ex-RNAS had their serial numbers reinstated, but those built for France had numbers given in the range reserved for experimental machines, becoming N524 and N541–N543. At least two of these returned aeroplanes were with the Seaplane Defence Sqn at St Pol in November 1917.

During February and possibly in light of operational experience, the Pup-type

tailplane was replaced by one of smaller area and revised profile. The chief advantage of adopting the new surfaces was the improvement it bestowed on the Triplane's radius of turn. Another structural alteration was tested on N5423. This was the use of wings that had increased chord, but the modification was not made on operational machines.

The Triplane and the RFC

The RFC had shown an early interest in acquiring the type and were prepared to order fifty on 7 June. The serial numbers A9000–A9099 were allotted for machines to be built by Clayton & Shuttleworth. Whether these one hundred incorporated the original planned fifty is not known. Later, another 106, A9813–A9918, were ordered from the same manufacturer. This latter batch may have replaced the earlier one.

The RFC had planned for the service use of its intended Triplanes. On 22 December 1916, it was stated that its first unit to equip with the type would be 81 Sqn, which was scheduled to form at Gosport on 1 January 1917, from elements of 1 RS, and move to Brattleby (Scampton) to work up to operational status. The following day, a list of intended unit establishments was circulated and 81 Sqn was planned to have, initially, six Triplanes, six Avros and six Bristol Scouts. The same list

indicated the training unit that would supply operational squadrons with their pilots. 54 RS was due to form at Wyton and it was planned to have the same establishment as 81 Sqn, 65 Sqn, also at Wyton, was to have been the first RFC squadron to take Triplanes to France but, in the event, none of these three units ever received the new Sopwith type.

There was no denying that the RFC was, by the winter of 1916, seriously deficient in modern combat scouts. The arrival of Albatros and Halberstadt scouts threatened to turn the tide of air superiority against the Allies. The RFC was receiving French Nieuport scouts and was expecting larger numbers of SPAD VIIs, but their numbers were deemed insufficient. Deliveries of RFC Triplanes were some way off. The RNAS also had SPAD VIIs on order, from British manufacturers. The Air Board summoned a meeting on 14 December 1916, at which it was agreed that 62 RNAS SPADs would be transferred to the RFC. It is not clear what pressure was exerted, but the RNAS had been in breach of protocol the previous year, when it bypassed the Air Board and acquired £3 million from the Treasury, for aircraft and engines. A subsequent meeting on 26 February 1917 agreed the transfer to the RFC of all RNAS SPADs, in return for the latter receiving the 106 Triplanes on order for the military. It is difficult to reconcile A9813–A9918 with known Triplane production and it seems likely that most, if not all were cancelled in favour of the Camel.

The RFC did, however, operate a Triplane. Before the arrangement to transfer the RFC order to the RNAS, N5430 had been delivered to the Testing Squadron at Upavon by November 1916. This was done so that the RFC could, presumably, conduct its own evaluation of the type. That evaluation was notified in Report 25. The Testing Squadron moved to Martlesham Heath in January 1917 and N5430 was one of the machines it took to its new station. A pilot who became enamoured with the Triplane, through his experience of this machine, was C.A. Lewis. In *Sagittarius Rising*, he remarked that 'It was so beautifully balanced, so well mannered, so feather-light on the stick, and so comfortably warm'. That last virtue must have been of great worth, when one considers the heights that these machines flew in combat. The Triplane had transferred to the RFC's other Experimental Station, at

Orfordness, by June, for armament trials. Its arrival coincided with the beginning of the Gotha raids on London and the South-East. Orfordness was one of the stations ordered to prepare what machines it could for Home Defence duty, and N5430 was one of those. It flew against four of the raids, making five sorties, and was flown by Lt N. Howarth, Lt Clarke and Capt V. Brown. Brown made contact with the enemy on 7 July, but his attack was frustrated by a jammed gun. Another Orfordness pilot to fly N5430 was Capt R.M. Charley. He first flew it on 14 January 1918 and noted that it was a 'nice machine'. His logbook records the Triplane as A5430 and N5430 is known to have been marked as such. In those pre-RAF days, someone must have considered the naval prefix letter to have been added in error and taken seemingly appropriate remedial action. The number A5430 had been allotted to an F.E.2b that was not built.

N5430 had a long and useful life at Orfordness, becoming a popular machine with those pilots who were allowed to fly it. On 12 March 1918, it was involved in a collision, which necessitated a major rebuild, but it was back at Orfordness by June and continued to serve there until at least October. Post-war, the Triplane ended its service days at Sutton's Farm, apparently with 78 Sqn. If it was on the strength of the Snipe unit, it can only have been as a 'personal' aeroplane that some fortunate (or high-ranking) pilot had managed to acquire. Only on 22 August 1919, was N5430 finally struck off charge.

Operational Service

Although 1N Sqn had received its full complement of Triplanes before 1916 was out, the unit saw very little action during its first two months on the type. However, on 15 February 1917, it was attached to the RFC for the forthcoming offensive, moved to Chipilly and came under the control of 4 Brigade. Twelve days earlier, 8N Sqn had returned to St Pol, after serving with the RFC on the Somme, and began to exchange its Pups for Triplanes. The third RNAS unit to be fully equipped with the type was 10N Sqn, which also began to receive the type that February. Both 8N and 10N were also subsequently attached to the RFC for the Battle of Arras and its aftermath. The Triplanes of these three units became involved in the intense air fighting that resulted from

that offensive and their combat performance brought fame to the type.

April 1917 has become known as 'Bloody April' to students of World War I aviation. It represented a time of hitherto unknown numbers of losses as the RFC pursued its policy of taking the offensive to the enemy. The naval Triplane squadrons were heavily involved in the aerial action, but losses were surprisingly few.

The first successful Triplane combat of that month occurred at midday on 5 April, when Flt Cdr R.S. Dallas DSC, in N5436, sent an Albatros D III down out of control. That Australian had already achieved a combat success on this machine, a previous

DSc of 8N Sqn, another Australian. He, too, was credited with eight combat 'victories' that month.

The next day, 6 April, brought two further successes, but these were offset by the loss of the first two Triplanes in combat, both from 1N Sqn. FSL N.D.M. Hewitt was brought down in N5457 apparently at the hands of Ltn K. Schaefer of *Jasta* 11, to become a POW. His machine was damaged, but its capture allowed the Germans an early opportunity to study the Triplane. FSL L.M.B. Weil was less fortunate, being shot down and killed by Hptm P. von Osterroht, *Jasta* 12. Only three more Triplanes were lost in action that month, 8N

N5379 had, like other later Clayton & Shuttleworth Triplanes, larger access panels to the carburettors and engine backplate. It was first issued to 10N Sqn on 25 June 1917 and flown by, among others, Flt Lt R. Collishaw. It was later with 12N Sqn and survived until January 1918. JMB/GSL

'victory' on 1 February. The other naval squadron then with the RFC, 8N, followed Dallas's victory with one of their own, FSL R.J.D. Compston getting the better of a Halberstadt D II. Both Compston and Dallas were to feature again in the combat record of these two squadrons during that month, the former being credited with another two 'victories' and the latter with seven. The other leading Triplane pilot to emerge during April was FSL R.A. Little

Sqn losing FSL E.B.J. Walter (killed in N5467 on the 24th) and FSL A.E. Cuzner (also killed, in N5463 on the 29th). The other casualty of 1N Squadron was FSL A.P. Heywood, who was wounded and, mistakenly thinking that he had force-landed in enemy-held territory, burnt N5441. This aeroplane had the name *Doris* painted in large white letters on the fuselage, under the cockpit, following what had become standard RNAS practice, that of marking girlfriends', wives' and relatives' names on aeroplanes. In this, the RNAS authorities were a lot more tolerant than those of the RFC, the latter forbidding the application of 'personal' markings.

The five losses during April were more than counterbalanced by the forty-eight combat 'victories' credited to Triplane pilots during that month. Many, admittedly, were classified as machines sent out of control, but the Triplane had proved its worth and its pilots had supreme confidence in the type's ability. The *Official History* paid due respect to the work of 1N and 8N Sqns at this time, citing as an example the success of Dallas and FSL T.G. Culling in breaking up a formation of fourteen enemy machines on the 22nd. The final 'victory' in April had been credited to FSL R. Collishaw of 10N Sqn, who destroyed an Albatros D II in N5490 on the 30th. That was the second of his successes on the type and in the following months his ability as a fighter pilot and supreme exponent of the Triplane was demonstrated by a mounting 'victory' list. 10N Sqn was then based at Furnes, but in early May it moved to Droglandt on attachment to the RFC.

Although the intensity of air fighting was reduced in May, all three Triplane squadrons

being killed. One was FSL G.G. Bowman of 1N Sqn, who was lost in N5461 on the 19th. Bowman had joined 10N Sqn on 1 April and encountered the Triplane on the 4th, recording, 'First time on Triplane. Nicest machine have flown.' He had some combat experience that month and an indication of the Triplane's performance is a logbook entry for the 28th. On a HA Patrol at 16,000ft (4,880m) he was attacked by two Albatros scouts and recorded 'Gun jambed [sic] after forty rounds so climbed away'. He was transferred to 1N Sqn at the start of May and was probably shot down by Obltn A. Ritt von Tutschek of *Jasta* 12.

Triplanes were delivered to 9N, 11N and 12N Sqns, but none of these

Its machines were given individual names: *Black Maria* (N5490, N5492 and later N533), *Black Prince* (N5487), *Black Sheep* (N5376), *Black Death* (N6307) and *Black Roger* (N5483). The usual pilots of these were FSL (later Flt Lt then Flt Cdr) R. Collishaw, FSL (later Flt Cdr) W.M. Alexander, FSL G.E. Nash, FSL (later Flt Cdr) J.E. Sharman and FSL E.V. Reid. Collishaw was the highest 'scoring' pilot in the British air services for both June and July, being credited with sixteen and fourteen 'victories' for those respective months. Reid was credited with nineteen, Alexander with eight, Sharman with seven and Nash with six. This gave the five a total of seventy 'victories' in those two months, but Shar-

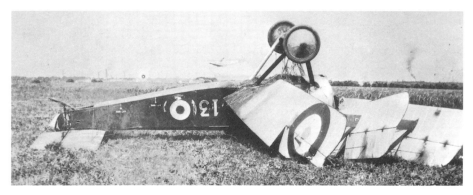

(Above) The French received Triplanes from the RNAS, as well as ten built especially by Sopwith's. All were marked with French cockades and rudder stripes in reverse sequence of colour. This is F13 after a major mishap. It had been N5386, was transferred to France in June 1917 and returned to its original identity with the RNAS during October. Whether it had been rebuilt for return is debatable. JMB/GSL

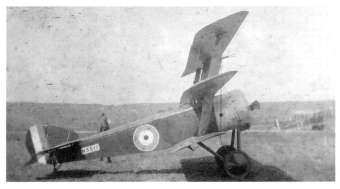

Oakley & Co. only delivered three of its two-gun Triplanes before its contract was terminated. All served with the RNAS at Manston but found new homes after the formation of the RAF. N5911, shown here, ended up with the SEAFIS at Shoreham, where it is seen in unarmed configuration. The three Oakley machines had ovular carburettor access panels. via K. Kelly

were involved in actions that consolidated the type's reputation and its pilots accumulated further successes. Little was credited with a further eight 'victories' during that month. His usual machine, since late April, had been N5493 and he was to amass a total of twenty successes in it. Compston and Dallas continued their runs of 'victories' and other pilots began to demonstrate their combat prowess. Flt Cdr C.A. Eyre and FSL T.G. Culling were rising 'stars' in 1N Sqn, while 8N Sqn had Flt Cdrs C.D. Booker and P.A. Johnston. Nine Triplanes were lost to enemy action during May, with five pilots

squadrons was fully equipped with the type. All saw limited combat, with 12N Sqn serving as a finishing school for RNAS scout pilots. The pace of air fighting escalated during June and 10N Sqn was in the thick of the action. Several of its pilots were ex-3 Wing RNAS and B Flt comprised mainly Canadian personnel. FSL R. Collishaw was Flight Commander and, under his leadership, its pilots ran up an impressive list of 'victories'. It became known as the 'Black Flight', that being the flight colour embellishing engine cowlings and wheel discs.

man and Reid were killed and Nash made POW. Collishaw had been the first RFC/RNAS pilot to claim six victories in one day, crediting himself with sending half a dozen Albatros scouts down apparently out of control on 6 July.

Triplane losses were, however, also escalating during that period. Eighteen pilots were shot down and killed, with 7 July being a particularly bad day for 1N Sqn. Flt Cdr C.A. Eyre (N6291) and FSLs D.W. Ramsey (N5480) and K.H. Millward (N6309) were all combat fatalities. A further four pilots were made

POW and six were wounded in action during those two months.

The Camel was, by then, reaching France in increasing numbers and 9N Sqn began equipping with the type in July. 11N Sqn was disbanded on 27 August, its pilots being used to reinforce other squadrons. The three fully equipped Triplane squadrons continued to fly the type, although the quality of enemy opposition was dramatically improving. The arrival of the handful of two-gun Triplanes, from the Clayton & Shuttleworth batch N533–N538, was a welcome bonus and Collishaw exploited the additional armament of N533 for his last two combat 'victories' on the type, destroying one Albatros D V and sending another down out of control on 27 July. These two-gun Triplanes had their armament fully exposed, which gave access to the gun-loading handles, unlike N5445. That Triplane was at the Grain experimental station and its twin Vickers were enclosed by a 'hump', in a similar manner to those of the Camel. It also featured a deeper fuselage decking and had a rudder of increased area.

August 1917 saw the re-equipment of 10N Sqn with Camels, but not before the unit suffered its last Triplane casualties. One of these was N536, one of the new two-gun machines that was lost on the 14th, with FSL S.H. Lloyd being killed. A further six Triplanes were lost in the air fighting that accompanied the Ypres offensive. 8N Sqn also sustained its last

casualties on the type, receiving Camels at the beginning of September.

That left 1N Sqn to continue to use the type operationally and as September progressed, its casualty rate rose. The unit lost eight pilots, killed or made POW, air fighting intensified. Two (N5490 and N6292) were shot down in combat on the 19th and another three (N5388, N5421 and N5440) on the 26th. One of these machines was N5388, which had been lent to the French authorities and later returned to RNAS service.

At the end of the month, 1N Sqn was withdrawn from operations, and, after a month at Dunkerque/Middle Aerodrome, it was retired to Dover for re-equipment with Camels. This began a phase wherein RNAS squadrons were returned to England for short periods of rest, a practice that was unique to that service. The Camels of 65 Sqn had taken the place of 1N Sqn at Bailleul. 12N Sqn continued to fly a few of the type in France, but still served in a non-operational capacity.

During the time of its first-line use by the RNAS, approximately one-third of all Triplanes were lost in action, with many others suffering combat damage. This figure may, at first, seem excessive but it averages at three losses per squadron per month. When that is compared with the combat successes achieved, the Triplane stands as one of the great fighting aeroplanes of the period.

One Triplane was delivered to 2 Wing RNAS in the Aegean. This was N5431 which was delivered there in January 1917. Initially, it served with E Flt of that Wing and suffered a mishap on 26 March, in the hands of Flt Lt J.W. Alcock (later of transatlantic flight fame). After a rebuild, it was with B Sqn at Thermi and was used in several successful combats by FSL H.T. Mellings. It underwent a further rebuild during the winter of 1917/18, but was damaged further and returned to the Repair Base at Mudros. It was not rebuilt again, but parts of it were used in the construction of the Alcock A.1, a small scout designed by the pilot of that name.

It had also served on home defence duties during the Gotha raids of 1917. N5424 was airborne from Manston against the first such raid on 25 May, being flown by Sqn Cdr C.H. Butler, who used it against two further raids. N5382 and N5383 were also on the strength of that station's War Flight, as was the first two-gun machine from Clayton and Shuttleworth. The closest any came to inflicting damage on a raider was on 12 August, when FSL H.C. Lemon, in N5382, made five attacks on a bomber that had been intercepted by nine RNAS machines.

A few ex-RNAS Triplanes continued after the formation of the RAF. There were twelve in service with the RNAS in England on 30 March 1918: N5910–N5912 were at Manston; N5366, N5384, N5460 and N5485 were at Eastchurch, along with the experimental N5445; N5378, N5386 and N6303 were at Chingford, and N5383 was at Cranwell. N6303 was only one of two home-based Triplanes known to have been given one of the fanciful colour schemes favoured by instructors.

The first Triplane to fall into enemy hands, in a reasonably intact condition, had been N5457 and this machine was examined by its captors. The wary respect given to the type by German fighter pilots, including von Richthofen, led to more exhaustive evaluations being made of others that suffered similar fates. At least one was at the Aldershof test aerodrome, fully restored to flying condition. The *Idflieg* was suitably impressed with the design layout and ordered experimental triplane types from a number of manufacturers. Although, it would seem, Fokker was not included in this, the Dutchman was aware of events and quickly produced his V4, which began the development of the DR 1 Triplane. That type became one of the

N5431 was the only Sopwith Triplane to serve in the Aegean. It is seen here with 2 Wing RNAS shortly after its arrival at Mudros. Crash damage subsequently resulted in its being fitted with a fin of local manufacture and resembling that shown on the captured machine shown in the following photograph. N5431 was later given a Lewis gun to supplement its Vickers. JMB/GSL

German fighting scouts most respected by Allied pilots during late 1917 and early 1918. However, by the time it reached the front in substantial numbers, the Sopwith design had been withdrawn in favour of the Camel. German AA fire had accounted for several Triplanes and it is interesting that at least one of the early Fokker products was brought down by this. Presumably the triplane layout was, at that time, accounted as being unique to Sopwith.

The Imperial Russian Air Service also received the Triplane, but only the solitary example N5486. That machine was delivered to the Central Stores Depot at White City during April 1917 and sent to Russia

(*Above*) **Several Triplanes were captured intact by German forces and this one, restored to flying condition, was photographed at Aldershof. The straight fin leading edge suggests that that component had been replaced, possibly by the captors. In this view, the Vickers gun does not seem to be mounted properly.** JMB/GSL

N5912 survives today at the RAF Museum, with its armament restored. It was with 2 Fighting School at Marske in 1918, unarmed and marked with the unit number 94. This photograph shows it in that condition, but the location is not Marske. via FA Yeoman

the following month. It was, apparently, reassembled near Moscow by the RFC contingent that operated there under the command of Maj J. Valentine. This aeroplane survived the Bolshevik Revolution and was, at one stage, fitted with skis in lieu of wheels on its split-axle undercarriage. At a later stage, it was re-marked with 'red stars' and a suitably patriotic legend. It survives today, although with non-standard wheels, in the Moscow Air Force Museum.

The inexperience of Oakley & Co. in aeroplane manufacturing was evident from the inordinate length of time taken for its products to appear. Whether the decision to have these Triplanes delivered with twin Vickers armament was the reason for the delay is not known, but it may have had some bearing. By October 1917, only the first three of its Triplanes had been completed, and 1N Sqn, the last unit in France to operate the type, was in the process of re-equipping with Camels so there was no operational need for further machines. The balance of the Oakley

order was, therefore, cancelled. Its three machines were taken on RNAS strength, probably unarmed, and all were at Manston by the end of March 1918. They found other homes upon the formation of the RAF. They can be readily identified in photographs from their ovular panels that gave access to the carburettors and engine backplates. N5910 was, probably, the colourful red, white and blue machine that was with 3 Fighting School at Sedgeford in the winter of 1918, while N5911 went to the South East Area Flying Instructors School at Shoreham and N5912 was delivered to 2 Fighting School at Marske. N5912 was frequently photographed, carrying its station number '94' on the rear fuselage and under its lower wings. Today, it is the sole survivor of its type in the UK, being exhibited at the RAF Museum, Hendon, with full armament but without unit identification. It would be interesting to know what happened to N5458, a Triplane that was sent to the USA for exhibition in December 1917.

Other Sopwith Triplanes

The Clerget-engined type was not the only Sopwith triplane design of 1916. There were two others, the two Hispano-Suiza-powered machines that employed a common airframe and the LRTTr. Neither achieved production status.

There was an obvious relationship between fuselage and tail geometry of the Clerget-engined Triplane and the Pup. The Hispano-Suiza machines, however, owed more to the 1½ Strutter, having bulkier proportions. However, the allotted serial numbers, N509 and N510, suggest that they were later designs than the production Triplanes. Certainly, those serials (if allocations were chronological) would have been allotted in the last four months of 1916. The design may have predated the serial allocation. The scarcity of Hispano-Suiza engines at that time could have delayed completion, making this a decided possibility.

Nos N509 and N510 were passed from Sopwith's at Brooklands to the RNAS

Specification – Sopwith Triplane (Hispano-Suiza)

Engine:	One 150hp Hispano-Suiza (N509) or one 180hp Hispano-Suiza (N510)
Weights:	Empty not known; loaded not known
Dimensions:	Length 23ft 2in (7.06m); height 10ft 6in (3.2m); wingspan upper 28ft 6in (8.69m), middle 28ft 6in (8.69m), lower 28ft 6in (8.69m); chord 4ft 3in (1.3m) (all on 150hp a/c), 5ft 1in (45.72cm) (all on 180hp a/c); stagger middle to upper 1ft 6in (45.72cm), lower to middle 1ft 6in (45.72cm); gap middle to upper 3ft 6in (106.68cm), lower to middle 3ft 6in (106.68cm); dihedral not known
Performance:	Max. speed 120mph (193km/h) Service ceiling not known Endurance not known
Armament:	One fixed Vickers gun, synchronized to fire through the propeller arc

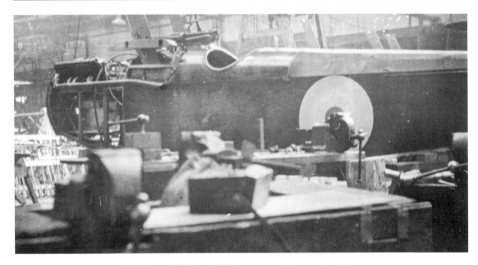

The two Hispano-powered Triplanes, N509 and N510, were much larger than the Clerget-powered machines. N509, fitted with a 150hp version of that engine, is seen here, armed, at Kingston during its construction and shows the small box rib on the centre-section strut for the attachment of the middle mainplane. JMB/GSL

The first Hispano-Suiza-powered Triplane, N509, assembled and ready for flying at Brooklands. N509 was delivered to Eastchurch on 26 October 1916 and was later with the War Flight at Manston, until damaged in a collision and subsequently deleted. JMB/GSL

Design Flight at Grain on the same date, 20 October 1916. Although employing the same airframe, the pair utilized different versions of the new French engine. N509 had the original 150hp type, whereas N510 was fitted with a geared 180hp engine. That reduction gearing caused N510 to have a raised thrust line.

The fuselage was slightly larger than that of the rotary-engined machine and carried tail surfaces that appeared to have been taken directly from the 1½ Strutter. There was a circular frontal radiator and the cylinder-head rocker covers protruded behind. The wing planform was essentially a slightly scaled-up version of those on the production triplane and employed similar 'plank' type interplane and centre-section struts. The wing bracing arrangement was similar to that of the rotary-engined type. Armament again comprised a single Vickers gun, mounted centrally on the decking ahead of the cockpit. Probably due to its more powerful engine, N510 had cooling slots in its engine cowlings. That machine also had a small gravity tank in its upper wing.

N510 did not last long. It was wrecked on the day of its arrival at Eastchurch. After an initial ten-minute flight by Flt Lt P.A. Johnston, Flt Lt L.H. Hardstaff took up N510 for a speed trial. The machine experienced tail flutter, before that assembly broke away. The machine crashed from 100ft (30m) and Hardstaff was killed.

No. N509 had a much longer existence, surviving for more than a year and performing some useful work. It was briefly tested at Dunkerque in November, spending less than a week in France. It returned to Eastchurch and was criticized for tail vibration by Sqn Cdr H.R. Busteed on 2 January 1917. The machine was transferred to the War Flight at Manston on 13 February and flew on four sorties against raiding German bombers from May to July. Flt Lt A.F. Brandon, who had achieved a shared success against a Gotha when flying a Camel, damaged N509 in a collision on 30 August. It seems likely that the machine then lingered at Manston until its deletion on 29 October.

While the Clerget Triplane could be described as looking dainty and the Hispano-Suiza machines as looking purposeful, the LRTTr could only be described as ugly. The Sopwith abbreviations have, again, never been fully explained, but most likely stood for Long-Range Tractor Triplane. A tractor it was, being designed to take advantage of the then new 250hp

Rolls-Royce engine that developed into the Eagle. It was also a private venture, never receiving any serial number, and was built to an RFC requirement for a long-range escort and anti-airship fighter. Its appearance was not that of a fighter.

It was under erection, fitted with its engine, at the same time as the first prototype Clerget Triplane, N500 (Spring 1916). With a span of 53ft (16.15m), it was the largest Sopwith wartime machine. Its fuselage owed nothing to previous designs and was a deep affair which incorporated a massive fuel tank that was located immediately behind the engine. There were twin cockpits and the vertical tail surfaces incorporated a ventral fin and a balanced rudder. The undercarriage was a cumbersome four-wheeled unit. Equally staggered wings were of constant chord and carried ailerons on all six main-planes. 'Plank'-type struts appeared similar to those on the other Sopwith triplanes of that period and were used to create a three-bay wing cellule on each side of the fuselage. The interplane struts were not of solid wooden construction, but employed a method patented by Fred Sigrist, whereby wooden nose and rear fairings were bolted to a metal strut of H section. Wing bracing was similar to that of the other triplanes, utilizing drag and anti-drag wires. High landing speeds must have been anticipated, because the lower wings carried air brakes, of similar form to those on the 1½ Strutter.

The most interesting feature of the LRTTr was its gunner's nacelle, carried in the centre section of the upper wing. That streamlined unit had a rather conical nose at first and was structurally weak. During an early test flight, carrying Sopwith employee E. Newman, it actually moved out of true, which must have provided a most disconcerting experience. The nacelle was later redesigned, with a more rounded nose. Initially, the LRTTr had an uncamouflaged finish, but with its redesigned nacelle it was given an upper surface covering a pigmented varnish and, perhaps in anticipation (or hope) of an RFC order, had a white serial 'box' marked on its rear fuselage. RFC authorities were, apparently, too sensible to want the type, but nothing is positively known about its subsequent fate.

The use of the triplane configuration did not disappear with these three types. The advantages that it gave in lift and manoeuvrability led the Sopwith design team to revive the format in 1918, in types such as the Cobham, Rhino and Snark.

The massive size and ungainly appearance of the LRTTr can be appreciated in this view of that machine on a trailer for transport between Kingston and Brooklands. The objects above the nose are struts to support the top-plane nacelle. JMB/GSL

The LRTTr looks somewhat cleaner in this front view, taken at Brooklands, which (again) emphasizes the size of the machine. The precarious position of the top-plane nacelle is well illustrated. JMB/GSL

Representative Clerget Triplanes with RNAS/RFC/RAF Units (*Twin Vickers)

1 Wing RNAS – St Pol: N500, N5420, N5422, N5428.
2 Wing RNAS – Mudros/Hadzi Junas/Thasos: N5431.
1N Sqn – Furnes/Chipilly/La Bellevue/Bailleul/Middle Aerodrome: N534*, N5352, N5372, N5387, N5435, N5475, N6291.
8N Sqn – Furnes/Auchel/St Eloi: N5351, N5366, N5421, N5429, N5434, N5439, N5446, N5449, N5467, N6290, N6292, N6299.
9N Sqn – St Pol/Furnes/Flez: N5356, N5358, N5360, N5365, N5371, N5374, N5377, N5378, N5427, N5443, N5451, N5462.
10N Sqn – St Pol/Furnes/Droglandt: N500, N533*, N536*, N5350, N5357, N5389, N5438, N5464, N5466, N5477, N6294.
11N Sqn – St Pol/Hondschoote: N500, N504, N524, N5351, N5355, N6293.
12N Sqn – St Pol/Petite Synthe: N504. N524, N533*, N534*, N537*, N538*, N541, N542, N5356, N5361, N5369, N5379.

Seaplane Defence Sqn – St Pol: N541, N543, N5386.
RNAS War School/War Flt – Manston: N535*, N5382, N5383, N5424, N5494.
RNAS Station – Eastchurch: N504, N5350, N5366, N5384, N5423, N5440, N5460, N5485.
RNAS Station – Chingford: N5378, N5386, N5485, N6303.
RNAS Station – Grain: N5445*.
RNAS Central Training Establishment – Cranwell: N5383.
78 Sqn – Sutton's Farm: N5430.
2 Fighting School – Marske: N5912.
3 Fighting School – Sedgeford: N5910(?).
SEAFIS – Shoreham: N5911.
201 TDS – Cranwell: N5383.
204 TDS – Eastchurch: N5366, N5384, N5460.
207 TDS – Chingford: N5378, N5386, N6303.
Experimental Station – Orfordness: N5430 (A5430).
CFS – Upavon: N5430.

CHAPTER SEVEN

The F1 Camel

The Legendary Dogfighter

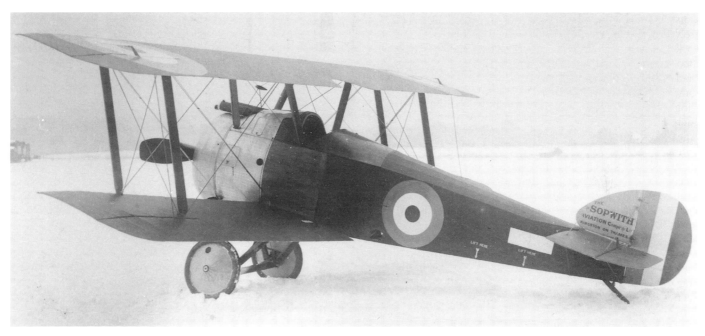

The prototype F1 Camel, powered by a 110hp Clerget, emerged in December 1916 and is shown in this well-known, yet classic, shot taken in the snow at Brooklands. Its one-piece upper wing, without any central cut-out is evident, as is the rounded and sloping fairing ahead of the cockpit that afforded protection to the pilot from the slipstream. JMB/GSL

Of all Sopwith designs, the Camel is the most famous and yet also the most infamous. Its fame has derived from its unsurpassed combat record during the Great War, when it was credited with the destruction of more enemy machines than any other Allied fighting scout. That success was, no doubt, due to the quality and bravery of its pilots, but a combat pilot was only as good as the machine he flew. It was often the unrivalled manoeuvrability of the type that enabled its pilots to achieve success. That same lightning manoeuvrability was also the reason for its infamy. Pilots new to the type were often slow to react to its idiosyncrasies and, consequently, accidents and fatalities occurred at an alarming rate.

Development

The first Camel prototype, designated F1 (F for fighter), first appeared during December 1916, only shortly after Pups had become operational with the RNAS and before the introduction into operational squadrons of either RNAS Triplanes or RFC Pups. The new design was drawn by Herbert Smith and was a synthesis of ideas generated by members of the Sopwith team. It must be remembered that the autumn of 1916 had seen the introduction of two-gun fighting scouts, most notably the Albatros D I and D II, into the German Air Service and that the impact of these on the balance of air power was immense. The newly introduced Pup and imminent Triplane squadrons were

already outgunned. The new design was significant; it was the first British fighting scout designed with what would become the classic armament for the next twenty years, two fixed machine guns firing forward through the propeller arc.

That unnumbered prototype was passed, as ready, by the Sopwith Experimental Department, on 22 December. It was an obvious descendant of the Pup and employed the same conventional contemporary construction techniques. It was, however, also significantly different. The major masses within the fuselage were concentrated more compactly and this gave a much more squat appearance. The engine and its backplate accessories, the armament and magazines, the pilot and

What might have been the second prototype is shown in this photograph. It had a 130hp Clerget and retained the use of a one-piece upper wing and short ailerons. No cut-out is visible in this shot, but one may have been incorporated at a later date in an attempt to overcome tail-heaviness. The sloping fairing ahead of the cockpit was more flattened. JMB/GSL

petrol/oil tanks were all fitted within the front third of the fuselage. The engine, again a rotary, was a 110hp Clerget 9Z. The squat appearance was made more pronounced by the adoption of a sloping and round-topped 'hump' over the Vickers guns. This served to deflect the airflow from its pilots, but must have had an adverse effect on the view forwards, especially on the ground. A major recognition point was the wing layout. The original idea was to have equal amounts of dihedral on the upper and lower wings, but to ease production the upper wing was made as a one-piece structure. As compensation, the dihedral on the lower wings was increased to 5 degrees. Ailerons were carried on all four planes and were relatively short.

It was an inspired design, which produced flight characteristics quite unlike those of its immediate predecessors. The torque of the engine, rotating clockwise from the pilot's viewpoint and combined with the concentration of masses, gave lightning turning ability. There was, however the tendency for the nose to drop in a steep starboard turn and for it to rise in one to the left. Consequently, left rudder had to be applied in both. The type's speed would be outclassed, but its turning ability was matched by few other designs during the remainder of the war.

The record of the full histories and sequence of the Camel prototypes has not survived. It seems certain, however, that another that had subtle design differences followed the first. This (second?) prototype had a revised and slightly flattened 'hump' over its machine-gun breeches. A small windscreen was fitted. More significantly, it had a 130hp Clerget 9B and a small centre-section cut-out that was too small to have been primarily for improved upward visibility. More likely, it was probably an attempt to reduce tail-heaviness, as had been tried on the Pup. The upper wing was, again, a one-piece structure and short ailerons were

The F1/3 is seen here at Martlesham Heath. Its forward decking was of the style adopted for production machines, although it too had a one-piece upper wing and short ailerons. There was a central cut-out to that upper wing. Like previous prototypes, F1/3 had square access panels to its carburettor and engine backplate. JMB/GSL

retained. Factory photographs of both machines show that they were marked with a white 'box' on the fuselage, in readiness for serial number application, the positions of which were slightly different.

A third prototype was given the designation F1/3, leading to the supposition that the second was F1/2. F1/3 retained the flying and control surface structures of its predecessors, but had another revision of the 'hump' over the machine guns. This was the close fitting, flat-topped aluminium panel that was adopted for production machines. On all three of these early prototypes, the access panels to the carburettors, set in the aluminium flank fairings, were square.

French interest in the type led to a machine, which was obviously a prototype, being sent for evaluation. It is not known whether this was a further machine, or a modification of one of the first three; certainly it had the one-piece wing and short ailerons. The machine-gun 'hump' profile resembles that of the (assumed) second machine, but had a revised aluminium portion. It had reached the French authorities by May 1917 and was wrecked in a crash that month, by a Sous-Lieutenant Canivet. By the time of its crash, a 110hp Le Rhone 9J had been fitted, this probably being the first installation of that engine in the Camel. It is not known whether the fitting of the Le Rhone had taken place before delivery. Despite the untimely end of the machine, French interest remained and a further specimen was sought. The replacement was, apparently, B2301, the first Ruston Proctor-built Camel, which arrived in Paris on 27 June. B3891, from the second Sopwith production batch, was later delivered and flown with a variety of engines, that included 130 and 185hp Clergets, a Gnome Monosoupape and a 170hp Le Rhone.

The first three British prototypes were regarded as naval machines, for the RNAS. Indeed, that service was quick to recognize the type's potential and an order for fifty machines was placed with Sopwith during January 1917. F1/3 was, however, diverted to the RFC and allotted the military serial number B381 during February, although it did not take up that identity until the following January. Delivered to the Experimental Station at Martlesham Heath, F1/3 was initially used for comparative engine tests and had also been fitted with a Le Rhone by 23 May.

Photographs show what may have been two further prototypes, with the basic F1 configuration; one with a one-piece upper wing, the other with a three-piece assembly and the final, longer ailerons. The disposition of the fuselage fabric lacing suggests that they were, at least, different machines. Both had the style of the forward-fuselage, aluminium panelling that was adopted as

The French government showed early interest in the Camel and a prototype was delivered for evaluation. Its forward decking was of the style used in probably the second prototype, but its aluminium panelling resembled that of F1/3. It was fitted with a 110hp Le Rhone, possibly by the French, and the extra cockpit instrumentation was probably a tachometer for that engine. It was crashed during May 1917 and this view of the scene shows that there was some form of covering over the centre of the one-piece upper wing. JMB/GSL

production standard, with ovular access panels to the carburettors. The disposition of the retaining studs on these panels was different to that of production machines.

That with the three-piece wing was, most likely, a reconstruction of F1/3. During 1918, that machine was again rebuilt, to something resembling the 'Comic' night-fighter (see below) and used for experiments in optical illusion as a means of distracting enemy aim. Photographs show just such a machine at Orfordness, where B381 re-emerged in May 1918. It had, by then, a three-piece upper wing, and its cockpit moved aft. The Vickers guns were retained and had become inaccessible in the event of stoppage. The machine was Sopwith built (evidenced by trademark transfers), was a prototype (with the unique studding arrangement on the carburettor panel) and

had been fitted with a Le Rhone engine (as revealed by the cowling slots characteristic for that engine).

The serial numbers N517 and N518 had been allotted by 24 February 1917 for two naval prototypes and on that date two further machines were allotted, one for the RFC and one for the French government. These naval serials may have been for existing machines. Certainly, there is some evidence to suggest that N517 was the second prototype. It was tested at Brooklands on 26 February and delivered to the Aircraft Depot at Dunkerque two days later. It was then passed between RNAS squadrons 6, 10, 9, 11 and 12, before being wrecked on 29 June. Returned to the Depot, N517 was struck off RNAS charge on 21 August.

February also saw the emergence of N518. Although a naval aeroplane, it went to the RFC Experimental Station at Martlesham Heath and spent a long career as an engine test-bed. During May, it was fitted with the first example of the AR1 engine. Those initials represented Admiralty Rotary and the engine was the brainchild of Lt W.O. Bentley (of motor car fame), whose genius was recognized by its being renamed BR1 (Bentley Rotary). That engine resembled a Clerget, but had a greater diameter and longer stroke. More significant was the fact that its cylinders were milled from aluminium and lined with steel sleeves. It developed 150hp and gave a vastly improved performance to the Camel.

A further prototype was built, with a new wing planform. The designation 4F1 was applied retrospectively and that machine was also known as the Taper Wing Camel. It had arrived at Martlesham by May 1917 and had been built in an attempt to increase performance. A wide and constant chord centre section supported mainplanes, which tapered from 5ft (1.52m) to 3ft 6in (1.07m) chord. The converging main spars enabled the adoption of a single, broad and I-section interplane strut in each wing cellule. These somewhat resembled those of the Triplane. The fuselage of this machine was similar to that of N518, but it was fitted with a Clerget 9B. Martlesham's report on its performance, M101, indicated that the machine was some 30lb (13.6kg) heavier than F1/3, but returned virtually identical speeds and rates of climb. However, mass production would have been more difficult

and the project was abandoned. The machine, itself, may have been a private venture by Sopwith's, because it was only subject to a contract in December 1917, by which time it had probably ceased to exist.

Into Service

Sopwith-built Camels, for the RNAS and from the initial production batch N6330–N6379, began leaving the production line

The Taper Wing Camel was produced in an effort to increase performance but that was not achieved. The wing layout would have been more difficult to mass produce and so the idea was abandoned. JMB/GSL

(*Left*) **The principal Camel engine was the 130hp Clerget 9B and one is shown here on a test rig at Marske.** JMB/GSL

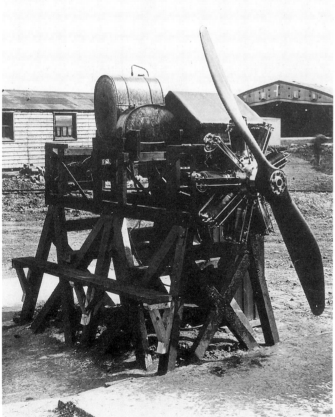

The Bentley BR1 Engine

The name of W.O. Bentley is best known in connection with luxury motor cars, but during the Great War he was responsible for designing the engine that gave the F1 and 2F1 Camels their maximum performance. Bentley was commissioned as a Lieutenant in the RNVR as an engineering officer and was seconded to various engine manufacturers, including Rolls-Royce, in an advisory capacity.

It was while Bentley was on detachment to Gwynnes, the English subcontractor for Clerget engines, that he formulated his ideas for a new engine. He was an advocate of using aluminium as a material for pistons and persuaded Gwynnes to adopt this idea. At the time, the 130hp Clerget engine was prone to cylinder distortion, due to uneven heat transfer. It had cast-iron cylinders and Bentley proposed substituting aluminium ones with steel linings. The reasoning behind this was that aluminium is a better conductor of heat. This was not accepted by Gwynnes but the Admiralty saw the logic and posted Bentley to the Humber engine works at Coventry and allowed the use of facilities to enable the construction of a prototype. The resultant engine was externally similar to the Clerget and, at 405lb (183.7kg), weighed only 5lb (2.27kg) more. It had a compression ratio of 5:9 to 1 and developed 150hp. It was tested at Martlesham Heath and ordered into production. Initially, it was named AR1 (Admiralty Rotary No1), but was rechristened BR1 (Bentley Rotary No1) in July 1917.

The Admiralty had a monopoly on BR1 deliveries and concentrated output into Camel production, with those machines produced by Clayton & Shuttleworth being almost exclusively given this power plant. The fact that most RNAS squadrons operated BR1 Camels led to their continuing to receive the type after the formation of the RAF, while ex-RFC units had to receive Clerget or Le Rhone-engined machines.

during early May 1917 and the complete batch had been delivered by the end of that month. These early Camels had the Vickers gun ammunition fed via canvas belts, which were rewound onto a drum. Cartridge case ejection was either down-over, through the bottom of the fuselage or into collection bags (surviving drawings do not show this detail, but the lack of ejection chutes on these machines indicates that one of these two methods was employed, probably the former).

This first batch was mainly fitted with the 130hp Clerget 9B, but eleven were given early examples of the BR1. Most of those eleven went to the first unit scheduled for re-equipment with the new type, 4 Sqn RNAS based at Frontier Aerodrome, Bray Dunes and under the command of Sqn Cdr B.L. Huskisson DSC. The first Camels had arrived, to replace its Pups, during the last week of May and the unit had ten by early June. This squadron was well placed to attack the Gothas that

had, at that time, begun attacking England by daylight. These enemy machines were especially vulnerable when returning to base with low fuel reserves.

The first recorded combat for the Camel was on 4 June, when Flt Cdr A.M. Shook sent an EA C type down out of control (OOC). That pilot had further successes the next day, another C type OOC and an Albatros scout that ended up crashing on the beach near Ostende. The squadron continued to build up its victory score, with Flt Lt (Flt Cdr from July) A.J. Chadwick, FSL A.J. Enstone and FSL R.M. Keirstead emerging alongside Shook as early exponents of the Camel's combat capability.

A second RNAS squadron re-equipped during the second half of June. This was 6N Sqn, which was at Flez, but moved to Frontier Aerodrome that month. The unit replaced its Nieuport 17bis with Clerget Camels and was soon in action. Among its successful pilots was Flt Lt B.P.H. de Roeper, who had accumulated a large

number of flying hours (including night Home Defence patrols) at RNAS Redcar and who was later to command the Flying Instructors' School in Egypt.

Sopwith's had received a second order for Camels from the RNAS in January, for fifty machines that were to be numbered N6530–N6579, but this was cancelled. The company did receive other contracts, but these were, unusually, from the RFC – Sopwith was regarded as a naval contractor. The RFC orders were received on 9 June and were for 450 machines, to be numbered B3751–B3950 and B6201– B6450. It was arranged that the RNAS would draw machines from these batches, which included both Clerget and BR1-powered versions. Production began immediately and the first of these new machines were delivered before the month was out.

At first, the BR1 was housed within a standard production cowling of constant diameter, but the engine was of greater diameter than the Clerget and this would

(Above) **The BR1 engine was almost exclusively used by naval squadrons and its greater diameter necessitated a wider cowling, as shown here.** via K Kelly

RNAS squadrons received Camels first and one such unit was 9N Sqn. This photograph shows what was probably B6358, a C Flt machine that was lost in action on 11 October 1917. The crescent marking is interesting, having been allocated as 9N's unit insignia in August but used very little. via K Kelly

have implications for cooling efficiency. As a result, a new cowling was introduced and used exclusively on BR1-powered machines. Its maximum diameter was greater than that at the engine backplate and so it was tapered to meet that item. This led, in turn, to a revised machine-gun 'hump', that was extended to overlap the cowling.

Further RNAS squadrons soon received Camels: 3N, 8N and 9N Sqns began re-equipping during July and 11N Sqn also had a small number on strength. A rationalization of RNAS units, resulting from a shortage of pilots, took place during late August, with 6N and 11N Sqns being disbanded and their pilots and Camels passed to 9N and 10N Sqns,

allowing the latter unit to re-equip with the type. 12N Sqn, which served almost as a French-based advanced training unit, received some Camels that autumn and the Seaplane Defence Flight at St Pol was redesignated the Seaplane Defence Squadron upon receiving the type during September. This squadron was brought into the RNAS numbering

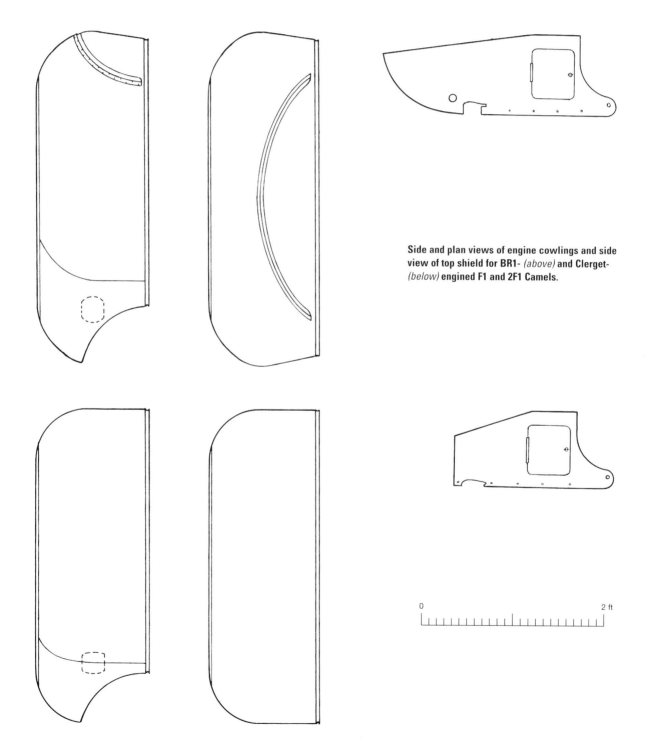

Side and plan views of engine cowlings and side view of top shield for BR1- *(above)* **and Clerget-** *(below)* **engined F1 and 2F1 Camels.**

A much later Camel of 209 Sqn, as 9N became after 1 April 1918, was this reconstructed machine, F5990. It had the revised unit marking, decreed on 22 March 1918, and blue coloured fin and wheel covers as flight markings. via author

sequence when it became 13N Sqn in January 1918.

The RFC had been slower to order the Camel and initial Sopwith output was for the RNAS. It was decided that the production of the type would be sub-contracted and, accordingly, the Lincoln-based Ruston Proctor & Co. Ltd was given orders for 250 machines on 2 March 1917. Further subcontractors received orders that summer, with others receiving them later. Contracts for the type were awarded until September 1918 and more than 5,700 F1 Camels were delivered, with others cancelled after the cessation of hostilities. The fact that Sopwith's ceased F1 production early was probably the result of that company becoming involved in the development and initial production of the 2F1, and of its being awarded a massive contract for the later Dolphin.

During its long production run, the F1 Camel was subject to numerous modifications, some to rectify design faults, others to incorporate lessons learnt from operational experience with the type. A good understanding of these can be obtained by examining the experiences of a typical manufacturer, such as Ruston Proctor and Co. Ltd, who built more Camels than any other manufacturer. The company had experience of aeroplane production, and had built batches of the B.E.2c/d/e and Sopwith 1½ Strutter for the RFC, but its initial batch of Camels was the largest production run that it had, so far, attempted. N6344, from the first Sop-

with batch, was diverted to Lincoln to serve as a pattern aircraft.

The first Ruston Camel was delivered to Lincoln Aircraft Acceptance Park on 1 June 1917 and was flown to France thirteen days later. After passing through 1AD and 2AD, where its cowling was modified, B2301 was delivered to the French government on the 27th. The second machine featured the addition of safety hinges to the engine cowling and the fitting of these was standardized from B2321 onwards. The first few machines lacked provision for gunsights, but brackets for the Aldis optical sight were fitted from B2308 onwards (except for B2330). The original fuel pump arrangement is not known, but from B2354, delivered on 29 August 1917, a Rotherham wind-driven pump was fitted to the rear starboard centre-section strut, as Alteration 490.

When B2361 was delivered on 5 September, it had a revised layout for the elevator control cables, which was standardized thereafter. Originally, these passed into the fuselage through a single fairlead under the top longeron and were prone to chaffing and subsequent failure. Alteration 585 provided a second fairlead, at fuselage mid-depth position, through which the lower cable was then passed. B2361 was the first to incorporate two other safety features, the packing of the gravity tank to prevent its moving and the provision of a bracing wire between the rear centre-section struts.

The earliest Ruston Camels, like those from Sopwith, were delivered with provision for Vickers gun ammunition to be fed on canvas belts. These belts had a tendency to absorb moisture, which froze at altitude and led to guns becoming inoperable. The remedy was the use of Prideaux disintegrating metal links and these were duly adopted. This led to a revision of the spent cartridge and link ejection system and a chute arrangement was adopted, which was complicated by the fact that only right-hand feed blocks were available for the Vickers guns. In this new layout, links and cases from the starboard gun were ejected from a chute that discharged via a slot in the starboard carburettor access panel. Cartridge cases from the other gun ejected from a slot in the port access panel, but the spent links were ejected through another chute that discharged sideways. Possible damage from spent links, blown in the slipstream, may be the reason why, from B2391, an aluminium plate (described as a shield) was fitted to the rear port centre-section strut.

New spar boxes were fitted from B2542, delivered on 17 November. These necessitated an alteration to the length of the interplane struts and must have posed problems, in terms of spares for earlier machines. Alterations to the oil, gravity and main tanks were incorporated during that month. Another modification to the fuel supply system was made from B5601, delivered on 28 November. This consisted of the addition of a strainer in the air intake tubes, a simple remedy for carburettors prone to jet blocking by foreign particles. The fuel supply was dependent upon efficient function of the Rotherham pump and early examples were prone to seizure. Modifications to that pump's lubrication system were adopted during December.

Camel tail-skids were prone to breakage and a modified version was introduced from B7388. This was a five-ply birch component and was stronger that the single lamination original. However, it was not infallible and it was not unknown for operational units to fabricate their own steel replacements.

It would be unfair to criticize Ruston Proctor for shoddy workmanship, because there are always examples of occasional failure with mass-produced articles. It is a fact, however, that at least four Ruston-built Camels were involved in crashes that could be attributed to the use of defective materials. B7456 had been sent to Lincoln AAP on 31 January 1918 and was delivered to the BEF. After a short spell with 43 Sqn, it was used by 3 TDS at Lopcombe Corner, where it crashed on 16 July with a total flying time of only 60 hours. Its pilot, 2 Lt Roy Mallett was killed after it tumbled in from 6,000ft (1,830m). Examination of the wreckage revealed that three of the four wing spars had failed and that the spiral graining of their timber had been the cause. E1436 had been delivered to Coventry on 13 June and was taken on charge by 4 Fighting School at Freiston. It crashed on 27 July, with only one hour of flying time. The use of defective materials had caused the port front bottom spar to fail and 2 Lt E.A. Kenny was lucky to land safely. Another casualty of spars with spiral graining was C8291, although its operational service was longer and more successful than that of B7456, being used by Lt E.G. Brookes of 65 Sqn in four successful combats. Upon return to England and while in use by 63 TS at Joyce Green, it crashed on 29 August, killing Flt Cdt P.G.D. Winchester. E1531 was delivered on 13 July and was allotted to 40 TS at Croydon. It too suffered spar failure, on 19 August, and this time it was due to the timber being cross-grained. Lt V.S. Parker was lucky to manage a forced-landing, without injury.

Modifications were made to improve the strength of lower wing spar joints, from C8218, and at the time of its delivery, in mid-February 1918, a new design of windscreen was adopted and heel-boards were added as concessions to pilot comfort. A new safety aspect was introduced on C8258, delivered on 23 February, which involved the provision of handed axle caps to retain the wheels. Previously, both had been of right-hand thread and led to port wheels eventually coming adrift. The new modification was applied to some machines, but not others, until D1896, whereupon its application was constant.

The inadequate performance that resulted from using the readily available Clerget 9B was improved somewhat by the introduction of that engine's long-stroke successor, the 140hp Clerget 9Bf. The widespread introduction of that more powerful engine led to a modification of the Camel's engine cowling, with the radius of the rounded front edge being increased to 7in (17.78cm). This, presumably, was done to improve air circulation and was introduced by Ruston's to machines from D1801 onwards.

Ruston's 1,000th Camel, D8249, was delivered to Lincoln AAP on 1 June 1918,

This close-up of F5990 shows two of the operational modifications made to Camels. The centre-section cut-out was widened to improve the pilot's field of vision upwards and forwards and the decking is cut away around the starboard gun to allow access to the cocking mechanism. via author

exactly a year after the first, which gave a respectable weekly production figure of about twenty machines. Subsequent airframe modifications included the lightening of the front wing spars, from E1481, and a strengthening of the sternpost, from E1590. Interestingly, and despite the fact that such a modification was ordered on machines already in France from July 1918, Ruston-built Camels were never built with the enlarged centre-section cut-out that did much to improve visibility both upwards and during turning manoeuvres. Production continued almost to the Armistice, with the last recorded delivery being that of F4037, to Burton-on-Trent, on 4 November. Some, if not all, of the balance of the final batch, F4048–F4067, were delivered, however, as several were recorded as being on the strength of the RAF's Syren Force in North Russia during 1919. This brought total production to 1,575 airframes, a quantity that was matched, but not exceeded, by only one other manufacturer, Boulton & Paul.

Not unnaturally, 4 (Lincoln) AAP was the usual initial destination for Camels leaving Ruston's factory, as may be gathered from the production history just outlined. Some, however, were delivered direct to other units. Machines intended

for service with the 7th Brigade in Italy were crated and delivered by rail to Southampton for shipment. Others were delivered by rail to home stations, such as D1935–D1937 which were dispatched to Driffield (Eastburn) for 2 SAF (listed by Rustons as SAG) on 22 April. Those for stations closer by were delivered by road, examples being E7144–E7155 which were delivered to 46 TDS South Carlton between 26 July and 1 August 1918. On that latter date, E7156–E7158 were delivered to 34 TDS Scampton, also by road. It will be noted that these were batches of consecutively numbered machines that were delivered to training units. This was not unusual and was part of the standard allotment process. Occasionally, training units found themselves short of machines and special delivery was authorized, such as to 63 TS at Redcar, which had been depleted of Camels by a series of accidents during mid-October 1918. Replacements were delivered from Lincoln, F4013–F4017 being dispatched between the 25th and 31st of that month.

Clerget engines, of either the 130hp 9B or 140hp 9Bf variety powered the vast majority of Ruston's Camels. This was not surprising, as the company also built that

Ruston's 1,000th Machine

25 January 1918 was an historic day for Ruston Proctor as, the firm's 1,000th machine, B7380, was delivered to Lincoln AAP. It had been completed three weeks earlier. Colonel Ruston was an Egyptologist and it may have been at his instigation that permission was sought to decorate it in a special paint scheme. It was decorated to represent Behudet, a winged sun, with blue, green, orange and grey striped fuselage and large 'eyes' painted on the cowling. Its wings and tailplane were in natural finish, with a sunburst effect painted on. Maj Gen W.S. Brackner visited Lincoln to inspect it on 1 February and, after participating in preparations for a forthcoming War Bond Week, it was delivered to the BEF in France on the 15th, still in its outlandish colour scheme. That scheme, not surprisingly, was deemed unsuitable for operational service and, rather than being redoped, B7380 was returned to the UK. Presumably it served with a training unit and one photograph shows it with the starboard decking ahead of the cockpit cut away; it had left the factory with a symmetrical cockpit cut-out.

Photograph via P. Jarratt

engine. What is interesting, however, is that Camels built by Ruston's, who were given repeated follow-on orders for the type, were regarded as being the least satisfactory of those from any subcontractor. Its machines had a reputation for tail-heaviness and English-built Clergets were notoriously poor at maintaining efficiency.

This engine inadequacy had revealed itself early in the Camel's career. The RFC hierarchy with the BEF had expected great things of the type, but were dismayed at the rate at which operational machines lost performance. Their optimistic expectations were based on the figures achieved in tests at Martlesham and their displeasure was soon and vehemently expressed. An investigation was called for and involved the sending of N518 from Martlesham to France on 1 September 1917. By that time, that machine had an AR1 engine fitted. Capt R.H. Carr took N518 to 1 AD St Omer, where comparative trials were held against six other Camels, three new and three, which had seen operational service, from 9N Sqn. All six had Clerget 9B engines. Not unnaturally, the three 9N Sqn machines returned the poorest performances and N518 the best. The sole Ruston Camel in the trials, B2338, returned the worst performance of the three new machines, although all three were fitted with Ruston-built Clergets.

The Clerget's problems centred on valve wear, with its consequent effect on ignition timing. There were also problems with the early versions of the Sopwith-

Specification – Sopwith F1 Camel

Engine:	One 130hp Clerget 9B or 140hp Clerget 9Bf or 150hp BR1 or 110hp Le Rhone or 100hp Gnome
Weights:	Empty 956lb (434kg) (130hp Clerget), 928lb (421kg) (140hp Clerget), 977lb (443kg) (BR1), 889lb (403kg) (Le Rhone); loaded 1,455lb (660kg) (130hp Clerget), 1,452lb (659kg) (140hp Clerget), 1,508lb (684kg) (BR1), 1,422lb (645kg) (Le Rhone)
Dimensions:	Length 18ft 9in (5.72m) (Clerget & Le Rhone), 18ft 6in (5.64m) (BR1), 18ft 8in (15.69m) (Le Rhone & Monosoupape); height 8ft 6in (2.59m); wingspan upper 28ft (8.53m), lower 28ft (8.53m); chord upper 4ft 6in (1.34m), lower 4ft 6in (1.34m); stagger 1ft 6in (45.72cm); gap 5ft (1.52m) (F1), 4ft 9in (1.43m) (F1/4); dihedral upper 0°, lower 5°
Performance:	Max. speed 105mph (169km/h) (Clerget), 118mph (190km/h) (Le Rhone), 111mph (179km/h) (BR1) Service ceiling 19,000ft (5,490m) Clerget, 24,000ft (7,315m) (Le Rhone), 20,000ft (6,100m) (BR1) Endurance 2½ hours
Armament:	Two fixed Vickers guns, synchronized to fire through propeller arc plus 4 × 20lb (9kg) bombs

Kauper gun interrupter gear and HQ RFC found itself in the position of having either to accept the Camel, with its faults, or struggle on with types that were becoming very outdated, namely the 1½ Strutter and Pup. Wisely it chose the Camel, in the expectation that initial problems could be ironed out. The RNAS was in a slightly more favourable position, having access to the AR1/BR1 engine, but that power plant was in short supply and several naval squadrons were also required to use Clerget-powered machines.

Apart from Sopwith and Ruston Proctor, a further seven contractors built F1 Camels. In terms of numbers delivered, Boulton & Paul Ltd matched Ruston's output of 1,575 and similarly concentrated on producing Clerget-engined machines. It did, however, install the 150hp Gnome Monosoupape in a proportion of those of its Camels that were delivered to the USAS. Clayton & Shuttleworth Ltd, another Lincoln firm, was a contractor for the RNAS and the vast majority of its output of 600 was given the superior BR1 engine. Camels built by Hooper & Co. of Chelsea were highly regarded and much of that firm's output of 370 F1s were Le Rhone powered, as were 146 machines delivered by the British Caudron Co. Ltd, of Cricklewood and Alloa. Most of the 185 Camels produced by March Jones & Cribb Ltd of Leeds also had that 110hp engine. Nieuport & General turned out 400 Camels from their Cricklewood factory, while Portholme Aerodrome Ltd of Huntingdon produced fifty.

Upon completion, machines were usually delivered to the nearest Aircraft Acceptance Park, where specially assigned service pilots tested them. The logbook of Lt P. Wilson, a former 1 Sqn Nieuport pilot who served in that capacity at 3 AAP Norwich, shows an average one or two acceptance tests per day during mid-1918, with a considerable proportion of machines being rejected until minor defects had been rectified. Some machines were delivered from factories directly to storage, while others went directly to units to which they had been allotted. Some machines intended for overseas service were crated for shipment and a case was designed and produced in the smallest possible proportions to take a dismantled airframe.

Further serial numbers were allocated for Camels and these were for machines that had been reconstructed from damaged airframes. Large numbers were rebuilt at the Aircraft Depots in France, and at home, under the Reserve Aeroplane Repair Scheme, training units were allowed to undertake their own reconstructions, while Aircraft Repair Depots, such as that at Yate, provided others in the wake of losses during the German spring 1918 offensive.

With the RFC in France

The RFC with the BEF had received its first Camel on 25 May 1917, when N6332 was transferred from the RNAS and delivered to 2 AD at Candas. By 13 June, it was with the operational RFC Camel unit, 70 Sqn at Boisdinghem, which was scheduled to replace its 1½ Strutters with the type. The problems with interrupter gear had been realized and N6332 was returned, briefly, to 2 AD for tests with the MkIII version of the Sopwith-Kauper device. Most of 70 Sqn's initial establishment of Camels were from the second Sopwith-built batch and its re-equipment was completed by early July. The unit soon had combat success, with Capts N.W.W. Webb and C.F. Collett emerging as its leading exponents on the new type.

As stocks of RFC Camels increased, a second 1½ Strutter squadron began re-equipment. This was 45 Sqn at Ste Marie Cappel, which received its first Camel on 25 July. The third of the squadrons with the Sopwith two-seater, 43 Sqn, had its re-equipment delayed and that for 45 Sqn was not as speedy as it might have been. This was due to the fact that, without the RFC-in-the-Field being consulted, 24 Camels were withheld from delivery to France and allotted on 10 July, for Home Defence duties as a result of aeroplane raids on London. During September, 43 Sqn re-equipped and four further Camel squadrons became operational the following month. 3 Sqn had flown a variety of Morane types since 1915 and had latterly operated the Type P two-seat parasol. It received its Camels at Warloy-Baillon and its observers, like those from the 1½ Strutter squadrons, were either transferred to other units or posted home for pilot training. 28 Sqn had no operational experience, having formed at Gosport almost two years earlier and serving as a training unit, with a brief spell on Home Defence duty. On 23 July, it had exchanged bases and equipment with 55 TS at Yatesbury and began mobilization for active service.

Camels, mainly from the third Sopwith-built batch, replaced its Pups, D.H.5s and Bristol Scouts and the unit arrived at St Omer on 8 October, moving to its operational base at Droglandt two days later. With the re-equipment of 1½ Strutter units completed, it was then the turn of Pup squadrons. The type had been flown operationally for seven months by 66 Sqn, with some success, but it was becoming rapidly outdated. Re-equipment took place, at Liettres, over a seven-day period,

46 Sqn RFC re-equipped from Pups and at first used the unit marking of two narrow bands ahead of the tailplane. B9199 was a B Flt machine, delivered to the unit on 29 January 1918 and was crashed on its nose by Capt D.W. Forshaw. JMB/GSL

from 14 October. A further unit arrived from England on the 27th. This was 65 Sqn, which established itself at Poperinghe on 4 November and its addition to the strength of 11 Wing in 2 Brigade allowed the withdrawal of 1N Sqn for re-equipment with the Camel. 65 Sqn had flown some Camels at Wye from August. These were early Sopwith-built machines that were used in the squadron's secondary, Home Defence, role and included, at least, one that was powered by a 100hp Gnome Monosoupape. During mobilization, from the beginning of October, the unit received its full complement of operational machines as an almost consecutive batch of Ruston Camels, two of which (B2401 and B2407) were lost in a training accident that resulted in their pilots ditching in the Channel. Its earlier training Camels were passed to the co-located 86 Sqn.

November and December saw the end of the Pup's service as a fighting scout with squadrons in France. 46 Sqn at Le Hameau and 54 Sqn at Bruay were re-equipped and in December 71 (Australian) and 73 Sqns arrived from England, with 71 Sqn being redesigned as 4 Sqn AFC from 14 January 1918. On the debit side, three Camel squadrons were withdrawn for service in Italy, in order to provide aerial protection for two accompanying R.E.8 units and to improve the aerial opposition to the Austro-Hungarian advance that followed the disaster at Caporetto.

It should be noted that all of the RFC's Camel squadrons, to that date, had the Clerget engine. The 130hp version was the standard, but the long-stroke 140hp was a prospect. RFC HQ preferred the 110hp Le Rhone and wanted its Camels thus powered, but unfortunately, the Le Rhone was in short supply and most Camel units had to be content with the Clerget. However, 54 Sqn received Le Rhone Camels upon its re-equipment and 3 Sqn was converted to that type in December. When 80 Sqn arrived at Boisdinghem, from England, on 27 January 1918, it too had that superior engine. A further advantage of the Le Rhone Camel

After March 1918, the unit marking for 46 Sqn was changed to a horizontal line running the length of the fuselage fabric. This is shown on B9329, a presentation machine, 'Huddersfield'. JMB/GSL

lay in its gun synchronization gear. This was the Constantinesco hydraulic gear, which was considered less susceptible to failure than earlier mechanical types. At the end of January, 46 Sqn also converted to Le Rhone Camels, but although 73 Sqn had them briefly, these four units were all that could be so equipped. It would seem that Home Defence units had greater priority in Le Rhone deliveries. As with the Clerget, a French-built Le Rhone was

considered superior to an English-built one. Deliveries of the 140hp Clerget 9Bf began during the early spring of 1918 and Camel units with the BEF started converting to the type from March.

As the number of Camel squadrons, with both the RNAS and RFC, had increased during the autumn and early winter of 1917, pilots began to develop a feel for the type and learnt its capabilities and limitations. Combat successes accumulated, but these were not gained without loss. However, it was soon realized that the optimum combat altitude was in the region of 9,000–12,000ft (2,740–3,660m). Within this height range, the machine was at its most manoeuvrable, without too much loss of speed or height during turns. The problem was that contemporary enemy fighting scouts could operate effectively at greater altitude. Consequently, Camels were often placed at an initial disadvantage by being attacked from above, but if combat was continued in an ensuing 'dogfight', the type came into its own and pilots could use its legendary turning ability to maximum advantage.

The day of the lone and roving fighter pilot was, however, effectively over by the time the Camel entered widespread service. Formation patrols had become the order of the day and squadrons were usually allocated patrol areas and altitudes that suited their machines. Deep penetration of enemy airspace was the usual province of

The widened centre-section that was ordered in July 1918 is seen here on a Le Rhone Camel of 3 Sqn C Flt. It is probably F6089 and the pilot is Lt J. Sellers. JMB/GSL

the Bristol Fighter, but the areas that lay within 15 miles (24km) of the Lines were more often patrolled by single-seaters, the S.E.5a (and, later, Dolphins) at higher altitude, with Camels below. The pilots that accumulated high 'victory' scores were often the patrol leaders, whose job it was to manoeuvre for favourable positions and then lead attacks that would minimize damage or loss to followers. In many combats, it was the first attacking shots that counted and it was the patrol leaders who usually fired these. Their followers might be successful if a prolonged combat developed, but that situation was not an everyday happening. A listing of the victories of high-scoring pilots as a proportion of the 'victories' of any Camel squadron will bear this out. Rather than giving a catalogue of Camel 'aces', inserts have been distributed throughout this chapter that highlight the exploits of three Camel pilots whose careers were connected, and who achieved varying degrees of combat success.

Successes there were, but the large-scale introduction of the Camel during the latter half of 1917 was not loss-free. The experience of 65 Sqn was typical. That unit, under the seasoned command of Maj J.A. Cunningham, had arrived in France on 27 October with eighteen pilots, only one of whom had seen active service in that capacity. Cunningham had, realistically, briefed his pilots at Wye by telling them that they were not going to France for the sake of their health and that casualties were bound to happen, but he did not want mention of these in the mess. The table below gives the unit's losses for its first two months of operations, the original members being noted with asterisks.

Camel Pilot 1 – Lt G.M. Knocker

Guy M. Knocker transferred to the RFC from the Royal Field Artillery and, after training was posted to 40 TS at Croydon, as an instructor. On 5 and 13 September 1917, one of his pupils was 2Lt V.M. Yeates. Knocker was then posted to 65 Sqn at Wye, a unit that was, at that time, in the process of 'working' up for operational service. He was one of the unit's original complement of pilots that flew to France on 27 October, flying and fighting with the unit for over five months. During that time, he was credited with sending two Albatros scouts down out of control, one on 18 December 1917 (shared with Lt G. Bremridge) and another on 4 January 1918. 65 Sqn, like most other fighting scout units, was tasked with ground attack work following the German advance that began on 21 March 1918. On 6 April Knocker was returning from such a mission and was flying over the lines at 2,000ft, when he was hit in the calf by a single rifle bullet. He landed at Bertangles and was sent to 46

CCS at Pecquigney, where the first person he met was his sister.

After convalescence, he was posted, on 11 July, to 63 TS at Joyce Green, where his CO was Maj T.E. Withington, a former 65 Sqn Flight Commander. 63 TS operated Avros and Camels, being tasked with turning out about eight pilots per month. Joyce Green was an unsatisfactory aerodrome for such duty and so the unit was transferred to Redcar on 5 October. By this time Knocker was commanding its Camel flight, but its was only then that he took an instructor's course, being graded as A1 by staff of the co-located North East Area Flying Instructors School. At Redcar, he flew a variety of other types, including the Sopwith Triplane and Bristol Fighter. He remained in the RAF post-war, flying Bristol Fighters on the North-West Frontier.

Photograph via author

65 Sqn Losses in its First Two Month's of Operation

Date	Pilot	Cause	Date	Pilot	Cause
3.11.1917	2Lt C.A. Maasdorp (RFC)	To hospital	26.11.1917	2Lt W.H. Cross (RFC)	HE
6.11.1917	Lt E.G.S. Gordon (Gordon Highlanders & RFC)*	POW	27.11.1917	Capt L.S. Weedon (Royal Fusiliers & RFC)*	To Hospital
6.11.1917	Lt W. Harrison (NZMR & RFC)*	POW	28.11.1917	Lt J.F. McKinnon (SR & RFC)	KIA
6.11.1917	2Lt E.H. Cutbill (RFC)*	POW	5.12.1917	Lt F.M.C. Noughton (RFC)	To Hospital
12.11.1917	Lt K.S. Morrison (RFA & RFC)*	POW wounded	7.12.1917	2Lt H.A. Dyer (RFC)	KIA
12.11.1917	Lt D.H. Scott MC (RFC)*	KIA – hit by AA	10.12.1917	2Lt A.E. Rudge (RFC)	HE
12.11.1917	2Lt W.H. Hemming (RFC)	KIFA	12.12.1917	Lt F.M. Cory (8th Sherwoods & RFC)	KIFA
12.11.1917	Lt G.A. Pitt (Nottingham Yeomanry & RFC)*	WIA	18.12.1917	2Lt D.M. Sage (RFC)	KIA
15.11.1917	2Lt T.P. Morgan (RFC)	POW	18.12.1917	2Lt R.H. Cowan (RFC)	POW
23.11.1917	2Lt L. Marshall (RFC)	KIA (collision)	18.12.1917	2Lt J.D. Cameron (RFC)	POW
23.11.1917	2Lt A. Rosenthal (RFC)*	KIA (collision)	25.12.1918	2Lt O. Darlington (RFC)	HE
23.11.1917	Lt C.F. Keller (6th London & RFC)*	POW	29.12.1918	Capt W.W. Higgins (6th Liverpools & RFC)*	To Hospital
23.11.1917	Lt C.P. Tiptaft (Connaught Rangers & RFC)	WIA	2.1.1918	Lt J. Boyd (Scottish Rifles & RFC)	To 43 Sqn
23.11.1917	2Lt G.S. Pilcher (RFC)	WIA	4.1.1918	2Lt R.E. Robb (RFC)	KIA

Although intended purely as a fighting scout, the Camel was pressed into other roles, as the need arose, and that most hated by most pilots was ground-attack work. The type had an introduction to this duty, with selected units, during the Cambrai battles, but the ferocity of the German push that began on 21 March led to the wholesale involvement of the Camel squadrons, in an attempt to stop the advance.

It was dangerous work and losses were high. Such missions tended to be of short duration and, consequently, pilots were able to fly a greater number of sorties. Capt A.H. Cobby, the leading Australian, recalled that these sorties involved 'getting to the line, loaded up with bombs and ammunition, as fast and as often as one could, and letting the enemy on the ground have it as hot and as heavy as possible'. An indication of this is the fact that on 25 March, 4 Sqn AFC expended more than 15,000 rounds of 0.303in ammunition. The bombs, mentioned by Cobby, were of the 20lb (9kg) variety and the fitting of a carrier for four of these became standard.

A variation on this type of work was attacks on enemy aerodromes. This was not a new idea, having been practised on an individual basis, but by 1918 it had been developed into well-organized raids that involved large numbers of attacking machines. A typical 'Wing Show' was that of 80 Wing on Haubourdin aerodrome on 16 August, led by 4 Sqn AFC, but involving 92, 88, 103 and 2 Sqn AFC machines. The attack was led by Cobby, who had painted the upper top wing of his Camel white, for easy identification. Col L.A. Strange, the Wing Cdr, flew alongside Cobby in his 'personal' Camel that was maintained by 4 Sqn AFC. Hangars and stationary machines were bombed and shot up with incendiary ammunition from all five squadrons and then 4 Sqn AFC proceeded to attack troops and transport in the surrounding area.

The March push had brought with it an increase in air combats and it was during that period that 43 Sqn gained distinction on two notable days, when two of its pilots succeeded in destroying greater numbers of enemy aeroplanes than had previously been achieved. On 24 March, Capt J.L. Trollope

MC flew two patrols, during the course of which he claimed the destruction of seven enemy machines, comprising an Albatros scout, two DFW C types, three Albatros C types and an unspecified two-seater. Nearly three weeks later, on 12 April, Capt H.W. Woollett MC came close to repeating this performance, destroying five Albatros scouts and an enemy C type.

Formation of the Royal Air Force occurred on 1 April 1918. Ex-RFC squadrons maintained their existing numbers, but the former RNAS units had 200

Another 3 Sqn Camel was C8374 and this view shows the cowling cut-out that was made to allow the use of the Le Rhone engine in a Clerget cowling. JMB/GSL

added to their numbers so that, for example, 1N Sqn became 201 Sqn. The Camel at that time equipped more single-seat squadrons of the BEF than any other type

and continued to do so until the Armistice. No further day-fighting squadrons of the BEF received the type, although two American squadrons were subsequently attached and two night-fighting squadrons arrived later in the year.

Training Service

Such widespread operational use of the type demanded that service pilots were familiar with its tendencies before posting to front-line units. Consequently, the type had an early introduction into training units. Six machines from the second Sopwith batch (B3799–B3804) were probably the first for the RFC and all served with B Sqn of the CFS at Upavon. The RNAS delivered some of its first machines to Eastchurch and Manston, the latter being the home of the War School, a finishing unit that prepared pilots for operational postings.

Certain RFC, and later RAF, Training Squadrons were dedicated to operating the Camel and suffered relatively high attrition rates as a consequence of the type's characteristics. It is interesting that, when the Training Depot Station (TDS) system was fully adopted from July 1918 with 61 such units, only five stations were for Camel training; Lopcombe Corner, Montrose, Shotwick, Chattis Hill and Hounslow. Very

Camels were notorious for their tendency to punish flying errors. B5184 was with 73TS at Turnhouse and is shown after coming to grief. It was repaired and later served with 36TS at Montrose. JMB/GSL

Another Camel crash was a spectacle for American personnel at Ternhill. The marking is that of 43TS and is similar to that shown earlier on a 1½ Strutter. via author

Another crash from Marske involved C1662, which spun in on 20 May 1918, killing Lt W.J. Knoll. JMB/GSL

This Camel crash near Marske cost Lt A.C. Doucet his life. D1933, with its 2 Fighting School number '59' crashed on 19 December 1918. JMB/GSL

few Training Squadrons survived, but most of those that did were the ones operating Camels: 10 TS at Gosport, 40 TS at Croydon, 42 TS at Wye and 63 TS at Joyce Green, later Redcar. The intended establishment of each was twelve Avros plus twelve Camels. Perhaps this was an indication of the intention to replace the type.

Upon graduation from the TDS system, pilots were usually posted to units dedicated to role-specific training. In the case of those pilots destined for service on Camels, this was one of the four Fighting Schools – Turnberry, Marske, Bircham Newton and Freiston. Gunnery and combat tactics were taught at these stations, but it must be said that the courses were often brief. 2 Fighting School at Marske was involved in attempts at air-to-air filming, presumably for training purposes, and it was during such an exercise that Maj L.P. Aizelwood AFC was killed in

E1456 on 29 September 1918, spinning in from 1,000ft (305m). The camera machine for these trials was an Avro 504J, apparently from the NEAFIS at Redcar. The Imperial War Museum holds footage from these trials and, in the background to one scene, a Camel can be seen spinning in to crash. Prospective fighting scout pilots had experience by the time they reached Marske, but Camel crashes were still plentiful and these also involved instructors. On 15 July 1918, C175 suffered an engine failure on take-off and crashed in an ensuing side-slip. Its pilot was no novice, but suffered near fatal injuries. This was Capt A.R. Brown DSC* who, for many years, was thought to have been responsible for the shooting down of Ritt M. Fr von Richthofen, Germany's leading fighter pilot.

Certain squadrons served in the UK without any operational role, instead acting as advanced training units. Several of these had Camels on strength, including 81, 86, 89, 91, 92, 93, 94, 95 and 96 Sqns. Most of these squadrons were disbanded during the summer of 1918, when the TDS system was more fully adopted. Other squadrons, even some earmarked to fly the S.E.5a operationally, had a few on charge.

Camels were favourites with instructors and many were given colourful finishes. C1660, with a blue and white chequered fuselage was flown by 73TS at Beaulieu and, later, 28 TDS Weston-on-the-Green. JMB/GSL

This unidentified Camel had a striped fuselage and embellished wheel covers. It was flown by 1 Fighting School at Ayr. JMB/GSL

From July 1918, UK-based training machines were ordered to display underwing serials. These are shown on F9574 of 32 TDS Montrose. JMB/GSL

At a large number of training units, Camels as well as Pups were often acquired as 'personal' machines by more senior officers. Perhaps an excuse was used that such machines needed to be highly visible for their instructional purposes, or maybe it was overlooked by higher authority, but a large number of these were given highly individualistic colour schemes. Striped and chequerboard examples were common, while others were marked in single colours overall. All, however, would have relied upon using the existing available colours, in other words black and those of the national markings.

Squadrons working up to operational status used Camels. B2511 was flown by 94 Sqn at Harling Road and displayed extra cockades on its cowling and wheel covers. JMB/GSL

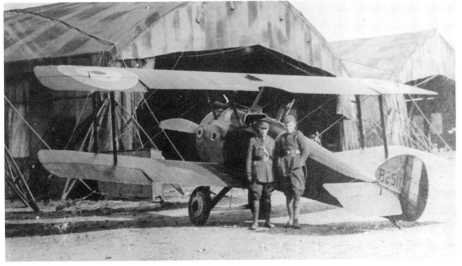

Camel Pilot 2 – Lt V.M. Yeates

Most of those interested in World War I flying will be familiar with this pilot through his novel *Winged Victory*, a semi-autobiographical account of life in a Camel squadron. Victor Maslin Yeates began his, unusually long, training with 4 TS at Northolt on 18 June 1917. After that preliminary training, he was posted to 65 Sqn at Wye, but only had one flight with that unit, on 15 August. A transfer to 40 TS at Croydon followed, where he flew Avros and Pups, before making his first Camel flight on 18 January 1918. Upon graduation, he was ordered overseas and posted to 46 Sqn on Le Rhone Camels. Yeates was, unusually for a World War I fighter pilot, married and, although a post-war study concluded that this status had an adverse effect on fighting efficiency, he achieved some success.

Yeates flew with 46 Sqn for more than six months, often alongside Capt D.R. MacLaren. He was credited with destroying a Pfalz D III on 15 May, a Fokker D VII on 3 August and shared in the destruction of three enemy two-seaters. Yeates did not, apparently, impress MacLaren, who regarded him as something of a dreamer who 'did not do much'. This, in some ways, reflects the impression gained, through Yeates' perception, when reading *Winged Victory*. He was temporarily with 80 Sqn during early August, returning to 46 Sqn on the 12th.

War flying led to Yeates suffering from stress and he was invalided home at the end of August. At this time he had 271 hours and 50 minutes flying time, 196 hours and 30 minutes of these on Camels. After a recuperative period, he was posted to 54 TDS at Fairlop, where he brought his total flying time to over 300 hours.

His wartime experience had an adverse effect on his health and he contracted tuberculosis. Yeates wrote his novel, which was not acclaimed at the time, but in doing so exacerbated his condition. He died on 15 December 1934, at the relatively young age of 37.

Photograph via W. Vandersteen

Service in Italy

As mentioned earlier, the Austro-Hungarian breakthrough after Caporetto and subsequent advance to the River Piave, during the autumn of 1917, had led to Allied reinforcements being made available. The RFC contingent comprised two R.E.8 corps squadrons and, in order to provide protection for these, 28, 45 and 66 Sqns with Camels were also dispatched. Of these, 45 Sqn had combat experience on the type, but 66 Sqn had only just re-equipped from flying Pups. 28 Sqn, although only recently operational, was fortunate to have Capt W.G. Barker MC* as a Flight Commander and his aggressive example to its, mainly inexperienced, pilots had been demonstrated during the few weeks that it had fought over France and Belgium. These three Camel squadrons entrained for Italy during October and all were at their designated operational bases by December, coming under the control of the newly-formed 7th Brigade.

Hitherto, the Austro-Hungarian forces, bolstered by several German *Jagdstafflen*, had enjoyed aerial supremacy over the opposing Italian units that were largely equipped with Hanriot and Nieuport scouts that were of inferior performance to the Albatros types of German and Austrian manufacture. The arrival of the RFC Camels, combined with the withdrawal of the German units in preparation for the forthcoming March push in France, led to a turning of the tide. The combat claims for the Camel squadrons mounted and several pilots amassed large numbers of 'victories'. In 45 Sqn, Capts M.B. Frew, C.E. Howell and J. Cottle were leading scorers, while in 66 Sqn Capt P. Carpenter and Lt H.K. Goode had similar success. Capt J. Mitchell and Lts C.M. McEwan and H.B.

Hudson were among 28 Sqn's leading aces, but the 'star turn' in the Italian theatre was George Barker, who transferred from 28 to 66 Sqn and was then promoted to command 139 Sqn, a Bristol F2B unit.

Barker had been credited with three successful combats during 28 Sqn's brief period of operation in France and he added a further nineteen with that unit in Italy. All of these were achieved in B6313. His transfer to 66 Sqn seems to have been the result of personal differences, but he was held in sufficient esteem to be allowed to take B6313 with him and he had a further sixteen successes. Upon receiving his majority with command of 139 Sqn, he again took B6313 with him and continued to fly operations, adding another eight 'victories' to his tally. Having been used to destroy forty enemy machines, send a further five down out of control and capture another, Camel B6313 was the most successful fighter of the war, possibly the most successful of all time. Upon his posting back to the UK, Barker delivered B6313 to 7 AP, where it was to be broken up. As a souvenir, he kept its unorthodox gunsight, but had to return its watch, which was RAF property.

Despite the many acts of bravery that were performed on the Camel, only one of its pilots was awarded the Victoria Cross. This took place in the Italian theatre and was not without controversy. The recipient was Lt A. Jerrard of 66 Sqn, who was brought down by Austro-Hungarian machines on 30 March 1918 and made POW. The award was made on the basis of accounts by survivors of the combat, although their claims bore little relationship to the facts that later emerged. More controversy, on that battle front, was aroused by the loss of commanding officers of 66 and 45 Sqns. On 14 January 1918, the 66 Sqn CO, Maj R. Gregory, was shot down and killed in B2475 and a similar fate befell Maj A.M. Vaucour DFC MC, in D8102 on 16 July. Italian pilots shot down both.

Just as in France, Camel squadrons were pressed into the ground-attack role during time of crisis and, in Italy, the major crisis came with the Austro-Hungarian advance across the River Piave that began on 15 June 1918. Pontoon bridges and troop concentrations were bombed and machine-gunned during an intense week, until the pressure was relieved by the forces of nature: floodwaters carried away the enemy bridges.

Squadrons 28 and 66 continued to fly and fight over Italy for the remainder of the war, but 45 Sqn was withdrawn during September 1918 and attached to the Independent Force (IF) in North-Eastern France. Although scheduled to receive Snipes, for long-range escort work, the unit continued to fly Camels and achieved some further combat successes. During this latter period, its most successful pilot was Capt J.W. Pinder DFC, who accounted for half of the ten victories claimed with the IF. However, activity was limited, as indicated by the experience of 2Lt G. Exley who only made 17 flights between 28 September and the Armistice.

Foreign-Flown Camels

The entry of the USA into the war, on the Allied side, signalled the ultimate neutralizing of the Central Powers. The March push had been made in the hope of achieving a breakthrough, before the American might in manpower and equipment could be brought to bear. The USAS had no shortage of personnel, but was lacking in machines. A large number of its pilots were attached to units of the RFC and RAF to gain combat experience. An arrangement was reached, during the late spring of 1918, whereby the RAF would supply sufficient Camels, with Le Rhone engines to maintain two American squadrons. The pilots of the 148th Aero Sqn were attached to 3, 43 and 4 AFC Sqns. Those of its sister unit, the 17th Aero Sqn, were with 65, 70 and 3 Sqns. Some had been with S.E.5a equipped units, but were transferred to those RAF Camel squadrons in anticipation of converting to that type.

The 17th Aero Sqn was formally activated on 20 June 1918, when its HQ and three flights were brought together at Petite Synthe under the command of 1Lt E.B. Eckert. The 148th was similarly activated at Capelle on 1 July, its CO being 1Lt M.L. Newhall. Both units were under RAF control, initially that of 65 Wing and drew their machines from RAF stocks. Standard RAF unit markings were allotted, a white dumbbell for the 17th and a white triangle for the 148th.

The RAF training soon brought dividends, as both squadrons began achieving combat success. During August, they moved south to the Amiens sector and transferred to the 13th Wing of 3 Brigade. More intense air fighting was developing and although combat successes mounted, so too did casualties. Both squadrons had their bad days. On 26 August, the 17th lost six aeroplanes in a fight with Fokker D VIIs that developed during its late afternoon patrol. Two pilots, 1Lt L.C. Roberts and 2Lt H.H. Jackson, were killed and the other four were made POW. These were 1Lt H.B. Frost, 2Lt R.M. Todd, 2Lt H.P. Bittinger and 1Lt W.D. Tipton. Six days later, the 148th lost four in a combat with *Jasta* 2; 1Lt L.H. Forster being killed, with 2Lt J.D. Kenyon, 2Lt O. Mandel and 2Lt J.E. Frobisher becoming POW. Despite such losses, both units took a toll on enemy machines and several of their pilots returned substantial numbers of 'victory' claims.

In the 148th Aero Sqn, the leading fighter was 1Lt E.W. Springs, who was posted to the unit after service and wounding with 85 Sqn on S.E.5as. In less than two months, Springs was credited with twelve combat 'victories', ten of which were over Fokker D VIIs. Elliot Springs is probably best known today as a novelist and he first came to the public eye in this field through his editorship of the book *War Birds*, based on the diary of his friend J.M. Grider. 1Lt G.A. Vaughn Jnr was a 'star turn' in the 17th. He had flown with 84 Sqn on S.E.5as and amassed seven 'victories' before his transfer to the American unit. He added a further six on Camels with the 17th.

Although the American war machine was gearing up for production, demands for machines (especially fighting scouts) could not be met. An agreement was reached, therefore, whereby the USAS could obtain Camels from British production. Although the exact extent of the subsequent order has not been established (one of 300 machines has been suggested), it is known that at least 208 were allocated and 143 were delivered. Boulton & Paul of Norwich was the contractor and American preference was for machines powered by the 150hp Gnome Monosoupape. Ninety-four of the machines delivered had this more powerful engine, the remainder having the standard Clerget, but there was little difference in performance. These machines were delivered in full American national insignia.

Further Aero Squadrons were equipped. The 27th had some Camels by early July 1918, but relinquished these in favour of SPAD XIIIs. The 147th had Camels by October, but they were transferred to the 185th, which was activated as a night-fighting squadron and adopted the appropriate unit insignia of a bat. The 41st and 138th Aero Squadrons were in the 5th Pursuit Group and both received Gnome-powered Camels as the war drew to a close. Other Camels, mainly those with the Clerget engine, were used at the American training centres at Toul and Issoudun. However, the US authorities had a preference for the SPAD and the vast majority of Camels had been withdrawn from front-line units by the time of the Armistice. A number of these machines were shipped to the United States after the cessation of hostilities.

Despite initial interest in the Camel, no French orders materialized. There was some Italian interest in acquiring the type, but this came to nothing. Other than the USA, the only other Allied nations to operate the Camel in wartime were Greece and Belgium. Mention has already been made of those supplied to the former and deliveries to the latter were of a slightly greater number. The Aviation Militaire Belge received

---

Known F1 Camels Transferred to/bought by the USAS

B3772, C3281, C3282, C3285, C3287, C3289, C3291, C3293, C3295, C3297, C3299, C3301, C3303, C3305, C3307, C3309, C3311, C3313, C3315, C3317, C3319, C3321, C3323, C3325, C3327, C3329, C3331, C3333, C3335, C3337, C3339, C3341, C3345, C3346, C3348, C3350, C3352, C3354, C3356, C3358, C3360, C3361, C3362, C3364, C3366, C3368, C3370, C3372, C3374, C3376, D9400, D9518, D9520, D9522, D9524, D9526, D9528, D9530, E1423, E1424, E1425, E1426, E1428, E1431, E1450, E1451, E1452, E1453, E1454, E1475, E1476, E7145, E7290, F1301, F1302, F1304, F1306, F1308, F1316, F1318, F1322, F1332, F1338, F1340, F1342, F1344, F1346, F1348, F1350, F1354, F1356, F1360, F1362, F1364, F1366, F1368, F1370, F1372, F1374, F1376, F1378, F1380, F1382, F1384, F1418, F1419, F1421, F1422, F1423, F1424, F1425, F1426, F1427, F1428, F1429, F1430, F1431, F1432, F1433, F1434, F1435, F1436, F1437, F1438, F1439, F1440, F1442, F1443, F1444, F1445, F1446, F1447, F1448, F1449, F1450, F1451, F1452, F1453, F1454, F1455, F1456, F1457, F1458, F1459, F1460, F1461, F1463, F1464, F1465, F1466, F1467, F1468, F1469, F1470, F1471, F1472, F1473, F1474, F1475, F1476, F1477, F1478, F1479, F1480, F1481, F1482, F1483, F1484, F1485, F1486, F1487, F1488, F1489, F1490, F1491, F1492, F1493, F1494, F1495, F1496, F1497, F1498, F1499, F1500, F1501, F1502, F1503, F1504, F1505, F1506, F1507, F1508, F1509, F1510, F1511, F1512, F1513, F1514, F1515, F1517, F1519, F1521, F1523, F1525, F1527, F1529, F1531, F1533, F1535, F1537, F1539, F1541, F1543, F1545, F1547, F1549.

These serials do not include Camels drawn from British stocks by the 17th and 148th Aero Squadrons when those units were attached to the RAF.

F1 Camels as early as November 1917 and fifty-four were initially intended for that force. Deliveries were essentially completed by the spring of 1918. Further machines were intended for delivery shortly before the Armistice and were parked ready for collection at 1 ASD Marquise, but the Belgian authorities were not informed until almost two months later. The intervening exposure to the elements meant that all nine Camels were totally unusable. In Belgian service, the Camel was operated by several units, including the 1ère, 9ère and 11ère Escadrilles de Chasse, but saw little combat. Pilots of the 1ère Escadrille preferred the Hanriot HD1 and exchanged their Camels for that poorer armed machine. Belgian observation squadrons were allotted small numbers of single-seat fighting scouts for escort duties and several operated Camels. The type did not disappear from the Belgian inventory until several years after the Armistice, some still being in service during 1923.

Home Defence

The Camel had an early introduction to Home Defence duties. The start of daylight aeroplane raids, mainly by Gothas and against London and the South-East from May 1917, coincided with the type's service introduction.

The RNAS, although intent on re-equipping its units in France, deployed small numbers of Camels to its bases at Eastchurch and Manston, machines from the latter also using Westgate. B3774, from Manston, flew that service's first anti-Gotha patrol for the type on 4 July, although an unspecified Camel (either B3751 or one of the prototypes) from Martlesham Heath beat it into the air by five minutes. More RNAS Camels intercepted the raid on 7 July and Flt Lt J.E. Scott in B3774 claimed one Gotha

destroyed, although this can be disputed. Three Gothas were destroyed during the raid of 22 August, but claims outnumbered victims. FSL E.B. Drake, in B3844 from Manston, almost certainly destroyed one and another was probably that claimed independently by Flt Lt A.F. Brandon, in a Manston Camel, and Pups from Dover and Walmer. It seems likely that the third was a victim of AA fire.

Despite the urgent need to replace the, by then, hopelessly outdated Sopwith 1½ Strutters in 43 and 45 Sqns, public outrage at the raids prompted urgent action by the RFC. The Home Defence force was still largely equipped with an assortment of B.E.2 and B.E.12 variants. While these had been adequate in countering the airship

menace of the previous year, such aeroplanes were hopelessly outclassed by the new threat. An initial response had been to redeploy certain Training Squadrons, that had single-seat fighting scouts as part of their establishments, to bases in the South-East, but the decision was then made, without reference to the RFC in France, to retain a proportion of Camel deliveries for Home Defence duty. Accordingly, twenty-four of the fifty-four Camels allotted to the RFC in the field during July were to be diverted to the Home Defence Group. These machines were drawn from the second Sopwith-built batch and the first so diverted were passed to 39 HD Sqn C Flt at Hainault Farm. This was, however, only a temporary measure, pending the

reformation of 44 Sqn in the Home Defence role. The Camel pilots of 39 Sqn were airborne against the 22 July raid, but failed to intercept the attackers.

44 Sqn duly reformed at Hainault Farm on 24 July and took over the machines from the colocated unit. The unit was provided with not only the latest fighting scout, but also an establishment of experienced pilots, many of whom had combat experience. Its initial personnel included Capts C.J.Q. Brand, T. Gran (the noted Norwegian pilot), G.W. Murlis-Green (who had achieved considerable combat success in Macedonia), J.I. McKay, G.A.H. Pidcock and Lt D.V. Armstrong. The latter two had each been credited with a victory on Nieuports, while serving with 60 Sqn

The outcry against the daylight Gotha raids caused Camels to be diverted to Home Defence duty. B2402 was an early machine with 44 Sqn at Hainault Farm and is shown in standard configuration. It was later converted to a 'Comic' night-fighter. JMB/GSL

and both would later improve upon that success. Armstrong has achieved lasting fame for his aerobatic prowess and it was with the Camel that this reputation was consolidated.

65 Sqn had been moved from Wyton to Wye in response to the Gotha raids. Its earlier equipment comprised Pups and D.H.5s and these were supplemented from early August with Camels. The unit was in the process of 'working up' for service in France, but remained on Home Defence duty until its final mobilization period. Although its Camels flew on some interceptions, no contact was made with the raiders.

A change in German tactics, probably as a result of losses incurred during August, led to a switch to night bombing. This made the raiding machines much more elusive and the night-flying B.E. types had virtually no chance of making contact. The machines of 44 Sqn, like those of Pup-equipped Home Defence units, were still regarded as day-fighting machines. Murlis-Green, although still a Captain, had been given command of 44 Sqn and had obtained permission, during the raid of 2/3 September, to mount a sortie. Along with Brand and 2Lt C.C. Banks, Murlis-Green made an uneventful patrol, in machines that were not fitted for night flying. It proved, however, that, despite its reputation, the Camel could be flown safely at night. As recorded by Cecil Lewis, in the classic *Sagittarius Rising*, the squadron began converting its pilots to night flying and soon came to be regarded as a night-fighting unit.

The initial conversion of 44 Sqn's Camels for their new role involved the installation of underwing brackets for Holt's flares, the fitting of wing-tip navigation lights and the lighting of cockpit instrumentation. The over-doping, in PC10/12 brown, of the white portions of national markings was a further concession to the need for camouflage.

A major problem with flying the Camel as a night fighter was the temporary blinding of its pilots when the Vickers guns were fired. This has been quoted as the reason for the adoption of the 'Comic' conversion that was armed with two Lewis guns on overwing mountings. The history of the 6th Brigade, written in 1919, gives a further reason for this conversion. 'RTS' ammunition had been introduced. It had both incendiary and explosive properties and, as such, was much more effective than existing types, such as Buckingham, but was highly sensitive. Firing such ammunition through the propeller arc was considered dangerous and required the transfer of guns to the upper centre section, from where the propeller arc could be cleared. A pair of the light Lewis guns was the obvious choice for this and should they be accessible to a Camel pilot, the cockpit had to be moved aft.

That was the basis of the conversion. The main pressure and gravity tanks were removed and the place taken by the cockpit. A B.E.2e main tank, of approximately half (18 gallons/82 litres) the capacity of the ones removed was placed in the former cockpit position. The forward decking 'hump' was eliminated and a lowered and rounded decking was extended from the cowling to the new cockpit position. The centre section was opened up and a pair of

S.E.5-type Foster mountings were fitted 16in (41cm) apart and aligned upwards at 15 degrees to the thrust line. A headrest was usually fitted behind the cockpit. The revised airframe and weight reduction gained from using a smaller capacity tank had a marvellous effect on performance. Although there was no improvement in speed, the climb rate and manoeuvrability at height were dramatically improved. A height of 20,000ft (6,100m) could be reached in just over 31 minutes and it could turn well at that height, being still below its ceiling (which has been quoted as 22,000ft/6,700m).

It is not known where and when the first 'Comic' conversion was made, but it seems likely that it was by 44 Sqn and during

flying a Camel armed with twin Lewis guns when he had so damaged a Gotha on the night of 18/19 December that it was forced to ditch in the Channel. That machine (B5196) may have been the original conversion. Another Lewis-armed machine of the unit was B3827, which had an armament arrangement to the suggestion of Lt F.W. Scarff RNAS. This may have been a Camel that was partially modified to 'Comic' standard. A photograph shows such a machine with the cockpit in the rear position, but still with Vickers armament – although the weapons and their associated magazines and tanks were moved rearwards so as to be accessible in case of jams. A single Lewis was fitted to the starboard side of the cockpit, angled to

The 'Comic' conversion involved transposing the positions of the pilot and fuel tank, as well as the replacement of the Vickers guns by a pair of overwing Lewis. Navigation lights and brackets for Holt landing flares were added. JMB/GSL

November or December 1917. The inspiration must, undoubtedly, have been the earlier and similar conversion of a 1½ Strutter by Capt F.W. Honnett of 78 Sqn at Sutton's Farm, which was only a short distance from Hainault. That conversion had proved the feasibility of such a layout. It is also likely that 44 Sqn had tried other means of fitting Lewis guns to its machines. One of its otherwise standard F1s of C Flt had a single Lewis mounted in a fixed position on the port side of its centre section. Murlis-Green, still Captain (although commanding 44 Sqn) had been

fire upwards at 45 degrees and sighted by a Neame illuminated sight. The beneficial effect on a bullet's trajectory when fired upwards at such an angle had been proven in experiments at the Orfordness Experimental Station.

The first Camels to be used by Home Defence units were powered by Clerget engines and the problems that were associated with these power plants have been described. The 'Comic' conversion was usually Le Rhone powered. Not only was this engine more reliable, but it was also lighter. From early 1918, most, if not all,

Home Defence Camels were fitted with that engine. Despite the amazing performance gains that were made by adopting the 'Comic' configuration, only a small proportion of Home Defence Camels was so modified. This may have been due to the fact that the conversion was to be made at unit level, where time and resources were scarce and maintaining operational readiness was a priority.

The success of 44 Sqn in using the Camel at night and the growing output of those machines from various sub-contractors led to further squadrons converting to the type. At Sutton's Farm 78 Sqn received its first machines in January 1918 and was soon operational on the type. 112 Sqn at Throwley followed in March, 61 Sqn in June, 37 and 50 Sqns in July and 143 Sqn in August. In June, the VI Brigade had sixty-six Camels on charge, but that number had risen to 181 by the end of October.

Several of 44 Sqn's pilots were posted to some of these new Camel units and Capt C.J.Q. Brand received his majority when transferred to the command of 112 Sqn on 15 February 1918. It was with this unit that he gained the second confirmed 'victory' given to a 6th Brigade Camel pilot. On the night of 19 May, he encountered a Gotha over Faversham, Kent, and, after a brief exchange of fire, disabled its starboard engine. Brand followed the bomber down, firing short bursts, which caused it to explode in flames. Both Brand and his Camel were scorched, indicating how close the combat had been. Brand was a South African and his countryman, D.V. Armstrong, was also promoted from 44 Sqn to his captaincy as a flight commander in 78 Sqn.

Nightfighting in France

The successful introduction of the Camel to nocturnal Home Defence duties was followed by the decision to use the type in a similar role with the BEF. This was prompted by an increase in enemy night bombing of rear areas by Gotha, AEG and Friedrichshafen twin-engine machines. The formation of 151 Sqn was made especially for night-fighting overseas and it received a flight from each of 44, 78 and 112 Sqns. Command was initially given to Murlis-Green and the pilots drawn from the three contributing squadrons were some of the most experienced available. The unit was hastily assembled, coming together on 12 June, and it began flying out to France four days later, becoming

established at Fontaine-sur-Maye. Most of its machines were standard F1s, fitted with night-flying equipment, as the 'Comic' had too short an endurance for its intended role. A concession to pilot comfort was the fact that the starboard sides of the Camels' cockpits were not cut away. Command soon passed to Brand, who exchanged postings with Murlis-Green. The squadron was operational for less than five months, but in that time proved its worth, not just in bomber interception, but also in what would later be known as night-interdiction sorties.

Capt D.V. Armstrong was one of the 78 Sqn pilots posted to 151 Sqn, and he brought his 'personal' Camel C6713 with him. He had named this machine *Doris* and it had sported a red colour scheme

(Above) Night flying had its perils and Lt Baird of 44 Sqn lost his life in this crash. JMB/GSL

The 'Comic' was all but abandoned by late 1918 and night-fighting Camels resembled H739. This machine was with 37 Sqn C Flt and its usual pilot was Lt McFadden. via GSL

while with 78 Sqn, but, presumably, its finish was changed to a more appropriate one for service in France. It was in this machine, on the late evening of 29 June, that Armstrong opened the scoring for 151 Sqn by sending a LVG C type down out of control. He used this machine to gain his three subsequent 'victories' and was awarded the DFC for this work. Lt J.H. Summers also flew C6713 on occasions and used it on 21 September, when he and

and, in its short spell overseas, the unit was credited with twenty-six combat victories.

The success of 151 Sqn resulted in the formation of a further such unit, 152 Sqn. This new unit formed at Rochford, under the command of Maj E. Henty, and again drew pilots from existing Home Defence squadrons. It should be noted that these night-fighting squadrons were regarded as an extension of the 6th Brigade and that the provision of pilots for them was the

Two-Seater Camels

The high attrition rate on Camel training stations has already been alluded to. A typical accident occurred after a machine had entered a spin subsequent to a stall, particularly when climbing out after take-off. Take-off required that the engine was given a rich petrol/air mixture, but the need for this gradually decreased with height. Should the mixture fine-adjustment lever

The two-seat Camel was produced in an attempt to reduce training losses. The basis of the conversion is seen in this photograph taken at Montrose. The main tank was dispensed with, to accommodate the second seat. The small tank shown held both fuel and oil, but only gave a 20-minute endurance. JMB/GSL

Brand destroyed an AEG G type. However, Armstrong was killed in C6713 on 13 November; spinning in during a bout of low-level aerobatics.

It should be noted that Brand was no chairborne CO and a further four victories were added to that achieved with 112 Sqn, making him the highest scoring RAF nightfighter pilot of the conflict. Several of 151 Sqn's other pilots achieved further successes

responsibility of that higher formation. To that end, the 6th Brigade operated its own training system and the best of its graduates were then posted (from 188, 189 or 198 TS) to such duties. On October 1918, 152 Sqn arrived at its designated French aerodrome, but it was too late for operational service. A further unit, 153 Sqn, formed at Hainault Farm on 4 November, but served in a training role.

be left in its take-off position, the engine would splutter, choke in the climb and then stall. All too often, trainee pilots would react too slowly to this and a spin would develop. Recovery was usually impossible from such a low altitude and the consequences were often fatal. It was in an attempt to reduce these training casualties that the two-seat trainer version of the Camel was developed.

Credit for the first conversion of a Camel to this configuration is usually given to the officers of the 23rd Training Wing at South Carlton in Lincolnshire and under the command of Lt Col L.A. Strange DSO MC. During the first part of 1918, that station housed 39 and 45 TS, while the other station in the Wing, Scampton, was home to 81 Sqn as well as 11 and 60 TS. All five of these units operated Camels in the training role. B3801, Sopwith-built as a standard F1, is fêted as the first such conversion, although the exact date of its metamorphosis is unknown. It may have been preceded by a more aggressive such conversion, for in June 1918 208 Sqn (ex-Naval Eight) modified one of its machines (possibly D1928) to two-seat form, with a Lewis gun for the passenger. The idea for this came from the fertile mind of the unit commander, Maj C. Draper DSC, with the thought of providing a shock for any enemy attacking from the rear. As soon as higher authority became aware of the conversion, orders were given for the machine to be returned to standard form.

The completed two-seat conversion is shown on B9140 of 42 TS at Wye. via GSL

As 1918 progressed, more home-based Camels were converted to two-seat trainers.

The conversion entailed extensive modifications to the fuselage. The Vickers guns,

Training unit Camels were usually unarmed and F9588 of the CFS was modified accordingly. It also had an unusual cut-away engine cowling. JMB/GSL

along with their magazines and ejection chutes, were discarded and the pilot's seat was moved slightly forward. This could cause the knee movement of that seat's occupant to be fouled by the carburettor induction pipe and so, in some cases, that pipe was raised to a position just below the upper longeron. The gravity tank and 30-gallon pressure tank were removed, allowing a second seat to be mounted in that location. Full dual control was fitted. A combined fuel/oil tank replaced the original oil tank under the front decking. Various styles of cockpit decking were added with most machines having separate cockpits, although B5575 (at least) had a communal cockpit.

Two-seat Camels, although never numerous, were operated on several training stations, additional to those mentioned above. Montrose, Upavon, Joyce Green, Cranwell, Eastchurch, Minchinhampton, Chattis Hill and Redcar are all known to have had examples on the strengths of their resident units. The revised fuel tank arrangement meant that the conversion had a very short endurance. G.M. Knocker was posted to 63 TS at Joyce Green after recovery from a wound received during April 1918. When that unit was moved to Redcar, he was tasked with flying its two-seat Camel to the new base but recorded that trying to do so, in a machine with only 20 minutes' endurance 'wasn't on'; he had managed to reach Fairlop on the first leg. The machine was returned to Joyce Green, dismantled and transported by rail.

Other Duties

Other F1 Camels had been used at home stations for Marine Operations. Flying boat and seaplane patrols, over the Channel and North Sea, began encountering determined opposition from German fighting seaplanes during 1917 and suffered losses. Camels replaced earlier types at such RNAS stations as Yarmouth, Dover and Walmer and flew on escort duties, although little contact was made with the enemy. Shortly after the formation of the RAF, these Defence Flights, along with other ex-RNAS units, were numbered in a sequence that ran from 300 upwards to avoid duplicating squadron numbers. Those flights still operating Camels were numbered as 470–487 Flts and, at home, these were 470 Flt at

Manston, 471 Flt at Walmer and 485/486 Flts at Burgh Castle (under Yarmouth control). From mid-1918, these flights were incorporated into squadrons that were numbered from 219 upwards. A further Camel unit, 487 Flt of 230 Sqn, was added during September.

The RAF and its predecessors had Experimental Stations at Grain, Martlesham Heath, Orfordness and, later, Butley, as well as the Royal Aircraft Factory (Royal Aircraft Establishment from 1 April 1918) at Farnborough. Camels were used at these for a variety of experimental and testing purposes. Much of the work done at Martlesham and Orfordness was related to performance and equipment testing. Some Camels were tested to provide official performance figures and others to assess the

was considered for all Camels and examples were sent to France, although were not used.

At Orfordness, most experimental work was concerned with armament and other equipment and some Camels were used for such work. An interesting modification was made to Camel B2541, which was fitted with a 150hp Gnome engine contained within an enclosed cowling. On 17 January 1919, Capt R.M. Charley recorded a height of 26,000ft (7,925m) in this machine, achieved during a flight of just 35 minutes. However, his barometer was found to be defective and the height was corrected to an estimated 21,540ft (6,565m) – still no mean achievement. Other Orfordness Camels were involved in testing pilot harnesses, as part of work involved in developing parachutes for air-

B2541 was modified at Orfordness for an attempted altitude record. Its modified cowling enclosed a 150hp Gnome engine. via H.S. Clarke

suitability of alternative engine installations. B3811 fell into the latter category, being fitted with a 100hp Gnome Monosoupape, which was replaced by a 130hp Le Rhone after being declared underpowered. The more powerful 150hp Gnome was the preferred engine of the USAS and both D6567 and F1336 were tested with that power plant. Towards the end of the war, F6394 was fitted with a 170hp Le Rhone and, perhaps due to the greater torque generated, was fitted with an enlarged rudder. Such a greater rudder area

crew. Pilots involved considered the harnesses restrictive to scanning the sky above and behind, an essential task for any scout pilot.

At Grain, F1 Camels were used for experiments in ditching machines and the development of suitable hydrovane and flotation gear. Successful ditchings were made during the summer of 1918, one machine used being B3878 which had earlier served with 8N Sqn. Another used for this purpose was B6229, which had also served with Naval Eight. At Felixstowe, at

After operational use, some Camels returned to the UK and training duties. One such was B3883. It had served with 9N Sqn and had several combat successes in the hands of H.F. Stackard and J.S.T. Fall. It was then used by the War School, later Pool of Pilots, at Manston and is seen here at Eastbourne. via A Kemp

least one F1 Camel, F3128, was used in the work to develop lighter-borne aeroplanes.

A further experimental programme was concerned with the dropping of machines from rigid airships. This was undertaken at the Pulham airship station and much of the final proving was done using 2F1s, but D8250 was used for the first successful unmanned drop on 3 November 1918. Another F1, H7343, was similarly dropped, in an experiment to assess the efficiency of Imber self-sealing fuel tanks. Other Camels served with naval units in the Adriatic and Aegean theatres of operations. One such unit, 2 Wing RNAS, had flown operations against the Turks in the Aegean since 1915. With HQ at Mudros, the Wing operated lettered squadrons and some of these received Camels. Some F1s from the first Sopwith-built batch were received as early as September 1917 and were operated by B, C, D and F Sqns form a variety of island bases. From April 1918, these units became numbered, and 2 Wing was redesignated 62 Wing, although it would seem that most squadrons kept their original identities until at least that summer. In the scheme of things, C Sqn at Imbros became 220 Sqn with three flights (475-477) and F Sqn became 222 Sqn with a further three (478-480). 221 Sqn, ex-D Sqn, is reported to have operated Camels, but was not assigned any flights in the numbered sequence allotted to that type. A small number of Camels, originally six but later increased, was transferred to the Royal Hellenic Naval Air Service, and operated by Z (Greek) Sqn, which was later absorbed into 222 Sqn.

Camel Pilot 3 – Maj D.R. MacLaren DSO DFC MC LdeH CdeG

Donald R. MacLaren was the most successful of all Camel pilots, being credited with fifty-four 'victories'. These were achieved in a combat career with 46 Sqn that lasted for more than ten months.

He had trained in Canada and served there on instructional duties before being posted to France and 46 Sqn in November 1917, as a 2nd Lt. His first 'victory' came some 3½ months later, a Hannover C type credited as being sent down out of control. From then on his scoring rate increased, especially after his promotion through to Captain and flight commander. He developed into a superb patrol leader, having the ability to place his formation in good attacking positions. Sixteen of his credited victories were shared with other 46 Sqn pilots and two of these included 2nd Lt V.M. Yeates, a

Halberstadt on 3 May and a DFW three days later. Six of his successes were against enemy kite balloons, which were usually exceptionally well-defended targets and another twenty-five were against enemy fighting scouts.

A 'victory' over an enemy C type, on 9 October, was his last. He broke his leg, playing football, the next day and was posted to England. Promotion to Major followed and he was involved in the creation of the Canadian Air Force at Upper Heyford and continued to serve with the CAF until the late 1920s, then went into civilian aviation. He died in 1969.

Photograph via N.L.R. Franks

Mediterranean Operations

The RNAS 6 Wing had set up bases in southern Italy during 1917, for bombing raids across the Adriatic. It became 66 Wing on 1 April 1918 and was joined by 67 Wing. Both of these parent formations operated Camels and each, eventually, had a dedicated Camel squadron for escort work: 225 Sqn (481–483 Flts) was based at Andrano in 66 Wing and 226 Sqn (472–474 Flts) operated from Pizzone with 67 Wing. Camels have also been reported as operating in small numbers by the other two squadrons of the Adriatic Group, 224 and 227 Sqns. As with the Aegean-based units, the Camel squadrons of the Adriatic Group saw little air-to-air combat and were frequently used as light bombers. In the post-war period, Camels from these two groups were used to help equip the RAF Mission sent to South Russia in support of the anti-Bolshevik cause.

The RFC and RAF also flew against the enemy in southern Europe. From 1916, 17 and 47 Sqns were based in Macedonia and each operated small numbers of fighting scouts for escort work. These fighter elements amalgamated on 1 April 1918 to form 150 Sqn and that new unit received some Camels the following month, which formed its C Flt. There was enough aerial opposition to provide combat opportunities and several of 150 Sqn's pilots had combat successes. Lt D.A. Davies was credited with ten 'victories', all enemy scouts, in the short period of two months from June 1918, all while flying C1599. Other successful Camel pilots with that unit included Lt J.C. Preston and Capt G.C. Gardiner. The unit's Camels were transferred to 17 Sqn from December 1918.

The type also flew in Egypt and the Middle East. At Heliopolis, 5 Fighting School had several Camels on strength and, towards the close of hostilities, 72 Sqn in Mesopotamia received a number of Boulton & Paul-built examples.

The Camel Post-War

The signing of the Armistice on 11 November soon resulted in a massive reduction of RAF units on the continent. On 31 October, the RAF with the BEF in France had 802 F1 Camels, the 5th Group had thirty-six, the Independent Force twenty-seven and seventy-five were with the 7th Brigade in Italy. Airframe stocks

were building up at home and new types, such as the Snipe, were beginning to enter service. The Camels were becoming redundant and there was no need to return them to the UK. Most were broken up. In Italy, this was done at 7 Aircraft Park and the crews returned home, most for demobilization, with a few remaining as squadron cadres. In France, 151 and 152 Sqns were designated as Demobilization Squadrons for those with RFC origins and 203 Sqn for those with RNAS connections. From January 1919, those squadrons that were not earmarked for policing duty in Germany delivered their machines to these Demobilization Squadrons where,

In the post-Armistice period, many pilots took the opportunity to 'paint up' their machines. One such was another 209 Sqn Camel, F6030. It too was a rebuild and had embellishments added to its decking, mainplanes and tailplane by Capt T. Gerrard, who is seen alongside his machine. via GSL

after guns and watches had been removed, the airframes were crushed before being burned or buried.

British operational use of the F1 Camel did not, however, end with the signing of the Armistice. RFC and RAF units had operated in Russia since 1917, first to bolster the Tsarist regime and, after the Revolution, in opposition to the Bolshevik government. There were two main centres of activity, in northern Russia around Murmansk and Archangel and in the south of that country, in the Caucasus.

At least five F1 Camels (F4054, F4055, F4058, F4061 and F4065) served with the Syren Force, in north Russia, from a

makeshift aerodrome at Lumbushi, on the northern shore of Lake Onega, some 450 miles (724km) south of Murmansk. The volunteer pilots were combat experienced and included Lt A. Jerrard VC (ex-19 and 66 Sqns), Capt F.O. Soden DFC (ex-60 and 41 Sqns) and Capt R Sykes DFC (ex-9N, 3N and 201 Sqns). They operated alongside a handful of R.E.8s and a detachment of Fairey IIICs. Aerial opposition was almost non-existent and so the Camels' main duty was attacking enemy communications. Sykes suffered the ignominy of being made POW, after the engine of F4055 failed during a bombing mission on 31 August 1919, but was later repatriated. The remainder of the unit had been withdrawn by early October and it seems likely that the machines were destroyed.

The RAF Mission in south Russia initially comprised 221 Sqn and members of 17 and 47 Sqns from the Macedonian front, these latter forming the basis of a revived 47 Sqn, under the command of Maj R. Collishaw DSO* DFC DSC, a successful exponent of the Camel. Volunteers from the UK replaced existing personnel in 47 Sqn and, just as in North Russia, these included several with existing combat success. The unit establishment included a flight of Camels and aerial opposition was greater on this front than in the north. Several of the pilots added to the combat successes that they had achieved during the Great War. Capt S.M. Kinkead DFC* DSC* (ex-201 Sqn) was credited with a further three 'victo-

Camels went to North Russia after the Armistice and were flown against Bolshevik forces, usually in the ground attack role. H2705 was with the RAF Contingent in north Russia. JMB/GSL

ries', Lt R.H. Daly (ex-10N Sqn) with four, and Collishaw one. The most successful was Capt M.H. Aten, who was credited with five enemy machines destroyed. The war in the Caucasus was a mobile one and the unit worked with the advancing forces of Gen Denikin, until internal feuding led to a collapse of the White Russian cause. 47 Sqn disbanded on 20 October 1919, its machines being

passed to the 11th, 12th and 13th Sqns of the 7th Division and its crews returning home.

The peacetime RAF had no place for the F1 Camel; it had outlived its usefulness. A few were retained for experimental purposes, but the type was soon declared obsolete. The 2F1 survived longer. Two F1s came onto the civil register, but the type was too idiosyncratic for regular pleasure flying. G-EBER (ex-F6302) was registered in Egypt, but only lasted three months in its civil guise before it crashed while performing aerobatics. G-EAWN was registered in 1919 and survived for three years before being dismantled. Three

others, G-CYFP to G-CYFR, appeared briefly on the Canadian civil register, having been Imperial Gift machines with the former identities of F6481, F6473 and F6310 respectively.

The USAS was short of indigenous fighting scouts at the end of the war and made arrangements to ship numbers home. This involved some of the F1 Camels that it had received and more than eighty were scheduled for shipment. No post-war army squadron was equipped with the type, but the US Navy received six from army stocks and these became A5658-59, A5721-22 and A5729-30. The USN had adopted the British idea of carrying aeroplanes on turret platforms and at least three of its Camels were allotted to the Ship Plane Units. Photographs show at least one of these Camels with full hydroplane and external flotation gear of the Grain type. USS *Texas* had two of these Camels during 1919, but no other American warship is known to have carried the type.

Despite the large numbers produced, few original F1 Camels survive. Pride of place must go to F6314, carefully restored and displayed by the RAF Museum at Hendon. In Brussels, B5747 is displayed in its Belgian markings as SC11, having undergone recent restoration. The fuselage of B7280, a 210 Sqn machine that was captured on 5 September 1918 after Capt H.A. Patey DSC had been brought down by Ltn Beckmann of *Jasta* 56, is dismantled at Krakow, Poland, where it was stored by its German captors during World War II. Another possible survivor is the machine on exhibition as 'E1537' in Arkansas, USA. There may be others and there are many more replicas, some flying, but most of the latter have radial engines.

Representative F1 Camels with RNAS/RFC/RAF Units

3 Sqn – Warloy/Vert Galand/Valheureux/Lechelle/Inchy: B2364, B2454, B2520, B5238, B5433, B5444, B5450, B6382, B7269, B7336, B7399, B9147, B9159, B9244, C1551, C1582, C1611, C1663, C1691, C8333, F6089, F6117, F6175, F6180, H801.

17 Sqn – Mikra Bay/San Stephano: C1598, C1600, D6551, D6553, F1911, F1913, F1914.

28 Sqn – Yatesbury/St Omer/Droglandt/Candas/Milan/Ghedi/Verona/Grossa/Sarcedo/Treviso/Sarcedo: B2303, B2316, B2362, B2422, B5622, B6251, B6306, B6314, B6315, C134, C1581, D8103, D8170, D8208, D8210, D8239, D8242, E1502, E1581.

31 Sqn – Risalpur: F1915.

37 Sqn – Stow Maries/Goldhanger/Biggin Hill: D9578, E1598, E5131, E5135, E5137, E5138, E5139, E5140, E5141, E5155.

39 Sqn – Hainault Farm/Gosport: B2536, B3752, B3763, B3764, B3765, B3767, B3776, B3815, B3816, B3827.

43 Sqn – Lozinghem/La Gorgue/Avesnes-le-Comte/Fouquerolles/Estrée Blanche/Touquin/Fienvillers: B2340, B2351, B2354, B2367, B2431, B2460, B5433, B5620, B5631, C8201, C8224, C8247, D1778, D1809, D6404, D9470, E1402, E1467, F5919.

44 Sqn – Hainault Farm: B5411, B5412, B9175, B9177, B9245, B9251, B9307, B9309, C8312, D6617, E5147, F1369, H739.

45 Sqn – Ste Marie Cappel/Fienvillers/Candas/Padua/San Pelagio/Istrana/Grossa/Bettoncourt/Izel-le-Hameau/Liettres: B2311, B2314, B2327, B2375, B2393, B2446, B2470, B5182, B5626, B6233, B6236, B6254, B6312, B7307, B7381, D1975, D9450.

46 Sqn – Filescamp Farm/Liettres/Serny/Poulainville/Cappy/Athies/Busigny/Baizieux: B2515, B3814, B4617, B4638, B5208, B5231, B5428, B5585, B5636, B9211,

Representative F1 Camels with RNAS/RFC/RAF Units *(continued)*

C1554, C1559, C1575, C1617, C1659, C3375, C6708, D6511, D6601, E5157, F6210.

47 Sqn – Beketovka: F1955, F6396, F6500.

50 Sqn – Bekesbourne: B7445, C6754, D6662, F2117, F2122, F2124, F2126, F2161, F2162, F5178.

54 Sqn – Bruay/ Lahoussoye/Flez/Champien/ Bertangles/Conteville/Clairmarais N/Caffiers/ St Omer/ Vignacourt/ Boisdinghem/ Liettres/Touquin/ Fienvillers/ Avesnes-le-Comte/ Rely/ Merchin: B2483, B5203, B5416, B5421, B6293, B6421, B7171, B7407, B7743, B9149, B9259, B9281, C1584, C1603, C3360, C3379, C8339, D1945, D6494, D6569, E5173, F2083, F6132, H7262.

61 Sqn – Rochford: E5130, E5131, E5137, E5162, F1309, F1311, F1325, F1369, F1389, F1393, F1997, F6389, H767, H4005.

65 Sqn – Wye/La Lovie/Bailleul/Poperinghe/ Droglandt/Clairmarais/Conteville/Bertangles/ Cappelle/Bray Dunes/Petite Synthe/ Bisseghem: B2380, B2383, B2414, B2419, B3847, B3977, B7744, B7804, B9144, B9166, B9188, C8250, C8264, C8290, C8291, D1807, D1810, D1815, D1876, D1903, D8118, D8148, D8158, D8172, D8193, D8204, E1415, E1537, F1938, H7007.

66 Sqn – Estrée Blanche/Candas/Milan/Verona/ Grossa/Treviso/San Pietro in Gu/Arcade/San Pietro in Gu: B2338, B2377, B2475, B2500, B3931, B4606, B5170, B5182, B5204, B5223, B5402, B5648, B6326, B7167, C46, C132, C135, D6640, E1577.

70 Sqn – Boisdinghem/Liettres/Poperinghe/Marieux/ Fienvillers/Remaisnil/Boisdinghem/Esquerdes/ Droglandt/Menin/Fort Cognelée/ Elsenborn/ Bickendorf: B2303, B2304, B2305, B2341, B2342, B2343, B2356, B2358, B2359, B2361, B2404, B2447, B2495, B3787, B3813, B3814, B5151, B5214, B5640, B6322, B7162, B7320, B7471, B9138, C1595, C8271, D9418, E7185.

71 Sqn/4 Sqn AFC – Castle Bromwich/St Omer/Bruay/ Clairmarais/Reclinghem/Serny/Auchel: B778, B2387, B2409, B2424, B2448, B2535, B4623, B5207, B5552, B5625, B7292, C8300, D1959, F1346, F1403, F1410, F1415, F1548, F1941, F5948.

72 Sqn – Baghdad: D6445, D6447, D6449, D6555, D6557, D6559, F6346.

73 Sqn – Lilbourne/St Omer/Liettres/Champien/Cachy/ Remaisnil/Beauvois/Fouquerolles/Planques/Touquin/ La Bellevue/Foucaucourt/Estrées-en-Chaussée/ Hervilly/Malincourt/Baizieux: B900, B2392, B2517, B2521, B2533, B4621, B5184, B5449, B5560, B5574, B5590, B5627, B6394, B7284, B7302, B7874, B9231, C1619, C8296, D6476, D6606, D8114, E7148, F1540.

74 Sqn – London Colney: B6222, B7789.

75 Sqn – Elmswell/North Weald Bassett: C3349, C3359, C6768, C8349, D6662, E5169, F1398, F2109, F2117, F2175, F2181.

78 Sqn – Sutton's Farm: B3752, B9253, B9297, B9305, B9311, C1563, C1582, C1625, C1689, C6714, C8312, D6688, F1371.

80 Sqn – Montrose/Beverley/Boisdinghem/Serny/ Champien/Cachy/Villers Bretonneux/Beauvois/ Remaisnil/Wamin/Belleville Farm/La Bellevue/ Fouquerolles/Liettres/Touquin/Vignacourt/Allonville/

Asseviller/Bouvincourt/Bertry West/Flaumont/Grand Fayt/Stree: B4625, B5447, B6264, B6265, B6266, B6304, B9165, B9170, B9171, B9173, B9175, B9179, B9201, B9209, B9223.

81 Sqn – Scampton: B6384, B7319, C7, C117, C118, C1602, C1604, C1608, C1666, C8209, D1807, D1808, D6472.

84 Sqn – Lilbourne: B3941, B3942, B3944, B3946.

86 Sqn – Wye/Northolt: B2380, B2383, B7230, B7396, B7425, B7772, B7789, C1682, C1684, C1688, C6789, E9977, F2093.

88 Sqn – Harling Road: B5196.

89 Sqn – Harling Road: B5201, B7336, B9264.

92 Sqn – Tangmere: B7828, D6510.

94 Sqn – Harling Road: B2510, B2511, B3847, B3945, B4603, B4640, B6315, B6324, B6395, B7308, B7321, B9226, B9266.

96 Sqn – North Shotwick: C8304, C8305, E9971, E9972, E9973, E9974, E9983.

112 Sqn – Throwley: B5215, B9301, C6748, C8349, D6403, D6415, D6429, D6437, E5129, E5153, F2090, F2109, F4175.

139 Sqn – Villaverla: B6313.

143 Sqn – Detling: C3349, C3359, E5169, F2175, F2181, H734, H737, H740.

150 Sqn – Kirec/Mikra Bay: C1586, C1587, C1597, C1598, C1599, C1600, D6551, D6553.

151 Sqn – Hainault Farm/Marquise/Fontaine-sur- Maye/Vignacourt/Bancourt/Liettres: B2504, B2517, B5412, B5446, B9301, C1629, C1653, C6717, C6725, C6753, C8229, C8277, D6405, D6423, D6573, D6660, D6682, D9441, E5142, F1887, F6090.

152 Sqn – Rochford/Carvin/Liettres: B5446, C6702, C6744, C6748, C8353, D6603, D8164, D9465, F1311, F1991, H6847.

153 Sqn – Hainault Farm: F1317, F1387, F1985, F1999.

1N Sqn/201 Sqn – Dover/Teteghem/Ste Marie Cap- pel/Fienvillers/Noux-les-Auxi/Baizieux/Beugnâtre/La Targette/Bethencourt: C63, C64, C144, C193, C195, D3363, D3393, D6431, D6434, D6528, D9586, E4379, E4407, F3227, F5918, F5941, F6022.

3N Sqn/203 Sqn – Furnes/Bray Dunes/Walmer/Bray Dunes/St Eloi/Treizennes/Liettres/Filescamp Farm/ Allonville/Filescamp Farm/Le Hameau/Bruille/ Auberchicourt/Orcq/Boisdinghem: B3855, B3856, B3857, B3858, B6401, B6408, B7184, B7185, B7187, B7219, B7220, B7222, B7223, C61, C191, C197, D3370, D3371, D3415, D3416, E4374, E4377, N6344, N6377, N6378.

4N Sqn/204 Sqn – Bray Dunes/Walmer/Bray Dunes/Teteghem/Cappelle/Teteghem/Heule: B3784, B3806, B3854, B3892, B3922, B3934, B6300, B6447, B7176, B7224, B7232, B7234, C72, C74, C75, D3332, D3361, D8187, D8188, D9600, E4384.

6N Sqn – Flez/Bray Dunes/Frontier Aerodrome: B3810, B3817, B3818, B3821, B3828, B3829, B3832, B3833, B3835, B3869, B3882, B3883, B3885, B3897, N6330, N6331, N6334, N6339, N6341, N6342, N6350, N6351, N6355, N6356, N6357, N6358.

8N Sqn/208 Sqn – St Eloi/Bray Dunes/Walmer/ Teteghem/La Gorgue/Serny/Tramecourt/Foucaucourt/ Estrées-en-Chaussées/ Maretz: B3757, B3758, B3759, B3853, B3854, B3857,

B3921, B3922, B3936, B6227, B6228, B6260, B6275, B6290, B6311, B6318, B6319, B6378, B6399, B7204, B7230, D1781, D3330, D3335, E1404, E1408, F1931, N6374, N6376, N6378, N6379.

9N Sqn/209 Sqn – Flez/Le Hameau/Frontier Aero- drome/Leffrinckhoucke/Frontier Aerodrome/Middle Aerodrome/Dover/ Middle Aerodrome/Teteghem/Bray Dunes/Cappelle/Bailleul/Clairmarais/Bertangles/Le Hameau/Bruille/Saultain/Froidmont: B3798, B3804, B3810, B3818, B3819, B3820, B3905, B3906, B3907, B5653, B5664, B5687, B6204, B6212, B6217, B6371, B6379, B7200, B7202, B7223, B7471, C58, C68, C198, D3326, D3327, D3328, E4393, E4394, F5990, H6998, N6356, N6370.

10N Sqn/210 Sqn – Droglandt/Leffrinckhoucke/ Teteghem/Treizennes/Liettres/St Omer/Ste Marie Cappel/Teteghem/Eringhem/Boussieres: B3760, B3781, B3808, B3809, B3860, B3912, B3919, B5658, B5659, B5750, B6202, B6203, B6204, B7153, B7155, B7202, B7205, C144, C200, D1883, D3332, D3336, E4404, E4407, N6354, N6357, N6359, N6371, N6373, N6376.

11N Sqn – Dunkerque/Hondschoote: B3785, B3809, B3934, B3935, B3937, N517.

12N Sqn – St Pol/Petite Synthe: B3759, B3760, B3810, B3834, B3882, B3897, B3905, B5551, B5651, B5666, B6259, B6297.

212 Sqn – Yarmouth: F3197, F3198.

Seaplane Defence Sqn/13N Sqn/213 Sqn – St Pol/ Bergues/Stalhille: B3761, B3773, B3774, B3865, B3935, B3936, B6239, B6240, B6390, B6400, B7226, B7234, C66, D3356, D3357, D3360, D8216, D8217, D3383, E4419, N6348, N6349, N6363.

219 Sqn 470 Flt – Manston/Bacton/Burgh Castle: E1518, F1518, F1520, F1522, F1524, F3918, F3926.

220 Sqn 475/476/477 Flts – Imbros/Pizzone/Mudros/ Imbros/Mudros: C51, D1970, D1971, D8140, D8141, D8142.

222 Sqn 478/479/480 Flts – Thasos/Stavros/ Marian/Mudros/Imbros/Mudros/San Stephano: C40, D1951, D8140, D9553, F1956.

225 Sqn 481/482/483 Flts – Alimini/Andrano/Pizzone: C56, D1914, D1915, D1916.

226 Sqn – Pizzone/Otranto/Andrano/Marsh/Mudros/ Pizzone: C42, C43, C44, C45, C53, C54, C55, C56, D1914, D1915, D1916.

230 Sqn 487 Flt – Butley: F3128, F3196.

233 Sqn 471 Flt – Walmer/Dover/Stalhille/Dover: D9434, D9436, D8179, F1526, F1528, F1530, F1534, F1536, F1537, F3956.

255 Sqn – Pembroke: D9542.

269 Sqn 484 Flt – Port Said:

273 Sqn 485/486 Flts – Yarmouth/Burgh Castle: C28, E1558, F3128, F3133, F3134, F8527.

AA Defence Flt – Gosport:

RNAS Station – Yarmouth: B3773, B3817, B5706, B5707, N6335, N6338.

RNAS Station – Redcar: B5720, B5721.

RNAS Station – Grain: B3878, B6229, N6375.

17th Aero Sqn USAS – Petite Synthe/Auxi- leChâteau/Soncamp: B7407, B7896, C141, D1938, D1940, D1941, D6513, H830.

148th Aero Sqn USAS – Capelle/Allonville/

Representative F1 Camels with RNAS/RFC/RAF Units *(continued)*

Remaisnil/Baizieux: B7349, D9555, D8180, D8195, D8196, F6169, F6185, H7379.
1 TS – Beaulieu: B885, B4620, B4639, B5167, B5631, B6287, B7142, B9324, C96, C172, C8210, C8322, F1357, F2199.
2 TS – Northolt: B5200.
3 TS – Shoreham: B2385, B9282.
6 TS – Montrose: B2335, B4621, B5617, B7436, C79, C80, C111, C112, D6672, D6676, D9535, E1445, E1447, E1448, E1449.
10 TS – Shawbury/Lilbourne/Gosport: B2310, B7316, B7359, B9132, B9242, B9316, C8, C15, C16, C92, E1507, E1508.
11 TS – Scampton: B4625, B7281, B7431, B7457, C114, D1808.
15 TS – Spittlegate: B7433.
18 TS – Montrose: B2502, B4637, B5189, B5225, B5618, B6295, B7345, B7371, B7421, B7422, B7423, C6, C11, C79, E1446.
29 (Australian) TS – Shawbury: B2515.
29 TS – Hendon/Stag Lane/Croydon: B3851, C172.
30 (Australian) TS – Shawbury/Ternhill: B2315, B6268, B6432, B6433, B6442, B9154, B9156.
34 TS – Ternhill/Chattis Hill: B2315, B3801, B3943, B4607, B4641, B6219, B6303, B6306, B6404, B6434, B7410, D8204.
36 TS – Montrose: B2504, B5184, B5185, B5189, B5555, B5617, B7455, B7461, B9244, C14, C16, D6678, D8132, D9533.
39 TS – South Carlton: B4122, B7301, B7319, B7391, B7433, D1806.
40 TS – Croydon/Tangmere: B5194, B5196, B5231, B5232, B5233, B5235, B6322, B6376, B7318, B9207, C152, C190, E1531.
42 TS – Wye: B2506, B5195, B5197, B5218, B7301, B7319, B7331, B7334, B7428, B7430, B7477, B7760, B7820, B9192.
43 TS – Ternhill/Chattis Hill: B7312, B7361, B7364, B7365, B7368, B7790, B7807, B9270, B9272, B9274.
45 TS – South Carlton: B4625, B7314, B9151, B9182, C13, C1612, C1618, D6466, D6668.
54 TS – Castle Bromwich/Eastbourne: B2480, B2486, B2519, B5215, B5589, B7363.
55 TS – Castle Bromwich/Lilbourne/North Shotwick: B2313, B6416, D8130.
60 TS – Scampton: B5598.
61 TS – South Carlton: B7133, B7443, C1666.
62 TS – Dover: B7464, B7476, C86, C171, D6430, D6510.
63 TS – Joyce Green/Redcar: B7435, B7760, B7821, B7822, C120, C130, E1574, F4013, F4014, F4015, F4016, F4017, F4187.
65 TS – Dover: B6315, B6395, B8830, B9146.
67 TS – Shawbury/North Shotwick: B2486, B2521, B4643, B6443, B7316, B9224, B9230, B9236, B9312, B9326, C10, C77.
68 TS – Bramham Moor: C158.
70 TS – Beaulieu: B5632, B7142, B7376, B7403, C66, C99, C184, E1525, F1361, F2199.
72 TS – Beverley: B4619, B4627, B7340, B7341, C8302, C8306, D8122, D8123, D8124, D8230, D9537, D9538.

73 TS – Turnhouse/Beaulieu: B2334, B2335, B2339, B2462, B2548, B4636, B5184, B5185, B5555, B6261, B6262, B6266.
74 TS – Castle Bromwich: B2519, B3946, B7793, B9232.
188 NTS – Throwley: C6738, D6683, F2004, F2017, F2088, F2105, F2107, H737.
189 NTS – Sutton's Farm: C3365, C8366, C8367, C8368, C8369, C8388, D6683, D9493, D9569, F1980, F1981, F1982, F2000.
198 NTS – Rochford: C3367, C3373, C8351, C8358, C8359, F1885, F1886, F1997, F1998, F1999, H747, H748, H7407.
5 TS AFC – Minchinhampton: B9158, C101, C104, C106, C110, C122, E1496, E1509, E5164, E7269, E7270, F1339, F1946.
6 TS AFC – Minchinhampton: B2315, B2318, B2515, B6432, B6433, B6436, B6442, B9162, B9215, B9248.
7 TS AFC – Leighterton: C108, C121.
8 TS AFC – Leighterton: C12, C121, C123, C127, E7267, E7287, F1347, F1948, F4170.
2 TDS – Gullane: B2335, B5613, B6295, B7421, C6742, C6743, C6750, C6751, C6766, C6767, C8222, C8325, C8330, D6670.
3 TDS – Lopcombe Corner: B6223, B6394, B7134, C124, C1678, C1680, D6478, D9532, E7138, E7275, E9973, F4177, H2688.
4 TDS – Hooton Park: B7297, C8.
5 TDS – Easton-on-the-Hill: B4664.
7 TDS – Feltwell: B3847, B4640, B7308, B7321, B9226, B9266, B9286, C8311, D9544.
8 TDS – Netheravon/Witney: B7401.
10 TDS – Harling Road: B2331, B6433, B7336, H7386.
16 TDS – Amria: D6533.
19 TDS – El Rimal: C1592, C1596, D6531, D6541.
26 TDS – Edzell: B7371, B7421, B7455, C6752, C6755, C6757, D9535.
28 TDS – Weston-on-the-Green: B7433, C68, C69, C1612, C1660, C8301, E1530, F6337, F6375, F6379, F6381, F6383, F6387.
29 TDS – Beaulieu: B2388, B3918, B7309, C96, C99, C184, C8321, C8322, F1359, F1922, F2205, F2206, F2207, F2208.
32 TDS – Montrose: B2504, B5185, B5250, B5555, B5618, B6218, B7136, B7177, C6752, C6755, D6676, D6678, E1441.
34 TDS – Scampton: B2547, B3801, B4625, B7136, B7431, B7457, D1808, D9564, D9565, D9566, E7156, E7157, F2189.
42 TDS – Hounslow: B7425, C190, E1532, E1561, E1571, E1572, E9975, H8253, F9637.
43 TDS – Chattis Hill: B5582, B6435, B7306, B7368, B7766, B7807, C95, C105, E7280, E7281, F1349, F1351, F9631, H8261.
46 TDS – South Carlton: B9172, D6668, E7147, E7148, E7149, E7152, E7154, E9966.
47 TDS – Doncaster: F6491.
51 TDS – North Shotwick: B2313, B6443, B7296, B7298, B7308, B9224, C107, D8126, D8128, E1462, E7271, E9972, F4184.
53 TDS – Dover: B2438, C2, C1676, E1566, E1567, F4188.
60 TDS – Aboukir: C1594, H760.

61 TDS – Tangmere: F6422.
RNAS Central Training Establishment/201 TDS/56 TDS – Cranwell: B5611, B5662, C23, C30, C93, D9546, F4213, F6024.
RNAS School/204 TDS – Eastchurch: B5570, B6280, B6281, C62, C1614, D1812, D9579, E1520, E1423, F4019, F4199.
RNAS School/205 & 212 TDS – Vendome: C8276, D6555, E1490, E1491, E1492, E1493, E1504, E1513, E1514, E1515.
206/50 TDS – Eastbourne: B888, B2438, B3819, B5717, B6230, B6291, B6318, B6340, C19, C57, C118, C3294, E1529, E7297.
RNAS School/207 TDS/54 TDS – Chingford/Fairlop: C88, C8328, E1420, E1421, E1422, E1533, F1417, F2104, F4196, F9508.
RNAS War School – Manston: B3761, B3773, B3774, B3798, B3819, B3822, B3843, B3923, B3924, B3925, B3926, B5666.
CFS – Upavon: B3802, B3901, B4623, B5165, B5166, B5643, B7369, B7370, H8291, H8292, H8294.
1 SAF – Ayr: B4640, B7146, B7465, B7467, B7470, B9134, B9207, C81.
2 SAF – Eastburn: D1935, D1936, D1937
1 SAF&G/1 FS – Turnberry & Ayr: B5560, B6398, B7479, B9212, B9262, C8207, C8211, C8305, D3367, E7181, E7225.
2 SAF&G/2 FS – Marske: B5554, B7449, B7451, C82, C83, C84, C167, C179, C180, E1401, E1532, E7295, F2094, H2720.
3 SAF&G/3 FS – Bircham Newton/Sedgeford: C91, C186, C187, C8318, C8320, E1474, E7236, E7237, E7239, E7253, H2724.
4 FS – Freiston: B3819, B5654, B5702, C18, C24, C27, C33, C34, C173, E1429, E1436, E1438, E7232.
SAF/5 FS – Heliopolis: C1591, D6533, D6537, D6539, F1902, F1908, F6318.
Grand Fleet SAF&G – East Fortune/Leuchars: E7255, E4415, F4210, F4211, F5014, F6356, F8497, F8529, F8541, F8545.
2 SSF/NEAFIS – Redcar: B3926, D3341, B7243, B7265, B7266.
NWAFIS – Ayr: B9134.
SEAFIS – Shoreham: E9968.
SSF/1 SSF/SWAFIS – Gosport: B5157, B5584, B6446, B7732, B9134, B7306, C9.
2 Wireless School – Penshurst: F2115.
Wireless Testing Park/WEE/IDE – Biggin Hill: B2534, B5234, B6303, C131, C1614.
Scout School 2 ASD – Candas: B5227.
RAF/RAE – Farnborough: B2312, B7756, B7863, D1965, F6456, H7363, N6340.
Experimental Station – Martlesham Heath: B2312, B3751, B3835, B3851, B3888, B4615, B4619, B5213, F6394, N518.
Experimental Station – Orfordness: B6218, N518.
Fleet Practice Station – Turnhouse: B5581, B5586, B5738, B5739, C6736, C6737, F1303, F1305, F3104, F3113, F3923, F3924.
Fleet Aeroplane Base – Donibristle: F5014, F5015, F5016, F5017, F5019, F5020, F5022, F5024, F5025, F8496, F8497, F8528.

CHAPTER EIGHT

Shipboard Sopwiths

The Royal Navy was preoccupied with the thought of bringing the enemy High Seas Fleet to battle and recognized the menace posed to its operations by the reconnaissance Zeppelins used by the German Navy. The RNAS, and later RAF, undertook much of the groundwork for future naval air operations in response to that threat. Initial ideas had concentrated on the use of seaplanes, but the limitations imposed on their operation led to the realization that more manoeuvrable landplanes were a better proposition, particularly if they could be operated from ships at sea. Sopwith types played a significant role in the development of naval flying; in the use of aeroplanes for fleet reconnaissance, fighting, strike operations and torpedo dropping.

Shipboard Pups

The idea of flying wheeled landplanes from ships was not a new one, even in January 1917. As early as 3 November 1915, Flt Cdr B.F. Fowler had flown a Bristol Scout C from a 64ft (19.5m) flying-off deck on HMS *Vindex*. The following day, Flt Lt R.J.J. Hope-Vere had flown a Deperdussin monoplane from a ramp fitted to the forecastle of HMS *Aurora*, but that type of machine, carried in that location, was too vulnerable to the elements. On 26 January 1917, Admiral Beatty set up the Grand Fleet Aircraft Committee, under the chairmanship of Rear Admiral Sir Hugh Evan-Thomas, whose brief was to make an assessment of the fleet's aircraft requirements. The subsequent report, prepared in only ten days, contained some far-reaching recommendations. These included the replacement of Baby seaplanes on HMS *Campania* by Sopwith Pups (as had already been done on HMS *Manxman*), the provision for such machines in certain light cruisers and the conversion of HMS *Furious*, then under completion on the Tyne, to an aircraft carrier. It was estimated that forty new aeroplanes would be needed.

Pups then being built by William Beardmore reflected the Admiralty's preoccupation with the Zeppelin menace and 42, from the batch 9901–9950, were completed as Type 9901a. This variation was not fitted with a Vickers gun, although the access panels for that weapon's magazine and feed were retained. A new centre section with an enlarged cut-out was fitted. A Lewis gun was mounted on a tripod ahead of the cockpit to fire forwards and upwards through this, at an angle that cleared the propeller arc. Alternative armament

Beardmore-built Type 9901a Ships Pup 9944 had a long career, serving aboard a selection of HM Ships, including Manxman, Yarmouth, Pegasus, Tiger, Southampton and Vindictive. It is seen here being transferred to its mother ship from a trawler. Like most Beardmore-built machines, it had a mounting for an upward-firing Lewis gun. JMB/GSL

comprised Le Prieur rockets, launching tubes for which could be mounted on the interplane struts. These Beardmore-built machines are easily recognizable in photographs, due to their having wing cockades marked in an inboard position, fuselage cockades further forward and elevators striped in national colours.

HMS *Manxman* received several of these early Beardmore-built Pups, including 9913, 9914, 9917, 9918, 9919 and 9920. The *Campania* soon had others, initially 9931–9934. The other seaplane carriers, *Vindex*, *Nairana* and *Pegasus* were later similarly equipped.

The Beardmore concern was allowed to redesign the Pup and its ideas were expressed in 9950, the last machine of its first batch of Pups. The new design was designated Beardmore WB.III and it incorporated a redesigned Pup fuselage that was mated to a new and folding wing structure. There were two basic versions, designated SB.IIIF (folding undercarriage) and SB.IIID (dropping undercarriage). Two production contracts were granted, with one hundred being produced (N6100–N6129 and N6680–N6749). Many of the second batch went directly to storage, the superior 2F1 Camel having entered service before they were delivered.

The conversion of carriers, cruisers and light cruisers to carry Pups involved the provision of flying-off platforms and decks. The term 'flying off' is significant, as at that time no thought had been given to retrieving machines, other than by salvaging them after they had been ditched. That machines could be flown off at all was due to the earlier development of a tail trestle, which placed them in flying attitude, and a quick release strop, which allowed them to be held until engine revolutions were sufficient for take-off. Five light cruisers were the first to be fitted with fixed platforms, in compliance with the committee's recommendations: HMS *Caledon*, *Cassandra*, *Cordelia*, *Dublin* and *Yarmouth*.

of ammunition and a signal pistol with cartridges. That Pup might have been 9901, which was transferred from HMS *Manxman* to Yarmouth on that date.

HMS *Furious*, completed with forward flying-off deck, had joined the fleet at Scapa Flow in July. Her initial complement of aeroplanes included five Beardmore-built Pups (N6450–N6454), which were delivered to the carrier at Tyneside during her final fitting out. The problem of aircraft retrieval was addressed by trials involving landing on that deck. This was achieved, with *Furious* under way, on 2 August, by Sqn Cdr E.H. Dunning DSC, in Pup N6452. The Pup had toggles fitted to its wing-tips and tail-skid. After flying parallel to *Furious* and past the superstructure, he then 'crabbed' across the deck and

satisfactory, requiring, as it did, great piloting skill. It was suggested that a more practical solution would be to provide a landing on deck at the rear of the ship. This met with some opposition, as it meant a further reduction in *Furious*'s armament, but was eventually adopted. The decision was made in October and the conversion completed by March 1918.

The problems of landing onto a deck were already being addressed at RNAS Grain. A dummy wooden deck was constructed on the aerodrome and Pups played a large part in the experiments that were conducted. Initially, thought was given to the use of arrester hooks and Sqn Cdr H.M. Cave-Brown-Cave tested this apparatus on 10 January 1917 using Pup 9497. The lightly loaded Pup was difficult to land in a restricted area and the next set of tests involved replacing the wheeled undercarriage with one of skids. 9922 was so fitted by 14 July, with an arrangement that incorporated the original undercarriage legs. It also had an arrester hook. The skid arrangement was pursued in further developments that did away with arrester gear and turned to fitting V-shaped horns to the undercarriage. These were designed to engage with closely spaced wires running the length of the deck and so bring the machine to a halt. Tests were first conducted during March 1918. N6438 was also used for such tests and these were extended to use the aft deck on HMS *Furious*. A successful landing was accomplished on 15 April, but a further attempt the following day resulted in the Pup coming to grief, after over-running into the barrier. Similar tests continued at Grain until the end of the war, but the idea of skid undercarriages was not adopted.

It was from HMS *Yarmouth* that the Grand Fleet Aircraft Committee's recommendations first bore fruit. *Yarmouth* sailed in support of a minelaying operation on 18 August 1917, carrying Pup N6430 and its pilot FSL B.A. Smart. A Zeppelin, the L23, was sighted on the morning of the 21st and N6430 was eventually launched. Smart climbed to 9,000ft (2,740m) and then used his height advantage to dive on the Zeppelin, some 3,000ft (915m) below. He made two attacks, diving after the second to 3,000ft. The Zeppelin had ignited and fell to the sea; there were no survivors. Smart had lost his parent ship and was preparing to make for Denmark when he saw smoke from the squadron. He ditched near to, and was picked up by the destroyer HMS *Prince*,

N6452 was the historic Ships Pup used by Sqn Cdr E.H. Dunning DSC to make the first deck landing on a carrier that was under way. That event took place on 2 August 1917 and a further attempt with that machine, five days later, resulted in a stall that caused N6452 to crash into the sea. Dunning was drowned and the mangled remains of his salvaged machine are shown in this photograph. JMB/GSL

The feasibility of using the Pup was put to the test on 28 June 1917. Flt Cdr F.J. Rutland had been a staunch advocate of the Pup as a shipboard aeroplane and his views may have influenced the committee. It was that pilot who made the type's first take-off from a platform, on HMS *Yarmouth* and his machine was fully loaded, with Lewis gun, two double drums

a handling crew grabbed the toggles. The engine was then cut and a safe landing made. Dunning repeated this five days later in N6453, but that Pup was damaged. A third attempt was then made, again using N6452. The engine faltered at the crucial moment and the Pup went over the bows. Dunning was drowned. The method itself was abandoned; it was not considered

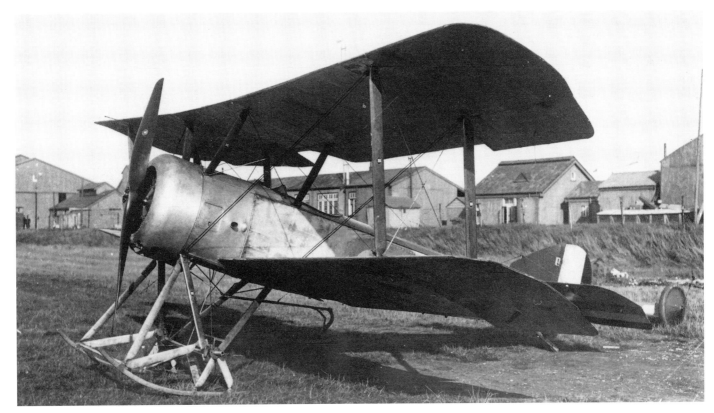

(Above) **Many deck-landing experiments were conducted at Grain, where a dummy deck was laid out. This Beardmore-built Ships Pup had any early form of skid undercarriage and an arrester hook for the purpose.** JMB/GSL

N6438 was initially issued to the Defence Flight at Walmer but later served on HMS Pegasus, Repulse, Tiger **and** Nairana. **It was subsequently fitted with skid undercarriage and used for deck landing experiments on** Furious. **It overshot on one of these and ended in the safety ropes at the forward end of the aft deck. Its fuselage name 'Excuse Me' seems quite appropriate to the occasion and is reminiscent of the names added to Pups of 3N Sqn. Like all Beardmore-built machines, it had its elevators marked in national colours.** JMB/GSL

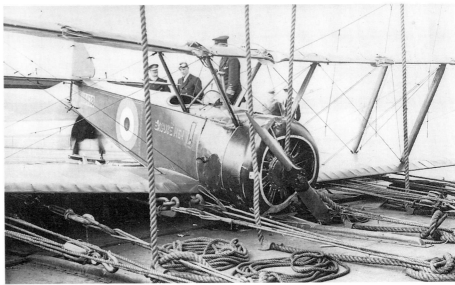

but his machine could not be salvaged. Smart was made a DSO.

Smart's success encouraged the Admiralty make it a policy that all future aeroplanes with the Grand Fleet would be of landplane configuration and to consider providing such machines for capital ships. This latter raised a problem, because hitherto ships had to turn into wind to launch aeroplanes. Were capital ships to do this, they would have to leave the battle-line,

something that went against the whole doctrine of naval battle tactics. The simple solution suggested by Lt Cdr C.H.B. Gowan was to have a rotating platform, that could be turned into the 'felt' wind, and the easiest way to achieve this was to employ the existing main gun turrets. HMS Repulse was selected for a trial of this method and a sloping platform, with tail trestle, was added to her forward B turret. Sqn Cdr F.J. Rutland was the pilot for the

test and on 1 October 1917 he had little difficulty in lifting off Pup N6453, with the turret at 42 degrees to starboard producing a felt wind of more than 30 knots. The platform was transferred to the aft Y turret and a similarly satisfactory take-off was achieved. These successes led to the widespread adoption of such platforms on capital ships, initially just for fighters, but later for reconnaissance machines as well. The Pup and Beardmore WB.III were, by

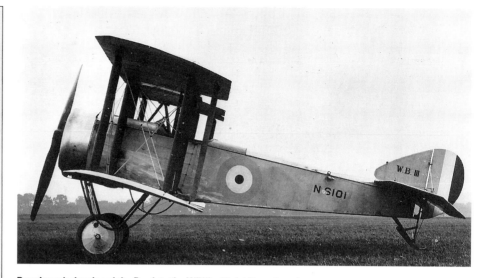

Beardmore's developed the Pup into the WBIII with folding wings for easy stowage aboard ship. N6100, the second production machine, had folding undercarriage to facilitate ditching and was designated SBIIIF, as was N6101. The others were SBIIID, with dropping undercarriage. via author

then, nearing the end of their useful lives and a further Sopwith design was ready to replace them.

The Camel Goes to Sea

The 2F1 is often thought of as little more than a shipboard version of the Camel but, in reality, there were fewer common components than may be thought. The 2F1 had its genesis in the desire to improve on the Baby seaplane, which was, after all, a development of the original Tabloid of 1913. The serial numbers N4 and N5 were allotted to Sopwith, during the week ending 1 December 1916, for two Baby (Improved) Seaplanes, to be powered by 130hp Clerget 9B engines and which were given the designation FS1. This was at the time that the company was finalizing the

prototype F1 and the design of that machine bore external similarities to the first FS1, N4, as it is depicted on manufacturer's drawings. No photograph of N4 is known to exist.

The FS1 floatplane had the fuselage shape and proportions of the F1, but embodied the split fuselage that had been adopted in the Baby. Only a single Vickers gun was mounted, to port, and the rounded forward decking swept upwards from the cowling, to serve as a windshield, as on the first F1. The wingspan was narrower, presumably to make accommodation aboard

N5 was the FS1 landplane and was the prototype for the 2F1 Ships Camel. It is seen here in its original guise, with an inverted Lewis gun on the top wing and a single Vickers on the port side of the fuselage. The FS1 was originally known as the Baby (Improved) Seaplane and had the split fuselage of the earlier type. N5 was delivered during March 1917 and is seen here at Martlesham Heath. JMB/GSL

ships easier, and this was accomplished by the adoption of a narrower centre section. Upper mainplanes were a common component of the F1, but the lower ones had, of necessity, reduced span. Long-span ailerons, of six full rib widths, are indicated on drawings, as is a small centre-section cut-out. A Lewis gun was mounted inverted on the centre section, whose struts were of steel tubing and of noticeably narrower chord than that of the F1. The main undercarriage was a pair of pontoon floats and a streamlined tail float, which incorporated a water rudder, supplemented this. Contemporary developments in the launching of aeroplanes from capital ships were recognized by the provision of a wheeled dolly that could be used on take-off.

N5 was built with a wheeled undercarriage, either as a landplane variant or to incorporate a more conventional method of launching from ships. It resembled the N4 drawings in most other respects, including the centre-section cut-out and inverted Lewis gun, but had a more flattened top to its forward decking, necessitating the provision of a small windscreen. N4 was delivered by Hawker to the RNAS Type Test Flight at Grain on 24 March 1917, presumably being flown off the Thames. It was reported wrecked three days later. Although it is not thought to have been rebuilt, it was not until 26 November that it was finally struck off charge.

N5 had a longer career. It flew from Brooklands to Hendon on 3 March and subsequently to the Testing Squadron at Martlesham Heath, where it crashed on the 27th. It was rebuilt, possibly by the RNAS Experimental Construction Department at Grain, where it was reported eight days later. Its reconstruction involved some modifications, the most obvious being to its armament. The Vickers gun was retained, but the Lewis gun was then carried on an early form of the Bowen & Williams (Admiralty) top-plane mounting, which allowed that weapon to be lowered for both reloading and upward firing. The latter ability, combined with the provision for Le Prieur rockets, hinted at the foreseen use of the type as an anti-airship weapon. A semi-retractable, wind-driven generator was mounted on the port fuselage side, to provide power for a W/T set, whose trailing aerial was fed through a fair-lead that protruded from under the cockpit area. An indication of its intended shipboard use was the provision of

slinging points above the centre-section struts. It has been suggested that flotation bags were fitted inside the rear fuselage, these being available in a range of sizes that allowed one to be fitted in each of the rear fuselage bays. If this were the case, then the bags would have hampered the control runs for the elevators, which were internal, as on the F1.

It would seem that plans were then made to convert N5 to floatplane configuration,

presumably to replace N4. These were not carried out and N5 had been returned to Grain by December 1917 and was eventually struck off charge on 9 July 1918.

Production versions had already been ordered, with Sopwith receiving a contract for fifty machines on 8 September. These were given the designation 2F1 and were referred to as Ships Camels. This may have been in response to an Admiralty paper of 30 August, which stated that 'The

N5 was involved in an accident and it may have been subsequent to that event that it is shown in this print, with a white rear fuselage serial. Later still, it was fitted with an early form of the Bowen & Williams top-plane mounting and WT generator. Its centre section had a deeper rear cut-out than production 2F1s. JMB/GSL

The split fuselage of the 2F1 Ships Camel is shown in this photograph of an unidentified, but light-coloured machine at Rosyth. The turnbuckles, which clipped onto the rear fuselage before being tensioned, are clearly visible. FW Weatherill

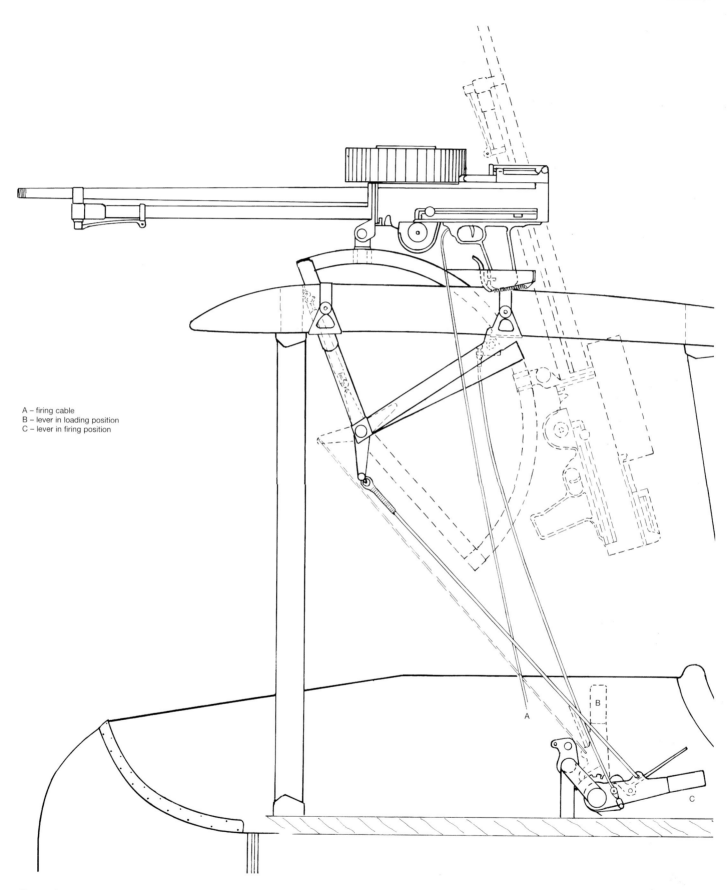

A – firing cable
B – lever in loading position
C – lever in firing position

Bowen & Williams (Admiralty) top-plane mounting for Lewis gun.

The principal features of the 2F1 are shown in this well-known but clear shot of N7146 and N7149 at
Turnhouse, the Fleet Practice Station. These 2F1s were from a batch of ten that were subcontracted to
Arroll Johnson of Dumfries, from Beardmore's. JMB/GSL

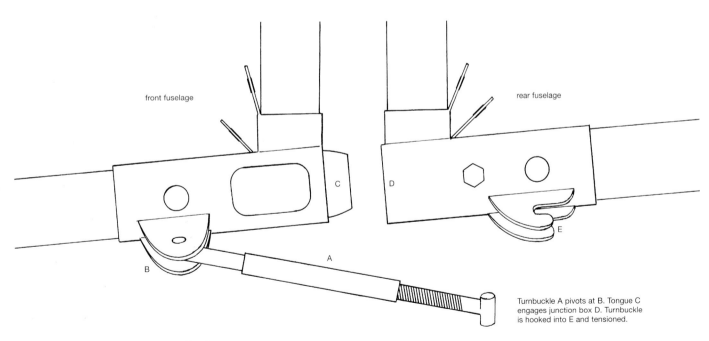

front fuselage

rear fuselage

Turnbuckle A pivots at B. Tongue C
engages junction box D. Turnbuckle
is hooked into E and tensioned.

Turnbuckle Arrangement Securing Rear Fuselage

The 2F1 Camel inherited the method, pioneered on the Baby, of making the rear fuselage detachable for
easy shipboard stowage. There were vertical and horizontal spacers at each side of the fuselage division
that provided rigidity. A joint box sleeved each longeron and these incorporated lugs for internal cross-
bracing. The four forward joint boxes also had lugs that were holed to accept the ends of turnbuckles. The
joint boxes on the rear fuselage were essentially similar but had simple hooked lugs to accept the other
ends of the turnbuckles. When the fuselage halves were mated, the turnbuckles were slipped over the rear
hooks and tensioned to create the correct alignment.

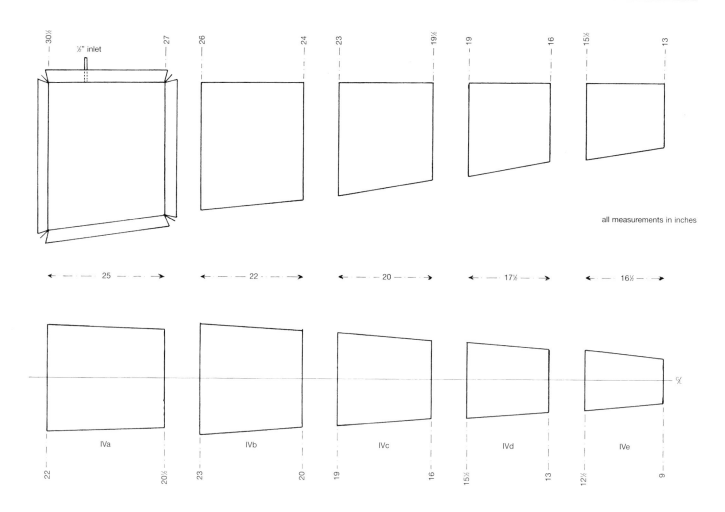

all measurements in inches

IVa   IVb   IVc   IVd   IVe

Flotation Bags (fuselage Mk IV illustrated)
Flotation bags were fitted to the rear fuselage bays of Sopwith aeroplanes designed for shipboard use. These bags were in a range of standardized sizes and were designed to fit each rear fuselage bay, being of diminishing depth and width.

Few 2F1s were presentation machines. N7149 'Swillington' shown in the previous photograph was one, and another was this unidentified machine marked 'Trimley St Martin'. The narrow, less splayed, steel tube centre-section struts of the 2F1 are evident, although the machine lacks its top gun. JMB/GSL

reply, or antidote, to hostile aircraft is better aircraft on our side'. Further contracts were placed with established contractors; Clayton & Shuttleworth, Hooper & Co. and Beardmore, the latter using Arrol-Johnston Ltd as a subcontractor. At least 230 production machines were delivered and these differed from the prototypes in having the 150hp BR1 engine, whose greater diameter necessitated the adoption of the revised cowling that had been introduced on the BR1-powered F1. Also, there were external elevator control runs, which connected to rocking levers at the forward end of the detachable rear fuselage and allowed full use to be made of flotation equipment. At last, the fleet had a truly effective fighter that was capable of intercepting Zeppelins on reconnaissance duty. The 2F1 proved its worth in this role and, perhaps more significantly, proved the concept of the shipborne strike aeroplane.

The first 2F1s were delivered from October 1917. A few of the first production batch were delivered to RNAS shore stations, but most were for service on light cruisers and capital ships, where they first replaced Pups and Beardmore WB.IIIs on flying-off platforms and, later, were standardized for operating from turret ramps. Turret ramps, as has been explained, were introduced on capital ships because they allowed the launching of aeroplanes without having to turn into the wind and out of the battle-line. Twenty-two cruisers and twenty-five battleships/battlecruisers are known to have embarked 2F1s, but few of these had the opportunity to launch their machines in action.

The concept of preventing enemy reconnaissance was tested on 1 June 1918, during an operation against the German Navy in the Heligoland Bight. The 2nd Light Cruiser Squadron was attacked by German seaplanes and launched 2F1s from HMAS *Sydney* and *Melbourne*. Flt Lt L.B. Gibson in N6756, from the latter, soon lost the enemy and ditched alongside HMS *Centaur* after 82 minutes. Flt Lt A.C. Sharwood, in N6783 from HMAS *Sydney*, had more success and engaged the enemy, claiming to have sent one down in a spin. His combat had taken him well away from his parent squadron and he was fortunate to find destroyers of the Harwich force, ditching alongside these. Both Camels were salvaged, but Sharwood's claim was disallowed.

Further such operations were conducted that month. HMS *Galatea* launched her 2F1 Camel on the 17th, its pilot being obliged to make a forced landing in Denmark and on the 19th, HMS *Furious* sent Lt M.W. Basedon up in N6810 after seaplanes, but the ensuing combat was indecisive.

Furious was the parent ship for what must be considered as the 2F1's most historically significant action, which took place exactly one month later. Seaplanes had previously been carried across the North Sea in order to allow attacks on German airship bases, but the action on 19 July was the first time ever that aeroplanes were flown off ships against a land-based target. That target was the airship station at Tondern and *Furious* launched seven

The most significant event in the 2F1's history was the raid on Tondern and the Camels used for that attack are almost certainly shown in this photograph taken on HMS *Furious*. **All have their upper-wing cockades toned down.**
JMB/GSL

2F1 Camels. The machines, in toned-down markings, were flown off at 03.22 hours. Capt T.K. Thyne was obliged to return early with engine trouble, but the remaining six all found their target and bombed with 60lb Coopers. Zeppelins L54 and L60 were destroyed in the subsequent explosions. Capts B.A. Smart DSO and W.F. Dickson managed to return, but Lt W.A. Yeulett was missing, presumed killed, and the remaining three Camels were force-landed in Denmark, with Capt

W.D. Jackson and Lts S. Dawson and N.E. Williams being interned. All pilots were decorated – Dickson was made a DSO and Smart received a bar to his existing decoration. The other five received DFCs, Yeulett posthumously. Smart was one of the war's unsung heroes, his achievements often being overshadowed by those of Lt S.D. Culley on 11 August 1918.

Culley achieved his deserved fame as a result of destroying Zeppelin L53. The means used to transport his 2F1 Camel to the scene of success was, however, different and stemmed from the wish to fly aeroplanes from destroyers as well as from larger ships. The Harwich Force worked in liaison with the RNAS station at Felixstowe and the addition of a forecastle ramp was considered detrimental to the stability of a destroyer. Cdr C.R. Samson, that great naval aviator, is credited with the idea of fitting platforms to towed lighters. These 58ft (18m) lighters had been developed as a means of transporting flying boats across the North Sea, in order to extend their radius of reconnaissance. Trials were conducted at Felixstowe, at first with a platform fitted parallel to the deck of Lighter H3 and 2F1 N6623, whose undercarriage was replaced by skids that ran in troughs along the deck, as an attempt at maintaining directional stability on take-off. Samson, always one to lead from the front, made the first attempt at take-off on 30 May 1918. Unfortunately, the effect of the high towing speed on the attitude of the lighter had not been considered and its nosing up meant that take-off was uphill. Samson may have increased engine revs accordingly, as N6623 was held on the quick-release strop, but the undercarriage skids jumped the troughs and the machine went over the side. Samson was lucky to survive. Subsequent trials involved a deck that was nose-down with the lighter at rest and incorporated a trestle for the tail-skid, which allowed the Camel to assume a horizontal attitude at towing speed. The first successful take-off was on 31 July, by Culley in N6812, a standard 2F1. Photographs

show that at least one F1 Camel was also used in these trials.

The Harwich Force conducted operations against German minesweepers and one such was launched on 10 August, with HMS *Redoubt* towing a lighter that carried Culley and N6812. Such operations had previously attracted the attention of reconnaissance Zeppelins and Culley had been well briefed by Samson as to methods of attacking such airships. N6812 was armed with twin fixed overwing Lewis guns for this operation, which suggests that RTS, or similar incendiary ammunition, was carried. Zeppelin L53 was seen shadowing the force on the morning of 11 August and N6812 was launched. Culley attacked from underneath at over 18,000ft (5,490m), firing 112 rounds (a full double drum from the starboard gun and 15 rounds from the port weapon, before it then jammed). L53 fell in flames. Culley and his machine were retrieved, after ditching, and N6812 later returned to service, being on the strength of 212 Sqn at Yarmouth by the end of the war.

As reported earlier, Camels and other types had a tendency to 'nose over' on ditching, due to the water drag created by the main undercarriage unit. Hydroplanes were tested as a possible remedy, but after his experience on 11 August, Culley suggested fitting a 2F1 with an undercarriage unit that could be jettisoned after take-off. He helped devise such a unit, one that was constructed of steel tubing, and it was installed on a 2F1 at Felixstowe. This, as yet unidentified, machine was also unusual in that it had a twin Vickers gun armament. Lt R.E. Keys DFC test-flew it on 20 September, with the undercarriage being successfully dropped.

212 Sqn also participated in 2F1 experiments which although not pursuing a new concept were to be developed further in the future. It has already been recounted that F1 Camels were used for initial experiments involving airships as another means of transporting aeroplanes and extending their range. The first 'live drop', with a pilot on board, was made from R23 by N6814 and Lt R.E. Keys DFC on 6 November 1918. Once the ability of airships to carry and launch aeroplanes had been proven, experiments were then conducted in their retrieval. These took place at Grain and among the machines utilized was N7352, which was fitted with roller gear that engaged an overhead wire. Once engaged, the aeroplane engine could be stopped and the machine allowed to roll to a halt along the wire. Other machines used in these experiments included Pups, an example being B2217. The post-war RAF did not

adopt the airship and it was the US Navy which developed the idea further, with the Akron and Macon during the 1930s.

The 2F1 Post-War

As with the F1 Camel, examples of the 2F1 were dispatched to Russia during 1919, in support of the interventionist forces. HMS *Vindictive* was used as a carrier and embarked at least thirteen 2F1s when she sailed for the Baltic in September (N6612, N6616, N6767, N7106, N7119, N7130, N7140, N7143, N8130, N8184, N8185, N8187, N8189). N6616 was disembarked at Biorko, Lithuania, with its pilot Capt C. Emery, who assumed instructional duties with the Estonian Aviation Company at Koivisto. His Camel was overmarked with Estonian insignia and survived until at least 1926. RAF pilots flew operations from Koivisto during October 1919, the principal target being the port of Kronstadt, and one of the pilots involved was Flt Lt S.D. Culley.

The neighbouring state of Latvia also received some of *Vindictive*'s 2F1s at Riga, at least seven being recorded (N6750, N7143, N8136, N8137, N8185, N8187 and N8189). These, too, were overmarked with appropriate insignia, the red swastika on a white disc, and given individual numbers.

White Russian forces in south Russia used other 2F1s, these machines (including N6803 and N6804) having originally been on the charge of the Aegean Group. It would seem likely that they were taken to south Russia by 221 Sqn.

At home, the 2F1 Camel continued in service for several years after its sister F1 had been withdrawn. Some were used for landing experiments on HMS *Eagle*, the

Specification – Sopwith 2F1 Ships Camel	
Engine:	One 150hp BR1 or 130hp Clerget
Weights:	Empty 1,036lb (470kg) (BR1), 956lb (434kg) (Clerget); loaded 1,530lb (694kg) (BR1), 1,523lb (691kg) (Clerget)
Dimensions:	Length 18ft 8in (5.69m) (BR1), 18ft 6in (5.64m) (Clerget); height 9ft 1in (2.77m); wingspan upper 26ft 11in (8.2m), lower 26ft 11in (8.2m); chord upper 4ft 6in (1.37m), lower 4ft 6in (1.37m); stagger 1ft 6in (45.72cm); gap 4ft 11in (1.5m); dihedral upper 0°, lower 5½°
Performance:	Max. speed 122mph (196km/h) (BR1), 114mph (183km/h) (Clerget) Service ceiling 17,300ft (5,270m) (BR1), 12,000ft (3,660m) (Clerget) Endurance 2½ hours
Armament:	One fixed Vickers, synchronized to fire through propeller arc plus one Lewis on top plane mounting

first 'flat top' with an 'island' and at least one had a raised undercarriage for that purpose. When 203 Sqn reformed at

Leuchars Junction on 1 March 1920, it was equipped with 2F1s which were retained until August 1922, the withdrawal of these signifying the end of the Camel's service with the RAF and its predecessors. Others had served with the Fleet School of Aerial Gunnery & Fighting, also at Leuchars.

There were 2F1 Camels still in store and, during 1925, the Canadian government bought eight (N7357, N7379, N7364, N7367, N8151, N8153, N8156 and N8204), supposedly to utilize as spares for its three F1s. The unarmed 2F1s had been fully refurbished at Brooklands and given a smart finish of aluminium pigmented dope. It would seem unlikely that they did much flying, but were used as ground instructional airframes at Camp Borden by 1928. N8156 survives today, restored to full 2F1 standard and displayed at National Aviation Museum, Ottawa. In the UK, the IWM holds N6812, Culley's Camel that was used to destroy L53. Its appearance and markings differ from those it had on that historic day in 1918.

(Above) **2F1s from HMS** Vindictive **found their way into the air services of some of the newly emerged Baltic nations in 1919. Three Latvian machines are shown, unarmed, at Riga.** JMB/GSL

The fore and aft cable used to arrest forward movement during landing on carrier decks necessitated the use of a propeller guard, which can be seen on this Beardmore-built 2F1. The undercarriage clips, that engaged the cables, can be seen, as can the centre-section slinging gear. JMB/GSL

Representative 2F1 Camels with Ships and Shore-Based Units

HMS *Ajax*: N6834.
HMS *Argus*: N6773, N6776, N6811, N6834, N7118, N7134, N8130.
HMS *Aurora*: N6756, N6770, N6816.
HMS *Australia*: N6786, N6790, N6822, N6826, N6828.
HMS *Barham*: N6750, N6762, N7103, N7136.
HMS *Birkenhead*: N6753, N6759, N6833, N6844, N6847, N7110, N7111.
HMS *Caledon*: N6602.
HMS *Calliope*: N6636, N6768, N6775, N6779.
HMS *Campania*: N6611, N6846.
HMS *Canada*: N7116.
HMS *Caroline*: N6602, N6617, N6637, N6766, N6768, N6831, N7108, N7121.
HMS *Cassandra*: N6794, N7122.
HMS *Chatham*: N6616, N6773, N6848.
HMS *Comus*: N6614, N6629, N6632, N6642, N6760, N6768, N6775, N6780, N6790, N6793, N6810, N6811, N6846.
HMS *Cordelia*: N6757, N6767.
HMS *Courageous*: N6619, N6645, N6751, N6752, N6763, N6773, N6775, N6793, N6842, N7128.
HMS *Dublin*: N6828, N7138.
HMS *Emperor of India*: N7129.
HMS *Furious*: N6771, N6772, N6788, N6789, N6798, N6800, N6810, N6823, N6825, N6832, N6840, N7140, N7141, N7147.
HMS *Galatea*: N6616, N6625, N6755, N6756, N6766, N6770, N6772, N6829, N7116, N7126, N7136.
HMS *Glorious*: N6604, N6605, N6614, N6776, N6778, N6788, N6835, N7117, N7121.
HMS *Inconstant*: N6631, N6640, N7100, N7116, N7119, N7123.

HMS *Indomitable*: N6614, N6647, N6759, N6780, N6791, N6792, N6813.
HMS *Inflexible*: N6759, N6786, N6787, N6792, N6817.
HMS *Iron Duke*: N6751, N6757, N6791, N6799, N7125.
HMS *Lion*: N6600, N6602, N6604, N6607, N6629, N6631, N6647, N6764, N6769, N6773, N6776, N6819, N6834, N7120.
HMS *Malaya*: N6789, N7146, N7148.
HMS *Manxman*: N6806, N6807, N6808.
HMS *Melbourne*: N6603, N6756, N6785, N6794, N6820, N6821, N6822, N7104.
HMS *Nairana*: N6602, N6604, N6605, N6606, N6614, N6646, N6648, N6770, N7102, N7118, N7134.
HMS *New Zealand*: N6617, N6832, N6833, N7109, N7134, N7140.
HMS *Orion*: N6819, N7119.
HMS *Pegasus*: N6638, N6643, N6646, N6770, N6772, N6773, N6785, N6788, N6793, N6820, N6826, N6836, N7103, N7127.
HMS *Penelope*: N6646, N6768, N6778, N6799, N6824, N6845, N7109, N7110, N7117.
HMS *Phaeton*: N6631, N6644, N6649, N6758, N6774, N6787, N6789, N6800.
HMS *Princess Royal*: N6604, N6633, N6642, N6758, N6768, N6770, N6830, N6839, N6849, N7114.
HMS *Queen Elizabeth*: N7120.
HMS *Renown*: N6606, N6611, N6617, N6619, N6630, N6633, N6641, N6751, N6838, N7101.
HMS *Repulse*: N6605, N6606, N6637, N6638, N7105, N7106.
HMS *Royalist*: N6611, N6639, N6751, N6754, N6762, N6782, N6795, N6831, N7113.
HMS *Royal Oak*: N6819.
HMS *Royal Sovereign*: N6752, N7103, N7108.

HMS *Southampton*: N6607, N6752, N6755, N6784, N6787, N6842, N7107, N7112.
HMS *Sydney*: N6629, N6631, N6635, N6638, N6783, N6789, N6797, N6798, N6820, N6822, N6838, N7101.
HMS *Tiger*: N6601, N6603, N6606, N6648, N6750, N6797, N6835, N7103.
HMS *Undaunted*: N6603, N6773, N6824, N6847, N7107, N7119, N7139.
HMS *Valiant*: N6769, N6795, N6838.
HMS *Vindex*: N6608, N6609.
HMS *Vindictive*: N6612, N6767, N7106, N7119, N7130, N7140, N7143, N8130, N8184.
HMS *Warspite*: N7120.
HMS *Yarmouth*: N6600.
Eagle Flt – Gosport: N6757, N8134.
War Flt – RNAS Yarmouth: N6600, N6608, N6620, N6621, N6622, N6623.
203 Sqn – Leuchars: N7355, N7360, N7361, N7362, N7366, N7368, N7374, N8130, N8146, N8147, N8149, N8150, N8191.
205 Sqn – Leuchars: N8191.
212 Sqn – Yarmouth: N6621, N6625, N6814.
219 Sqn 470 Flt – Manston: N6634.
220 Sqn – Imbros: N6803, N6805.
222 Sqn – Mudros: N6803.
273 Sqn 485/486 Flts – Burgh Castle: N6620, N6621, N6624.
RNAS War School – Manston: N6610, N6613, N6624, N6625, N6626, N6627, N6628.
Fleet SAFG – Leuchars: N6777, N6824, N6825, N6832, N8140, N8141, N8142, N8143.
205 TDS – Vendome: N6610, N6613.
RNAS ECD/MAEE – Grain: N4, N5, N6603, N7352.

Ships Strutters

Another original recommendation of the Grand Fleet Aircraft Committee had been that the fighters to be flown from ships should be fitted with short-range W/T sets. This would enable an enhancement of the cruiser lines' reporting range and may be the reason why the FS1 landplane, N5, was fitted with such a set. The success of Pup, Beardmore WB.III and 2F1 Camel operation led to thoughts of providing the fleet with dedicated reconnaissance machines. The Sopwith 1½ Strutter was an obvious choice and a trial was first made on 4 March 1918, by Flt Cdr D.G. Donald in 9744, from an extended turret platform fitted to HMS *Repulse*. The turret platform's extension was flexible and the machine's propeller was struck by it, causing Donald to ditch 9744. On 7 March, that same pilot flew N5644 from an extended and presumably inflexible platform on HMS *Australia*. FSL Simonson repeated the operation the following day, in the same machine. With the theory proved, plans were made to introduce the 1½ Strutter onto capital ships and the usual procedure was for such vessels to carry a fighter (a 2F1 by 1918) over a rear turret and a 1½ Strutter over a forward one. The platforms for the Camels were some 10ft (3.05m) shorter than those used for the two-seaters. The problem was that the RNAS did not have sufficient 1½ Strutters.

A Westland-built Ships Strutter ready for take off on fixed platform, with the wind-driven generator for its wireless set clearly visible on the cockpit side. The officer at the front of the platform is, apparently, testing wind direction. via CCI

The RAF was formed on 1 April and, in the period leading up to that event, surplus ex-RFC machines became available. These were put forward for conversion to what became known as Ships Strutters. The conversion, at its simplest, involved the installation of slinging points, internal flotation gear and a W/T set, along with an appropriate wind-driven generator. Some of the machines, however, had been originally built as single-seat bombers, which had a revised fuselage structure and fuel tank arrangement. These had to be converted to two-seater configuration. Despite these arrangements, there was still a deficit of machines and the RAF had to seek further supplies. As has been related, large numbers of 1½ Strutters were built in France and seventy were obtained in two batches, F2210–2229 (delivered during May 1918) and F7547–7596 (most of which arrived during that September). These were converted to Ships Strutter standard at 2 (Northern) ARD, Coal Aston, most of the first batch and some of the second being issued to ships of the fleet.

These turret-flown 1½ Strutters were not the first to go to sea, however. HMS *Furious* had already had the type on board, drawing machines from another RNAS F Sqn, at East Fortune (F for *Furious*). During December 1917 and January 1918, F Sqn received eighteen single-seat bomber

The Ships Strutter was for fleet reconnaissance and one is seen here on the A turret of a capital ship, possibly HMS Renown. K Kelly

versions of the 1½ Strutter, a consecutive batch (A5982–5999) of Morgan & Co-built machines. These were converted Ships Strutter standard and, by 22 March, eighteen were embarked on the *Furious*.

The 1½ Strutters also featured in the variety of ditching and deck-landing trials that were conducted at Grain. 9390 was used in early tests, being fitted with a hydrovane and external flotation bags. It was so equipped by September 1917 and featured in ditching trials on 22 March 1918. These were successful. By the following month, 9390 had a skid undercarriage, but retained its flotation gear. It was used for tests on Grain's dummy deck. A6987, a converted ex-RFC bomber, was similarly equipped and also featured an X form of bracing for the inner part of each wing bay. This allowed each bay to be detached as a separate unit and allowed for easy transport to, and reassembly on, ships at anchor, after being delivered by lighter. Others used at Grain included N5245 and N5246, for flotation bag experiments, N5601 and A8255, fitted with skid undercarriages, and A6918, which had a hydrovane fitted.

Most, if not all, Ships Strutters retained their wheeled undercarriages, with horns for the engagement of arrester wires being fitted to the spreader bars of those intended for carrier use. That engagement raised the wires and necessitated the fitting of

Ships Strutter A5992 was one of a number that were delivered to East Fortune and F Sqn for use aboard HMS Furious. Its fuselage is seen being transported by whaler to its parent vessel. N5992 subsequently served on HMS New Zealand and Argus. via CCI

Representative Ships Strutters with Ships and Shore-Based Units

F Sqn – East Fortune/HMS *Furious*; A5254, A5951, A5952, A5985, A5986, A5987, A5988, A5989, A5990, A5991, A6971.
HMS *Argus*: A5951, A5992.
HMS *Australia*: A6968, F7562, N5606, N5644, N5985.
HMS *Barham*: A5988, A6006, F2225, F2228.
HMS *Bellerophon*: A5984, A5985.
HMS *Campania*: A6014, A6015, A6920, A6921, A6922, B2566.
HMS *Courageous*: A5994, A5998, F2210, F2222, F2227.
HMS *Emperor of India*: F7561.

HMS *Glorious*: A5990, A6905, B744, N5644.
HMS *Indomitable*: A5988, A6952, A6966, A8277, F2216.
HMS *Inflexible*: A6010, A6980, A8224.
HMS *Malaya*: A6967, A8277, F2221.
HMS *New Zealand*: A6981, F2220.
HMS *Queen Elizabeth*: A6006.
HMS *Renown*: A5987, A5993, A5995, F2215, F2225, F2228, F2229.
HMS *Repulse*: A5982, A6967, A8300, F2224, F2228, N5644.

HMS *Valiant*: A6952.
HMS *Warspite*: A5987.
Fleet Practice Station – Turnhouse: A5983, A5989, A5991, A6006, B4016, B4044, N5164, N5636, N5643, N5649.
RNAS Experimental Depot – Grain: A6019.

Disembarked machines used the Fleet Bases at Turnhouse, East Fortune and Donibristle for storage/maintenance/repair.

---

propeller guards, as extensions of the undercarriage units. The practicality of such an arrangement was tested on HMS *Argus*, the first true 'flat top', on 1 October 1918, by that distinguished naval pilot, then Lt Cdr R. Bell Davies VC DSO in F2211. The venerable Sopwith two-seater continued in service for a short period after the war, but by the end of 1919, most, if not all, had been retired.

The Ships Strutter lasted slightly longer on the other side of the Atlantic. A large number of the French-built machines that had been bought for the American Expeditionary Force were returned to the USA during 1919 and a number of these were transferred to the US Navy. Known 1½ Strutter with the USN included (American numbers) A5660, A5625–5628, A5634–5644 and A5749–52, a total of twenty machines. These were of the two-seat variety and most, if not all were fitted with hydrovanes of Grain pattern and external generators for W/T equipment. It was intended to operate them from US warships that were fitted with turret platforms. The first flights were made from USS *Texas* and seven other capital ships had platforms mounted. The USN operated its Ships Strutters in its Ship Plane Units and the disbandment of these in mid-1920 heralded the end of the type with that service.

The Sopwith B1 was a consequence of interest in a replacement for the Sopwith 9700 which was expressed by both British and French authorities, but was built for the latter. French interest in the type may have been the reason for a break in what had become a Sopwith tradition, namely the use of a water-cooled engine, the engine neatly cowled behind a circular frontal radiator. The pilot was placed well forward, giving a good field of vision for bombing purposes, but a poor one to the rear and above. A fixed Lewis gun, mounted ahead of the cockpit, was to be the only defensive armament. It was intended to use the type as a high altitude bomber and

That the first Sopwith B1 was intended for the French government is evident from the reversed colours of its national markings. This photograph also shows the inspection panel for the internal bomb bay and its fixed, forward-firing Lewis gun. The French did not want the machine. It was numbered N50 and served with 5 Wing RNAS, before being returned home and converted to the prototype Grain Griffin. JMB/GSL

The B1 and B2

The Sopwith B1 and B2 bombers are included in this chapter, partly because of the influence that their design had on the subsequent Cuckoo. It must also be noted, however, that the former was converted (at a late stage in its career) to what may have been intended as a Ships Strutter replacement.

French Hispano-Suiza 8B. It is also worth considering that, at that time, Sopwiths were also engaged in the design of the Dolphin and that might have influenced the choice of engine, or vice-versa. The B1 was ready at Brooklands by 23 April 1917. It was a large machine for a single-seater, with its two bay wings having a (reported) span of 38ft 6in (11.73m). Its design was a lot cleaner than that of the 9700, with the

it was hoped that superior speed would suffice for defence. Its bomb load was carried internally, its inspection being through access panels in the fuselage sides, similar to those on the 9700.

The machine was delivered to Dunkerque that May, for assessment by the French authorities. There had obviously been a breakdown of communications, for the French were expecting the, apparently unbuilt, FR2 that had also been designed for the Hispano-Suiza. The French rejected the B1 and it was with 5N Sqn at Dunkerque by the middle of the month, being numbered N50, remaining for some two weeks and actually flying operationally alongside that unit's D.H.4s. It failed to make a significant impression, no production orders were forthcoming and it was returned to England. N50 went to the Grain experimental station for further trials, which included the fitting of a BR1 rotary engine. It was restored to Hispano-Suiza configuration and later had a Wolseley Adder fitted. More significantly, it was converted to a two-seater and fitted with a hydrovane. In this guise, it served as a prototype for what became the Grain Griffin, a type that achieved limited production. During December 1918, N50 was allotted to the Mediterranean Area, but the reasoning behind that allocation is not known.

A second Sopwith Bomber was built and given the designation B2. This was also powered by a 200hp Hispano-Suiza, but may have had an increased wingspan of 40ft (12.19m). It had little to distinguish it externally from the B1, except for its military number B1496. It would seem that the RFC was also interested in acquiring a new bomber, possibly to replace its Martinsyde Elephants. B1496 was ready by January 1918 and went to Martlesham for assessment. It returned figures that were no improvement on those of the D.H.4 that was already on RFC strength, and D.H.9s were already on order and Hispano-Suiza engines were scarce, so production was never a prospect.

The T1 Cuckoo

The Sopwith T1, later to be named Cuckoo, shared several design features with the B1. The type was developed as a consequence of the RNAS desire to take the war to the enemy and was the direct result of a letter sent from Commodore M. Sueter to T.O.M. Sopwith during October 1916, asking that Sopwith's investigate the possibility of developing a torpedo-carrying aeroplane. The idea of launching torpedoes from the air was not a new one, but the machine that emerged was well suited to the task. The fuselage was, apparently, completed by January 1917, but it was not until 6 June that the completed machine was passed by the Sopwith experimental

Specification – Sopwith B1	
Engine:	One 200hp Hispano-Suiza
Weights:	Empty 1,700lb (771kg); loaded 2,945lb (1,336kg)
Dimensions:	Length 27ft 6in (8.38m); height 9ft 8in (2.95m); wingspan upper 38ft 6in (11.73m), lower 38ft 6in (11.73m); chord upper 6ft 3in (1.91m), lower 6ft 3in (1.91m); stagger 0; gap 6ft (1.83m); dihedral 2½°
Performance:	Max. speed 118mph (190km/h) Service ceiling 22,000ft (6,700m) Endurance 3¾ hours
Armament:	One fixed Lewis gun firing through the propeller arc plus 560lb bomb load

B1496 was the second B1 and was referred to as the B2. It was unarmed and was tested at Martlesham Heath. Its engine cowling differed from N50's. JMB/GSL

The Sopwith T1 was a development of the B1 and N74 was the prototype. This photograph was taken at Grain and shows the split undercarriage that allowed the carrying of a torpedo. JMB/GSL

department. It is not known whether the B1 was developed during this hiatus, or earlier, but the fuselages of the two designs were very similar.

With a circular radiator at the front and a Hispano-Suiza 8B engine, the first T1 fuselage resembled that of the bomber, except that the cockpit was further to the rear. Tail surfaces were almost identical. The wing layout was, perforce, different. Whereas the B1 was intended to lift 560lb of bombs, the T1 had to contend with a 1,000lb torpedo and consequently required a larger wing area. An extended lower centre section carried a divided undercarriage, which allowed a torpedo to be carried under the fuselage. The upper centre-section was necessarily wide, to match the span of the lower one. The mainplanes were designed to fold, indicating shipboard use. Wing cellules were two-bay structures,

with the inner pair of struts mating against the outer ones of the centre section, when the wings were extended.

The first machine, at first marked with just a T in its serial number box, was allotted the number N74. It was delivered to Grain in July and tested prior to flotation gear experiments on 2 August. It moved north to the Forth, being recorded at East Fortune, Donibristle and Rosyth before testing from HMS *Furious* on 2 November. It is worth recording that the T1 was never intended to land on carriers, just to take off from them and so was not fitted with any form of arrester gear. This aeroplane was then returned to Grain for the fitting of torpedo carrying and release gear. It had been re-engined with a Sunbeam Arab by March 1918 and ended its days at East Fortune.

Admiral Sir David Beatty was an advocate of the torpedo plane concept. He had

proposed using such machines for attacks on the German fleet in its home anchorages during the spring of 1918. This would have required suitable carriers to transport the aeroplanes close enough to their targets to allow flight home, but such carriers were not available. The Admiralty Operations Committee had, therefore, to turn down this proposal. The T1, however, was already on order, although not from Sopwith's. The parent firm was too busy with the production of its fighting scouts and so the initial order was given to the Glasgow firm of Fairfield Engineering. These and subsequent machines were to have the 225hp Sunbeam Arab engine, the Hispano-Suiza being in short supply and required for S.E.5a production. The Glasgow firm had little experience and deliveries ran well behind schedule, as did those from a further contractor, the

The production T1 was named the Cuckoo. Blackburn's produced most and N6954 has the company logo on the fin. N6954 was delivered at the end of June 1918 and served with 201 TS at East Fortune. It was a Cuckoo Mk1 with 225hp Sunbeam Arab engine. JMB/GSL

Specification – Sopwith T1 Cuckoo	
Engine:	One 200hp Sunbeam Arab, 200hp Wolseley Viper or 275hp Rolls-Royce Falcon III
Weights:	Empty 2,199lb (997kg) (Arab), 2,233lb (1,013kg) (Viper), 2,585lb (1,173kg) (Falcon); loaded 3,883lb (1,761kg) (Arab), 3,974lb (1,803kg) (Viper), 4,350lb (1,973kg) (Falcon)
Dimensions:	Length 28ft 10in (8.79m); height 11ft (3.35m); wingspan upper 46ft 8in (14.22m), lower 45ft 9in (13.94m); chord upper 6ft 3in (1.91m), lower 6ft 3in (1.91m); stagger 0; gap 6ft (1.83m); dihedral upper 2½°, lower 2½°
Performance:	Max. speed 81kts (150km/h) (Arab), 90kts (167km/h) (Viper), 101kts (187km/h) (Falcon) Service ceiling 12,000ft (3,660m) Endurance 4 hours
Armament:	One 18in (46cm) torpedo weighing 1,099lb (499kg)

N7990 was converted to Cuckoo Mk.III, by the installation of a 275hp RR Falcon III engine. It went to Grain for type trials. JMB/GSL

HMS *Argus*, with an unobstructed deck, underwent sea trials in September 1918 and was designated to carry the T1, which became known as the Cuckoo about that time. 185 Sqn was formed at East Fortune, as the unit for the *Argus* and received its complement of Cuckoos. It embarked on the carrier during the week that the Armistice was signed and so saw no action. A sister unit, 186 Sqn, was formed on *Argus*, on 31 December, from elements of 185 Sqn and was intended for operations in Russia. The plan was shelved and 186 Sqn disembarked at Gosport, where it served as a development squadron until redesignated 210 Sqn on 1 February 1920. 185 Sqn was effectively disbanded on 14 April 1919.

The Cuckoo was the only operational RAF torpedo aeroplane capable of operating from carriers and so was retained on the post-war order of battle. 210 Sqn continued to operate the type until it disbanded on 1 April 1923 and had been joined at Gosport by 1 Training Flight, which also had several of those machines. A considerable number never saw service, having been delivered direct to storage at either 6 (Renfrew) AAP or 9 (Newcastle) AAP.

Post-war, the Japanese armed forces provided a ready market for British aeroplanes and six Cuckoo Mk.IIs were bought for the Imperial Navy in 1921, these being (presumably) the longest surviving examples. Of greater historical significance is the fact

Doncaster-based firm of Pegler. The latter's production fell so far behind schedule that the Blackburn Aeroplane and Motor Co. of Leeds took over both production of its initial batch and responsibility for design development, notably the substitution of the Arab engine.

Blackburn's were awarded their own contracts for T1 production and were experienced enough in aeroplane manufacturing to implement the design changes. In the post-war RAF, the Arab-engined T1 became the Cuckoo Mk.I. Arab-engined machines had no reduction gear to their propellers and can be recognized from a lower engine thrust line and revised radiator shell that was of horseshoe shape. The Mk.II was given the Wolseley

Viper engine; another without reduction gearing and the Mk.III was powered by a Rolls-Royce Falcon. The Mk.III returned surprisingly poor performance figures and so was not put into production.

Production T1s began to emerge from Blackburn's Leeds factory during May 1918; it was not until August that Fairfield could follow and October before a Pegler machine was completed. The initial deliveries were to 201 TS at East Fortune, that unit's predecessor, 1 Torpedo Training Squadron, having received (probably) just one machine. 201 TS was charged with proving the type and it conducted torpedo-dropping experiments in the Forth. A Special Duty Flight was formed at Gosport, for the same purposes.

Representative Cuckoos with Ships and Shore-Based Units

185 Sqn – East Fortune/HMS *Argus*: N6929, N7011, N7022, N7023, N7024, N7025, N7150, N7151, N7152, N7153, N7154.

186 Sqn – HMS *Argus*/Gosport: N6926, N6927, N7193.

210 Sqn – Gosport: N6975, N7155, N7161, N7195, N7197, N7994, N7995, N7996, N7997, N8003, N8011.

201 TS – East Fortune: N6930, N6953, N7000, N7001, N7002, N7003, N7004, N7005, N7006, N7007, N7008, N7017, N7021.

Development Sqn – Gosport: N7152, N7154, N7188, N7193, N7198, N7982, N7986, N7992, N7993.

1 Training Flt – Gosport: N6923, N7155, N7161, N7173, N7984, N7993, N7994, N7995, N7996, N8000, N8001, N8003.

Experimental Station – Martlesham Heath: N8005.

Marine Experimental Station – Grain: N7990, N8005.

HMS *Furious*: N6953, N6980, N6985, N6993.

The Scooter was a monoplane version of the Camel and used as a 'runabout' before entering the civil register, where it eventually became G-EACZ. JMB/GSL

The Swallow was a development of the Scooter and utilized the fuselage of Boulton Paul-built Camel B9276. It was intended as a fleet fighter and armed with twin Vickers guns. B9276 was tested at Martlesham, but not adopted for service. JMB/GSL

Specification – Sopwith Swallow	
Engine:	One 110hp Le Rhone 9J
Weights:	Empty 889lb (403kg); loaded 1,420lb (644kg)
Dimensions:	Length 18ft 9in (5.72m); height 10ft 2in (3.1m); wingspan 28ft 10in (8.79m); chord 5ft 9in (1.75m); dihedral 0; sweepback 6in (5.24cm)
Performance:	Max. speed 113mph (182km/h) Service ceiling 18,500ft (5,640m) Endurance not known
Armament:	Two fixed Vickers guns, synchronized to fire through propeller arc

that Herbert Smith, Sopwith's designer, went to Japan to work for the Mitsubishi concern, developing indigenous shipborne torpedo-carrying aeroplanes from 1922 and partly paving the way towards the events of 7 December 1941.

The Sopwith Swallow

The 2F1 Camel had inherited the F1's poor field of vision for its pilots. A further Camel development, the Swallow, was intended as a fleet aeroplane and its monoplane configuration was designed to overcome that problem. The Swallow itself was developed from an earlier design, the Scooter, which had been built as a 'runabout' for Harry Hawker. Subsequently given the designation Sopwith Monoplane No. 1, the Scooter was completed during July 1918 and was, in essence, a Camel fuselage fitted with a parasol wing, which incorporated a degree of sweepback. It had no armament and so the distinctive machine-gun 'hump' was removed. The wing was set very close to the top of the fuselage and incorporated a trailing edge cut-out that was necessary for cockpit ingress/egress. Contemporary reports indicate that the machine was very manoeuvrable, Hawker using it for some spectacular displays of his piloting ability. The Scooter survived, in various guises, until 1927, when it was scrapped.

The Swallow was, essentially, an armed version of the Scooter, but had an enlarged wing, which was set slightly higher above the fuselage to accommodate twin Vickers guns. These weapons were set further apart than on the Camel. The basis for the Swallow was the fuselage of Camel B9276. That identity was displayed in typical Sopwith fashion, but the machine was Boulton & Paul-built. It is tempting to suggest that the fuselage was that which had been delivered, but not used, for the TF1 programme. The Swallow had a 110hp Le Rhone engine, rather than the 130hp Clerget that appeared in the Scooter. It was delivered to Martlesham Heath for trials on 28 October 1918, but these were not reported on until May 1919. Its performance was no great improvement on that of the 2F1, although its rate of climb and service ceiling were marginally better, but the war was over and the RAF had standardized on the Ships Camel as its fleet fighter. There was no place for the Swallow and the prototype was scrapped.

124

CHAPTER NINE

The Dolphin

The Underrated Sopwith

The 5F1 Dolphin was, undoubtedly, the best Sopwith design of fighting scout to achieve production during the Great War, having superior performance than either its predecessors or the subsequent 7F1 Snipe. That is significant because it was the only operational Sopwith fighter to be powered by a water-cooled engine and was treated with wary respect by new pilots because of the pronounced back-stagger given to its wings. It was produced in numbers comparable to those of the Sopwith Pup and yet only saw operational service in France with four RFC/RAF squadrons. Pilots who flew the type operationally, however, were almost unanimous in their praise for its design.

Development

Design of the 5F1 was taking place in the months leading up to the operational introduction of the Camel. It may be that the limited field of upward and forward vision afforded to a pilot of the Camel had already been recognized, because the design drawn up by Herbert Smith gave precedence to that combat requisite. The choice of a water-cooled engine, the 200hp Hispano-Suiza 8B, was interesting. It may be that Sopwith's were keen to use the make of engine in the early Camel's rival, the S.E.5, or perhaps it was due to the firm already having utilized that engine in one of its two experimental triplanes, N510, and earmarked it for two other contemporary designs, the B1 and T1. It was not realized at the time, however, that the engine would be the source of problems, both in terms of availability and mechanical reliability.

The first prototype, 5F1, emerged during May 1917 and was, it has to be agreed, a rather ugly machine after the more dainty Pup, Triplane and, even, Camel. There was nothing unconventional about its construction. The fuselage was a typical

The Hispano-Suiza Engine

There were two major strands to aero engine development during the Great War. One was epitomized by the rotary and radial layout that sought to provide the greatest engine power for the lightest possible weight. The other was the refinement of the water-cooled motor car engine of either inline or V-cylinder layout. The Hispano-Suiza was an example of the latter.

The name Hispano-Suiza translates, of course, as Spanish-Swiss and the company, La Sociedad Hispano-Suiza was based in Barcelona. Its designer was Marc Birkigt and his first engine in the series developed 150hp named 8A, 8 being the number of cylinders and A to indicate the first in the series of that engine.

The Dolphin I had the 200/220hp development of the original engine, the Hispano-Suiza 8B. That engine followed the V8 configuration of the original, but was fitted with reduction gearing for its propeller. What made the Hispano-Suiza such a brilliant design was its use of a cast aluminium block, with steel linings for the cylinders. This gave not only a lighter weight compared with other water-cooled engines, but also better heat dissipation. In addition, casting of the aluminium crankcase allowed a stronger component and therefore its walls could be made thinner to save further

weight. Aluminium was also used for the pistons. Like all V8s, the engine was smooth running with a firing order of 1L, 4R, 2L, 3R, 4L, 1R, 3L, 2R (L = left, R = right). Fuel consumption was less than that of rotary engines of equivalent horsepower.

The reduction gearing was the weakness in the 200hp and 220hp engines and units made by the French firm of Brasier were particularly vulnerable to the gears shearing off. The remedy was to remove the gearing and allow direct drive and machines with engines so modified were known as the Dolphin II. That removal served to lower the thrust line of the engine and allows easy identification of the two marks.

The 300hp Hispano-Suiza 8F, as fitted to the Dolphin II, was essentially a 220hp unit with increased bore and stroke. It too was fitted with reduction gearing.

The Hispano-Suiza engine with its reduction gearing is shown here with the Vickers guns and their timing mechanisms. The port gun has a right-hand feed, the starboard a left-hand one. JMB/GSL

(Top) **The first prototype Dolphin was fitted with a frontal radiator that is clearly evident in this frontal view taken at Martlesham Heath in June 1917.** JMB/GSL

(Above) **This rear view of the first prototype well illustrates the narrowness of the Dolphin's fuselage, the negative stagger of the wings and the good forward and upward field of vision afforded to the pilot.** JMB/GSL

box-girder structure, with wooden members and wire cross-bracing. The wings, similarly, followed the usual Sopwith method of construction. Spruce spars carried plywood ribs, with AP121 oval section tubing forming the wing-tips and trailing edges. The horizontal tail surfaces were of similar construction, while the Camel-like fin and rudder were fabricated from shaped tubing. The deep fuselage was created by the addition of formers, which formed a decking that reached the level of the centre section. That centre section was of steel tubing and formed an open square of tubing, through which the pilot's head projected. The depth of the fuselage was accented by the adoption of a deep, frontal radiator. The armament, consisting of two Vickers guns, was encased in the top

decking of the engine cowling. The back-staggered wings had slight dihedral and were of two-bay form. This prototype never wore and, as far as is known, was never allotted a serial number, which suggests that it was built as a private venture.

It had its first trials on 22 May and exhibited a performance that was far superior to its predecessors. A report submitted to the Progress and Allocations Committee credited the type with a speed of 145mph (233km/h) at 5,000ft (1,525m). Its performance during those trials was compared with that of a Camel, but the new type had outclassed its stablemate. The machine was passed to the Experimental Station at Martlesham Heath, after minor modifications had been made. By this time, it was already known as the

Dolphin, the name being bestowed by Sopwith's. Martlesham pilots had little time to evaluate the type's performance thoroughly, as it had been allotted for service trials in France, presumably to satisfy the curiosity of Trenchard, who had heard of its maker's trials. Capt H. Tizard delivered it to 1 AD St Omer on 13 June, and the Martlesham Report M104A was published three days later. That report was not uncritical, but it did recognize the Dolphin's attributes. The main adverse comments concerned the exposed position of the pilot's head, the need for a larger rudder (to counteract engine torque at full speed) and the nose-heaviness of the type. It would appear that Sopwith's were aware of the nose-heaviness, as it had already been decided to move the lower wing further forward.

On 14 June Capt W.A. Bishop DSO MC of 60 Sqn tested the Dolphin at St Omer. Although scheduled to receive S.E.5s, 60 Sqn was still operating Nieuports and Bishop was a noted exponent of that type. He reported favourably on the Dolphin's speed, manoeuvrability, armament and field of vision. Of especial interest is the fact that its turning performance was not compared

Patrick MC, another experienced pilot. Lewis, at that time, had the greater combat experience and it is likely that the opposing machine, as much as its pilot, was the cause of his humiliation.

Trenchard, however, had already made up his mind and, whatever the Dolphin's qualities, remained committed to having the S.E.5a as the principal stationary-

(C8001–C8200). When the second prototype emerged, it had obviously been built with the Martlesham comments in mind. The ungainly frontal radiator was dispensed with, no doubt reducing nose-heaviness, and the lower longerons were brought up at a sharp angle from the front undercarriage sockets to meet the upper ones. This permitted the adoption of a close-fitting cowling,

The second prototype had radiators let into the upper wing surfaces and that permitted the revision of the nose contours, as seen in this photograph taken at Brooklands. It had an Aldis optical sight fitted to the front centre-section spar and this again emphasizes the high seating position of the pilot. JMB/GSL

unfavourably with that of the nimble Nieuport, on which Bishop had, to that date, been credited with twenty-six combat 'victories'. Another pilot who encountered the Dolphin, during its sojourn at St Omer, was the combat-experienced Lt C.A. Lewis MC of 56 Sqn, the only unit thus far equipped with the S.E.5. Lewis, in his classic *Sagittarius Rising*, recounted how, while air-testing his squadron's first S.E.5a (presumably A4563) he engaged the Dolphin in mock combat. Both machines had the same type of engine but, as Lewis recalled, the Dolphin was 'all over' him. Lewis attributed his 'defeat' to the fact that the Dolphin was being flown by Capt W.J.C.K. Cochran-

engined fighting scout with the BEF. He conceded that the Dolphin could be an alternative to the SPAD 13, provided it could be delivered on time and with satisfactory engines of English manufacture. French-built Hispano-Suizas would be required for the S.E.5a programme.

A second prototype was under construction and there must have been official confidence in the type because on 28 June, Hooper & Co. of Chelsea was given an order for 200 (D5201–D5400). The following day, Sopwith's was contracted to build 500 production Dolphins (C3777– C4276), its largest order to date. A fortnight later, Darracq received an order for a further 200

which angled downwards from the cockpit to the nose, no doubt improving visibility in that direction. This arrangement exposed the barrel casings of the twin Vickers guns. Twin radiators were let into the inner, upper mainplanes, each with its own header tank. The rear decking was still brought up to cockpit level, as was the front cowling, and a small windscreen was fitted to the front cross tube of the centre section. An Aldis sight was passed through that screen. The tail fin was reduced in height and a balanced rudder was fitted. Visibility, downwards and forwards from the cockpit, was enhanced by the provision of interspar cut-outs, each of one rib width, in the lower mainplanes.

It should be noted that the slab-sided fuselage was only 27in (68.6cm) wide and this precluded the use of two right-hand-fed Vickers guns – there was insufficient room for the magazine of such a starboard gun. A left-hand-fed breech had been developed for the weapon and the Dolphin had priority for guns so fitted. Both of the Vickers guns on a Dolphin were fed from the centre of the fuselage and this allowed the use of simplified ejection chutes for cartridges and spent belt links.

This second prototype, again unnumbered, was tested at Brooklands in July and the arrangement of the radiators in the upper wings was found to be unsatisfactory, providing insufficient cooling. It was returned to Kingston for modification and given flank radiators, positioned below the rear of the cockpit. The balanced rudder's shape was also revised and a redesigned fin, of greater area, was fitted. It was in this form that the machine was delivered to Martlesham Heath, on 27 July, for official type trials that generated Reports M137 and 137A. The performance figures revealed improvements over those obtained with the first prototype. A four-bladed airscrew was tried, but performance was impaired and so the standard two-bladed type was reinstated. The reports were very favourable as regards the machine's handling qualities and noted the effectiveness of the revised radiator layout. The pilot's view forwards and downwards was criticized, but it was suggested that the former could be improved by lowering the height to which the cowling was brought at the cockpit.

A third prototype was under construction and resembled the second. It did, however, dispense with the lower-wing cut-outs and shutters were added to its radiators. When it arrived, rather belatedly, at Martlesham on 18 October, it was fitted with a four-gun armament. The original twin Vickers guns had been supplemented with a pair of Lewis guns stripped of their barrel casings and mounted at an upward angle on the front of the centre-section frame. This fitting may have been in response to the Air Board specification for a new fighting scout, Type A1 (a), to which the subsequent Snipe was to aspire. This armament arrangement also attracted the interest of the RNAS, presumably due to its possibilities as an anti-airship weapon. The Lewis guns were not fixed in a forward firing position, but were carried on a mounting that incorporated a three-position ratchet, which allowed limited sideways movement.

Flank radiators were adopted on the modified second prototype and retained on the third, which is shown here at Brooklands. That machine retained the high rear decking of its two predecessors and produced the streamlined fuselage, whose lines are emphasized in this photograph and may have led to the name Dolphin being adopted. This machine had the full armament of twin Vickers plus two Lewis guns. JMB/GSL

The RNAS was involved in discussions regarding the Lewis gun armament, its representative being Lt F.W. Scarff.

While at Martlesham, the third prototype had modifications made to its fuselage and these involved the lowering of the decking behind the cockpit, to improve rearward visibility, and a reduction in the height of the engine cowling in front of the cockpit, presumably in response to the suggestions made after the trials with the second prototype. The new machine was not reported on until 22 January 1918, by which time production Dolphins were becoming operational. Report M172 recorded that without the Lewis guns, performance was similar to that of the earlier prototypes, but that, with one gun, it was slightly reduced. That delay in reporting had been due to problems with the machine's oil tanks.

Trenchard had heard of the increase in armament and wisely insisted that he did not want performance handicapped by too much extra armament. He was reassured that the Lewis fittings were not permanent and the machine could operate with one, if required. In operational use, when a Lewis was fitted on the centre section, it was (almost invariably) mounted to starboard.

A fourth prototype had been constructed and was of the form adopted by production machines. It was originally intended for Martlesham, but was sent to France on 29 October, arriving at 1 AD St Omer. It was tested there, with full four-gun armament, and the ensuing report was again very favourable. The machine was not returned to England, but instead was passed to 19 Sqn at Bailleul. That squadron had been selected as the RFC's first Dolphin unit and was then flying SPAD VIIs. Its pilots liked the new machine and reports on it were unanimous in their praise.

Early Service

The first production Dolphins were, by then, coming off the production line at Sopwith's Kingston works and it is interesting that the first operational unit to receive any of these was an RNAS one, not RFC. C3786 was delivered to Guston Road, Dover, on 6 December and was taken onto charge by 1N Sqn, in England for re-equipment with Camels, having only recently given up its Triplanes. This aeroplane remained at Dover when 1N Sqn returned to France on 16 February 1918. It had been joined at that station by C3785 on 6 January. This second aeroplane remained at Dover until, at least, the beginning of June, latterly on the strength of 491 Flt, a Marine Operations unit that was primarily equipped with D.H.9s. C3786 had a more active career. It went to

France and joined 4N Sqn at Bray Dunes on 23 March, remaining with that unit when it became 204 Sqn RAF. It was damaged on 7 April and, after rebuilding, was with 23 Sqn, with which unit it was used in two successful combats.

19 Sqn began to receive its first production Dolphins on 28 December and was fully equipped with the type within a fortnight. The unit retained the fourth prototype and it was given the serial number B6871, a number from the range allotted to airframes rebuilt in France by the two Aircraft Depots. This aeroplane continued to serve in 19 Sqn until 26 February 1918, when it was lost in combat near Comines with a Fokker Dr I; its pilot, 2Lt J.L.

Sqn, working up at Beaulieu, had suffered three days earlier (2Lts C.D. Chapman and A.R. Taylor in C3800 and C3860). The prejudice that surrounded the type's back-stagger may have been the cause for urgent remedial action, which involved strengthening the wing root fittings for the front spars in both upper and lower wings. That done, and the modification applied retrospectively to existing machines, the problem did not arise again.

The first three production Dolphins (C3777–79) from Sopwith's had been delivered to Martlesham for continued trials and they had returned performance figures that were not significantly different from those returned using the prototypes.

breech casing of the gun uncomfortably close to the pilot's face. Tests with the cabane, using the third prototype, indicated a slight loss of performance, in terms of speed, rate of climb and service ceiling.

These three production machines continued to be used at Martlesham, although C3779 was lost in a crash on 5 February 1918. Its pilot, Lt L.M. Barlow MC**, had a distinguished combat record from his service with 56 Sqn the previous year. C3777 was later employed as a ground-instructional airframe at Uxbridge.

It was unfortunate that Dolphin production was getting into its stride at a time when there was a shortage of Hispano-Suizas, and this would seem to be the reason for the new fighting scout's delayed entry into service in significant numbers. Sopwith's had delivered more than 120 airframes by the end of 1917 and further orders were placed with the parent firm and its two subcontractors. Experience with the 200hp Hispano-Suiza revealed shortcomings, which were never fully rectified. The lubrication system was an endless cause of trouble and the use of reduction gears brought its own problems. Not only were these gears often of poor-quality material and prone to shearing, but they were also made to different ratios by different manufacturers, causing inevitable problems of requisition on the squadrons using that engine (whether Dolphin or S.E.5a).

It was hoped, during late 1917, that the Dolphin could be adopted as a Home Defence machine. The Camel had not yet been standardized as the VI Brigade's single-seater night-fighter and the Dolphin seemed to be a better, more stable proposition than its radial-engined stablemate. In addition, its Lewis guns could be used to fire the new RTS ammunition, which was not entirely suitable for firing through the propeller arc from fixed and synchronized Vickers guns. Discussions took place between Sopwith's and RFC representatives, which included Maj E.R. Pretyman, the CO of 61 Sqn. It was considered that increased dihedral would make the machine more stable and that an adjustable, enlarged tailplane would make it easier fly. Overturning after landing at night was a common occurrence on Home Defence stations and the exposed position of Dolphin pilots would make them vulnerable to injury in such a type of accident. The simple solution was suggested as being two semicircular steel tubes, one mounted above each pair of inner interplane struts. These would prevent injury

Production Dolphins had the lowered rear decking that was introduced on the modified third prototype and retained on the fourth. This view shows a pair of early Dolphins on a muddy Beaulieu aerodrome on 15 February 1918. The main subject is probably C3816 of 79 Sqn. At the time, the full four-gun armament was still being fitted. The protective covering of the rear centre-section spar and the leather headrest below can be discerned. JMB/GSL

McLintock, was killed. It was on that same day that 19 Sqn achieved its first combat success on the type, with Lt J.D. de Pencier being credited with sending another triplane down out of control. McLintock was not 19 Sqn's first Dolphin fatality – 2Lt A.A. Veale had been killed when C3826 crashed on 22 January.

It was at this time that concern arose about the structural integrity of the Dolphin, after a crash had resulted from wing failure. That crash may have been Veale's, or it may have been one of two that 79

All three, as well as the third prototype, were fitted with a raised cabane structure of tubular steel. This was done to develop a concession to pilot safety in the event of a machine turning over on landing; the pilot's head was exposed and severe injury in such a circumstance was a decided possibility. The cabane comprised a pair of triangular tubular fittings that mounted on the centre-section spar attachments. These were connected at their apexes by a cross tube, which was then utilized as the mounting for a Lewis gun, bringing the

and give sufficient clearance to allow a pilot to extricate himself safely from the cockpit. Sopwith's modified C3858 to meet these suggestions, the dihedral angle of the wings being twice that of standard machines. Photographs do not suggest an enlarged tailplane, but that member was adjustable, the sternpost being replaced by sliding tubes that moved through a worm gear. That gear was operated by cables, which were fed around a control wheel on the port side of the cockpit. C3858 was not ready, in its modified form, until 19 February 1918, by which time standard Dolphins were already in service with VI Brigade.

Formation of 141 Sqn had taken place at Rochford on 1 January and it moved to Biggin Hill on the 9th of the following month. It received at least six Dolphins, the concessions to their intended night-fighting role being simply the provision of underwing brackets for Holt magnesium flares and wingtip navigation lamps, the addition of Hutton illuminated gunsights and (presumably) cockpit lighting. Available photographs of 141 Sqn Dolphins (showing

The RNAS received C3785 and C3786. The former is shown here at Guston Road, Dover. Again, there is a full armament and the machine was decorated with an early example of shark mouth and eye markings. JMB/GSL

the first 'Comic' conversions showing improvements in performance over the standard F1. In addition, problems with the geared Hispano-Suiza were becoming apparent and so Dolphins were then withdrawn from that duty, 141 Sqn giving up its machines in April.

at Shotwick and 91 Sqn at Chattis Hill. Forward planning by the RFC anticipated that all six of these squadrons would be operational with the type during the spring of 1918, alongside 19 Sqn and 23 Sqn, which was scheduled to re-equip from SPAD XIIIs. 23 Sqn had only received

The first operational Dolphin unit was 19 Sqn, which had the distinctive dumbbell unit marking. B7855 of that unit was a reconstructed airframe from the SARD at Farnborough and had that depot's characteristic apostrophe added to its serial. It is seen here visiting Izel-le-Hameau and was lost in action on 30 October 1918, with Capt J.W. Crane killed. via author

B7928 was another SARD reconstruction and is here shown, unarmed, at Farnborough. It is interesting to note that the serial, in its SARD style, was also marked on the rear fuselage. JMB/GSL

C3803, C3862, C3942 and C3962) reveal that no cabanes or protective hoops were fitted. C3803 and C3942, at least, had their national markings altered to eliminate the white portions and C3862 was also recorded with 78 Sqn.

As recounted earlier, the decision was made during early 1918 to standardize on the Camel as the VI Brigade night fighter, rotary engines being easier to start and

In Service in France

It had been planned that further squadrons would be equipped and 79 Sqn, then mobilizing at Beaulieu, began to receive its Dolphins during December, as did 87 Sqn at Hounslow. 85 Sqn, colocated with 87 Sqn, was also intended to have the type and further units earmarked for service in France were 81 Sqn at Scampton, 90 Sqn

that latest model of the famous French fighting scout, also powered by the 200hp Hispano-Suiza, during December 1917 and its adoption must have been seen as a stop-gap measure – certainly it did not interfere with other programmes, having been acquired in lieu of contracted examples of the SPAD VII.

The RFC in France expected these new units and when the 22 March reallocation of unit-markings was circulated, it included devices for all eight Dolphin squadrons. 19 Sqn was allotted its famous dumb-bell, 23 Sqn a white disc, 79 Sqn a white square and 87 Sqn a horizontal 'S'. These markings, of course, were subsequently adopted and retained for the duration of hostilities. 81 Sqn was allotted a horizontal crescent, 91 Sqn a white triangle and 90 Sqn a white bar that sloped downwards on the rear fuselage. These were never worn in France. 85 Sqn was given a white hexagon which was not carried on its Dolphins, but which became famous on its S.E.5as and was retained on that unit's machines through to the 1970s.

Dolphins and 90 Sqn continued at Shotwick, serving in a training capacity until it was disbanded in July. It had received a few Dolphins (for example C3878, C3909, C4002, C4063, C4101, C4169 and C4170), as had two other Shotwick-based units, 95 Sqn (C4101, C4139, C4062 and C4064) and 96 Sqn (C3909).

The date for 81 Sqn to join the BEF was set for April 1918, with 96 Sqn to follow in May and 86 Sqn in June. As it transpired, all three were disbanded during the summer, into the expanded system of Training Depot Stations. In addition 93 and 95 Sqns, which were expected in France during September, were also disbanded. 91 Sqn continued to

The back-staggered wing layout of the type evoked memories of the D.H.5 among service pilots and, at first, the Dolphin was regarded with trepidation. Once operational pilots had overcome whatever prejudices the Dolphin's initial reputation had generated, they discovered that it was a superb fighting scout and began to use it to its potential. An indication of the type's capabilities was the fact that the four squadrons that flew it suffered only twenty-seven combat fatalities. After its initial 'victory' in February, 19 Sqn continued to achieve combat success and an early exponent of the type in that unit was Maj A.D. Carter DSO. His rank was from his service

D5315 served with 23 Sqn and was photographed in the summer of 1918. The balance area of its rudder appears to have been marked in a darker colour. JMB/GSL

C4147 was one of 23 Sqn's early Dolphins and is shown overturned after a landing accident. The obvious danger of the exposed nature of the pilot's head in such an accident is well illustrated. JMB/GSL

79 Sqn had received some early Sopwith-built machines for training and lost two, as mentioned earlier. It began mobilizing for active service at the start of 1918 and joined the BEF on 20 February. 87 Sqn did not join the BEF until after the formation of the RAF, flying from Hounslow to St Omer on 24 April, by which time 23 Sqn had started exchanging its SPAD XIIIs for Dolphins. Although other units were subsequently intended to operate the type in France, none materialized and these four squadrons were the sole ones to use it on active service.

The reduction to half of the intended squadrons becoming operational with the type was a reflection of the shortage of engines, S.E.5a production evidently having priority. 85 Sqn was re-equipped with SE5as and was operational by May, its Dolphins (such as C3845, C4145, C4172) going to other units in the process of formation. At Northolt, 86 Sqn received

operate the type from Tangmere and Kenley, while 81 and 93 Sqns were reformed and their departures to France again rescheduled, but never undertaken. Unit markings were once more designated, 91 Sqn again being allocated a white triangle, while 81 Sqn was given the white hexagon and 93 Sqn the crescent that had originally been intended for 81. It should be noted that the same marking could be given to two squadrons, as long as they operated different types of aeroplane. The reformed 93 Sqn had been planned as an all-Canadian unit, but its intended personnel were transferred to 81 Sqn at Upper Heyford, which received Dolphins during November and had the dual identity of 1 Sqn, Canadian Air Force. Its Dolphins never carried the hexagon marking, but did carry the appropriate (and probably unofficial) one of a maple leaf. 91 Sqn did mark its triangle onto Dolphins but it is not known whether 93 Sqn adopted its marking.

in the infantry, as in 19 Sqn he was a flight commander. Carter had already achieved considerable success on the squadron's earlier SPAD VIIs and this was continued with the Dolphin. Between 15 and 24 March, he was credited with destroying two enemy machines and sending a further two down out of control.

The German spring offensive, which began on 21 March, saw the RFC fling as many machines as possible into ground-attack work, and the Dolphin was no exception. A standard carrier for four 20lb bombs was fitted under the fuselage to give added punch to work on such sorties. At first, 79 Sqn was involved in flying covering patrols and suffered both its and the Dolphin's first casualty to enemy action when 2Lt A.F.G. Clarke was shot down in C8244 to become a POW on 23 March. On the 26th, 19 Sqn suffered its first casualties on low-flying operations when 2Lts E.J. Blyth (C3793) and F.W. Hainsby

(C3790) were shot down. The following day was a bad one for 79 Sqn, losing four Dolphins, with two pilots killed and another made POW. However, in the next three weeks 79 Sqn suffered only a further two casualties and 19 Sqn none, a low rate compared to those suffered by other (particularly Camel) units.

Once the spring crisis had subsided, the Dolphin was brought into its own in the role for which it was intended. The introduction of the German *Jagdgeschwadern* and *Jagdgruppen*, combat wings, brought about a revision of RAF tactical formations. The RAF response was for similar large patrols, usually comprising machines from squadrons with varying equipment. Where this was the case, machines were disposed at heights that gave optimum performance. Usually this meant Camels at about 10,000ft (3,050m), with S.E.5as above at about 15,000ft (4,570m) and Dolphins as 'top cover' at 18,000–20,000ft (5,490–6,100m).

Dolphin pilots continued to notch up combat successes. Carter, in 19 Sqn, increased his 'victory' total to fourteen on the type, out of his total 'score' of twenty-nine. Eleven of these were in C4017, including credit for three Pfalz D IIIs on 23

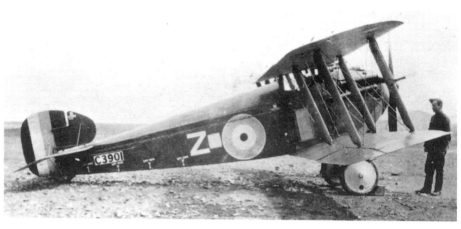

C3901 was one of 79 Sqn's early Dolphins, marked with the unit symbol of a white square, its individual letter 'Z' and its wheel covers doped in white. JMB/GSL

C8043 was another Dolphin with 79 Sqn's C Flt and had its individual letter repeated on the turtle decking. Its wheel covers had light coloured centres. JMB/GSL

April. The final three were achieved in C4132, then on 19 May he was made POW after being brought down in C4017 by Ltn P. Billik of *Jasta* 52.

In 79 Sqn, the 'star turn' was Capt F.W. Gillet DFC CdeG(B), who was also the leading Dolphin 'ace'. He flew with the squadron from 29 March until the

Armistice and was first credited with the destruction of an enemy machine on 3 August. His eventual total of twenty included the destruction of three kite balloons.

However, 23 Sqn did not achieve the success on the Dolphin that it had with its earlier SPADs, although an American, Lt (later Captain) J.W. Pearson had a string of twelve 'victories' that made him the unit's leading scorer on the type. In 87 Sqn

it was Capt A.W. Vigers MC DFC, who matched Carter's achievement of fourteen enemy brought down while flying the type. Other Dolphin pilots who distinguished themselves in combat were Lt H.A. White of 23 Sqn, Capts J. Leacroft MC* and O.C. Bryson MC of 19 Sqn, Capts R. Bannerman DFC* and F.I. Lord DFC of 79 Sqn

and Capt A.A.N.D. Pentland MC DFC of 87 Sqn.

The Dolphin had been intended to have a four-gun armament, but RFC authorities had dictated that this be reduced to three. In operational service, pilots often preferred to remove the Lewis gun, its use in combat being limited. Despite its drawback of being drum fed, the Lewis was probably a better weapon in the close combat situations that World War I pilots often found themselves in, due to its narrower cone of fire. It was left to 87 Sqn to turn the Dolphin into the first RAF fighter with a forward firing armament of four machine guns. During the summer of 1918, some of its pilots began to mount a pair of Lewis guns, one on each of the lower wings of their Dolphins. The chosen location was just inboard of the inner interplane struts, from which position the propeller arc was cleared. The reason(s) for the adoption of this armament layout were not documented. It may have been done simply to increase the volume of fire, or to allow the use of RTS ammunition, or it may have been to make use of the greater accuracy of the Lewis. If the latter was the case, the oft-repeated criticism of the installation (that ammunition drums could not be changed) can be negated, as the 194 rounds of ammunition carried in two double drums would have a greater proportion on target than a much greater number of Vickers rounds.

The RFC/RAF training programme had to take the introduction of the Dolphin into account and some of the higher Training Squadrons were designated as those for prospective pilots of the type. Training Depot Stations, specializing in the type, were created from the disbandment of

(Above) **C3900 was another early Dolphin with 79 Sqn and is shown, apparently, without unit or individual markings.** JMB/GSL

4 TDS at Hooton Park was one of the home-based units dedicated to training pilots especially for Dolphins. One of its machines is shown here with the fittings for the Lewis guns prominent. The strops on the rear centre-section spar may have been aids to cockpit entry. The pilot shown was J.S. Swales, who was posted to 43 Sqn – not a Dolphin unit. JMB/GSL

Training and (some) home-based Service Squadrons from July 1918. It should be noted that many training units (of all types) that were intended to have a full establishment of Dolphins did, in fact, operate small numbers alongside other types. In addition to those service squadrons already mentioned that did not achieve operational status, 1 and 70 TS at Beaulieu and 60 TS at Scampton were the main original units tasked with training Dolphin pilots. Under the TDS system, 4 TDS at Hooton Park, 29 TDS at Beaulieu, 34 TDS at Scampton, 46 TDS at South Carlton and 51 TDS at Shotwick were all noted in the Autumn 1918 Survey of Stations as each having an intended establishment of thirty-six Dolphins and thirty-six Avros. It is unlikely that these establishments were ever reached; certainly 34 TDS was still operating numbers of Camels and Pups at the time of the Armistice and on into 1919.

At least one Dolphin was converted to become a two-seat trainer, following the precedent set by the Camel. The conversion was again under the auspices of the 23rd Wing, 34 TDS at Scampton utilizing C8022 for this purpose. No report has emerged of such a conversion's handling and performance.

Dolphins were issued to Fighting Schools in England. C8090 and C8091 are shown with 4FS at Marske. They were Dolphin IIIs and the lowered thrust line is evident. JMB/GSL

The Dolphin II and III

Although the Martinsyde F.4 Buzzard was scheduled to replace Dolphins with the BEF during 1919, a development of the Sopwith type could have made that unnecessary. The Buzzard was powered by the 300hp Hispano-Suiza 8Fb and that same engine was installed in the Dolphin, with these machines then designated Dolphin IIs, with the retrospective designation Dolphin I being given to those with the 200hp Hispano-Suiza.

The 300hp engine was recognized for the great potential it had, but it was up to the French to consider the Dolphin II for production. An early Dolphin had been received in France at the beginning of 1918 and fitted with an early 300hp engine, apparently with assistance from Sopwith representatives in Paris. Harry

Specification – Sopwith Dolphin	
Engine:	One 200hp Hispano-Suiza (geared Dolphin I, ungeared Dolphin III) or 300hp Hispano-Suiza (Dolphin II)
Weights:	Empty 1,400lb (635kg) (Dolphin I and Dolphin III), 1,566lb (710kg) (Dolphin II); loaded c2,000lb (907kg) (Dolphin I and Dolphin III), 2,358lb (1,070kg) (Dolphin II)
Dimensions:	Length 22ft 3in (6.78m); height 8ft 6in (2.59m); wingspan upper 32ft 6in (9.91m), lower 32ft 6in (9.91m); chord upper 4ft 6in (1.37m), lower 4ft 6in (1.37m); gap 4ft 3in (1.3m); stagger 1ft 6in (46cm) negative; dihedral upper 2°, lower 2°
Performance:	Max. speed 120mph (193km/h) (Dolphin I), 140mph (225km/h) (Dolphin II), 117mph (188km/h) (Dolphin III) Service ceiling 21,000ft (6,400m) (Dolphin I), 24,600ft (7,500m) (Dolphin II), 19,000ft (5,790m) (Dolphin III) Endurance 2 hours
Armament:	Two fixed Vickers guns, synchronized to fire through propeller arc plus two optional Lewis guns

The Dolphin II had the 300hp Hispano-Suiza, whose greater bulk necessitated the use of an enlarged cowling. This machine appears to be one of those built in France. JMB/GSL

Hawker crossed the Channel to test-fly the conversion and was confident enough in its strength to perform aerobatics on its first outing. The machine was crashed, due to pilot error, on 18 April and was almost immediately replaced by D3615, which was similarly converted. Trials with this machine returned spectacular performance figures. Despite its heavier loaded weight, due partly to an increased fuel load, the Dolphin was capable, according to British figures, of 140mph (225km/h) at 10,000ft (3,050m) and had a service ceiling of 24,600ft (7,500m). Figures from French trials were very similar, although they recorded the service ceiling as a more impressive 26,000ft (7,925m).

The Dolphin II was instantly recognizable by the more bulbous cowling that was needed to enclose the engine ancillaries. The Vickers guns were then, once again, buried within the fuselage and the ungeared engine resulted in a lower thrust line. Long exhaust pipes were led along the upper fuselage longerons, being cranked to pass over the radiator blocks. An adjustable tailplane was fitted.

The RAF was informed, but expressed little interest in acquiring a specimen, presumably because it was anticipating the service introduction of the Martinsyde F.4 Buzzard. The United States Air Service was, however, deficient in combat aeroplanes and its own domestic aircraft

industry was unable to make that good. It was agreed therefore that Dolphin IIs for the USAS would be produced in France, orders for 2194 being placed with the Société Anontme de Constructions Aéronaubiques of Paris. There is no known record of how many Dolphin IIs were actually produced, but it cannot have been many, the Armistice having been signed before any production machine was delivered.

The French government was also looking for a SPAD XIII replacement and the exciting Nieuport C1 was just a prospect in mid-1918, the prototype only flying in June. Evaluations of both types were made, but again the Armistice intervened. Post-war, the French, not unnaturally, adopted their indigenous design.

The USAS did, however, receive Dolphins, probably Mk.1s. Eight were allotted to the Americans during October 1918, for conversion to Mk.II standard. These were E4662–4663 and E4465–4650. A further five, E4642–4643, E4646–4647 and E4650, have also been reported as being delivered to that service and these may have been the ones to be shipped across the Atlantic at the beginning of 1919. A Dolphin was reported at McCook Field by the end of the year, but it is unlikely that it was used for any flying from that experimental station.

The 200hp Hispano-Suiza had continued to give trouble and its unreliability can have done little to increase novice pilot confidence in the Dolphin. The same problems were encountered on the S.E.5a. The introduction of the ungeared Wolseley Viper engine, a development of the Hispano-Suiza, did much to eliminate problems with the S.E.5a, but that engine was not available for Dolphin production. It was not until late 1918 that a, seemingly obvious, solution was implemented. The engines of a considerable number of Dolphins were de-geared. That involved modifications to the crankcase and the resultant lowering of the thrust line meant that the nose cowling had to be modified. A variety of nose cowling shapes is evident from photographs and it would seem that

modifications were made on a local basis. The designation Dolphin III was given to such machines and they were being introduced to the four squadrons of the BEF at the time of the Armistice, where they were operated alongside Dolphin Is. The de-gearing of the engines had a slightly detrimental effect on performance, but this was, no doubt considered a price worth paying for the improved reliability.

Post-War

The Dolphin did not last long in the post-war RAF. 19 Sqn gave up its machines and was reduced to a cadre on 18 February 1919, as had 87 Sqn nine days earlier; 23 Sqn followed on 15 March. 79 Sqn lasted a little longer, taking its Dolphins to the Rhineland as part of the Army of Occupation and setting up base at Bickendorf. It continued on policing duties until disbanded on 15 July.

In the UK, 81 Sqn (1 Sqn CAF) exchanged its Dolphins for S.E.5as in April and 91 Sqn disbanded on 3 July 1919. 93 Sqn had already disbanded, ten days after the signing of the Armistice. Thereafter the few Dolphins on RAF strength were with experimental establishments. Among other experiments, the Dolphin was used in pursuing the RAF's increasing interest in providing operational pilots with effective

parachutes and in trials to test the Lott petrol tank. That tank was designed to be jettisoned in case of emergencies. The RAE at Farnborough had used a few, including C3747, C4191 and D8194, but these had been withdrawn by September 1919.

Many Dolphins had been delivered direct to storage and the Aircraft Disposal Company at Croydon acquired numbers of the type. Only one, however, ever entered the civil register, G-EATC (ex-D5369) which was registered to Handley Page Ltd on 7 May 1920.

The last surviving operational Dolphins were flown in Poland. Post-war, the British government presented aircraft to the newly emerging nations of Eastern Europe and thirty, including ten Dolphins, were given to Poland. Initial allocations included E4821 on 19 March and D5331, E4666 and E4721 on 20 March 1920. These were cancelled and the machines that eventually arrived in Poland during May were E4815, F7120, F7128, J139, J151, J153, J162, J169, J178 and J181. These were used operationally by Polish forces, but a lack of spares soon made the type unserviceable. By 1921, the Dolphin had been withdrawn.

No intact Dolphin is in known existence, although the RAF Museum at Cardington has parts that are currently being incorporated into a reconstruction for display at Hendon.

Representative Dolphins in Unit Service

19 Sqn – Bailleul/Ste Marie Cappel/Savy/Abscon/Genech: B6871, B7855, C3769, C3789, C3770, C3793, C3794, C3818, C3820, C3828, C3833, C3838, C3902, C4026, C8158, D5236, D5237, E4501, E4514, E4546, E4547.
23 Sqn – St Omer/Bertangles/Cappy/Hancourt/Bertry East/Clermont: B7894, C3785, C3807, C3824, C3870, C3871, C3903, C3905, C4130, C4149, C4181, D3581, D3691, D3749, D3752, D5232, D8531, E4319, E4492, E4717, E4729, F5961, H7243.
78 Sqn – Sutton's Farm: C3862.
79 Sqn – Beaulieu/St Omer/ Estrée Blanche/Champien/Cachy/Beauvois/Ste Marie Cappel/Reckem/Nivelles/Bickendorf: B7927, C3797, C3816, C3879, C3887, C3900, C3901, C4059, C4131, C4182, C8043, D3771, D8075, E4512, E4715, E4859, F7065.
81 Sqn – Scampton: C8023, C8602, D3729.
81 Sqn/1Sqn CAF – Upper Heyford: C8002, E4764, E4768, F7076, F7085, J1, J2, J3, J6, J8, J10, J12, J14, J15, J16, J30, J33.
85 Sqn – Hounslow: C3845, C4028, C4145, C4168, C4172.
87 Sqn – Hounslow/St Omer/Petite Synthe/Estrées-les-

Crécy/Rougefay/Soncamp/Boussières: C3827, C4136, C4155, C4156, C4157, C4158, C4159, C4162, C4163, C4165, C4173, C4230, C4239, C8072, C8109, C8163, D3590, D3718, D3774, E4493.
90 Sqn – North Shotwick/Brockworth: C3670, C3878, C3909, C4002, C4028, C4063, C4101, C4169, C4170, D3739, D3764.
90 Sqn – Buckminster: (J5, J7, J20, J21 allocated).
91 Sqn – Kenley/Lopcombe Corner: C3818, D5295, D5296, D5298, D5300, E4441, E4730, E4733, E4757, J1, J4, J9, J11, J13.
92 Sqn – Tangmere: C4172.
93 Sqn – Tangmere: C4428.
93 Sqn – Port Meadow: D5276, D5277, D5282, E4428, E4764, E4765, F7056, F7085, (J2, J3, J6, J8, J9, J10, J11, J12 allocated).
95 Sqn – North Shotwick: C4062, C4064, C4139, C4161.
96 Sqn – North Shotwick: C3909.
141 Sqn – Rochford/Biggin Hill: C3803, C3862, C3942.
1N Sqn – Dover: C3786.
4N Sqn/204 Sqn – Dover: C3786.
491 Flt – Dover: C3785.
1 TS – Beaulieu: C3848.

27 TS – London Colney:
60 TS – Scampton:
70 TS – Beaulieu: C3797, C3881, C8001, D7554.
4 TDS – Hooton Park: C3862, C3875, C3876, C3911, C3997, C3998, C3999, C4138, C4142, D3670, D3698, D3753, E4505.
10 TDS – Harling Road: E4772.
29 TDS – Beaulieu: B7954, C8061, D5339, E4449.
30 TDS – Northolt: D5261.
34 TDS – Scampton: C4065, C8018, C8024, C8128.
46 TDS – South Carlton: D3686, D3594.
51 TDS – North Shotwick:
56 TDS – Cranwell: E4698.
CFS – Upavon: C4054, D3769.
SSF – Gosport: C4172.
NEAFIS – Redcar: C8090.
1 FS – Turnberry: C3783, E4437.
2 FS – Marske: C3854, C4145, C8090, D3765.
3 FS – Bircham Newton:
4 FS – Freiston:
Experimental Station – Martlesham Heath: C3777, C3778, C8194, D3615, D6567.

CHAPTER TEN

The Snipe and Dragon

The Quest for the Fighter of 1919

The Snipe has, invariably and inevitably, been compared unfavourably with the Martinsyde F.4 Buzzard and its radial-engine development, the Dragon, was undoubtedly a failure. However, a point often overlooked is that both of these Sopwith designs resulted from, initially, a private development of the existing Camel, that may or may not have been drawn to the Air Board specification for Type A1 (a), its next generation of scout (fighter) machines. This specification had been drawn up in April 1917 and anticipated a new machine to be the replacement for the scout types that were then coming into production, namely the S.E.5 and Camel. The performance and armament provision demanded by the specification required a machine that would be vastly superior to existing types, no matter how greatly modified.

This was later combined with the quest for a standardization of engine types, that led to the development and introduction of the B.R.2 and Dragonfly. The airframe design was modified to one that came closer to the Type A1 (a), then the later Type I specification and was finally selected for service on the, apparent, whim of the RFC hierarchy.

The Camel had been a welcome replacement for the under-armed Pup, but one of its major shortcomings was the poor upward view afforded to its pilots. Sat closely under the centre section, the pilot of a Camel could see little above and this deficiency became a liability in the tight turns of a dogfight combat. If the Camel was turning behind an enemy machine, visibility could be lost. It has already been related that centre-section modifications were made to counteract this, but it would seem that an attempt at early rectification of the fault led to the genesis of the design that was to become the Snipe.

Development of the Snipe

Herbert Smith produced drawings, in August 1917, for a single-seat fighter that was to carry an armament of two machine guns, synchronized to fire through the propeller arc, and capable of taking most of the rotary engines then in service. The design owed much to the Camel, with mainplanes of similar planform and an apparently identical tail unit. The mainplanes were, however, rigged with equal dihedral but the

significant difference lay in the fuselage. This was a deep unit, which brought the pilot's level of vision up to the rear of the centre section and gave an uninterrupted view forwards and upwards. This had been, of course, a feature of the Dolphin and it is possible that Smith borrowed that successful feature to overcome one of the Camel's obvious shortcomings. The design was ready for construction as a private venture by September, under Licence No.14, and a BR1 engine was requested from the Air Board. The choice of the BR1 was an obvious one. That power plant had been successfully installed in RNAS Camels and gave that type a performance that was far superior to that of the standard, Clerget-powered design.

When it emerged from the factory at the end of October, the machine was a single-bay biplane of conventional design and closely resembled Smith's original drawings. Only an open centre section, of full interspar chord which may have been an attempt to overcome tail-heaviness, as well as the absence of a fairing over the Vickers guns, showed as obvious modifications. Although a white 'box' was painted on the rear fuselage, no serial was yet added. Serials B9962–B9967 were allocated on 10 November to cover the six prototypes that had been officially ordered eleven days previously. That the machine was seen as a development of the Camel is evident from the wording of that order, which described it as 'Sopwith Single Seater Camel (Snipe)'. The name Snipe was the Sopwith nomenclature for the new design.

The first prototype was soon modified and, although retaining the vertical centre-section struts, had an increased dihedral on its mainplanes and a more substantial fairing around the breeches of its Vickers guns.

A second prototype was ready during that November and was delivered to Farnborough on the 23rd. It resembled the

The first Snipe prototype in its original guise. The centre section was more open than it later became and the shape of the upper mainplane trailing edge was different. In this view, the derivation of the Snipe from the Camel is obvious. JMB/GSL

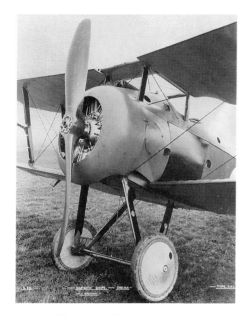

After modification, the first prototype was given a revised cowling and forward decking. The centre-section cut-out was altered and the shape of the upper-wing trailing edge was rounded. JMB/GSL

The first prototype was also given greater dihedral to its mainplanes, as shown in this photograph taken at Brooklands. JMB/GSL

modified first prototype, but was fitted with one of the first six Bentley BR2 engines, which necessitated a taller under-carriage, and had a different fuel system. A direct reading ASI was, at that time, carried on the port interplane struts. The machine was marked with its military number, B9963. After tests at Farnborough, it returned to Brooklands in March 1918 and was then sent to Hendon, where it became one of the small fleet, of various types, that were available for the use of

senior RFC/RAF officers. It was still at Hendon in July, when that heterogeneous collection of machines became The Communications Squadron, later 1 (Communications) Sqn, and served with that unit until at least December.

The exact sequence and numbering of the Snipe prototypes then becomes confused. This problem is compounded by the fact that the annotations to Sopwith factory photographs of these machines are the result of misidentification. For example,

that of a single-bay machine with fully faired fuselage and BR2 engine is labelled as '2nd machine', when it must surely have been B9965, the fourth prototype, in its original guise. It is not known whether B9964, the third prototype, ever existed. It was reported as awaiting its BR1 engine during November 1917 and all six prototypes were reported as having been delivered, but nothing further is known.

B9965 was in existence by the second week in November and scheduled for trials

B9963, the second prototype, served at Hendon with the Communications Squadron and that machine is probably the subject of this photograph. The machine has white wheel covers, coloured bands around its fuselage and flies a streamer from its interplane rear strut. JMB/GSL

The Bentley BR2 Engine

The BR2 engine was rated at 230hp and was another of W.O. Bentley's engineering masterpieces which, although weighing only 70lb (32kg) more than its predecessor, returned 1hp per 2lb (as opposed to 1hp per 2.6lb for the BR1) and produced 50% more torque. It had resulted from an Air Board order for three prototypes of an improved BR1 and, when first tested in October 1917, had produced 234hp in bench runs. The engine was a piece of precision machinery, with the crankcase and cylinders being milled from blocks of solid metal. Aluminium was again used, with steel linings for the cylinder walls.

The Air Board saw the solution to a problem that had persisted up until that time. With no other serious contender on offer, there was now an opportunity to standardize rotary engine production and thus increase output. Accordingly, plans were made for BR2 production that, it was anticipated, would reach an output of 1,500 engines per month.

A variety of manufacturers were subcontracted to build the BR2. Crossley Motors, Daimler, Gwynnes, Humber and Ruston Proctor received orders for a total of 7,300 units but there was no way that such a precision piece could be produced at the rate anticipated by the Air Board. In the event, only 2,567 had been produced by December 1918, but it was undoubtedly the ultimate British rotary engine of the war.

at Martlesham Heath. It retained, at this stage, the single-bay wings, but had fully faired fuselage sides and a redesigned vertical tail unit that appeared totally inadequate in area. Again, a direct reading ASI was fitted to the port interplane struts. An accident and its subsequent repair delayed arrival at the Experimental Station until 18 December. It was the subject of Trials Report M.165, but this was concerned with performance only. It recorded a speed of 119mph (192km/h) at 1,500ft (460m) and a ceiling of 21,500ft (6,550m), but produced no assessment of its shortcomings or potential, on the understanding that these were not required. B9965 was involved in another mishap, during December, and returned to Sopwith's for rebuilding.

It may be that B9964 was statically tested to destruction, using the standard contemporary sand loading tests – but why then would it have needed an engine? Either the second or the fourth prototypes were proposed for this purpose, but the existence of both, fully completed and fitted out, is recorded in photographs and so their use seems unlikely.

It would seem probable that the first three machines were regarded as little more than developments of the Camel and that the Snipe proper began with B9965, which also had a BR2 fitted. Again, it was a single-bay machine, but had fully faired fuselage sides and a wider span centre section that required the splaying of its struts to the fuselage. The centre-section cut-out was reduced to a semicircular one ahead of the rear spar. The fin was much reduced in area and a balanced rudder was fitted. This machine was ready during the same month as the two previous machines, but was involved in an accident. It had been allotted to the Experimental Station at Martlesham Heath and eventually arrived there on 18 December. The Experimental Station Report M.165 recorded a speed of 119mph (192km/h) at 5,000ft (1,525m) and a service ceiling of 21,500ft (6,550m). The accident occurred during late December and the aeroplane was returned to its makers for reconstruction.

Concurrently, a new specification, Type I, had been issued for a high altitude, single-seat fighter and the BR2, whose mass-production had been authorized, was the designated power plant. It would appear that Sopwith took the opportunity to modify B9965 in an attempt to match this requirement. New, two-bay mainplanes were fitted and the third (Lewis) gun, although an optional fitting, was mounted to starboard on the centre section, outside the existing cut-out. In this form it returned to Martlesham and was the subject of a critical report, M.176A. The trials for this took place with a full military load, unlike those for M.165, and this, combined with the increased weight of the new mainplanes, served to return poorer performance figures. More importantly, the handling was criticized and some of this must have been due to the retention of the original fin and rudder.

Sopwith was not alone in looking for a machine to meet the specification for the Type I. Austin, Armstrong Whitworth, Boulton & Paul and British Nieuport had their own contenders. However, only the Snipe had undergone any assessment and its most serious rival, the British Nieuport BN1, was crashed during March. The outcome was the decision to adopt the Snipe,

although much development work was still required.

B9965 was allotted to the BEF for assessment and went to 1 AD at St Omer on 11 March 1918. Reaction, from service pilots, was mixed. The pilot's field of vision was praised, as was its manoeuvrability, speed and climb, but the tail-heaviness and inefficient rudder were criticized.

Despite its shortcomings, the Snipe had been selected and large contracts were placed before any service evaluation of B9965 was finalized. Optimistically, production deliveries were expected to begin that June. The table below shows that the type was not such a great improvement over its predecessor and was less promising than either its radial engined development or potential competition.

B9965 returned to Martlesham during early April, only to be passed to Sopwith's for the fitting of a spinner and modified cowling. While this conversion was under way, B9966 arrived at Martlesham and had modifications that included a slightly enlarged rudder, increased fuel capacity, revised fuel delivery system and an adjustable tailplane. The latter was not of the control-wheel operated, worm gear type that had been used on earlier designs. Instead, a ratchet lever, mounted on the

The fourth prototype, which became B9965, at first retained the single-bay wings, but had a faired fuselage. Its centre section cut-out was a small semicircular opening.
JMB/GSL

Specification:	Camel (BR1)	Snipe	Snipe (Dragonfly)	Buzzard
Speed at 10,000ft	111mph (179km/h)	121mph (195km/h)	148mph (238km/h)	143mph (230km/h)
Climb to 10,000ft	10min	9min 25sec	6min 30sec	6 min 30sec
Endurance	2½ hours	3 hours	?	3 hours

(Above) **B9966 was fitted with the two-bay wings that had subsequently been added to B9965. It too had a small centre-section cut-out and was fitted with a direct reading ASI on its outer port interplane struts.** JMB/GSL

This close-up of B9966 shows how the layout of the production Snipe was evolving. B9966 was later given a rectangular centre-section cut-out and was fitted with an experimental triangular tailplane. JMB/GSL

The ABC Dragonfly Engine

The Air Board decision to standardize on the BR2 could have been undermined because, within days of its having been made, a new engine design was brought to its attention. This was the ABC Dragonfly radial, developed to meet the April 1917 specification for an engine to power the next generation of fighting scouts. On paper, the design was tempting. It was rated at 300hp, had a better power–weight ratio than the BR2 and, it was thought, would be cheap to manufacture. The problem of heat dissipation from the steel cylinders was addressed by a novel method that involved coating the cooling fins with electrically deposited copper, which has better conductive properties. Unusually, it had three valves per cylinder (one inlet and two exhaust) and required twin carburettors. The engine was, however, untried.

The Air Board wisely decided against reducing or abandoning the BR2 programme, but entrusted Vickers to develop the new engine. Standardization was compromised, but this was outweighed by the advantages that would result if the engine achieved its potential. The problems associated with the Dragonfly are detailed in the main text but it was ordered on a massive scale. Seventeen contractors received orders that totalled 11,848 engines, but only thirteen had been delivered by 31 October 1918 and another ten by the end of the year. The vast majority of the balance was cancelled. In the event, it was not a cheap alternative to the BR2; at £1,072 per unit, it was £198 more expensive than Bentley's masterpiece.

upper starboard longeron in the cockpit, controlled cables, which caused the forward end of an actuating arm to move along an arcuate guide. The rear end of the arm was then forced to move up or down the sternpost. In doing so, its connection to the tailplane rear spar caused that surface to pivot about its forward spar. Movement allowed an angle of incidence of between 1 degree 20 minutes and 5 degrees 50 minutes. The new fuel system was of the Badin type, which eliminated the need for wind-driven fuel pumps. Instead, a venturi was used to create suction, which transferred fuel from the main tank, located under the pilot's seat, to the gravity tank and thence to the carburettor.

Trials with B9966 revealed continuing shortcomings, when performance was compared with the Type I specification and service comments regarding its handling characteristics. Attempts at remedial action included the fitting of inversely tapered and balanced upper ailerons, an alteration to the mainplane dihedral angle, a more enlarged

rudder that was coupled with a fuller fin and even a triangular tailplane which resembled, somewhat, that of the Fokker Dr 1.

Production deliveries did not match expectations. Sopwith-built machines began to be delivered during August and resembled B9966 in its original form. The layout had been shown in Air Board Office drawing No. SH D2316, dated 11 April, with the only noticeable difference being an extension of the cockpit side decking back to the line of the rear interplane strut on the port side, presumably in the interest of pilot comfort. That on the starboard side was left open, to allow access to the cocking handle of the Vickers gun. As a result operational pilots were destined to receive machines that retained the problems of control that were the result of the unbalanced ailerons and small vertical tail surfaces. Although orders had been placed with five other contractors, these were slow off the mark and their production rate was only 25 per cent of that expected by the time of the Armistice.

The Dragon

As related, the ABC Dragonfly radial engine had been ordered as an alternative to the BR2 and, although the 200hp Clerget 11E was viewed as the official alternative engine for the Snipe, an example was installed in B9967, the final prototype, during April 1918. The machine had its rear fuselage lengthened by some 22in (56cm), to compensate for the greater weight of its new power plant, but retained the original design of fin and rudder. A bulbous nose cowling enclosed the engine's crankcase, to give a streamlined frontal aspect. The Dragonfly was, however, extremely temperamental. When it performed properly, it gave the Snipe an outstanding performance, with speeds of 140+mph (225km/h), an increased service ceiling and rates of climb that were approximately double those produced using the BR2. Unfortunately, proper performances were few, as the engine gave repeated problems. In the expectation that these difficulties could be overcome, orders were placed for a production version of the Dragonfly Snipe as early as May 1918 and that type was given the new name Dragon.

The promise that had been shown by B9967 led to a similar installation being made on E7990, a production Snipe from the first Sopwith-built batch, that had the large fin and rudder. At one stage, this machine was scheduled for transfer to the USA, but that never materialized. It was delivered to Martlesham for tests, but engine trouble again delayed these and it was sent for repair.

F7017, a production Dragon with the final airframe features, was sent to Martlesham as a replacement for E7990, but it, too, was plagued with engine difficulties. Nevertheless, large orders had been placed

Specification – Sopwith 7F1 Snipe and Dragon	
Engine:	One 230hp BR2 (Snipe), one 360hp ABC Dragonfly (Dragon)
Weights:	Empty 1,305lb (592kg) (Snipe), 1,329lb (603kg) (Snipe 1a), 1,405lb (637kg) (Dragon); loaded 2,015lb (914kg) (Snipe), 2,271lb (1,030kg) (Snipe 1a), 2,132lb (967kg) (Dragon)
Dimensions:	Length 19ft 2in (5.84m) (Snipe, early rudder), 19ft 10in (6.05m) (Snipe, final rudder), 21ft 9in (6.63m) (Dragon); height 9ft 6in (2.9m); wingspan upper, unbalanced ailerons 30ft (9.14m), upper, balanced ailerons 31ft 1in (9.47m), lower 30ft (9.14m); chord upper 5ft (1.52m), lower 5ft (1.52m); stagger 1ft 4in (40.64cm); gap 4ft 3in (1.3m); dihedral upper 4°, lower 4°
Performance:	Max. speed 121mph (195km/h) (Snipe), 117mph (188km/h) (Snipe 1a), 150mph (241km/h) (Dragon) Service Ceiling 19,000ft (5,790m) (Snipe), 23,000ft (7,100m) (Dragon) Endurance 3 hours (Snipe), 4½ hours (Snipe 1a)
Armament:	Two fixed Vickers guns, synchronized to fire through propeller arc, plus 4 × 20lb (9kg) bombs

for Dragons and even as late as September 1921 it, along with the Snipe and Salamander, was specified as a standardized RAF type. The engine's problems were never overcome and the Dragon never reached squadron service. Belatedly, in April 1923, it was withdrawn from the RAF's inventory. It is difficult to reconcile this abject failure with the fact that Granville Bradshaw, who had convinced the authorities of the Dragonfly's worth, was awarded £48,000 by the post-war Royal

Commission on Awards to Inventors and yet W.O. Bentley received only £8,000.

The RAF in the field anticipated great things of the BR2 Snipe and it was preceded by glowing reports that overstated its performance. The two units that flew the type on operations, in the bitter and intense air fighting of the few weeks leading up to the Armistice, achieved some notable combat success, but no more than that achieved by many units that had still to soldier on with the Camel.

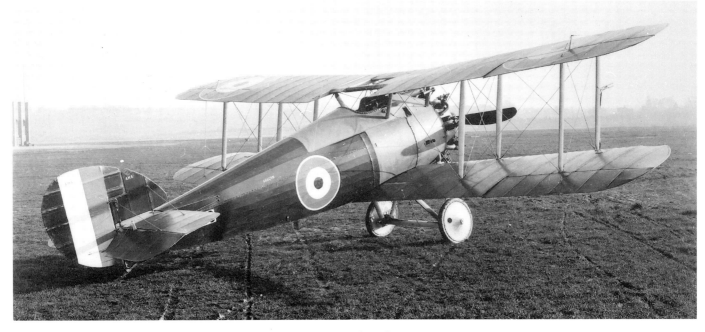

E7990 was the first true Dragon and its lengthened rear fuselage is evident in this view taken at Brooklands. JMB/GSL

The Snipe in Service

The operational unit earmarked to introduce the Snipe into service was 43 Sqn, under the command of Maj C.C. Miles MC, which had a distinguished history of combat with the Camel and 1½ Strutter. The squadron was based at Fienvillers and began taking delivery of the new type, in its initial form, from 2 ASD at the end of August. There followed a long period of working up, that occupied most of September, weather damage to several of its new machines on the 7th prolonging this process. In this, its pilots were most fortunate. Some of the bloodiest air fighting of the war took place during that month and the inadequacies of the type were not put to what would have been a most severe baptism of fire. It was 27 September before the squadron could claim combat victory, its first being a Fokker D VII that Capt R. King (E8031) and Lt C.C. Banks (E8028) sent down, out of control, near Cambrai. The unit had been flying as part of the escort for D.H.9s of 107 Sqn that were detailed to bomb railway targets at Bohain, when Fokkers interfered. King and Banks were both experienced air fighters, this victory raising their credited 'scores' to twenty and ten respectively. A few minutes later, Lt R.S. Johnston sent another down in a similar manner. The unit flew on patrols until the Armistice, but significant combat success was elusive. Victories, as was usual, came mainly to patrol leaders, but the unit's two most experienced pilots only managed to add two more to each of their totals – King and Banks both claiming Fokker D VIIs on 1 and 30 October.

The intended large-scale introduction of the Snipe produced a need for replacement pilots. By July 1918, the RAF had rationalized its training programme to create Training Depot Stations. These took pilots from the *ab initio* stage through to qualification on service types. Each TDS had a type specialization and those intended for Snipes were 30 TDS at Northolt and 41 TDS at London Colney and 42 TDS at Hounslow, whose establishments were intended as thirty-six Avros + thirty-six Snipes, twenty-four Avros + twenty-four Snipes and thirty-six Avros + thirty-six Snipes respectively. It is unlikely that these units ever reached their intended establishments and all three certainly still had a variety of types on strength during late 1918. Before being posted to operational units, scout pilots were given a short

43 Sqn was the first operational unit to receive Snipes. E8006 was flown by 2Lt E.G. Weaver and had the original fin and rudder and unbalanced ailerons. JMB/GSL

course at one of the Fighting Schools, such as Turnberry and Marske, and these, too, were issued with a handful of the new type.

As more Snipes came forward, it became possible to re-equip a further operational

The early forms of fin, rudder and ailerons are seen in this view of E8027, an unarmed machine, apparently with a training unit. JMB/GSL

unit. This was 4 Sqn AFC, another ex-Camel squadron with an enviable combat record. The Australians were withdrawn from operations for a working-up period at Ennetieres and its machines, as delivered, were also of the initial production form.

The first operations with the new type were on 26 October and an afternoon patrol of nine, led by Capt T.C.R. Baker MM (E8069) and 2Lt T.H. Barkell (E8032) became embroiled with fifteen

Fokker D VIIs at 14,000ft (4,270m) over Tournai. In the ensuing dogfight, the Australians were credited with five victories – two for Barkell and one each for Baker, Lt H.W. Ross and Lt E.J. Richards. On the debit side, Barkell was hit in the leg and force-landed near Peronne. It was an auspicious beginning and two days later the unit followed this success with a further six victory claims, with King being credited with three of them.

What was to be 4 Sqn AFC's greatest action, with the Snipe, took place on the 29th. The mid-afternoon patrol of fifteen machines, two Flights led by Capts E.R. King (E8050) and T.C.R. Baker (E8092), tangled with an estimated sixty Fokker D VIIs over Tournai. Another ferocious dogfight developed. Captain G. Jones (E8052) quickly destroyed two and Lt A.J. Palliser (E8064) followed suit, before being attacked by four of the enemy, one of which strayed into his path and was sent down out of control. A further five were claimed by others in the patrol, one to Lt P.J. Sims (E8070) who was then shot down and killed. Further successes were recorded on the 30th, with Baker and King emerging as two of the leading exponents of the Snipe in combat.

Despite its increasingly weakened position, the German Air Service was far from defeated, as the Australians found to their cost on 4 November. It was a day of heavy fighting all along the British Front and, by the end of it, 4 Sqn AFC had lost five of its pilots. Capt Baker (E8062), Lt P.W. Symons (E8038) and Lt A.J. Palliser (E8064) were all killed in an early afternoon tangle with Fokker D VIIs of, probably, *Jasta* Boelke. The other casualties were made that morning, again in combat with Fokkers, and resulted in Lts C.W. Rhodes (E8073) and E.J. Goodson (E8072) being made POW.

The Snipe served operationally with one other unit of the BEF, 201 Sqn at Beugnatre. Only one Snipe, E8102, was on charge alongside its BR1-engined Camels and this was on attachment from the UK. However, it was destined to bring more fame to the type than the collective actions of 43 Sqn and 4 Sqn AFC. It was allotted to Maj W.G. Barker DSO* MC* whose resting after combat in Italy was followed by a posting to Hounslow. Barker argued that he hardly could instruct in the fighting techniques, required for service in France, if it had been a year since he had last fought there, with 28 Sqn. As a consequence, he was allowed a ten-day refresher period and flew E8102 over on 17 October. This Snipe, according to Capt R. Sykes of 201 Sqn, was destined for 43 Sqn but was decorated to Barker's taste and was reminiscent of his beloved Camel, B6313,

with five white bars painted around the rear fuselage. Its port Vickers gun was fitted with the famous red devil, thumbing its nose, as a sight. This was not a flat sheet metal cut-out, as has been previously reported, but a small figurine of a type that Barker and other pilots acquired and used in Italy. The choice of 201 Sqn as host unit was not the logical one. Although engine fitters were familiar with the Bentley engine, there were differences between the BR1 and BR2 and 43 Sqn should have been the obvious choice. The reasoning would seem to have been that 201's commanding officer, Maj C.M. Leman MC DFC, was a friend of Barker's; they had flown together as a B.E.2c crew in 9 Sqn. For the designated ten days, Barker vainly sought combat and diverted during his early morning flight back to 1 ASD, where E8102 was due on the 27th, in order to have 'one last look'. What followed has to be one of, if not the, most epic combats of the war. Patrol flying and fighting had long since become the norm and so the subsequent single-handed combat against overwhelming odds was an exception that demands attention.

Barker encountered a Rumpler C type over Mormal Woods and promptly sent it down, with its crew bailing out. Shortly after, he was 'jumped' by fifteen Fokker D VIIs and received a thigh wound that caused him to faint. Recovering consciousness, Barker found himself surrounded by his attackers and, in a furious fight, sent three of them down to crash. He received further wounds in the process, to his other leg and his left arm. The combat was clearly visible to troops in the Allied front area and his injuries and the combat damage to the machine forced Barker to bring E8102 down to a landing in Allied lines. Barker was awarded the Victoria Cross for this gallantry. The Snipe was salvaged and, after display in the UK, was handed to the Canadian Government. Today, the fuselage is on display in the Canadian War Museum, Ottawa, as a proud memorial to a great fighter pilot.

The Independent Force, based in northeastern France, had been carrying the war to the enemy, by its bombing of targets in southern Germany. The losses inflicted on its day-bombing D.H.4 and D.H.9/9A units in particular were high and thought was given to providing fighter escorts. To this end, 45 Sqn was withdrawn from operations in Italy, and by 22 September had been established at Bettoncourt. The

Camels of the unit lacked the range needed for long-range escort duties. A development of the Snipe was already in hand for this purpose, as a stopgap until a long-range version of the Martinsyde F.4 Buzzard was ready. 45 Sqn was scheduled to re-equip with this variant. Designated the Sopwith 7F1a, Snipe Mk1a, the new machine had increased tankage that gave an endurance of 4 hours and 30 minutes, over an hour more than the standard machine's. Three prototypes, E8089–E8091, were produced, although the serials H9964–H9966 were allotted for these. The variant could be distinguished from standard machines by the presence of an extra fuel filler port behind the cockpit on the port side and a slight sweepback of 1 degree 30 minutes on the mainplanes. The former fed a redesigned main tank of 50 gallons (227 litres) capacity that was shaped to fit below and behind the pilot's seat, while the latter was in compensation for the resultant change to the centre of gravity. The first prototype, for whatever reason, had a vertical tail unit that resembled that of the Dolphin. It had been completed by 18 September, but was not tested at Martlesham until after the Armistice. The Trials Report M.244 recorded speeds that were marginally slower, for given heights, than those of the standard machine. The rate of climb was, however, significantly poorer, but this was to be expected from a machine which carried an extra 230lb load. Fifty Snipe Mk1a were ordered, apparently E8211– E8260, from within the first Sopwith-built batch. These production machines were fitted with the final form of fin and rudder. Deliveries were made to the BEF and Independent Force, but their arrival came post-Armistice. 45 Sqn, the IF unit to receive the Snipe, had E8017 and E8081 by the end of the war, but these must have been standard 7F1s. This was just as well, because when testing of the 7F1a was belatedly carried out, it was discovered that the design was structurally unsafe and orders were given that prohibited aerobatics in the type.

On 30 October, a further unit began to re-equip. 208 Sqn, formerly the famous Naval Eight and under the command of the extrovert Maj C. Draper DSC, drew its first machines from 2 Air Issues. It had not fully re-equipped by the time of the Armistice, but having done so it was tasked for duty with the Army of Occupation, as were 43 Sqn and 4 Sqn AFC.

70 Sqn received Snipes to replace its Camels with the Army of Occupation. E8057 is shown in front of the distinctive hangars at Bickendorf. JMB/GSL

(Below) Another of 70 Sqn's machines is shown in this rear view. It has the unit number '17' on its fuselage and the 'V' on its upper mainplane would suggest that it had seen service with another unit, probably 4 Sqn AFC. JMB/GSL

Eventually, all three units were established on aerodromes around Cologne. The Australians soon returned to their homeland and handed their equipment to the RAF at the end of February 1919. This enabled 70 Sqn, also with the Army of Occupation, to exchange its Camels for Snipes and it continued on policing duties alongside 43 and 208 Sqns until returning to the UK in August. In December 1918, 80 Sqn had received Snipes and in May 1919, after duty in Belgium, was dispatched, via

(Right) E7337 was built by Ruston Proctor and displays the large form of serial number presentation that was introduced in late 1918. This machine saw service with 112 Sqn at Throwley. JMB/GSL

(Below) E6140 had the later form of fin and rudder, but retained unbalanced ailerons. It was one of the handful of Snipes issued to 2 Fighting School at Marske. JMB/GSL

Marseilles, for service in Egypt, being based at Aboukir.

RAF pilots did not have the luxury of parachute equipment, although the Central Powers had adopted this in the spring of 1918. Perhaps spurred on by this, experiments began that examined the potential use of the Guardian Angel parachute for aeroplane pilots, and Snipe E8137 was a machine used for this purpose. The parachute was not worn, but stowed in a sack and connected to its user's harness by a cord. It was deployed by static line. E8137 had its rear upper decking modified to provide stowage for this apparatus, but it cannot have been used for any live jump.

By the end of 1918, the Snipes being delivered were incorporating combinations of the airframe modifications that had been developed on B9966. The enlarged fin and rudder became standard and the balanced upper ailerons were progressively introduced. By that time, however, the war was over, and although many contracts were allowed to continue, the majority of machines delivered were consigned straight to storage.

Home-Based Snipes

Despite the fact that the 'Comic' conversion of the F1 Camel had been identified by the 6th Brigade as the best night-fighting aeroplane of 1918, that machine did not remain long in the hands of the LADA squadrons, once the Armistice had been signed. The type chosen as its replacement was the Snipe. On 31 October 1918, one Snipe was in service with the Home Defence organization. This was probably E8076, which was with 78 Squadron at Sutton's Farm and fitted with full night-flying equipment that included navigation lights, signalling lamps and underwing brackets for Holt magnesium flares. Its national markings were suitably amended to exclude the white portions of the cockades and rudder stripes, but it retained the white surround to its fuselage and upper wing cockades. Interestingly, a Snipe is visible in photographs of the VI Brigade Home Defence Competition, held at the end of August. It would appear that the intention was to replace the Camels of those units that were based immediately around London in the 49th, 50th and 53rd Wings and pass that equipment on to their component units that were still flying F.E.2Bs and Avro 504K(NF)s. The reasoning behind this is unclear. A comparison of the performance figures for the Snipe and the Le Rhone-powered 'Comic' reveals no significant increase in speed or ceiling. Only the greater endurance and increased ammunition stowage of the Snipe can be seen as a possible cause, although a more likely reason is the fact that, by the time of the Armistice, Camel production was running down while that of Snipes was increasing. Given a substantial stock of airframes and the chance to increase engine standardization, the Snipe was an obvious choice. The Snipe was, however, significantly deficient

Representative Machines with Wartime and Army of Occupation Units	
4 Sqn AFC – Serny/Ennetières/Bickendorf: E8050, E8052, E8063, E8064, E8065, E8069, E8070, E8073, E8082, E8085, E8092.	153 Sqn – Hainault Farm: E6143, E6236, E6826, E7367, E7383, E7401, E7405, E7407, E7410, E7413, E8171.
37 Sqn – Biggin Hill: E6153, E6205, E6213, E6830, E6831, E6938, E6939, E6940, E6941, E7407, E7433, E7446, E7530, E7583.	208 Sqn – Maretz/Strée/Heumar/Eil: E6173, E6175, E7343, E7356, E7361, E7363, E7364, E7988, E7996, E8042, E8048, E8051.
43 Sqn – Fienvillers/Senlis/Bouvincourt/Bisseghem/ Cognellée/Bickendorf/Eil: E7989, E7996, E8013, E8021, E8025, E8028.	5 TS AFC – Minchinhampton: E7375, E8138.
44 Sqn – Hainault Farm: E6310, E7504, E7517, E7571, E7572, E7579, F2396.	30 TDS – Northolt: E6157.
45 Sqn – Bettoncourt/Liettres/Izel-le-Hameau: E8017, E8081.	41 TDS – London Colney: E7998.
50 Sqn – Bekesbourne: E7425.	42 TDS – Hounslow: E8079, E8271.
51 Sqn – Marham/Suttons Farm: E7426, E7427, E7432, E7569, E7574, E7575, E7578, E7580, E7582.	56 TDS – Cranwell: E7416.
61 Sqn – Rochford: E6138, E6230, E6235, E6238, E6242, E6246, E6251, E6942, E6944, E7382, E7414, E7415, E7591, E7592.	204 TDS – Eastchurch: E8171.
70 Sqn – Bickendorf: E8057, E8099, E8230, E8323, F2339, F2351, F2367, F2370.	1 Fighting School – Turnberry:
78 Sqn – Suttons Farm: E6230, E6231, E6830, E6831, E7391, E7426, E7427, E7433, E7434, E7446, E7569, E7574, E7575, E7578.	2 Fighting School – Marske: E6140, E6142, E6258, E8077, E8114, E8189, E8316.
112 Sqn – Throwley: E6643, E6839, E6842, E6844, E6848, E7426, E7427, E7429, E8018.	3 Fighting School – Bircham Newton:
143 Sqn – Detling: E6230, E6238, E6843, E7382, E7591, E7593, E7425, E7431.	4 Fighting School – Freiston: E6274.
	Fleet SAFG Leuchars Junction: E6864, E6865, E6866, E6896.
	Fleet Practice Station – Turnhouse: E8111, E8112.
	SEAFIS – Shoreham: E7991, E7992.
	1 School of Navigation & Bomb Dropping – Stonehenge: E6198.
	2 School of Navigation & Bomb Dropping – Andover: E6201.
	2 Wireless School – Penshurst: E6164.

in comparison with its predecessor in terms of the types of ammunition that could be carried. It has already been related that the Camel 'Comic' was produced to allow the firing of RTS incendiary bullets, which were too unstable to be fired through the propeller arc and the reversion to the twin Vickers arrangement can only be viewed as a retrograde step.

Camels had also performed satisfactorily on Marine Operations from shore bases in the UK, but the type's range was limited. It was intended to create five Snipe squadrons for this sort of duty, which involved escorting seaplanes and flying boats over the North Sea. That, presumably, is why E8068 was delivered to the Experimental Station at Grain. There it was fitted with flotation gear and an undercarriage unit that incorporated a hydrovane and allowed for the wheels to be jettisoned in the event of ditching. The machine was successfully ditched and recovered on 19 October 1918, before being sent to Martlesham for trials, which returned performances that were marginally below those of a standard. It subsequently returned to Grain. Another Snipe at that station was fitted with lifting eyes

on the centre section and used in slinging trials. This would suggest that the type was also being considered for shipboard use.

Although the war in Western Europe was over, the new regime in post-revolutionary Russia was regarded as a major threat and so Britain gave support to the various counter-revolutionary forces that had grown in that country. This included air support and the RAF Missions, in both north and south Russia, were provided with a miscellany of operational machines as well as volunteer, combat-proficient aircrew to fly them.

To Russia

The RAF Mission in north Russia was centred on Archangel. In early 1919, it was intended to provide this unit with twelve Snipes, plus spares and at least five (E6350, E6351, E6360, E6375 and E6884) are known to have been operated by the Slavo-British Air Corps at Bereznik. The operations in that theatre were mundane and, although there was some action, any cohesive application of air power was inhibited by the infighting among the anti-Bolsheviks, which developed to such a pitch that their cause collapsed. Foreign support was withdrawn and the RAF Mission prepared to return home in July 1919. A leading figure at Bereznik was Maj Alexander Kozokov (Kazokov), Imperial Russia's foremost fighter pilot. Despondent at the thought of Allied withdrawal, Kozokov took off in Snipe E6350 in the late afternoon of 1 August, maintained a very low height and then pulled up into a loop. The machine lacked the necessary speed and stalled. Kozokov died in the resulting crash, beyond the help of those British and Russian comrades who had rushed to the scene.

Snipes of 1 Sqn flying over Baghdad in loose formation. JMB/GSL

The Snipe Post-War

There was little foreign interest in acquiring either the Snipe or the Dragon. The French Government received Snipe E8267 for evaluation. This was a machine that incorporated the finalized design features and it was tested at Villcoublay during 1918, but no further interest was shown. The Canadian Government acquired three Snipes and one, ex-E7649, received a civil registration, G-CYDZ. The others were E8213 and Barker's E8102. Dragon J3628 was delivered to the US Government (originally E7990 was to have gone), but the type fared no better in trials that took place at McCook Field during the summer of 1921. A few Snipes also went to the United States and at least one was tested at McCook Field. The only foreign government to acquire the Snipe in any quantity was Brazil, whose government bought twelve of the type for its naval aviation service during 1922. These came from stocks held in the UK, presumably by the Aircraft Disposal Company of Waddon, Croydon.

Very few Snipes came on to civil registers. In the UK, only five did so (G-EATF, G-EAUU, G-EAUV, G-EAUW and G-EBBE – ex-J465, J459, J453, J455 and J461 respectively). The Canadian specimen has already been mentioned and at least one appeared in the USA, being used for film work.

The post-Armistice rundown of the RAF was rapid and, by the end of 1919, no home-based squadron was equipped with the Snipe. The parlous state of the nation's defences was recognized the following year with the re-formation on 26 April of 25 Sqn, with Snipes at Hawkinge. This was the sole UK-based fighter squadron but, in September 1922, it was detached to San Stephano in Turkey in response to the Chanak Crisis. It was supported in that venture by, among other units, a detachment of 56 Sqn Snipes.

Other Snipe squadrons were operational overseas. 56 Sqn was re-formed at Aboukir on 1 February 1920, by renumbering 80 Sqn, and served in the Canal Zone until disbandment two years later. In India, 1 and 3 Sqns were re-formed in 1920 and designated originally as B and A Squadrons, respectively. The latter was short-lived, but 1 Sqn was transferred to Mesopotamia and based at Hinaidi as part of the RAF contingent that was charged with upholding the British Mandate for the policing of the region. This often involved flying ground support and low-bombing missions against outbreaks of tribal unrest, for which purposes a carrier for four 20lb bombs could be mounted under the fuselage.

Snipes in post-war service were given overall aluminium finishes from 1923. By then, the balanced ailerons were standard. This view shows a machine of 1 Sqn, which served on policing duty in Mesopotamia. JMB/GSL

A gradual build-up of the RAF at home began in 1923 and, as new fighter squadrons re-formed, the large stock of Snipe airframes was drawn upon to provide their initial equipment. Many of these machines were in need of refurbishment and contracts were placed for this. Much of the reconditioning work was undertaken by Hawker's, in the same Kingston factory where some of the Snipes had originally been built. The reconditioning involved a complete strip-down of both airframes and engines, with suspect parts repaired or replaced. Upon reassembly and recovering, the machines were given a new finish. The drab PC10 Brown and Battleship Grey of wartime origin gave way to the bright 'silver' finish that characterized interwar RAF fighters. Aluminium-pigmented dope was applied to fabric areas that had been primed with brick-red iron-oxide pigmentation, to provide the material with a more effective protection from sunlight. Metal panels were left in their natural finish and often polished. Perhaps in response to the new appearance of their machines, fighter squadrons began to adopt colourful unit markings, most of which have been retained until the present day, and some of these first appeared on the Snipe.

Just as a two-seat version of the Camel had been developed for training, so too was a two-seat Snipe. Sopwith's had prepared drawings for such a machine as early as February 1919, but none were specifically manufactured. The forty or so two-seater Snipes were conversions of existing airframes, which had their armament removed and a second cockpit installed behind the original. Dual control was fitted. These machines were issued, in ones and twos, to the Snipe squadrons of the 1920s and used for continuation training. Others were on the strengths of Flying Training Schools, but never in great numbers.

The reintroduction of the Snipe was, however, purely a stopgap measure, pending the arrival of a new generation of fighters that included the Gloster Grebe and Gamecock, Hawker Woodcock and Armstrong-Whitworth Siskin. 43 Sqn was, probably, the last home-based squadron to have a full complement of Snipes, converting to Gamecock Is in May 1926. Abroad, 1 Sqn operated its Snipes until disbanded on 1 November of that year.

The type continued in service, from 1920, with the CFS at Upavon, the RAF (Cadet) College at Cranwell and 1, 2 and

Representative Snipes with Post-war Units

1 Sqn – Risalpur/Bangalore/Hinaidi: E6655, E6801, E6939, E6960, E6965, E7373, E7514, E7534, E7638, E7639, E7642, E7645.

3 Sqn – Bangalore/Ambala: F2387, H4880, H4883.

3 Sqn – Manston/Upavon: E6342, E6343, E6531, E6648, E6837, E6942, E7415, E7712, F2476.

17 Sqn – Hawkinge: E6478, E6490, E6544, E6622, E6804, E6826, E6862, E7432, F2484.

19 Sqn – Duxford: E6316, E6336, E6338, E6530, E6625, E6838, E6955, E6965, E7599, E7605, E8148, E8245, F2430, F2444.

23 Sqn – Henlow: E6235, E6311, E6340, E6615, E6616, E7713, F2408, F2419.

24 Sqn – Kenley: F2409.

25 Sqn – Hawkinge/San Stephano: E6156, E6243, E6266, E6307, E6339, E6493, E6600, E6623, E6632, E6651, E6944, E6961.

29 Sqn – Duxford: E6595, E6838.

32 Sqn – Kenley: E6268, E6308, E6629, E6646, E6651, E6792, E6794, E6839, E6974, E7550, E7556, F2433, F2434, F2442.

41 Sqn – Northolt: E6316, E6618, E6646, E6825, E6965, E7599, E8245.

43 Sqn – Henlow: E6530, E6612, E6622, E6644, E6836, E6944, E7432, E7538, E7565, E7724, E8165, F2435.

56 Sqn – Aboukir/San Stephano: E7511, E7512, E7513, E7518, E7520, E7521, E7522, E7523, E7525, E7526, E7528, E7530.

56 Sqn – Hawkinge/Biggin Hill: E6309, E6335, E6481, E6484, E6525, E6601, E6616, E6791, E6819, E6841, E6951, E6961, E694.

80 Sqn – Aboukir:

111 Sqn – Duxford: E6617, E6643, F2441, F2527.

203 Sqn – Leuchars: E6570.

205 Sqn – Leuchars: E6525, E6611.

208 Sqn – San Stephano: E7511, E7523, E8105, F2336, F2487, H8694.

1 FTS – Netheravon: E6150, E6311, E6340, E6348, E6480, E6482, E6487, E6529, E6546, E6615, E6616, E6625, E6840, E6876.

2 FTS – Duxford/Digby: E6190, E6470, E6477, E6483, E6528, E6614, E6620, E6647, E6835, E6842, E6844, E6943, E6958.

5 FTS – Shotwick (Sealand): E6311, E6591, E6594, E6837, E6938, E7551, E7714, E7717, E7722, F2466, F2479.

RAF (Cadet) College – Cranwell: E6173, E6184, E6278, E6524, E6530, E6592, E6620, E6656, E6789, E7720, E8365, E8369.

CFS – Upavon: E6310, E6311, E6340, E6348, E6357, E6487, E6492, E6493, E6499, E6501, E6566, E6570, E6599, E6615, E6616.

Meteorological Flt – Duxford: E6525, E6625, E6964, E6965, E7539, F2385.

Armament & Gunnery School – Eastchurch: E6310, E6479, E6612, E6621, E7470, E7531, E7992, F2411.

Air Pilotage School – Andover: E6611, E6870, E6876, F2420.

IDE – Biggin Hill: F2338.

RAF Base – Gosport: E6317.

RAF Base – Leuchars: E6467, E6592.

5 Flying Training Schools, respectively at Netheravon, Digby and Shotwick. It served with these training units in both single- and two-seat forms. The crash, on 21 June 1921, of CFS Snipe E8220 robbed the RAF of one of its most distinguished pilots. Flt Lt A.W. Beauchamp-Proctor VC DSO DFC MC* lost control of the machine while attempting to perform a slow loop and was killed when the machine spun in near Enford, Wiltshire. More than five years later, a further crash, on 26 November 1926, claimed the life of another of the RAF's Great War 'aces'. An, as yet unidentified, Snipe two-seater of 3 Sqn at Upavon crashed in a nosedive, shortly after take-off. Both occupants were killed, P/O J.R. Early and Flt Lt J.A. Slater MC* DFC, the latter having been credited with bringing down twenty-four enemy aircraft.

Known Dual-Control Snipes

E6307, E6478, E6480, E6484, E6487, E6493, E6531, E6594, E6597, E6604, E6618, E6625, E6840, E6862, E6977, E7714, E8224, F2430,

By 1928, the Snipe was obsolescent. It had been used as an advanced trainer for prospective fighter pilots, but the new generation of fighters were powered by static radial engines, which bestowed different handling characteristics to those resulting from a rotary-engined machine. The type was then finally withdrawn from RAF flying units, although some airframes continued to be used for ground instructional purposes.

No Snipe remains in Britain today, but there are three on the other side of the Atlantic. The fuselage of Barker's E8102 has already been mentioned, but Canada also has E6938, which was originally restored by Jack Canary and is now housed in the National Aviation Museum at Rockliffe, Ottawa. Across the border, the former Cole Palen Snipe is no longer flown, but is housed in the National Air and Space Museum of the Smithsonian Institution and marked as E8105. Other serials have been associated with this Snipe and in the early 1960s, it was identified as 6949 (E?) from its days at Roosevelt Field.

CHAPTER ELEVEN

Ground-Attack Sopwiths

The destructive and demoralizing effects of low-flying, single-seater aeroplanes in support of, and as a counter to, ground advances had been well proven during the battles of 1917. The idea was not a new one, but had previously been conducted on an individual basis. A different ploy was brought in by the RFC for the Third Battle of Ypres – the co-ordinated use of scouts to 'soften up' enemy positions, to destroy strongpoints that held up advances and to break up rallying concentrations of defenders. These tactics brought some successes during August 1917, with the D.H.5 proving its worth for such work.

The Battle Flights

The preparations for the Battle of Cambrai, that November, envisaged an expansion of this work, with dedicated Battle Flights being allocated from the squadrons involved for the duties listed and charged additionally with the reporting of enemy gun positions that could threaten advancing tanks and troops. The D.H.5s of 64 and 68 (Australian) Squadrons were regarded as

specialists for this work, although Cambrai was to be the swan song for this machine. The Camel was, by then, in widespread service and was brought into ground-attack operations, notably by 3 and 46 Squadrons, being fitted, as required, with an under-fuselage carrier for four 20lb Cooper bombs.

The Battle Flights from these squadrons achieved some successes, notably at Bourlon Wood on 23 November, but the value of such work had not been lost on the enemy. When the German counterattack began on 30 November, it too was preceded by attacking aeroplanes of the *Schutzstaffeln* (Protection Flights) that were subsequently renamed *Schlachtstaffeln* (Battle Flights).

Success was bought at a high price. The D.H.5 units may have been trained for low work while the Camel squadrons had not, but casualties for both types were unsustainably high. The majority of losses were to ground fire, but low-flying aeroplanes were also vulnerable to attack from above. On 23 November, 46 Squadron had six Camels lost or damaged, 64 Squadron six D.H.5s and 68 (Australian) Squadron three D.H.5s. Pilot losses were three

wounded and three fatalities. The *Official History* records daily losses as high as 35 per cent for units operating in this role, with 30 per cent being the average. The average monthly wastage rate for aeroplanes on scout units was around 66 per cent, using them for constant ground-attack work would have increased this figure to 900 per cent. Pilot losses may not have been as high, but they were nevertheless unacceptable and the mental stress caused by the work and the knowledge of probable casualties can hardly have led to the efficient operation of fighting units.

It was against this background that the need was realized for a specialized ground-attack single-seater. During that November the RFC with the BEF had expressed the requirement for such a machine, specifying an armament of three guns, two of which were to be fitted for firing downwards, at medial 45° to the line of flight and movable through a 20° arc of fire. Concurrently, the Aircraft Inspection Directorate proposed a machine with a similar armament layout and an armoured forward fuselage. Type 2 on the RFC requirement list of types needed for 1918 was a ground-attack machine, to be armed with one Lewis and two Vickers guns, capable of carrying four 20lb bombs.

The TF1

When the RFC's Technical Department examined these proposals, it was realized that there were two problems to be resolved. One was that of armouring the vital parts of an aeroplane, the other the aiming of fixed guns that were not aligned to the thrust line. The latter was, quite rightly, handed over to the experts of the Armament Experimental Station at Orfordness. There was still debate over which configuration of machine, tractor or pusher, was best suited to ground-attack work and, by January 1918, the Technical Department requested that Sopwith's should convert a Camel to the Type 2

3 Sqn RFC/RAF was one of the Camel squadrons that were heavily involved in ground-attack work. Here, one of its Le Rhone Camels, 'Z', is shown fitted with the standard carrier for four 20lb bombs. JMB/GSL

specification. Sopwith's had, by this time, ceased the production of F1 Camels, but the scheme must have already been in the pipeline as, during the previous month, two Camel fuselages had been allocated for this purpose and dispatched to Kingston from from Boulton & Paul factory at Norwich. Apparently, the delivery of these was delayed and it has been reported that a further Camel was sent to Kingston from Martlesham for conversion, to become the Sopwith TF1. It is, therefore, interesting to note that this TF1 was B9278, a Boulton & Paul-built machine that would have left the production line during December and that its serial number presentation was in that Norwich-based manufacturer's characteristic style. Also, its underwing cockades were of differing styles, the port side one having a white outline, which suggests assembly from spare components. It is equally interesting to note that the Sopwith Swallow monoplane was B9276 – could it have utilized the other fuselage?

B9278 emerged as the TF1 and was first flown on 15 February. At first glance, it differed little from the standard Camel, but there were significant modifications. Foremost was the addition of armour. Externally, there was an under-fuselage plate that extended aft from the front engine mounting plate for some 6ft (1.83m) with lateral extensions to protect the lower wing to fuselage attachments. Further, internal armour protected the engine backplate, magneto and carburettor. It may have been that the protective plates were not true armour plating, but merely steel sheets cut to shape in order to test the practicality of the idea. The under-fuselage armour precluded the use of the typical V-shaped exhaust channel in that position and so the side ones, at the base of the aluminium flank panels, were enlarged. A 110hp Le Rhone was carried within a standard Clerget cowling, which lacked the additional cut-outs that were associated with the former engine. The lack of Vickers guns led to a modified 'hump' being added to the front fuselage decking. The armament comprised three Lewis guns. Two were mounted in the cockpit and were fixed to fire downwards and forwards at 45°, in a position that must have been both uncomfortable for the pilot and made it almost impossible to change ammunition drums. The third Lewis was carried above the top wing, on a Bowen and Williams top-plane mounting that had been standardized for

Boulton & Paul-built Camel B9278 was converted by Sopwith's to become the TF1 and underwent service evaluation in France. It was fitted with twin downward-firing Lewis guns and a further Lewis on a Bowen and Williams top-plane mounting. The design was not adopted. JMB/GSL

the 2F1 Camel. A direct-reading ASI was mounted on the port interplane struts and the undercarriage struts were of the broad-chord variety. There may have been other internal differences, such as within the wings, as there had been a request for these to be strengthened.

The choice of the Le Rhone engine was not a random one. It was appreciated that the additional weight of the armour would require compensation elsewhere and, at 245lb (111kg) dry weight, the Le Rhone was some 155lb (70kg) lighter than the alternative 130hp Clerget, while consuming only marginally more fuel (0.75lb (0.34kg) as opposed to 0.723lb (0.33kg) per BHP hour).

In the meantime, the question of sighting the downward firing guns was addressed at Orfordness and the only practical solution was an optical device, based on the periscope principle, that comprised two mirrors, one under the upper wing and the other at the cockpit front. These were marked, respectively, with a ring and a dot and aiming was correct when the latter was centralized in the former. How such a system would have stood up to war flying is open to question, as is how it should have functioned in condensation. However, the device was fitted to B6218, a Clerget Camel that had seen considerable experimental work at Martlesham Heath since September 1917.

It was ordered that B6218 and B9278 should fly to France for evaluation and this was done on 7 March, in the skilled hands

of Capts L.J. Wackett and O. Stewart. B6218 spent some time with 3 Sqn, a unit that had experience of low work. The impracticalities of the designs were quickly realized and it was suggested that it would be better to have Camels with the standard armament arrangement but fitted with underside armour. Eventually, armour plates for the pilots' seats of Camels were developed and found some, limited, use in the squadrons of the BEF. Value was also placed on having ground-attack machines in camouflaged finishes, as machines flying at low height were very vulnerable to attack from above. The two experimental machines were returned to England, B9278 on 13 March and (with no apparent reason for the delay) B6218 on 11 April. The latter was at Orfordness by 26 April and was recommended for striking off charge, but was also reported as a two-seater at 32 TDS Montrose later that year. B9278, presumably devoid of armour and armament, found its way to Hendon, for use by the Controller of the Technical Department and ended its days at Westland's, Yeovil, where it was destroyed by fire on 7 November.

Birth of the Salamander

While the TF1 was still undergoing development, Sopwith's was invited to submit a design to meet the RFC Type 2 requirement. An outline design proposal was quickly produced and, from the beginning, the firm suggested the use of an armoured box as a forward fuselage and the new Bentley BR2 engine, which promised 230hp, as the power unit. The armament was to conform to the RFC requirement of two downward-firing and one forward-firing machine gun, with provision to carry four 20lb bombs.

Drawings were quickly produced and what emerged as the TF2, by early February, was a design that was obviously based on the geometry of the Snipe. Mainplane and tailplane planforms were identical to those of the existing design, but were to have stronger spars. The fin and rudder

were interchangeable with those of the earlier type. An open-topped armoured box was to encase the pilot, fuel, ammunition tanks and engine backplate fittings. The armour was to be of single thickness, except for that behind the pilot, which was a double skin. The rear fuselage was designed around a typical wooden box girder structure, with a semicircular turtle decking that carried a headrest for the pilot. Flank panels, over the sides of the armoured box, would fair the engine cowling to the slab sides of the rear fuselage. A typical Sopwith split-axle undercarriage was to be fitted.

Six prototypes were put into construction but the future of these was jeopardized by the adverse reports from the BEF on the TF1 trials. Whether the expected German spring offensive, when it came on 21 March, had any bearing on the subsequent decision to continue development of the type is conjectural, but once again the RFC scout units were flung into the ground-attack role and again began to sustain heavy casualties. The serial numbers E5429–E5234 had already been allocated to the intended six prototypes and the suggested Sopwith name of Salamander accepted, but it was decided, in light of the TF1 experience, to fit twin forward-firing Vickers and make provision for a free-

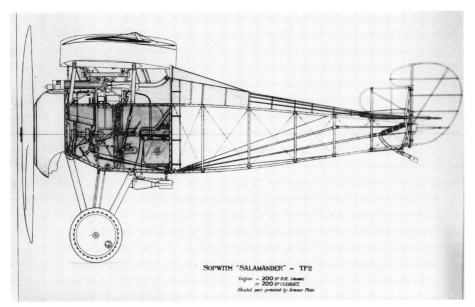

This factory drawing shows the Salamander in its original form, with unbalanced ailerons and small fin. The shaded area shows the extent of the armoured 'bathtub'. JMB/GSL

E5429 was the first prototype Salamander and is seen here at Brooklands in April 1918. It had unbalanced, single-acting ailerons and unstaggered Vickers guns. E5429 flew to France for service evaluation on 9 May and was struck off charge twenty days later, after an aerodrome accident. JMB/GSL

mounted Lewis on the centre section. In order to expiate development, the first prototype was to have the armoured portion of its fuselage fabricated from ordinary, non-hardened steel plates. Its aileron controls were simplified to single action by the use of rubber cording, elastic returns, rather than using the usual span-wise balance cable that would have allowed dual action. This machine first flew on 27 April, some two and a half weeks later than initially anticipated.

A further view of E5429, again taken at Brooklands. During its brief service evaluation, pilots were critical of the type's lateral control and recommended the introduction of balanced ailerons. JMB/GSL

At this early stage it was realized that the typical side-by-side arrangement of the Vickers guns would restrict the size of their magazines and, consequently, the amount of ammunition carried. Provision for a thousand rounds had been envisaged and this was increased to 1,850 rounds by the simple expedient of staggering the guns by some 3in (7.6cm) to allow the fitting of larger magazines. This modification was to be incorporated in the second and subsequent prototypes.

Salamander E5429 was flown to France on 9 May 1918 and, after initial testing at 1 ASD, was passed to 73 Sqn, then 3 Sqn and finally to 65 Sqn. While with the last unit it was badly damaged on 19 May in an aerodrome accident. It was passed to 2 ASD and was to be struck off charge on 29 May. However, it was still recorded as being on BEF charge as late as that December, albeit still in a wrecked condition and classed as being unworthy of reconstruction. During its ten-day evaluation, E5429 had made enough of an impression to

prompt a report stating that it was 'very promising' for its intended role, although some design improvements were suggested, such as balanced ailerons.

The other five prototypes were built with true armour plating. The steel sheets for this were cut and drilled by Sopwith's, before being delivered to Thomas Firth & Sons Ltd of Sheffield for tempering. Upon their return, some were found to be distorted, to the extent that this interfered with airframe assembly. Reheating steel plate, in order to eliminate impurities, creates armour plating. Just as with welding, heat distorts the metal. The extent of the distortion can be due to the subsequent type of cooling process used – water, sand beds or even just atmospheric cooling can be

used. Which of these was practised at Firth's has not been recorded, but that firm had to resort to using smiths to hammer the cooling sheets back to their original shapes.

Even before the BEF's evaluation of the type had been reported, plans were in hand for production and, on 18 June, Sopwith's received an order for 500 of the type. Shortly after this, the third prototype (E5431) was delivered, in standard finish for the time, to the Experimental Station at Martlesham Heath for official tests, which were completed by the end of the month and culminated in the publication of Report M211. This machine still had single action ailerons, but did have the staggered Vickers guns. The recorded service ceiling was only 13,000ft (3,960m) and its climb rate was unspectacular, but these figures were not detrimental for a ground-attack machine. Low-level speed was good, 125mph (202km/h) at 500ft (150m), and decreased only slightly with height.

Further production orders were placed, initially with Wolseley Motors of Birmingham and later with the Air Navigation Company, the Glendower Aircraft Company, Palladium Autocars and National Aircraft Factory No. 1. By 31 October 1918, 800 had been ordered, although only thirty-seven (including the remaining prototypes) were on RAF charge. A further 600 were ordered during November.

Mention has already been made of the value of camouflaged finishes for low-flying machines and the Experimental Stations at Martlesham and Orfordness had spent time on developing suitable schemes. These were tested on a Pup, an AW FK3, a B.E.2e, a B.E.12a and an F.E.2b. E5431 was so camouflaged during the early summer of 1918

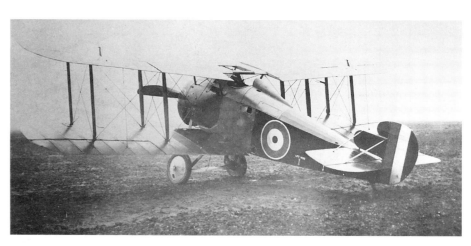

This rear view of an early Salamander shows the original style of fin and rudder, with strut-braced tailplane, and the slab-sided nature of the fuselage. JMB/GSL

and was to be sent to France, for evaluation. It was damaged before this could be effected, but from the results of initial tests the decision was made that production machines should be camouflaged.

Perhaps as a replacement, the fourth prototype went to the BEF in September and generated criticism of its lateral control. Balanced upper ailerons were again suggested, but these were already being fitted to production aircraft and followed the geometry of those fitted to later production Snipes.

Delivery of production machines was slow. Whether there was a delay due to the incorporation of suggested modifications is a matter for speculation, but the availability of engines can also be considered. Planning during 1917 had decided upon the BR2 becoming the standard engine and production was forecast at 1,500 per month by mid-1918. In reality, only 718 had been delivered by 31 October 1918, against a background of booming orders for Snipes. The 200hp, eleven-cylinder Clerget 11E was viewed as an alternative power plant to the BR2 for the Salamander and the RAF intended to have squadrons using both in service by the spring of 1919.

In view of Sopwith's splendid reputation as a manufacturer of quality machines, it was surprising that the company could be labelled as negligent. There is no evidence of deliberate negligence or of cost-cutting, as could (perhaps) have been levelled against Fokker, but a large number of early Salamanders were delivered with Snipe centre sections. Due to the similar geometry, these were interchangeable, but those of the scout were less highly stressed than those of the ground-attack machine and could have caused problems had the type been subjected to the airframe strains imposed by operational flying. Once identified, the error was both notified and rectified.

The Salamander in Service

The first Salamander unit was 157 Squadron. This unit had formed at Upper Heyford on 14 July 1918 and it worked up with a variety of training types that included Pups. Its mobilization establishment was of nineteen Salamanders, and by 23 October 1918 it had received F6504 as a training machine. It was scheduled to be fully equipped by the last day of that month and the balance of its machines was at 7 AAP Kenley, in various stages of readiness.

Airframe Costs

The use of an armour-plated forward fuselage and strengthened components in the rest of the airframe made construction of the Salamander more complicated than that of other Sopwith landplanes and this was reflected in the price. The BR2 engine was also the most expensive British rotary to be fitted in a Sopwith landplane and combined with airframe price to make the Salamander dearer than all production Sopwith landplane types. Only the much larger Cuckoo, a ships aeroplane, was more expensive. The following table gives airframe with engine costs but does not include guns and instruments.

	Airframe	Engine	Total Price
1½ Strutter	£842-6s-0d	£907-10s-0d (Clerget 9B)	£1,749-16s-0d
Baby	£1,072-10s-0d	£907-10s-0d (Clerget)	£1,980-0s-0d
Pup	£710-18s-0d	£620-0s-0d (80hp Le Rhone)	£1,330-18s-0d
Ships Pup	£770-0s-0d	£620-0s-0d (80hp Le Rhone)	£1,390-0s-0d
Camel	£874-10s-0d	£907-10s-0d (130hp Clerget)	£1,782-0s-0d
	£874-10s-0d	£771-10s-0d (110hp Le Rhone)	£1,646-0s-0d
	£874-10s-0d	£643-10s-0d (BR1)	£1,518-0s-0d
Ships Camel	£825-0s-0d	£643-10s-0d (BR1)	£1,468-10s-0d
Snipe	£945-17s-0d	£880-0s-0d (BR2)	£1,825-17s-0d
Dolphin	£1,010 -13s-0d	£1,004-0s-0d (Hispano)	£2,014-13s-0d
Salamander	£1,138-0s-0d	£880-0s-0d (BR2)	£2,018-0s-0d
	£1,138-0s-0d	£951-0s-0d (200hp Clerget)	£2,089-0s-0d
Cuckoo	£1,613-10s-0d	£1,017-10s-0d (Arab)	£2,631-0s-0d

F6508 was ready and six others (F6503, F6505, F6511, F6514, F6516 and F6517) were undergoing flight tests. A further four (F6506, F6512, F6513 and F6515) were undergoing final inspection; F6510 was having its petrol tank repaired; F6518 and F6521 were having rigging inspections; F6520 and F6528 were undergoing engine tests; and F6519 was having guns fitted. Six others (F6522– F6527) were being rigged. This gave a total of twenty-four machines with or allocated to the squadron which,

Salamander F6504 was allocated to 157 Sqn at Upper Heyford and delivered to that unit with the early form of fin and rudder, strut-braced tailplane and unbalanced ailerons. JMB/GSL

151

F6518 was of similar configuration to F6504 and was likewise delivered to 157 Sqn. It was marked with the letter 'H' and came to grief in the snow during the winter of 1918–19. JMB/GSL

J5913 was built by the Glendower Aircraft Co. Ltd, fitted with balanced ailerons and was finished in a variation of the official camouflage scheme for the Salamander. The black dividing lines between the camouflage colours are clearly shown. The upper mainplanes should have carried cockades. This photograph was taken, post-war, at Minchinhampton. JMB/GSL

Salamander Camouflage

The need for an effective camouflage scheme for low flying machines was realized in 1917. Hitherto, day-flying aeroplanes had been finished in standardized doping schemes to specifications PC10 and PC12. Both relied on iron oxide and lampblack as basic pigments and resulted in a drab brown appearance. From 1916, the fuselages and upper surfaces of machines with the BEF had been so finished, while undersides were clear doped before varnishing. Metal and plywood-covered airframe components could be covered in either PC10/12 or in battleship grey dope/varnish. National markings were superimposed and from May 1917 the cockades were made more distinctive by the addition of white surrounds. The resultant appearance from above was of a dark mass, against which the cockades stood out.

Protection for low-flying ground-attack aeroplanes was deemed to lie in the use of camouflage and the Experimental Station at Orfordness was entrusted with the task. Although recognizing that a machine could not be made to blend in completely with the background over which it was flying, it was accepted that its identification and retention in view could be reduced dramatically by use of appropriate colours applied in a pattern that broke up the outline.

The scheme evolved for the Salamander relied on lightening those areas that appeared darkest from the air (i.e. the lower wings and fuselage) and then breaking up the whole outline with patches of colour. Black lines separated the patches of colour and were considered vital to the effectiveness of the scheme. National markings on the upper wings had the red and blue portions darkened and the white ring replaced by one of light grey-green. No fuselage cockades or rudder stripes were carried. The wing cockades were positioned asymmetrically. The light grey-green colour was also used for the fuselage sides and a light earth-brown covered most of the lower wings. Dark purple-earth and green patches were applied to the remainder of the upper surfaces, breaking up the leading edges of wings and cowling.

In contrast, the underside national markings were required to stand out as much as possible, to prevent incidences of 'friendly fire' over terrain that would probably see hostile aeroplanes operating as well.

The lessons learnt from this scheme were not forgotten. When 74 Sqn reformed with Demons in 1935 and was sent to Malta in response to the Abyssinian Crisis, its machines were finished in a similar scheme. Similarly, three years later, when the RAF's home-based fighter force was camouflaged as a result of the Munich Crisis, Furies, Demons and Gladiators had lighter shades of earth and green applied to their lower wings and cockades reduced to red/blue only.

---

after several postponements, was scheduled to join the BEF on 21 November. The full complement was delivered, but the Armistice intervened and the unit stayed in England until disbandment on 1 February 1919, having lost F6524 but gaining F6544 and F6547. Further Salamander units were to follow: 158 Sqn was to mobilize at Upper Heyford; 86 Sqn at Bircham Newton; and 96 Sqn at Wyton. However, only the last squadron was even allocated any of these machines (F6532 and F6534). These early production machines had dual-action ailerons, with a span-wise balance cable, but lacked balances to these surfaces and were fitted with the prototype form of fin and rudder. Later production machines were given the balanced ailerons and an

enlarged fin that followed the form of that on later Snipes, but most of those built were consigned straight to store. Less than half of those ordered were actually delivered, the majority being cancelled in the wake of the Armistice.

Thought had also been given to the training of pilots for the type. From mid-1918 the emphasis of the RAF's training programme had moved to all-through flight training at Training Depot Stations, rather than pilots progressing from Elementary to Higher Training Squadrons. Each of these TDSs had a type specialization and 28 TDS at Weston-on-the-Green, hitherto a Camel TDS, was selected to train Salamander pilots. The RAF Autumn 1918 Quarterly Survey of Stations gave the (intended)

establishment of that unit as thirty-six Salamanders plus thirty-six Avro 504s. It is not known whether any of the former actually reached Weston-on-the-Green, although the 31 October disposition of machines, given in the appendices to the *Official History*, records one with 'Areas' – a generic term that covered TDSs and the few remaining Training Squadrons.

There was some foreign attention paid to the Salamander, notably from the French who were becoming interested in the use of aeroplanes for ground-attack work. Upon its withdrawal from 157 Sqn, F6524 was delivered to France, for evaluation by Section Technique de l'Aéronautique at Villacoublay where, at one stage, it was fitted with a direct reading ASI on its inner port interplane struts. F6533 was transferred to America, for evaluation at McCook Field and survived until 1926, although how much flight testing it did is a matter of conjecture.

The Buffalo

The Salamander was not the last Sopwith venture into armoured aeroplanes. It had been designed purely for ground-attack work, to harass enemy troops ahead of an advance. There was another duty associated with advance against the enemy and this was Contact Patrol work. Contact patrols were vital tasks that had been performed previously by such machines as Moranes, B.E.2 variants or R.E.8s from the Corps squadrons and involved following and reporting the front line, as well as any points of resistance such as enemy concentrations, anti-tank guns or strongpoints. Losses of

Specification – Sopwith TF2 Salamander	
Engine:	One 230hp BR2 or 200hp Clerget 11EB
Weights:	Empty 1,852lb (840kg); loaded 2,613lb (1,185kg)
Dimensions:	Length 19ft 6in (5.94m); height 9ft 6in (2.9m); wingspan upper, unbalanced ailerons 30ft 1⅛in (9.18m), upper, balanced ailerons 31ft 2⅛in (9.51m), lower 30ft 1⅛in (9.18m); chord upper 5ft (1.52m), lower 5ft (1.52m); stagger 1ft 5in (43cm); gap 4ft 3in (1.3m); dihedral upper 4°, lower 4°
Performance:	Max. speed 124mph (200km/h) Service ceiling 13,000ft (3,960m) Endurance 2 hours
Armament:	Two fixed Vickers guns, synchronized to fire through propeller arc, plus 4 × 20lb (9kg) bombs

The Buffalo was an armoured contact patrol machine and two prototypes were produced. The first, H5892, underwent service evaluation and had its pillar mounting for the observer's Lewis gun replaced by the Scarff ring shown in this photograph. JMB/GSL

The second Buffalo, H5893, is seen here at Brooklands, with a Dragon for company. It can be distinguished from the modified first prototype by the cut-outs in the lower-wing trailing edge. JMB/GSL

Corps machines, when dedicated to such work had (again) been disproportionally high. The Buffalo was the Sopwith solution and can be seen as a development of both the Salamander, from which its armoured fuselage evolved, and the Bulldog, which provided the geometry of its flying surfaces.

Design work on a new type, with the Sopwith name Buffalo, was under way by the early summer of 1918 and again the BR2 was the designated engine. The air-frame had a compact fuselage, built around an armoured box that protected the engine backplate components, the pilot and the observer. The two-bay mainplanes had slight sweepback and dihedral, while the setting of the upper plane close to the fuselage ensured good views from the cockpits. Armament was envisaged as a single forward-firing Vickers for the pilot and a Lewis gun, mounted on a Scarff ring for use by the observer. Two prototypes were ordered on 6 September 1918, H5892–H5893, to include the first machine that was already under construc-tion. The first machine flew that month, with its Lewis gun on a pillar mounting, and was delivered to the BEF for evalua-tion on the 27th. It was quite well received and suggested modifications were incorpo-rated into the second machine. This had a Scarff ring fitted and had revised designs of rudder and forward fuselage fairings. Its armour was also extended further aft.

In November 1918 H5893 was sent to Martlesham Heath for the official trial report M252, a process that took some five months. H5892 had, by then, returned from France and was also fitted with a Scarff ring. In April 1919, both Buffalos were dispatched to the BEF and 43 Sqn at Bickendorf, with the Army of Occupation. What the planned use of the type was, by then, to be is conjectural and the choice of 43 Sqn can only have been due to the fact that the engine fitters on that Snipe unit were familiar with the workings of the BR2. Mishaps occurred to both machines and H5892, at least, was back in England by early 1920, but what its subsequent fate was, or that of H5893, is not known.

Specification – Sopwith Buffalo	
Engine:	One 230hp BR2
Weights:	Empty 2,175lb (987kg); loaded 3,071lb (1,393kg)
Dimensions:	Length 33ft 3½in (10.15m); height 9ft 6in (2.9m); wingspan upper 34ft 6in (10.52m), lower 34ft 6in (10.52m); chord upper 5ft 6in (1.68m), lower 5ft 6in (1.68m); stagger 1ft 3in (38cm); gap 4ft 6in (1.37m); dihedral upper 2½°, lower 2½°
Performance:	Max. speed 114mph (183km/h) Service ceiling 9,000ft (2,740m) Endurance not known
Armament:	One fixed Vickers gun, synchronized to fire through propeller arc plus Lewis gun on Scarff ring for observer

This port front view of H5893 illustrates the manner in which the engine cowling of the Buffalo was faired into the armoured box section of the fuselage and the good upward view afforded to the pilot. JMB/GSL

H5893 went to Martlesham Heath for the compilation of Trial Reports and is seen at that station in this rear view. JMB/GSL

Post-War

Although the Salamander had not the opportunity to prove itself in combat and despite the tendency of the type's fuselage to warp and misalign the airframe rigging, it was retained in service by the post-war RAF until at least 1922. This was long after types such as the F1 Camel had been declared obsolete. F6608 and F6660 were still being used in camouflage tests at the RAE Farnborough during the early part of 1920. Some were recorded in Egypt as late as 1922, perhaps in response to the Chanak Crisis, and F6607 was with 1 Sqn at Hinaidi that September. Possibly this was because metal airframes were deemed to be less susceptible to heat distortion than wooden ones. Whatever the case, the type had outlived its usefulness and could not have survived much longer in service.

CHAPTER TWELVE

The Final Designs

Triplanes, Engine Troubles and the Civil Market

Although Sopwith's Ham works were busy from 1917 in the production of Camels, Dolphins, Snipes and Salamanders, those at Kingston were used for the development of a range of experimental types, none of which achieved production status. Certain design features can be attributed to these later types. Firstly, there was limited use of the established BR2 engine, but attempts were made to utilize the unsuccessful Dragon or adopt the official alternative to the BR2, the 200hp Clerget 11Eb. Secondly, there was a reversion to the triplane configuration that had been so successful during 1917. Then there was experimentation with the monocoque fuselage that offered greater structural strength and had been employed by enemy manufacturers, notably Pfalz. Finally, with the war at an end, there was an attempt to produce machines that would appeal to the new and burgeoning civilian market. In order to review these designs chronologically, a return has to be made to April 1917. French production of the 1½ Strutter was in full swing, but the type was by then becoming outdated. With this in mind, and the possibility of another potential export/licensed production market as a prospect, a new design was drawn up as a possible successor. The Dolphin had just emerged and the new design also incorporated negative stagger. It was given the designation 3F2 (the 2 for two-seater) and the name Hippo. It could, at first, be mistaken for a Dolphin in rear view photographs, but from the front there was no such possibility. It was designed for a rotary engine and the Clerget 11Eb was chosen, possibly with the potential French market in mind. The Hippo made its first flight on 13 September 1917 and, with the number X11 in the series reserved for machines licensed to be built under Defence Regulations, went, unmarked, to Martlesham Heath for evaluation on 29 December. The number X10 was also reserved for the Hippo, but there is no definite proof that it was built.

The Hippo

The Hippo, with pronounced back-stagger and two-bay wings of 40ft (12.2m) span, was initially given balanced ailerons in an attempt to ensure maximum lateral control. The centre-section struts were very short, giving the impression that the upper wing was integral with the fuselage. It also had a truncated fin and balanced rudder. The undercarriage struts were of wooden construction.

The wide separation of the pilot and observer in the 1½ Strutter was an accepted drawback for that type in combat and yet the Hippo had a similar crew layout. The pilot sat with the centre-section front spar at the back of his cockpit, with the breeches of a pair of Vickers guns buried in the decking ahead. The observer occupied a cockpit that was let into a centre-section trailing edge cut-out. The main fuel tank, with a gravity tank above, occupied the fuselage space between the two cockpits.

The deep fuselage and negative stagger of the Hippo gave its crew of two a superb field of vision, as is evident in this photograph of X11, which also emphasizes the dihedral of the mainplanes. JMB/GSL

Specification – Sopwith 3F2 Hippo	
Engine:	One 200hp Clerget 11EB
Weights:	Empty 1,867lb (847kg); loaded 2,590lb (1,175kg)
Dimensions:	Length 24ft 6in (7.47m); height 9ft 4in (2.84m); wingspan upper 38ft 9in (11.81m), lower 38ft 9in (11.81m); chord upper 5ft(1.52m), lower 5ft (1.52m); stagger 2ft 3in (69cm) negative (original), 1ft 9½in (55cm) (later); gap 4ft 6in (1.37m); dihedral 3° (original), 5° (later)
Performance:	Max.speed 115mph (185km/h) Service ceiling 18,000ft (5,490m) Endurance not known
Armament:	Two fixed Vickers guns synchronized to fire through propeller arc plus two Lewis guns for observer

The initial armament for the observer was a pair of Lewis guns that were mounted on pillars, one at each end of the cockpit. The field of view, especially forwards and upwards, was excellent for both of the crew.

The Martlesham report M170 and M170A were lukewarm and, with little chance of an order from the British services, the Hippo returned to Sopwith's, where its engine was removed and given to the first of the Bulldog prototypes. The opportunity was taken to fit new wings, which had plain ailerons, and a fuller rudder, possibly in a continued hope for an order from the French government. Later, during the spring of 1918, with the number X11 then marked, its engine was reinstated and the degree of back-stagger was reduced. Steel tube undercarriage struts were fitted and a Scarff ring added to the rear cockpit. All was to no avail. No production orders materialized and development was arrested. The serial numbers H4420–H4421 were allocated to Hippos when the X series was discontinued in 1918. The number X18 is also associated with the type and may have been a second prototype. It would seem likely that the service serial numbers were allocated for striking-off purposes, after the X series was discontinued during 1918.

The Bulldog

If the Hippo was reminiscent, in some ways, of the Dolphin, another two-seater of 1917 design was similarly so of the Snipe. Sopwith's had received the official Licence number 14 to build four examples of a two-seater fighter-reconnaissance machine that was allotted the designation 2FR2. That appellation suggests that there may have been a previous attempt at designing such a type. The Licensed numbers X2–X5 were allocated

It was given the rather apt name of Bulldog for, as it first appeared, the 2FR2 (presumably) X2 was a very squat machine, whose span of 26ft 6ins (8.08m) was only marginally greater than its 23ft (7.01m) length. The single bay wings had forward stagger and, as with the Snipe, there was an open centre-section. Plain ailerons were fitted and, from the front, the first Bulldog could easily be mistaken for an early prototype of the Snipe, were it not for its eleven cylinder Clerget 11Eb. The fin was of typical Sopwith shape and was partially surmounted by the overhang of the

The pugnacious appearance of the Bulldog is shown in this view of the prototype with single-bay wings and provided a possible reason for the choice of name. The full armament of twin Vickers and two pillar-mounted Lewis guns is visible. JMB/GSL

Specification – Sopwith 2FR2 Bulldog	
Engine:	One 200hp Clerget 11EB or 360hp ABC Dragonfly
Weights:	Empty 1,441lb (654kg) (Clerget); loaded 2,495lb (1,132kg) (Clerget), 3,100lb (1,406kg) (Dragonfly)
Dimensions:	Length 23ft (7.01m) (Clerget), 23ft 2in (7.06m) (Dragonfly); height 8ft 5½in (Clerget), 8ft 9in (Dragonfly); wingspan upper 34ft 6in (10.52m), lower 34ft 6in (10.52m); chord upper 5ft 6in (1.68m), lower 5ft 6in (1.68m); stagger 1ft 3in (38cm); gap 4ft 6in (1.37m); dihedral upper 2½°, lower 2½°
Performance:	Max. speed 109mph (175km/h) Service ceiling 15,000ft (4,572m) Endurance 2 hours
Armament:	Two fixed Vickers guns synchronized to fire through propeller arc plus two Lewis guns for observer

The Bulldog with two-bay wings and fitted with a Scarff mounting for the observer's armament. This photograph was taken at Orfordness. via H.S. Clarke

comparatively large and balanced rudder. Twin Vickers guns were, again, provided for the pilot and the observer had a pair of pillar mounted Lewis guns. The cockpits were also widely separated, that of the pilot being under the centre section, while the observer's was behind the upper-wing trailing edge. The machine first flew during late 1917 and is not known to have undergone any service evaluation. Handling performance was, however, poor and the small wing area must have made for a heavy loading.

X3 was ready by March 1918 and featured two bay wings of increased span. Balanced ailerons were, at first, fitted, but were soon replaced by plain ones, which brought the span to 33ft 9in (10.29m). This aeroplane was delivered, in its revised form, to Martlesham Heath on 22 April 1918, for evaluation that generated Report M197. Although it handled satisfactorily, the performance was not good. It had subsequently moved to Orfordness, by July, where a BR2 was fitted, and was used for a variety of experimental work. It should have received the serial number H4422 but was consistently recorded as X3, even on its departure from Orfordness for Hendon on 2 September 1919. On that flight, it hit a tree, just short of Hendon, and this caused sufficient damage to warrant striking it off charge.

The third machine was fitted with a Dragonfly engine and delivered to the RAE at Farnborough as X4. There it was used in a series of unsuccessful trials that attempted to overcome the problems inherent in that engine. It was still at Farnborough on 16 June 1920, by which time it should have received the service serial number H4423. It is doubtful whether X5 was ever built.

The Rhino

A return was made to the triplane configuration when the next experimental type, the Rhino, appeared in October 1917. The Rhino had the designation 2B2 and, as indicated by the letter B, was to be a bomber. As such, it marked something of a breakaway from what was becoming Sopwith tradition as a designer of fighting scouts. It was regarded as a possible contender for the bombing role later taken by the D.H.9 and D.H.10.

The new triplane looked somewhat ungainly as a result of its deep fuselage that accommodated a 230hp BHP inline engine. The nose was made as streamlined as possible and Dolphin-type flank radiators were fitted on each side of the cowling. The Rhino had a low-aspect fin and taller rudder that had an almost square balance area. That combination of vertical tail surfaces that had begun with the Hippo was to be continued on the remainder of Sopwith's wartime designs. The single-bay wings had equal gap and balanced ailerons on all three mainplanes. The ailerons were linked by struts between the bottom and middle planes, but those on the upper wing were connected by cable. The undercarriage looked proportionally small. The pilot's cockpit was under the upper wing and a forward-firing Vickers gun was provided. Interspar cut-outs were made in the inboard rib bay of the middle plane, to give some degree of view forwards and downwards. The observer's cockpit had provision for armament, in the form of a pillar for the mounting of a Lewis gun. There were cut-outs in the inboard trailing edges of the bottom mainplanes to improve the observer's view forwards and downwards. A novel feature, and one of the first examples of an armament pack, was the case for bombs that, ready loaded, could be winched into place within the deep fuselage and replaced with similar ease. That first prototype was built under Licence regulations and received the experimental serial X7.

The Rhino went to Martlesham Heath, for evaluation, on 16 January 1918,

Specification – Sopwith 2B2 Rhino	
Engine:	One 230hp BHP
Weights:	Empty 2,185lb (991kg); loaded 3,590lb (1,628kg)
Dimensions:	Length 27ft 8in (8.43m); height 10ft 11in (3.33m); wingspan upper 33ft (10.06m), middle 33ft (10.06m), lower 33ft (10.06m); chord upper 6ft (1.83m), middle 6ft (1.83m), lower 6ft (1.83m); stagger middle to top 5in (13cm), lower to middle 5in (13cm); gap middle to top 4ft (1.21m), lower to middle 4ft (1.21m); dihedral top 2½°, middle 2½°, lower 2½°
Performance:	Maximum Speed 103mph (166km/h) Service ceiling 12,000ft (3,660m) Endurance 3¾ hours
Armament:	One fixed Vickers synchronized to fire through propeller arc plus Lewis gun for observer plus bomb load

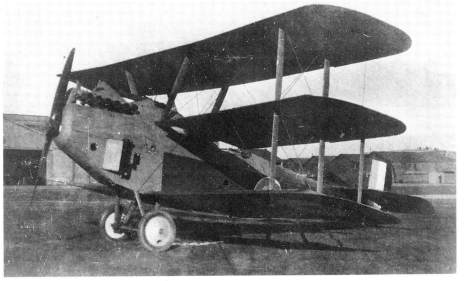

The almost comical appearance of the Rhino is apparent in this view. Despite its ungainly configuration, it introduced novel ideas of design and returned quite good performance figures. JMB/GSL

remaining there until 4 April, and test reports M167, M167A and M167B were produced. X8, the second example, was flying at Brooklands by February and differed little from the first machine. It did, however, have plain ailerons, a revised fairing around the breech of its Vickers gun and a Scarff ring for the observer's Lewis. The RAF had no use for the Rhino, being committed to the D.H.9 and, later, the D.H.10 for medium-range bombing. The only use for the two Rhinos was experimental work by their manufacturer and they did not receive any military serial numbers

The Snail

The static radial engine attracted the interest of the Air Board and the problems associated with the Dragonfly have been recounted. Another ABC radial engine, the 170hp Wasp, was in prospect by late 1917 and Sopwith's were asked to produce four examples of a fighting scout with this power plant on 24 November. The number of machines was increased to six the following month. The revised order was due to the fact that the first four were of conventional, if faired, box girder fuselage construction and the Air Board was interested in evaluating monocoque fuselage construction, which was specified for the extra two machines.

Sopwith's allocated the type number 8F1 and the serials C4284–C4289 were authorized. Not all were built, but C4284 was and emerged as a clean design with conventional fuselage and single-bay wings that were given slight negative stagger. The cockpit was placed under the centre section that had a large central cut-out to enable entry and provide an upward field of view. The wooden centre-section struts joined the fuselage just above the centre line. The seven-cylinder engine was neatly enclosed in an almost conical cowling, through which the cylinder heads protruded. Armament comprised the usual pair of Vickers guns, but these were, somewhat unusually, mounted just above the centre line with only the tips of the barrel casings exposed. C4285–C4287 were not built, although some work was undertaken on the first two. Had they been completed, C4285 and C4286 would have had a reduction in the negative stagger of the wings.

C4288 had the monocoque fuselage, constructed of plywood strips nailed and glued to elliptical formers and hoops that had no interconnecting longerons. The

C4288 was the Snail with a monocoque fuselage. Unlike its predecessor, it had positive stagger to its wings. JMB/GSL

cockpit was moved aft and the wings given positive stagger to compensate for this and the weight of the fuselage. The disposition of the centre-section struts was altered and their construction was of steel tubing. There is no evidence, in factory photographs, of any armament being fitted, but after evaluation at Martlesham from 9 May to June 1918 (test report M203), C4288 was the subject of armament report ARM21 and so presumably it received Vickers guns. The Snail was seen as a possible contender for the same Specification A1(a) as the Snipe and as such also had provision for a moveable Lewis gun on its centre section. That weapon was to be mounted to starboard, fixed to fire forwards and capable of being swung inwards for the changing of ammunition drums. C4289 was to have had the monocoque fuselage, but was not built, C4284 and C4288 found no useful employment, but existed until at least November 1919.

The Snark

The monocoque form of fuselage was also employed on Sopwith's last design for a triplane fighting scout, the Snark. That design also attempted to make use of the ABC Dragonfly and, as such, was fated to suffer from that engine's protracted developmental problems. Had it entered service, the Snark would have been the RAF's first six-gun fighter.

Specification – Sopwith 8F1 Snail	
Engine:	One 170hp ABC Wasp
Weights:	Empty 1,390lb (631kg) (Snail II); loaded 1,478lb (670kg) (Snail I), 1,920lb (871kg) (Snail II)
Dimensions:	Length 18ft 9in (5.72m) (Snail I – conventional fuselage), 19ft (5.79m) (Snail II – monocoque fuselage); height 8ft 3in (2.51m) (Snail I), 7ft 10in (2.39m) (Snail II); wingspan upper 25ft 9in (7.85m), lower 25ft 9in (7.85m); chord not known; stagger 5in (13cm) negative (Snail I); gap not known; dihedral not known
Performance:	Max. speed 114½mph (184km/h) (Snail I), 124mph (200km/h) (Snail II) Service ceiling not known Endurance not known
Armament:	Two fixed Vickers guns synchronized to fire through propeller arc plus one moveable Lewis gun

Specification – Sopwith Snark	
Engine:	One 360hp ABC Dragonfly
Weights:	Empty not known; loaded 2,283lb (1,036kg)
Dimensions:	Length 20ft 9in (6.32m); height 10ft 1in (3.07m); wingspan upper 26ft 6in (8.08m), middle 26ft 6in (8.08m), lower 26ft 6 in (8.08m); chord upper 4ft 6in (1.37m), middle 4ft 6in (1.37m), lower 4ft 6in (1.37m); stagger middle to upper c.9in (23cm), lower to middle 1ft 0½in (32cm); gap middle to top 2ft 10½ (88cm), lower to middle 3ft 6in (1.07m); dihedral not known
Performance:	Max. speed 130mph (209km/h) Service ceiling not known Endurance not known
Armament:	Two fixed Vickers synchronized to fire through propeller arc plus four wing-mounted Lewis guns

This rear view of the Snark gives the impression that the upper wing was added as an afterthought. The access panels for the wing-mounted Lewis guns are visible on the lower mainplanes. JMB/GSL

Designed by 20 April 1918, a contract for three Snarks (F4068–F4070) was issued on 14 May and it was intended to match RAF Specification Type I, for a high-altitude fighter. The airframe of F4068 had been completed by September 1918, but events were then delayed by the unavailability of a suitable engine. One was finally delivered during December, but it was not until the following April that it was fitted.

As completed, the first Snark had a compact fuselage, with its Dragonfly enclosed by a rounded cowling that was fretted to allow the cylinder heads to protrude, as on the Snail. The wings were of greater chord than those of the earlier Clerget Triplane but, again, all six mainplanes had ailerons. What made the Snark unique was the unequal stagger between its sets of wings. That between the middle

and upper wings was much less than the stagger between the lower pair, giving the impression that the upper wing had been added as an afterthought. Armament comprised a pair of fuselage-mounted Vickers guns, with provision for two Lewis guns to be mounted under each lower mainplane.

F4068 had not flown by July 1919, when an engine change was made. It finally took to the air in September and was delivered to Martlesham by 12 November. With the war then over for a full year, there was little chance of any orders for the type. However, F4069 and F4070 were completed and joined the first machine at the Experimental Station, during April and September 1920 respectively. F4070, at least, had a modified front fuselage, with a hemispherical spinner fitted to its propeller. When the Dragonfly could be persuaded

to function properly, the Snark was capable of 130mph (209km/h) at 300ft (91m). F4068 was re-engined with the 360hp Dragonfly 1A during September, becoming the Snark Mk II. The 320hp version was then designated Mk I. The monocoque fuselages were not, however, as sturdy as might be imagined, suffering rapid deterioration and subsequent misalignment that resulted in the machines being struck off charge by 1922.

The Snapper

The final Sopwith fighter to be built was the biplane that was a near contemporary of the Snark, the Snapper. It, too, was designed to meet Specification Type I for a high-altitude fighting scout. A monocoque fuselage was also envisaged for this machine, but that idea never came to fruition and the production of three prototypes went ahead using the conventional method of fuselage construction. The serials F7031–F7033 were allocated on 4 June 1918. The Snapper was beset by the same problem as the Dragon, Snark and later Cobham – it was designed to have the Dragonfly engine.

As with the Snark, the Snapper employed a wide centre section in its single-bay wings. Those wings were of noticeably deep chord and had ailerons on all four mainplanes. The fuselage was very slab-sided, with its engine cowled in a similar manner to the original Snark. The pilot sat well back and his upward and forward fields of view were enhanced by a trailing edge cut-out in the upper centre section. The almost negligible fin was virtually identical to the Snark's and carried a balanced rudder. Armament was a pair of Vickers guns that were widely spaced and slightly staggered to accommodate the magazines in the relatively narrow fuselage. Spent cartridge cases and used belt links were ejected via common chutes that terminated above the upper fuselage longerons. The machine had a purposeful appearance.

The airframe of F7031 was ready by September 1918 but there were delays with its engine and it was not flown until May of the following year. That first machine went to Martlesham on 1 August, where tests were protracted due to engine problems. By that time, its appearance had been altered by the enlargement of its engine cowling diameter and the addition of a spinner that had a small frontal opening for access to the propeller boss. When its Dragonfly engine

Specification – Sopwith Snapper

Engine:	One 360hp ABC Dragonfly
Weights:	Empty 1,462lb (663kg); loaded 2,190lb (993kg)
Dimensions:	Length 20ft 7in (6.27m); wingspan upper 28ft (8.53m), lower 28ft (8.53m); height 10ft (3.05m); chord not known; stagger not known; gap not known; dihedral not known
Performance:	Max. speed 140mph (225km/h) Service ceiling 23,000ft (7,010m) Endurance not known
Armament:	Two fixed Vickers guns synchronized to fire through propeller arc

The Snapper was intended as a high-altitude fighter and its generous wingspan is evident here in this view taken at Martlesham Heath. JMB/GSL

could be coaxed into functioning correctly, the Snapper could achieve a good performance – 138mph (222km/h) being recorded at 10,000ft (3,050m). It returned to Sopwith's for wing modifications and was back at the Experimental Station by December. There were plans to fit two-bay wings but these were never implemented.

The second and third machines were built, although there was no possibility of a service contract. One of these may have been the civilian-registered K-149 (allocated G-EAFJ) that appeared at Brooklands in June 1919 and was intended to participate in the 1919 (Victory) Aerial Derby. Both F7032 and F7033 were delivered to the RAE at Farnborough, on 29 January and 26 February 1920 respectively. There, both were subjected to static load tests, using sand, and F7032 is recorded as having been used for aerodynamic research. F7031 had, apparently, joined them by June, but the ultimate fates of all three is not known.

The Cobham

The final Sopwith military design was, against tradition, a bomber and unique in being the only Sopwith twin-engined machine. Its characteristics as a triplane

that was intended to have the Dragonfly engine followed the traits of its immediate predecessors, but its name broke with established tradition – the Cobham was named after a small town and had no animal connotation.

The Cobham was designed during 1918 to be either a day bomber or escort fighter, much the same as the D.H.10. A mock-up was prepared by that August after the construction of three prototypes (H671–H673) had been ordered on 12 July. That contract envisaged that the Cobham would meet Air Board specifications for Types VI and VIII, short- and long-range day bombers respectively.

H671 had not been completed by the time of the Armistice and the emerging problems with the intended Dragonfly led to the decision being made to fit high compression 290hp Siddeley Pumas. A pair of those engines had been delivered to Kingston by November 1918, but the pace of development slowed down in peacetime. As a result, H671 did not fly until mid-1919 and was designated Cobham Mk.II to distinguish it from the Dragonfly version, the Mk.I.

The airframe had a conventional, deep and slab-sided fuselage of box-girder construction that could accommodate a crew of three. The pilot's cockpit was set forward of the wing leading edges, with a bomb-aimer's position in the nose and a gunner's behind the wing trailing edges. The latter two positions were fitted with Scarff gun rings. Again, there was a small fin and balanced rudder. The 54ft (16.5m) span, triplane wings had ailerons on all six mainplanes. Each outer wing cellule comprised two bays, with pairs of wooden interplane struts. Pairs of V-struts that supported the engine

Specification – Sopwith Cobham

Engine:	Two 360hp ABC Dragonfly (Cobham I), two 290hp Siddeley Puma (Cobham II)
Weights:	Empty not known; loaded 6,300lbs (2,858kg) (Cobham II)
Dimensions:	Length 38ft (11.58m); height 13ft (3.96m); wingspan upper 54ft (16.46m), middle 54ft (16.46m), lower 54ft (16.46m); chord not known; stagger not known; gap middle to upper 4ft 6in (1.37m), lower to middle 4ft 6in (1.37m); dihedral not known
Performance:	Max. speed not known Service ceiling not known Endurance not known
Armament:	Two Lewis guns mounted on Scarff rings plus bomb load

mountings connected the extremities of the wide centre sections. A further pair of such struts connected the fuselage to the upper wing. The Puma cowlings on H671 filled the gap between the lower and middle wings, which were perpendicular to the line of flight, although the upper one was given slight negative stagger. Twin undercarriage wheels were placed under each engine position and connected by an extremely long axle that had to be supported by a V-strut from under the fuselage. That undercarriage was damaged and H671 was at 10 (Brooklands) AAP, for repair, in November 1919.

H672, the Cobham Mk.I, was almost completed at that time. It differed in having Dragonfly 1A engines that were enclosed in circular sectioned fairings of minimal diameter. Its upper wing had slight positive stagger and the rudder was given an extra balance area, below the fuselage, that necessitated the use of a taller tail-skid. This aeroplane first flew in January 1920 and was passed to Martlesham the next month. It was at the Experimental Station until June, when it went to Farnborough for disposal.

H673 was built and it too had Dragonfly 1As. It joined H672 at Martlesham in February 1920, but only stayed a month. It was back with Sopwith's in May, before moving on to the RAE at Farnborough in June. Both H672 and H673 had been struck off charge when H671 arrived at Farnborough on 29 November 1920. It last flew there on 27 January 1921 before meeting the same fate as the other two.

The Atlantic

The Snark, Snapper and Cobham had not, as has been related, flown by the time of the Armistice and the arrival of peacetime conditions brought an end to service contracts. Even before the year was out, Sopwith's mind had turned to the £10,000 prize money, still unclaimed, that had been offered by the *Daily Mail* in 1913 for the first non-stop transatlantic flight. A machine was designed and built in the minimum of time, as there were several possible contenders. What emerged, and was flying by February 1919, was a relatively small machine, of 49ft 9in (15.16m) span. The planform of its two-bay wings resembled those of the Cuckoo, but the fuselage was a very deep and angular structure with a diminutive fin and rudder. There was a crew of two

H672 was the Dragonfly-engined Cobham and this photograph was taken at Brooklands. The twin balance areas of the rudder are visible. JMB/GSL

and these were placed in staggered cockpits at the level of the upper wing trailing edge. The single engine was a 375hp Rolls-Royce Eagle VIII, chosen for its reliability. The massive tanks necessary to contain the fuel for such an undertaking occupied the fuselage interior, between the engine and the cockpits. The undercarriage was jettisonable, to reduce drag, and a wireless set was carried for use in emergencies. A wind-driven generator, whose retractable propeller was mounted on the rear port side of the fuselage, provided power for the wireless set. The possibility of ditching was provided for by the second function of the rear fuselage decking, which was an inverted lifeboat. The machine was popularly known as the Sopwith Atlantic.

The Atlantic was flying by February 1919 and, with a two-bladed propeller (rather than the original four-bladed one) was shipped to its proposed take-off point in Newfoundland. The crew was Hawker, the natural choice for pilot, and Lt Cdr K. Mackenzie-Grieve as navigator. The pair

took off in the dark on the morning of 18 May 1919 and, after jettisoning the undercarriage, set off eastwards. Cooling problems developed and could not be rectified, and in the early morning of the 19th Hawker was obliged to ditch the machine. He had made for the shipping lanes to the south, and came down after sighting the Danish steamer SS *Mary*.

Both crew were picked up safely, but the vessel was without wireless. Fears for the safety of Hawker and Mackenzie-Grieve developed and it was eventually assumed that they had perished in the attempt. Hawker's wife even received a telegram of condolence from the King. SS *Mary* reached the Hebrides on 25 May and notified the presence of its passengers. The Navy took control and provided a ship to Scapa Flow, from where the airmen were conveyed to Thurso for entrainment south. The Sopwith Atlantic had not sunk and was picked up by the SS *Charlotteville*, en route from Canada to Danzig. The remains were brought back to England and exhibited on the roof of Selfridges in Oxford Street.

Specification – Sopwith Atlantic	
Engine:	One 375hp Rolls Royce Eagle VIII
Weights:	Empty 3,000lb (1,364kg); loaded not known
Dimensions:	Length 32ft (9.76m); wingspan upper 46ft 6in (14.18m), lower 46ft 6in (14.18); height 11ft (3.36m); chord upper 6ft 3in (1.9m), lower 6ft 3in (1.9m); stagger 3in; gap 6ft (1.83m); dihedral upper 2½°, lower 2½°
Performance:	Max. speed 118mph (189km/h) Ceiling 13,000ft (3,965m) Endurance not known

The Gnu

Sopwith recognized the potential of the post-war civilian market for both sporting and commercial aeroplanes. The company's first attempt at entering this market was with a three-seater passenger/transport machine that was named the Gnu. It was completed and at Brooklands by 31 March 1919, and was a very clean-looking aeroplane. The Gnu had two-bay, staggered wings and an enclosed cabin for two passengers sat side-by-side. That space could also be occupied by an equivalent weight of cargo. The pilot's cockpit was not enclosed and he was placed forward, under the centre section. The tail, typical for its time, incorporated a balanced rudder. A rotary engine was fitted, a BR2 in the first machine and the 110hp Le Rhone in subsequent examples.

The registration K-101 was given to the prototype, which was flying by May. Its passenger comfort was commented on favourably but, of the total of thirteen produced, seven were left unsold. This may have been due to the fact that rotaries had greater fuel and oil consumption than other types of engine. Three Gnus were exported to Australia. Nos K136 and K163 lasted until 1926, as G-EADB and G-EAGP, when both were crashed. Gnu G-EAGP had its moment of glory, however, when it was used on 23 June 1923 by Flt Lt W.H. Longton to win the Grosvenor Challenge Cup, on the first occasion of that trophy's availability.

The Dove

With the late wartime preference by RAF instructors and senior officers for the Pup as a 'personal' machine, it is not surprising that the first civil sporting machine should have been based on that airframe. The Dove was, however, a tandem two-seater, but retained the 80hp Le Rhone engine. The extra weight of a second occupant altered the centre of gravity and so the wings were given sweepback in compensation for this. The fin and rudder resembled those of the Camel and may have accounted for the Dove's slightly increased length over a Pup.

The first Dove was K-122 (later G-EACM) and it was first flown in May 1919 by Maj W.G. Barker VC DSO MC*, with the Prince of Wales as passenger on a subsequent flight, even though Barker was still

Specification – Sopwith Gnu	
Engine:	One 230hp BR2 or 110hp Le Rhone
Weights:	Empty not known; loaded 3,350lb (1,520kg) (Le Rhone)
Dimensions:	Length 25ft 10in (7.87m); height 9ft 10in (3m); wingspan upper 38ft 1in (11.61m), lower 38ft 1in (11.61m); chord not known; stagger 1ft 2in (36cm); gap 5ft (1.52m); dihedral upper 2½°, lower 2½°
Performance:	Max. speed 93mph (150km/h) (BR1), 91mph (146km/h) (Le Rhone) Ceiling not known Endurance 3½ hours

The first Gnu had a cabin for its passengers and freight, but most of those produced lacked that luxury. Most went to Australia and the demise of one of those is shown here. JMB/GSL

recovering from his famous final combat. Nine other Doves followed and most were exported: K-133 (G-EACU) to Sweden; K448 (G-EAFI) to Norway; G-EAJI, G-EAJJ, G-EAKH and G-EAKT to Australia; G-EAGA and G-EAHP to unknown foreign buyers. The last machine was G-EBKY and this survives today, rebuilt to Pup configuration and part of the Shuttleworth Collection.

The Wallaby

The Sopwith Wallaby owed much to the design of the Atlantic and also employed the 375hp Rolls-Royce Eagle VIII. It had, however, three-bay wings. A novel feature was its crew seating, which could be lowered deeper into the fuselage to give protection from the elements. The Wallaby was built to compete for another prize of £10,000,

Specification – Sopwith Dove	
Engine:	One 80hp Le Rhone
Weights:	Empty 1,065lb (483kg); loaded 1,430lb (649kg)
Dimensions:	Length 19ft 4in (5.89m); height 9ft (2.74m); wingspan upper 24ft 9½in (7.56m), lower 24ft 9½in (7.56m); chord upper 5ft 1½in (1.56m), lower 5ft 1½in (1.56m); stagger 1ft 6in (46cm); gap 4ft 4in (1.32m); dihedral 3°
Performance:	Max. speed 100mph (161km/h) Ceiling not known Endurance 2½ hours

The derivation of the Dove from the Pup is apparent in this view of the prototype, which also illustrates the twin-seating arrangement and the slight sweepback of the mainplanes. JMB/GSL

even completing the journey. The aeroplane, however, was shipped to Australia and rebuilt as G-AUDU.

The Antelope

A development of the Wallaby, with two-bay wings and constant-chord balanced ailerons, was produced as another passenger/transport with enclosed cabin. It was named the Antelope but its lines were functional, rather than graceful. The fuselage was rectangular, save for a slightly rounded top decking and it was deep enough to accommodate two passengers in enclosed comfort. As with the Gnu, the pilot sat in an open cockpit under the centre section. Its vertical tail unit had an outline reminiscent of the Camel's, but incorporated a balanced rudder. There was a V-strut undercarriage that was later replaced by an ungainly four-wheeled unit. The machine incorporated several minor design features; some were of novelty value (such as an elevating passenger seat that allowed head exposure to the slipstream), but others (especially easily folded engine cowlings) were of a more practical nature. The chosen power plant was the 200hp Wolseley Viper that, despite its drag-inducing frontal radiator, gave a maximum speed of 110mph (177km/h).

The solitary Antelope was built in 1919 and exhibited at the following year's Olympia Show, where it attracted some attention. After the show, it was entered in the Small Commercial Aeroplane Competition, held by the Air Ministry at Martlesham Heath, as G-EASS. It was refitted with tapering, but still balanced, ailerons and a four-wheeled undercarriage unit that had a braking system. These brakes were added to enable a landing run with the limit specified in the competition's rules. Hawker flew the Antelope at Martlesham and won a £3,000 prize. The Antelope was returned to V-strut undercarriage and won a further competition in June 1922, The Surrey Open Handicap Race. It was then exported to Australia in 1923 and, as G-AUSS, flew alongside the Wallaby on mail runs.

offered by the Australian government to the first Australian airman to return home by air in a machine of all-British or Commonwealth construction. A time limit of thirty days was set for such an epic return.

The Wallaby had dual control and its crew was Capt G.C. Matthews and Sgt T.D. Kay (ex-4 and 3 Sqns AFC respectively). They left Hounslow, the designated departure point, on 21 October 1919, but their journey was slow and they had no hope of reaching Australia within the time limit. The Wallaby was crashed at Bali on 17 April 1920, ending any possibility of

The Grasshopper

There was one other Sopwith venture aimed at breaking into the civilian market and that, too, resulted in the production of

Specification – Sopwith Wallaby	
Engine:	One 360hp Rolls Royce Eagle VIII
Weights:	Empty 2,780lb (1,261kg); loaded 5,200lb (2,359kg)
Dimensions:	Length 31ft 6in (9.6m); height 10ft 8in (3.25m); wingspan upper 46ft 6in (14.17m), lower 46ft 6in (14.17m); chord upper 6ft 3in (1.91m), lower 6ft 3in (1.91m); stagger 3in (8cm); gap 6ft (1.83m); dihedral upper 2½°, lower 2½°
Performance:	Max. speed 115mph (185km/h) Ceiling not known Endurance not known

Specification – Sopwith Antelope	
Engine:	One 180hp Wolseley Viper
Weights:	Empty 2,387lb (1,083kg); loaded 3,450lb (1,565kg)
Dimensions:	Length 31ft (9.6m); height 11ft 3in (3.43m); wingspan upper 46ft 6in (14.17m), lower 46ft 6in (14.17m); chord upper 6ft 3in (1.91m), lower 6ft 3in (1.91m); stagger 1ft 6in (48cm); gap not known; dihedral not known
Performance:	Max. speed 110mph (177km/h) Ceiling not known Endurance not known

Specification – Sopwith Grasshopper	
Engine:	One 100hp Anzani
Weights:	Empty not known; loaded 1670lb (758kg)
Dimensions:	Length 23ft 1in (7.04m); height 9ft (2.74m); wingspan upper 33ft 1in (10.08m), lower 33ft 1in (10.08m); chord upper 5ft (1.52m), lower 5ft (1.52m); stagger 1ft 5in (43cm); gap 4ft 9in (1.45m); dihedral upper 4°, lower 4°
Performance:	Max. speed 90mph (145km/h) Ceiling not known Endurance not known

a single example. The Grasshopper was an attractive two-seater 'tourer', the planform of whose two-bay wings proclaimed its manufacturer. Its fuselage was slab-sided and the vertical tail unit also harked back to that of the Camel. The engine was a ten-cylinder, 100hp Anzani radial. Completed and at Brooklands by 31 July 1919, the Grasshopper was not granted its Certificate of Airworthiness until 22 March of the following year. The reason for the long delay is unclear, but it may have been connected with engine troubles, the radial design still being in its infancy and beset with teething troubles.

The intended market for the Grasshopper was, unfortunately for Sopwith's, flooded with war surplus Avro 504Ks that were cheap to buy and simple to maintain and repair. No orders were forthcoming but the existing machine entered the Civil Register. It passed through the hands of four owners before being bought by the well-known female pilot, Constance Leathart, in February 1928 and was based at Cramlington. It ended its active career and was withdrawn from use in May 1929.

The Schneider and Rainbow

Peacetime conditions brought a resurrection of the Schneider Trophy competition and Britain, as the holder, was set to stage the 1919 event, set for September. Bournemouth was the chosen location. Sopwith's, as the designers of the 1913 winner, was keen to repeat the previous success and the seaplane produced for that purpose and again named the Schneider was, undoubtedly, the most attractive to emerge from Kingston. Needless to say, the quality of its finish was superb.

A radial engine was chosen, on account of the greater power delivered by that layout. The chosen type was a new engine, the Cosmos Jupiter that delivered 450hp. Naturally, such a powerful engine had a large diameter, but careful design work by W.G. Carter ensured that it was neatly installed in a circular sectioned nose and faired into that profile by a hemispherical spinner. Aluminium panels covered the forward fuselage and fairings were set behind each of the protruding cylinder heads to minimize their disturbance to the airflow. The rear fuselage tapered into a rectangular cross-section, but not to a tubular sternpost. This was because a further drag-reducing tactic was the use of a rudder with a bulbous lower half that was some 6in (15cm) wide and doubled as a tail float. The rear fuselage tapered to that width. The Schneider's single-bay, equal-span wings had ailerons on all four planes and were set with slightly negative stagger. The floats had rectangular cross-section and were reminiscent of those fitted to the Baby.

The Schneider was registered as G-EAKI and taken to Hythe for assembly that was finished by 29 August. Hawker, the natural choice of pilot for the event, attempted the Schneider's first flight on 10 September, but the float position had been wrongly calculated and the machine nosed over. Remedial action took two days. A speed of 180mph (290km/h) was achieved in the eliminating round of the competition, but the final stages were aborted due to fog. The Schneider was unlikely to have won, its floats having been damaged on arrival for the main event.

G-EAKI was reconstructed to landplane configuration over the winter and re-emerged with the new name Rainbow. The name and wheeled undercarriage were not the only changes. The Jupiter engine was not available and a Dragonfly was installed, necessitating some revision of the nose contours. The less powerful

engine reduced the maximum speed by some 10mph (16km/h). The Rainbow was entered in the 1920 Aerial Derby, with its race number '13' added to the rear fuselage. The superstition surrounding that number was realized. Hawker miscalculated his run and was disqualified.

It had been planned to enter the Rainbow in the 1920 Gordon Bennett competition but the liquidation of the company preceded that event by three weeks. The Rainbow still existed and was re-engined with another Jupiter. With its airframe overhauled by the new Hawker company, it was flown in the 1923 Aerial Derby, in the hands of Flt Lt W.H. Longton AFC DFC**, and achieved second place, with a speed of 164mph (264km/h). There were plans to enter the Rainbow in the 1923 Schneider Cup competition but, before the necessary reconversion could be undertaken, it was crashed and wrecked at Brooklands by Longton.

There is little doubt that the Schneider and Rainbow were the ultimate in Sopwith design and the culmination of eight years' experience. Those eight years had seen the company grow into one of the major aircraft manufacturers of the Great War era and make a major contribution to the Allied war effort. Appendices I and II give information on production and reconstruction and show the vast number of Sopwith machines available to the flying services. An evaluation of their impact on the air war has to be positive. Although many of the early designs were not particularly successful, they did attempt to define new roles for the RNAS and their presence contributed to the early expansion of that arm. The Schneider and Baby can be seen as workhorses which performed useful, if unspectacular, duties. It was the development of the rotary-engined fighters, beginning with the 1½ Strutter, that set Sopwith's at the forefront of the industry. The combat record of the subsequent Pup, Triplane and Camel speaks for itself and was a consequence of putting good designs in the hands of the brave men of the RNAS, RFC and RAF. Sopwith fighter design probably reached its peak with the Dolphin, although the Snipe achieved greater status. Had the war continued into 1919 and the Dragonfly engine achieved its potential, the Dragon and other later designs could have made a great impact. That was not to be, however, and the Sopwith Company is probably best remembered for its 1916–1917 designs.

Contracted Sopwith Machines

The following tabulation gives the serial numbers allocated to Sopwith aeroplanes, seaplanes and flying boats that were ordered from the parent company and its subcontractors.

SERIAL BLOCK	MANUFACTURER	TYPE	ORDERED	PRODUCED	REMARKS
27 only	Sopwith	School Biplane	1	1	for Naval Wing, rebuilt as D1
33 only	Sopwith	D1	1	1	ex-1913 Olympia Show machine
38 only	Sopwith	Bat Boat Type 1	1	1	for Naval Wing
58–60	Sopwith	Type HT	3	3	for Naval Wing
61 only	Sopwith	Type S	1	1	for Naval Wing
93 only	Sopwith	Pusher Seaplane	1	1	for Naval Wing
103–104	Sopwith	D1	2	2	for Naval Wing
118 only	Sopwith	Bat Boat Type 1	1	1	ex-1913 Olympia Show machine
123–124	Sopwith	Pusher Seaplane	2	2	for Naval Wing
127 only	Sopwith	Bat Boat Type 2	1	1	for Naval Wing
137–138	Sopwith	Type 137	2	2	for Naval Wing
149 only	Sopwith	Sociable	1	1	for Naval Wing
151 only	Sopwith	Tractor Seaplane	1	1	1913 'Circuit of Britain'
157–159	Sopwith	Type C	3	3	for RNAS
160 only	Sopwith	Single-Seat Biplane	1	0	no evidence of delivery
167–168	Sopwith	SS	2	2	904 & 905 renumbered
169 only	Sopwith	StB	1	1	Tabloid prototype, ex-RFC 604
170 only	Sopwith	Special Seaplane	1	1	for Naval Wing
243 only	Sopwith	D1	1	1	for Military Wing
246–247	Sopwith	D1	2	2	for Military Wing
300 only	Sopwith	D1	1	1	for Military Wing
315 only	Sopwith	D1	1	1	for Military Wing
319 only	Sopwith	D1	1	1	for Military Wing
324–325	Sopwith	D1	2	2	for Military Wing
333 only	Sopwith	D1	1	1	for Military Wing
326 only	Sopwith	SS	1	1	for Military Wing
362 only	Sopwith	SS	1	1	for Military Wing
378 only	Sopwith	SS	1	1	for Military Wing
381 only	Sopwith	SS	1	1	for Military Wing
386–387	Sopwith	SS	2	2	for Military Wing
392 only	Sopwith	SS	1	1	for Military Wing
394–395	Sopwith	SS	2	2	for Military Wing
604 only	Sopwith	StB	1	1	Tabloid prototype, to RNAS as 169
611 only	Sopwith	SS	1	1	for Military Wing
654 only	Sopwith	SS	1	1	for Military Wing
801–806	Sopwith	Type 806 Gunbus	6	6	for RNAS
807–810	Sopwith	Type 807	4	4	for RNAS
851–860	Sopwith	Type 860	10	10	for RNAS
879 only	Sopwith	Bat Boat Type 2	1	1	impressed for RNAS
880 only	Sopwith	Type 880	1	1	impressed 'Circuit of Britain
896 only	Sopwith	Type 880	1	1	impressed from Greeks
897–901	Sopwith	Pusher Seaplane	5	5	impressed from Greeks
904–905	Sopwith	SS	2	2	ex-RFC 394 & 395
906 only	Sopwith	D1	1	1	for RNAS
919–926	Sopwith	Type 807	8	8	for RNAS
927–938	Sopwith	Type 860	12	9	last 3 cancelled

SERIAL BLOCK	MANUFACTURER	TYPE	ORDERED	PRODUCED	REMARKS
1051–1074	Sopwith	Spinning Jenny	24	24	for RNAS
1201–1212	Sopwith	SS3	12	12	for RNAS
1213 only	Sopwith	SS	1	1	impressed for RNAS
1214 only	Sopwith	Gordon Bennett	1	1	impressed for RNAS
1215 only	Sopwith	Gordon Bennett	1	1	impressed for RNAS
1347–1350	Sopwith	Type 860	4	0	cancelled
1436–1447	Sopwith	Schneider	12	12	for RNAS
1556–1579	Sopwith	Schneider	24	24	for RNAS
3686 only	Sopwith	Strutter (Type 9400)	1	1	prototype
3691 only	Sopwith	Pup	1	1	prototype for RNAS
3698–3699	Sopwith	Biplane (150hp)	2	0	cancelled
3707–3806	Sopwith	Schneider	100	100	production order
3833–3862	Robey & Co. Ltd	Type 806 Gunbus	30	30	at least 13 delivered as spares
5719–5721	Sopwith	Strutter	3	3	ex-RNAS machines for RFC
7762–7811	Ruston Proctor & Co. Ltd	Strutter	50	50	initial RFC production
7942 only	Sopwith	Strutter	1	1	ex-RNAS machine for RFC
7998–8000	Sopwith	Strutter	3	3	ex-RNAS machines for RFC
8118–8217	Sopwith	Baby	100	100	initial production
9376–9425	Sopwith	Strutter (Type 9400)	50	50	15 transferred to RFC
9496–9497	Sopwith	Pup	2	2	pre-production for RNAS
9651–9750	Sopwith	Strutter (9400 & 9700)	100	100	49 transferred to RFC
9891 only	Sopwith	School Biplane	1	1	trainer version of Strutter
9892–9897	Sopwith	Strutter	6	6	1 transferred to RFC
9898–9900	Sopwith	Pup	3	3	pre-production for RNAS
9901–9950	Wm Beardmore & Co. Ltd	Ships Pup Type 9901a	50	50	for RNAS
A377–A386	Sopwith	Strutter	10	10	ex-RNAS machines for RFC
A626–A675	Standard Motor Co. Ltd	Pup	50	50	for RFC
A878–A897	Sopwith	Strutter	10	10	ex-RNAS machines for RFC
A954–A1053	Fairey Aviation Co. Ltd	Strutter	100	100	for RFC
A1054–A1153	Vickers Ltd	Strutter	100	100	for RFC
A1902–A1931	Sopwith	Strutter	30	30	ex-RNAS machines for RFC
A2381–A2430	Ruston Proctor & Co. Ltd	Strutter	50	50	for RFC
A2431–A2432	Sopwith	Strutter	2	2	ex-RNAS machines for RFC
A2983–A2991	Sopwith	Strutter	9	9	ex-RNAS machines for RFC
A5138–A5237	Wells Aviation Co. Ltd	Pup	100	0	cancelled
A5238–A5337	Wells Aviation Co. Ltd	Strutter	100	100	for RFC
A5950–A6149	Morgan & Co.	Strutter (bomber)	200	100	for RFC, transfers to RNAS, last 100 cancelled
A6150–A6249	Whitehead Aircraft Ltd	Pup	100	100	for RFC
A6901–A7000	Hooper & Co. Ltd	Strutter (bomber)	100	100	for RFC, transfers to RNAS
A7301–A7350	Standard Motor Co. Ltd	Pup	50	50	for RFC
A8732–A8737	Sopwith	Pup	6	0	for intended transfers from RNAS
A8141–A8340	Ruston Proctor & Co. Ltd	Strutter	200	200	for RFC
A8726–A8731	?	Strutter	6	0	intended for ex-RNAS machines
A8744–A8793	Vickers Ltd	Strutter	50	50	for RFC
A8970–A8973	Sopwith	Sparrow	4	4	numbers allotted for striking off ?
A9000–A9099	Clayton & Shuttleworth Ltd	Triplane (Clerget)	100	0	cancelled RFC order
A9813–A9918	Clayton & Shuttleworth Ltd	Triplane (Clerget)	106	0	cancelled RFC order
B331	Sopwith	Pup	1	0	cancelled
B381	Sopwith	Camel	1	1	F1/3 transferred from RNAS
B1496	Sopwith	B2	1	1	For RFC
B1701–B1850	Standard Motor Co. Ltd	Pup	150	150	for RFC
B2151–B2250	Whitehead Aircraft Ltd	Pup	100	100	for RFC, most 100hp Monosoupape
B2301–B2550	Ruston Proctor & Co.	F1 Camel	250	250	for RFC, 11 to RNAS
B2551–B2600	Ruston Proctor & Co. Ltd	Strutter	50	50	for RFC
B3751–B3750	Sopwith	F1 Camel	200	200	for RFC, 104 to RNAS
B3977	Sopwith	F1 Camel	1	1	ex-N6338
B4601–B4650	Portholme Aerodrome Ltd	F1 Camel	50	50	for RFC
B5151–B5250	Boulton & Paul Ltd	F1 Camel	100	100	for RFC
B5251–B5400	Whitehead Aircraft Ltd	Pup	150	150	for RFC
B5401–B5450	Hooper & Co. Ltd	F1 Camel	50	50	for RFC

SERIAL BLOCK	MANUFACTURER	TYPE	ORDERED	PRODUCED	REMARKS
B5551–B5650	Ruston Proctor & Co. Ltd	F1 Camel	100	100	for RFC, 19 to RNAS
B5651–B5750	Clayton & Shuttleworth Ltd	F1 Camel	100	100	for RNAS
B5901–B6150	Standard Motor Co. Ltd	Pup	250	250	for RFC training
B6151–B6200	Sopwith	F1 Camel	50	0	renumbered as 2F1s N6600–N6649
B6201–B6450	Sopwith	F1 Camel	250	250	for RFC, 131 to RNAS
B7131–B7180	Portholme Aerodrome Ltd	F1 Camel	50	50	for RFC, 21 to RNAS
B7181–B7280	Clayton & Shuttleworth Ltd	F1 Camel	100	100	for RNAS, 3 to Belgium
B7281–B7480	Ruston Proctor & Co.	F1 Camel	200	200	for RFC, 6 to RNAS
B7481–B7580	Whitehead Aircraft Ltd	Pup	100	100	for RFC training
B9131–B9330	Boulton & Paul Ltd	F1 Camel	200	200	for RFC
B9962–B9967	Sopwith	Snipe	6	6	prototypes
B9990	Sopwith	F1 Camel	1	1	ex-N6344
C1–C200	Nieuport & General Aircraft Co.	F1 Camel	200	200	for RFC, 81 to RNAS
C201–C550	Standard Motor Co. Ltd	Pup	350	350	later machine to storage
C551–C750	British Caudron Co. Ltd	F1 Camel	200	0	cancelled
C1451–C1550	Whitehead Aircraft Ltd	Pup	100	100	some transfers to RNAS
C1551–C1600	Hooper & Co. Ltd	F1 Camel	50	50	for RFC
C1601–C1700	Boulton & Paul Ltd	F1 Camel	100	100	for RFC
C3281–C3380	Boulton & Paul Ltd	F1 Camel	100	100	for RFC, delivered to RAF
C3707–C3776	Whitehead Aircraft Ltd	Pup	70	70	for RFC
C3777–C4276	Sopwith	Dolphin	500	500	initial production order
C4284–C4289	Sopwith	Snail	6	2	C4284 and C4288 only completed
C6701–C6800	British Caudron Co. Ltd	F1 Camel	100	100	for RFC
C7901–C8200	Cubitt Ltd	Snipe	300	0	mistaken allocation ?
C7901–C8000	Fairfield Engineering	Cuckoo	100	0	reallotted to N7000–N7099
C8001–C8200	Darracq Motor Engineering Co.	Dolphin	200	200	for RFC, not completed until 9.1918
C8201–C8300	Ruston Proctor & Co. Ltd	F1 Camel	100	100	for RFC
C8301–C8400	March Jones & Cribb Ltd	F1 Camel	100	100	no evidence of last 3 delivered
D1776–D1975	Ruston Proctor & Co. Ltd	F1 Camel	200	200	for RFC, later RAF
D3276–D3325	Pegler	Cuckoo	50	0	cancelled
D3326–D3425	Clayton & Shuttleworth Ltd	F1 Camel	100	100	for RNAS
D3576–D3775	Sopwith	Dolphin	200	200	for RFC
D4011–D4210	Whitehead Aircraft Ltd	Pup	200	200	for training
D4211–D4360	Wm Beardmore & Co. Ltd	F1 Camel	150	0	cancelled
D5201–D5400	Hooper & Co. Ltd	Dolphin	200	200	for RFC
D6401–D6700	Boulton & Paul Ltd	F1 Camel	300	300	for RFC, later RAF
D8101–D8250	Ruston Proctor & Co. Ltd	F1 Camel	150	150	for RAF
D9381–D9530	Ruston Proctor & Co. Ltd	F1 Camel	150	150	for RAF
D9531–D9580	Portholme Aerodrome Ltd	F1 Camel	50	50	for RAF
D9581–D9680	Clayton & Shuttleworth Ltd	F1 Camel	100	100	for ex-RNAS RAF units
E1401–E1600	Ruston Proctor & Co. Ltd	F1 Camel	200	200	for RAF
E4374–E4423	Clayton & Shuttleworth Ltd	F1 Camel	50	50	for ex-RNAS RAF units
E4424–E4623	Sopwith	Dolphin	200	200	for RAF
E4629–E5128	Sopwith	Dolphin	500	200	last 300 cancelled
E5129–E5178	Portholme Aerodrome Ltd	F1 Camel	50	50	for RAF
E5429–E5434	Sopwith	Salamander	6	6	prototypes
E6137–E6536	Boulton & Paul Ltd	Snipe	400	370	last 30 possibly cancelled
E6537–E6686	Coventry Ordnance Works	Snipe	150	110	last 40 possibly cancelled
E6787–E6936	Napier & Son	Snipe	150	135	last 15 cancelled
E6937–E7036	Nieuport & General Aircraft Co.	Snipe	100	100	for RAF
E7137–E7336	Ruston Proctor & Co. Ltd	F1 Camel	200	200	for RAF
E7337–E7836	Ruston Proctor & Co. Ltd	Snipe	500	472	last 28 cancelled
E7987–E8286	Sopwith	Snipe	300	300	for RAF
E8307–E8406	Portholme Aerodrome Ltd	Snipe	100	100	for RAF
E9997	Sopwith	Dolphin	1	1	one of 4, possibly for prototypes
F1301–F1550	Boulton & Paul Ltd	F1 Camel	250	250	for RAF and USAS
F1883–F1957	Boulton & Paul Ltd	F1 Camel	75	75	for RAF
F1958–F2007	Portholme Aerodrome Ltd	F1 Camel	50	50	for RAF
F2008–F2082	Ruston Proctor & Co. Ltd	F1 Camel	75	75	for RAF

SERIAL BLOCK	MANUFACTURER	TYPE	ORDERED	PRODUCED	REMARKS
F2083–F2182	Hooper & Co. Ltd	F1 Camel	100	100	for RAF
F2210–F2229	ex-France	Ships Strutter	20	20	converted at 2 (Northern) ARD
F2333–F2532	Sopwith	Snipe	200	200	for RAF
F3096–F3145	Clayton & Shuttleworth Ltd	F1 Camel	50	50	for ex-RNAS RAF units
F3196–F3245	Nieuport & General Aircraft Co.	F1 Camel	50	50	for ex-RNAS RAF units
F3918–F3967	Nieuport & General Aircraft Co.	F1 Camel	50	50	for ex-RNAS RAF units
F3968–F4067	Ruston Proctor & Co. Ltd	F1 Camel	100	100	for RAF
F4068–F4070	Sopwith	Snark	3	3	prototypes
F4974–F5073	Clayton & Shuttleworth Ltd	F1 Camel	100	100	for ex-RNAS RAF units
F5174–F5248	March Jones & Cribb Ltd	F1 Camel	75	75	for RAF
F6301–F6500	Boulton & Paul Ltd	F1 Camel	200	200	for RAF
F6501–F7000	Sopwith	Salamander	500	102	later machines cancelled
F7001–F7030	Sopwith	Dragon	30	30	for RAF
F7031–F7033	Sopwith	Snapper	3	3	prototypes
F7034–F7133	Darracq Motor Engineering Co.	Dolphin	100	100	for RAF
F7144–F7146	Sopwith	F1 Camel	3	0	cancelled
F7547–F7596	ex-France	Ships Strutter	50	50	converted at 2 (Northern) ARD
F7601–F7750	Wolseley Motors Ltd	Salamander	150	0	cancelled
F7801–F7950	Air Navigation Co. Ltd	Salamander	150	0	cancelled
F8231–F8280	Blackburn	Cuckoo	50	0	reallotted N6950–N6999
F8496–F8595	Nieuport & General Aircraft Co.	F1 Camel	100	100	for ex-RNAS RAF units
F8646–F8695	Portholme Aerodrome Ltd	F1 Camel	50	50	for RAF
F9446–F9495	British Caudron Co. Ltd	F1 Camel	50	0	cancelled
F9846–F9995	Coventry Ordnance Works	Snipe	150	0	cancelled
H351–H650	Ruston Proctor & Co. Ltd	Snipe	300	98	last 202 cancelled
H671–H673	Sopwith	Cobham	3	3	prototypes
H734–H833	Hooper & Co. Ltd	F1 Camel	100	100	for RAF
H2646–H2745	Boulton & Paul Ltd	F1 Camel	100	100	for RAF, many to store
H3996–H4045	British Caudron Co. Ltd	F1 Camel	50	46	last 4 cancelled
H4865–H5064	Sopwith	Snipe	200	98	last 102 cancelled
H5892–H5893	Sopwith	Buffalo	2	2	prototypes
H7343–H7412	Hooper & Co. Ltd	F1 Camel	75	75	for RAF
H8513–H8662	Nieuport & General Aircraft Co.	Snipe	150	0	cancelled
H8663–H8762	Portholme Aerodrome Ltd	Snipe	100	53	remainder cancelled
H9964–H9966	Sopwith	Snipe 1a	3	0	duplicated E8089–E8091
J1–J150	Hooper & Co.	Dolphin	150	109	last 41 cancelled
J151–J250	Darracq	Dolphin	100	65	last 35 cancelled
J301–J400	March Jones & Cribb	Snipe	100	0	cancelled
J451–J550	Boulton & Paul Ltd	Snipe	100	25	last 75 cancelled
J651–J680	British Caudron	Camel	30	0	cancelled
J681–J730	March Jones & Cribb	Camel	50	10	last 40 cancelled
J2392–J2541	British Caudron Co. Ltd	Snipe	150	0	order changed to Nighthawks
J2542–J3041	Grahame-White Aviation Co. Ltd	Dragon	500	0	order changed to Nighthawks
J3042–J3341	Gloucestershire Aircraft	Snipe	300	0	cancelled
J3617–J3916	Sopwith	Dragon	300	100	last 200 cancelled
J3917–J3991	Barclay Curle & Co.	Snipe	75	0	cancelled
J4092–J4591	National Aircraft Factory No3	Snipe	500	0	cancelled
J5892–J5991	Glendower Aircraft	Salamander	100	50	last 50 cancelled
J5992–J6091	Palladium Autocars	Salamander	100	0	cancelled
J6092–J6491	National Aircraft Factory No1	Salamander	400	0	cancelled
J6493–J6522	Kingsbury Aviation	Snipe	30	30	delivered to store
N4–N5	Sopwith	Strutter	2	2	cancelled
N4–N5	Sopwith	FS1	2	2	N5 became 2F1 prototype
N50	Sopwith	B1	1	1	intended for French government
N74	Sopwith	Cuckoo	1	1	prototype
N300	Blackburn	Baby	1	1	replacement for 8201 (to Japan)
N500	Sopwith	Triplane (Clerget)	1	1	prototype
N503	Sopwith	Pup (110hp Le Rhone)	1	0	cancelled
N504	Sopwith	Triplane (Clerget)	1	1	2nd prototype
N509–N510	Sopwith	Triplane (Hispano)	2	2	150 & 200hp respectively

SERIAL BLOCK	MANUFACTURER	TYPE	ORDERED	PRODUCED	REMARKS
N517–N518	Sopwith	F1 Camel	2	2	Naval prototypes
N524	Sopwith	Triplane (Clerget)	1	1	from French
N533–N538	Clayton & Shuttleworth Ltd	Triplane (Clerget)	6	6	for RNAS, twin gun armament
N541–N543	Sopwith	Triplane (Clerget)	3	3	from French
N1010–N1039	Blackburn	Baby	30	30	110 hp Clerget, 5 intended for French
N1060–N1069	Blackburn	Baby	10	10	110hp Clerget
N1100–N1129	Blackburn	Baby	30	30	100hp Clerget
N1190–N1219	George Parnall & Co. Ltd	Hamble Baby	30	30	130hp Clerget
N1320–N1329	Fairey Aviation Co. Ltd	Hamble Baby	10	10	110hp Clerget
N1330–N1339	Fairey Aviation Co. Ltd	Hamble Baby	10	10	130hp Clerget
N1340–N1359	Sopwith	Daily Mail	20	0	cancelled
N1410–N1449	Blackburn	Baby	40	40	130hp Clerget
N1450–N1479	Fairey Aviation Co. Ltd	Hamble Baby	30	30	130hp Clerget
N1960–N1985	George Parnall & Co. Ltd	Hamble Baby	26	26	130hp Clerget
N1986–N2059	George Parnall & Co. Ltd	Hamble Baby Convert	74	74	at least 53 to store
N2060–N2134	Blackburn	Baby	75	75	130hp Clerget
N5080–N5119	Sopwith	Strutter	40	40	Types 9400S & 9700 for RNAS
N5120–N5169	Westland Aircraft Works	Strutter	50	50	Type 9700 for RNAS
N5170–N5179	Sopwith	Strutter	10	10	Type 9400S
N5180–N5199	Sopwith	Pup	20	20	initial production
N5200–N5219	Mann, Egerton & Co. Ltd	Strutter	20	20	Type 9700 for RNAS
N5220–N5249	Mann, Egerton & Co. Ltd	Strutter	30	30	Type 9400S
N5350–N5389	Clayton & Shuttleworth Ltd	Triplane (Clerget)	40	40	for RNAS
N5420–N5494	Sopwith	Triplane (Clerget)	75	75	for RNAS
N5500–N5549	Sopwith	Strutter	50	38	Type 9700, last 12 cancelled
N5550–N5559	Sopwith	Strutter	10	0	cancelled
N5550–N5559	Sopwith	Triplane (Clerget)	10	0	cancelled
N5600–N5624	Westland Aircraft Works	Strutter	25	25	first 5 Type 9700, rest 9400S
N5630–N5654	Mann, Egerton & Co. Ltd	Strutter	25	25	6 Type 9700, rest Type 9400S
N5910–N5934	Oakley & Co.	Strutter	25	0	order amended to Triplanes
N5910–N5934	Oakley & Co.	Triplane (Clerget)	25	3	last 22 cancelled
N5940–N5954	Sopwith	Strutter	15	0	cancelled
N6100–N6129	Wm Beardmore & Co. Ltd	Pup	30	0	order amended to WB.III
N6160–N6209	Sopwith	Pup	50	50	for RNAS
N6290–N6309	Sopwith	Triplane (Clerget)	20	20	for RNAS
N6330–N6379	Sopwith	F1 Camel	50	50	for RNAS
N6430–N6459	Wm Beardmore & Co. Ltd	Pup	30	30	Type 9901a
N6460–N6529	Sopwith	Pup	70	20	last 50 cancelled
N6530–N6579	Sopwith	F1 Camel	50	50	cancelled
N6600–N6649	Sopwith	2F1 Camel	50	50	for RNAS
N6750–N6799	Wm Beardmore & Co. Ltd	2F1 Camel	50	50	for RNAS & RAF
N6800–N6849	Wm Beardmore & Co. Ltd	2F1 Camel	50	50	for RAF
N6900–N6929	Blackburn	Cuckoo	30	30	replaced D3276–D3325
N6930–N6949	Pegler	Cuckoo	20	10	last 10 probably cancelled
N6950–N6999	Blackburn	Cuckoo	50	50	initial deliveries
N7000–N7099	Fairfield Engineering	Cuckoo	100	50	last 50 cancelled
N7100–N7139	Wm Beardmore & Co. Ltd	2F1 Camel	40	40	for RAF
N7140–N7149	Arrol Johnston Ltd	2F1 Camel	10	10	sub contracted from Beardmore
N7150–N7199	Blackburn	Cuckoo	50	50	built as Mk.I, 2 became Mk.II
N7200–N7299	Fairey Aviation Co. Ltd	2F1 Camel	100	0	cancelled
N7300–N7349	Pegler	2F1 Camel	50	0	cancelled
N7350–N7399	Arrol Johnston Ltd	2F1 Camel	50	25	last 25 cancelled
N7650–N7679	Wm Beardmore & Co. Ltd	2F1 Camel	30	0	cancelled
N7850–N7979	Frederick Sage & Co. Ltd	2F1 Camel	150	0	cancelled
N7980–N8079	Blackburn	Cuckoo	100	32	last 68 cancelled
N8130–N8179	Hooper & Co. Ltd	2F1 Camel	50	35	last 15 cancelled
N8180–N8229	Clayton & Shuttleworth Ltd	2F1 Camel	50	25	last 25 cancelled

The Sigrist Bus

As recounted in Chapter Four, the origins of the 1½ Strutter lay in the Sigrist Bus of late 1914. For many years it was thought that no photographs of this significant aeroplane had survived but, purely by chance, historian Phil Jarrett found these two as part of a larger collection bought in a sale. At first their significance did not register with him and Jarrett was not entirely sure that these were, indeed, the Bus. As a result he did not buy the album, at first, but waited over a year and bought it at a later sale. A telephone call to the eminent historian Jack Bruce settled the matter and as Phil later remarked, 'Jack went very quiet for a few moments!'. The location for the photographs is not known and the Bus is shown in a later form, having lost the central undercarriage skid; it is most probably in use as a Sopwith company hack. The photographs are reproduced here for the first time, with grateful thanks to Phillip Jarrett.

Reconstructed Sopwiths

The attrition rate for World War I aeroplanes was high and many machines were damaged during training and non-operational sorties. Others were damaged in combat and if repair was beyond that possible at unit level, machines were handed over to specialist formations for rebuilding. These included the Aircraft Depots in France, the numbered Aircraft Repair Depots at home and the Aircraft Repair sections of home-based Wings. If damage was limited, a machine could be repaired and reissued, but sometimes it was necessary to strike an aeroplane off RFC/RAF charge. When this latter happened, all possible components were salvaged and used to reconstruct further airframes. New serial numbers were then allocated. Special blocks of serials were set aside for such reconstructions by the major depots and others were allocated for rebuilds (or machines assembled from spares) by training units. Given the huge number of Sopwith aeroplanes in service, large numbers re-emerged under new identities. Naturally, there were more Camels than any other type – this being a reflection of the vast number of that type in service. The situation could occur where a reconstruction could itself be reconstructed, an example being F6067 (formerly C8257) which became F6267. It should be noted that the 1½ Strutter and Pup reconstructions were done by home depots, those types having been in the process of withdrawal from the RFC with the BEF when the practice of allocating new numbers was introduced. The lists below give known serial numbers for reconstructed RFC and RAF Sopwith aeroplanes by type. Although the RNAS undoubtedly followed the practice of reconstruction, it was not that service's policy to allocate new serial numbers.

Sopwith 1½ Strutter (21 known)
B711, B714, B715, B729, B744, B745, B762, B816, B827, B862, B4016, B4044, B7903, B7914, B7915, B7916, B7946, B8911, B8912, B9910, C4300.

Sopwith Pup (34 known)
B735, B803, B804, B805, B849, B1499, B4082, B4128, B4131, B4136, B7752, B8064, B8784, B8785, B8786, B8795, B8801, B8821, B8829, B9440, B9455, B9931, C3500, C3501, C3502, C3503, C4295, C8653, C8654, C9990, C9991, C9993, E9996, F4220.

Sopwith F1 Camel (577 known, including 64 incorrectly numbered and later remarked)
B778, B802, B847, B885, B886, B888, B889, B893, B895, B898, B900, B3977, B3980, B4122, B7728, B7732, B7733, B7735, B7736, B7742, B7743, B7744, B7745, B7746, B7755, B7757, B7760, B7766, B7769, B7772, B7774, B7776, B7777, B7783, B7784, B7785, B7786, B7789, B7790, B7791, B7793, B7797, B7798, B7806, B7807, B7808, B7817, B7820, B7821, B7822, B7828, B7829, B7834, B7835, B7856, B7859, B7860, B7862, B7863, B7864, B7867, B7868, B7869, B7870, B7873, B7874, B7875, B7883, B7889, B7895, B7896, B7897, B7905, B7906, B7907, B7923, B8013, B8025, B8055, B8830, B8920, B8921, B8926, B9990, E9964, E9965, E9966, E9967, E9968, E9969, E9970, E9971, E9972, E9973, E9974, E9975, E9976, E9977, E9978, E9979, E9980, E9981, E9982, E9983, F2189, F2190, F2191, F2192, F2193, F2194, F2195, F2196, F2197, F2198, F2199, F2200, F2201, F2202, F2203, F2204, F2205, F2206, F2207, F2208, F4170, F4175, F4177, F4178, F4179, F4180, F4181, F4182, F4183, F4184, F4185, F4186, F4187, F4188, F4189, F4190, F4193, F4194, F4196, F4197, F4199, F4200, F4201, F4202, F4203, F4204, F4205, F4207, F4208, F4209, F4210, F4211, F4212, F4213, F4214, F4215, F4216, F5913, F5914, F5915, F5916, F5917, F5918, F5919, F5920, F5921, F5922, F5923, F5924, F5925, F5926, F5927, F5928, F5929, F5930, F5931, F5932, F5933, F5934, F5935, F5936, F5937, F5938, F5939, F5940, F5941, F5942, F5943, F5944, F5945, F5946, F5947, F5948, F5949, F5950, F5951, F5952, F5953, F5954, F5955, F5956, F5957, F5958, F5959, F5960, F5964, F5965, F5966, F5967, F5968, F5969, F5970, F5981, F5982, F5983, F5984, F5985,F5986, F5987, F5988, F5989, F5990, F5991, F5992, F5993, F5994, F6021, F6022, F6023, F6024, F6025, F6026, F6027, F6028, F6029, F6030, F6031, F6032, F6033, F6034, F6035, F6036, F6037, F6038, F6039, F6051, F6052, F6053, F6055, F6056, F6058, F6061, F6062, F6063, F6064, F6067, F6068, F6069, F6076, F6082, F6083, F6084, F6086, F6087, F6088, F6089, F6090, F6100, F6102, F6105, F6106, F6107, F6110, F6111, F6115, F6117, F6122, F6123, F6126, F6129, F6132, F6135, F6138, F6140, F6147, F6148, F6149, F6150, F6151, F6152, F6153, F6154, F6155, F6156, F6157, F6175, F6176, F6177, F6180, F6182, F6183,F6184, F6185, F6188, F6189, F6190, F6191, F6192, F6193, F6194, F6197, F6198, F6199, F6200, F6201, F6202, F6210, F6211, F6216, F6219, F6220, F6221, F6223, F6224, F6225, F6226, F6227, F6228, F6230, F6238, F6240, F6241, F6242, F6243, F6244, F6245, F6246, F6247, F6249, F6250, F6251, F6252, F6253, F6255, F6256, F6257, F6258, F6259, F6260, F6261, F6262, F6263, F6264, F6265, F6267, F6268, F6269, F6271, F6272, F6275, F6281, F6282, F6285, F6287, F6290, F6291, F6292, F6293, F6293, F6294, F6295, F6296, F6297, F6298, F6300, (F6301, F6302, F6303, F6304, F6305, F6306, F6307, F6308, F6309, F6310, F6311, F6312, F6313, F6314, F6315, F6316, F6317, F6318, F6319, F6320, F6321, F6322, F6323, F6324, F6325, F6326, F6327, F6328, F6329, F6330, F6331, F6332, F6333, F6334, F6335, F6336, F6337, F6338, F6339, F6340, F6341, F6342, F6343, F6344, F6345, F6346, F6347, F6348, F6349, F6466, F6467, F6468, F6469, F6470, F6471, F6472, F6473, F6474, F6475, F6476, F6477, F6478, F6479, F6489 – these 64 renumbered incorrectly and later given new serials in H6843–H7342 block), F9407, F9410, F9411, F9413, F9417, F9548, F9574, F9575, F9576, F9579, F9588, F9592, F9608, F9617, F9623, F9624, F9628, F9629, F9630, F9631, F9632, F9634, F9635, F9636, F9637, F9695, H6844, H6847, H6848, H6850, H6851, H6852, H6853, H6854, H6855, H6856, H6860, H6861, H6862, H6863, H6864, H6867, H6868, H6869, H6871, H6872, H6874, H6875, H6876, H6877, H6878, H6884, H6886, H6889, H6890, H6891, H6892, H6897, H6898, H6899, H6901, H6902, H6903, H6904, H6993,

H6994, H6995, H6996, H6997, H6998, H6999, H7000, H7001, H7002, H7003, H7004, H7005, H7006, H7007, H7008, H7009, H7010, H7011, H7012, H7013, H7014, H7015, H7016, H7077, H7078, H7079, H7080, H7081, H7082, H7083, H7084, H7085, H7086, H7087, H7088, H7089, H7090, H7091, H7092, H7093, H7094, H7095, H7096, H7097, H7098, H7099, H7100, H7101, H7102, H7103, H7104, H7105, H7106, H7107, H7108, H7109, H7110, H7111, H7112, H7113, H7114, H7115, H7116, H7117, H7151, H7205, H7206, H7207, H7208, H7209, H7210, H7211, H7212, H7213, H7214, H7215, H7216, H7217, H7218, H7219, H7220, H7221, H7222, H7223, H7224, H7225, H7226, H7234, H7235, H7236, H7237, H7238, H7239, H7240, H7241, H7255, H7269, H7270, H7271, H7272, H7273, H7274, H7275, H7276, H7277, H7278, H7279, H7280, H7281, H7282, H7283, H7284, H7285, H7286, H7287, H7288, H7289, H7290, H8200, H8201, H8202, H8253, H8258, H8259, H8260, H8261, H8262, H8264, H8271, H8291, H8292, H8293, H8294.

Sopwith 5F1 Dolphin (24 known)

B7849, B7851, B7855, B7861, B7876, B7877, B7927, B7928, B7937, B7953, B7955, B7978, B8189, F5961, F5962, F6020, F6144, F6145, F6146, H6866, H7243, H7244, H7245, H7246.

Sopwith 7F1 Snipe (10 known)

H6846, H6880, H6894, H6895, H7149, H7150, H7152, H7153, H7154, H7227.

Index